V&R

Schriftenreihe der FRIAS School of History

Edited by
Ulrich Herbert and Jörn Leonhard

Volume 4

www.frias.uni-freiburg.de

American Foundations and the Coproduction of World Order in the Twentieth Century

Edited by
John Krige and Helke Rausch

Vandenhoeck & Ruprecht

Mit 2 Tabellen

Umschlagabbildung: Rückseite der Sonderprägung einer Eindollarmünze
der Smithonian (Silver Dollar, Smithsonian 150th Anniversary – 1996 –
mit einer den Globus überragenden Allegorie und Motto
»FOR THE INCREASE AND DIFFUSION OF KNOWLEDGE«.)

Bibliografische Information der Deutschen Nationalbibliothek

Die Deutsche Nationalbibliothek verzeichnet diese Publikation in der
Deutschen Nationalbibliografie; detaillierte bibliografische Daten sind
im Internet über http://dnb.d-nb.de abrufbar.

ISBN 978-3-525-31043-4
ISBN 978-3-647-31043-5 (E-Book)

Satz: Dörlemann, Lemförde
Druck und Bindung: ⊕ Hubert & Co, Göttingen
Redaktion: Agnes Fellner, Jörg Später, Valentine Meunier
Assistenz: Jonas Wegerer
Gedruckt auf alterungsbeständigem Papier.

Table of Contents

John Krige and Helke Rausch

Introduction – Tracing the Knowledge: Power Nexus of American Philanthropy

The rise and international expansion of large-scale American foundations is widely recognised as one of the key features of the "American Century".[1] Various Carnegie philanthropies as well as the rapidly expanding range of initiatives taken by the Rockefeller Foundation testify to the unprecedented international strength of US philanthropy beginning shortly after the First World War. Their agendas successively evolved from ad hoc charitable programmes to highly professionalised interventions[2], and from a domestic to a transatlantic, if not to say global, scale reaching out primarily to Europe, but also to Asia and Latin America.[3] After the Second World War they were joined by the Ford Foundation, which explicitly used its extensive resources to promote American-style democracy and decidedly Western values world-wide.[4] All of these organisations adopted institutional reform, education and training as part of their philanthropic goals. Progressivist and New Deal ideals of social reform in the inter-war period gave way to the more instrumental use of knowledge as power in the Cold War, when America's vast system of knowledge production was harnessed for its global transformative

---

1 See Brinkley, "Concept"; De Grazia, *Irresistible Empire*. Against the background of the existing bulk of research, we focus on more recent publications of roughly the last decade, mentioning older studies only where crucial to our argument.

2 See Friedman/McGarvie, *Charity, Philanthropy and Civility*.

3 See, amongst the more recent of the many publications that deal with specific instances of global philanthropic commitment in and beyond Europe, Fangerau, "Private Wissenschaft"; Sachse, "Gereinigte Wissenschaft"; Hammack/Heydemann, *Projecting Institutional Logics*; Nemchenok, "So Fair a Thing"; Brier, "AIDS"; Hull, "Conflict and Collaboration"; Korey, *Repressive Regimes*; Berghahn, "America's Cultural Cold War"; Birn, *Marriage of Convenience*; Shepherd, "Imperial Science"; Stein, "Vital Times"; Lawrence, *Rockefeller Money*; Hewa/Stapleton, *New Political Culture*. Interventions in Europe are more specifically dealt with especially by Gemelli et al., see below. Among the more recent insider accounts are Geithner, "Ford Foundation in Southeast Asia"; Sutton, "Nation-Building"; Bresnan, *At Home Abroad*.

4 See Krige, *American Hegemony*; Berghahn, *Intellectual Cold Wars*; Rausch, "Scientific Philanthropy"; Rausch, "Verordnetes Wissen?".

agenda. Improved scientific knowledge and understanding, embedded in a tissue of social relations that tied centre to periphery, became a preferred instrument for exporting American ideas and models abroad with the purpose of improving the human condition and warding off rival ideologies.[5]

While there seems to be a consensus on the general shape of the historical trajectory that integrates US philanthropy into a broader context of both global and US-American history, our sense is that there needs to be a sharper focus, in both current and future research, on the intricacies of this worldwide philanthropic expansion. Indeed, in this volume we tackle a specific set of important issues that demand further study and that are conspicuously under-theorised – notwithstanding the interesting research still being conducted into the activities of the foundations along the lines of the now-current master narrative. This collection of articles is interested both in a diachronic *longue-durée* perspective of philanthropic encounters during the twentieth century as well as in the specificities philanthropists had to deal with when building their social networks. How are we to make sense of the confusing plethora of parallel processes in US philanthropy from the 1920s to the 1970s? How should we rate their range and effects? And how can we connect apparently disparate instances of philanthropic funding and eventual knowledge transfers especially in Europe to a broader, more complex analysis of twentieth-century transnational or global history?

When it comes to answering these questions, even the ever-growing body of scholarly research on the multifaceted interventions of the Carnegie, Rockefeller and Ford foundations throughout the world has major lacunae. On the one hand, a host of studies tend to confine themselves to small-scale analyses of the funding of individuals or institutions.[6] While this is certainly invaluable for a sound understanding of local constellations and action, it often tends to ignore the more general regional or (trans)national circumstances and logics of philanthropic activities. On the other hand, many broad-brush studies of US philanthropy proliferate.[7] While it is obvious that current research projects – including this volume – still avail themselves of some of these, others tend to restrict the history of US philanthropic activities to a domestic dynamic and thus do not explore the relationship with the

---

5 See generally Engerman, "American Knowledge"; Guilhot, *International Relations Theory*; Tournès, *Sciences de l'homme*; Müller, *Krieger und Gelehrte*; Parmar/Cox, *Soft Power*.

6 For US philanthropy in Western Europe see the many invaluable contributions especially by Giuliana Gemelli et al. such as Gemelli/Macleod, *American Foundations in Europe*; Gemelli, *"Unacceptables"*; eadem, *Ford Foundation and Europe*. See also Fleck, *Transatlantische Bereicherungen*; Tournès, *L'Argent de l'influence*.

7 See Zunz, *Philanthropy in America*; Curti, *American Philanthropy Abroad*.

"periphery" in any detail.[8] More to the point, many still seem to ignore the critical question of whether the international history of philanthropy is in actual fact simply about transferring knowledge from the North American West to the rest of the world, a diffusionist model of knowledge circulation that we emphatically reject in this book.

For all the richness of existing research, there is ample reason to insist that the issue of US philanthropy still requires sustained reconsideration. This volume accordingly sets out from the proposition that US philanthropy needs to be integrated into a bigger picture – without underestimating its internal polymorphism on the one hand or squeezing it into an all-too-narrow and static frame on the other. To this end, our point of departure is the hypothesis that US philanthropic initiatives and multiple research activities sponsored around the world (in Western Europe in particular) must be understood as embedding knowledge in all its forms in international political, social and cultural power alignments. Thus, we aim to link the production and circulation of knowledge promoted by US philanthropy to a broader twentieth-century inter- or transnational history, shaped not only by such fundamental processes as inter-war Wilsonian Internationalism and Cold-War bloc antagonisms, but also by both US and European late colonialism and development as well as, not the least, by modernisation ideologies that, as we know from recent research, were not monopolised by the United States or the northern hemisphere but proliferated throughout the world.[9]

This volume focuses on the knowledge–power nexus that lay at the core of US philanthropic activity during the inter-war period and for the first two or three decades after the Second World War. The horrors of the Great War provided the recently established foundations with an opportunity to extend the scope of their activities from the domestic to the international sphere, and to support initiatives as diverse as the promotion of public health in Europe and the creation of organisations that were supposed to make another war politically impossible. The transformations of world order in the 1970s set the upper limit to our analysis. This decade is marked by a decline of the nation-state as an autonomous historical actor along with renewed global interdependence typified by the oil crisis of 1973–74, the rise of neo-liberal economics and its emphasis on deregulation, the turn to increasingly sovereign market forces, and the proliferation of non-governmental organi-

8 See among many others Khurana/Kimura/Fourcade, "How Foundations Think"; Buxton, *Patronizing the Public*; Rojas, "Mission in Black Studies"; Lagemann, *Politics of Knowledge*; Sealander, *Private Wealth*.

9 See Latham, *Right Kind of Revolution*; Ekbladh, *Great American Mission*; Engerman et al., *Staging Growth*; Bright/Geyer, "Globalgeschichte"; Büschel/Speich, *Entwicklungswelten*.

sations.[10] If previously the foundations had operated in a world in which they could count on American leadership, if not to say dominance, they now had to reposition themselves in a rapidly changing global regime. These radical transformations call for a separate study of their own, though the transnational focus of this book undoubtedly provides useful raw material for such an analysis.

With these considerations in mind, we adopt a twofold research perspective: First, we propose to account for the extent to which transnational processes affected American philanthropists over the period in question. As we have suggested, they obviously benefitted from the economic superiority of the foundations during the inter-war period and even more so from a world order underpinned by US military and political hegemony after 1945.[11] The structural ascendance of the Carnegie, Rockefeller and Ford foundations over their institutional or individual grantees abroad is not to be underestimated; it definitively shaped philanthropic encounters and actions throughout the twentieth century to an extent that needs careful study in each case. Second, this volume aims to historicise the knowledge–power nexus at the core of philanthropy by systematically incorporating additional substantial factors that influenced negotiations over knowledge circulation in different places and periods. Taken together, the following contributions argue that the asymmetries in favour of American foundations can only partly explain the terms of encounters and negotiations between philanthropists and their potential and actual counterparts, especially in Europe. The articles stress that it is imperative to take seriously the role and importance of the foundations' respective negotiating partners in the dyadic relationship. Only then do we no longer expect the philanthropic endeavour to merely mirror international power imbalances. As many contributions in this volume suggest, foundations could not unilaterally impose US scientific paradigms or "Atlantic" values on the world. Rather, each time philanthropists entered different local, regional and national stages and settings abroad, their ambition to reconfigure substantial parts of the academic sector or social, cultural and political practices met with incongruous traditions of disciplines and politics, institutional settings and complex actor constellations. Their funding activities in fact exposed the philanthropists to a whole set of asymmetries both in spatial as well as in chronological terms to which foundation officers in their turn had to adapt.

10 See Ferguson et al., *Shock of the Global.*
11 See Maier, *Among Empires*; Ninkovich, *Diplomacy of Ideas.*

1. American Foundations and the Coproduction of World Order in the Twentieth Century: Explorations in an Open Field

The contributions to this volume all take the knowledge–power nexus in philanthropic activities as a point of departure. While each author adopts his or her own timeframe and explores specific settings, they all deal with the role of agency – whether it concerns foundations as self-proclaimed vectors of knowledge circulation (Section I) or local grantees as their distinct and avowedly self-interested counterparts (Section II). While many of the characteristics illustrated pertain to both inter-war and Cold-War situations, it is obvious that these two periods remain decidedly distinct (Section III). Thus, this volume presents case-studies that throw light on how US philanthropy, as a driver of knowledge circulation, operated in different structural, regional and personal contexts abroad.

The collection begins with a discussion from three perspectives, exploring representative instances of philanthropic initiatives in Western Europe after the First World War. All of them contrast attempts at diffusionist control with the regulating effects of the role played by the foundations' local counterparts. Jens Wegener traces the tactics adopted by the Carnegie Endowment for International Peace (CEIP) in its promotion of the "international mind" campaign in Europe, intended to diplomatically counteract US isolationist foreign policy. The CEIP's hope of furthering both educational exchange and a more scientific approach to foreign relations was undermined by the conflict-prone power politics of the European grantees. The next two contributions deal with the Rockefeller Foundation as the most bustling transatlantic US philanthropy with a strong historical impact. Ludovic Tournès focuses on both country- and knowledge-specific dimensions in his discussion of the foundation's intervention in the field of French biomedicine. By virtue of prior French commitments in this particular area of knowledge and of various pre-established transatlantic interchanges, much of what might be superficially interpreted as strong US interference in French science emerges as an attempt to modernise a pioneering research field by adapting philanthropic activities to local peculiarities. Helke Rausch explores inter-war Rockefeller philanthropy from a comparative angle, focussing on anthropology as a major knowledge input to social planning in crisis-ridden late colonial contexts. By comparing and contrasting parallel funding commitments in France and Britain, she identifies the specific circumstances that favoured knowledge co-production. European grantees emerge as idiosyncratic actors (and as modernising agents in their own right, in fact) who were quite capable of manipulating their benefactors when it came to negotiating what was deemed to be an American agenda.

The contributions in the larger, second group of articles deal with the changed context in which both philanthropists and their grantees were active after the Second World War. Paul Weindling begins with a view from inside the Rockefeller Foundation and shows how a major organisational change both reflected and pre-empted a more basic reorientation of priorities. The closing of the Rockefeller Foundation's International Health Division in 1951 testifies to a major politics- and generation-induced shift from international health issues to population and nutrition programmes intended to support future-oriented knowledge in a world that segregated a prosperous West from a "backward" Southern hemisphere. While endorsing the fundamental imprint of East–West ideological rivalry in US philanthropy, Tim B. Müller then traces the myriad intricacies of early Cold-War philanthropy. He not only profiles central Rockefeller funding initiatives that testified to the philanthropic power politics of US-contingent knowledge production, but also illustrates that this attempt at "high modernity" was at times deliberately unconventional and pluralist. Alternative ideological approaches that were not easily harmonised with the Western liberal consensus of the day were encouraged, if only to demonstrate the pre-eminence of the United States' capacity for tolerance and openness as compared to its closed and secretive rival.

The next three articles in this part of the book track crucial varieties of knowledge circulation and network building from the 1950s to the 1970s. John Krige revisits his earlier study of the Ford Foundation's support for European physics in Copenhagen and Geneva. This time, rather than reading the programme through the lens of the transmission of cultural values, he focuses on it as an example of the transnational circulation of sensitive knowledge. The approach privileges the role of the State Department and the CIA, alongside the Ford Foundation, in the awarding of these grants and demands an analysis of the foundation's articulation with the national security state. It also highlights the role of physicists themselves as fellows, rather than that of officers, trustees and laboratory directors, and invites us to understand international scientific exchange as the pursuit of sometimes less noble national interests, including informal intelligence gathering.

Giles Scott-Smith illustrates the core elements of hegemonic knowledge co-production in a study of Ford Foundation funding for international law institutions in the Netherlands. The Ford Foundation hoped these would become intellectual stepping-stones and multipliers for expanding the scope of US norms of jurisprudence and Atlanticism throughout Europe. A transatlantic convergence in legal practices would supposedly facilitate US relationships with a diverse and complex continent. Lastly, Nicole Sackley moves beyond this region and looks into Ford Foundation strategies for co-producing "development" knowledge in India via a specially installed field office in New Delhi. This initiative had to contend with local circumstances, which differed substantially from those encountered in a post-war Europe under reconstruction. Co-operation with the Ford Foundation office allowed Indian elites to camouflage controversial decisions on development policies in a language of technocratic expertise. Notwithstanding the differences, the situation in India resembled that in European settings in the sense that potential and actual grantees could exploit their privileged position in order to gain strategic political influence within their respective local environments.

Sackley's is the only article that deals with America's relations outside of Western Europe. This partly reflects our determination to do a longitudinal study that throws into relief the changes in motivation brought about by the Cold War as well as the centrality of the situation in Europe in 1945 that triggered that change. Because the US emerged stronger than ever from the Second World War – and because Europe was in ruins – the American transformative project could move centre stage in the thinking of the foundations and successive US administrations: Their overriding goal was controlled modernisation and the construction of an American-led regime of world order, and they had the resources to make that goal meaningful. In the 1950s, as the process of decolonisation took off along with the rise of peasant power and the danger of Communism in the "Third World", the transformative agenda became also a global struggle for the soul of mankind.[12] Even if this broader agenda is represented by only one article in this volume, we hope that the insights presented in the collection are portable to other regions of the globe and to other case-studies, and that they can be used to enrich the growing body of excellent work on issues like post-war population control and agricultural development.[13]

2. Foundations as Vectors for Circulating Modernisation Knowledge

Philanthropists had a characteristic way of legitimising their programmatic goals and action in their voluminous annual and official reports and, ever so often, when officially negotiating with potential grantees. They conveyed an often self-congratulatory altruism coupled with the claim that their efforts were driven solely by the desire to contribute to the social and moral progress of mankind. These actor-centred declarations of an allegedly disinterested liberalism (or even humanitarianism) need historically based critical deconstruction – albeit one that is free of the ideological commitments that

---

12 See Westad, *Global Cold War*; Leffler/Westad, *Cambridge History of the Cold War*.
13 See Cullather, *Hungry World*; Connelly, *Fatal Misconception*.

have often marked such critiques in the past.[14] It would be hard to deny that US philanthropy was not least a matter of geo-politics – the attempt at virtually buying loyalty and ultimately making the world a site for implementing the modernising fantasies[15] of foundations who always claimed to be acting independently of the US Administration. To identify such self-perceptions, however, is not to say that this defined the substance of their accomplishments, or, perhaps more to the point, that this was how foundations were contemporarily perceived by others. Indeed, the following articles reveal a wide spectrum of visions and modes of philanthropic operation that allow us to historically qualify and categorise the American philanthropists as (self-proclaimed) vectors of global stabilisation and modernisation. At the same time, many articles illustrate how this materialised in very different funding patterns of the "big three", especially in Europe.

Together with the Rockefeller Foundation, the Carnegie Endowment was one of the first major philanthropies to engage in the European theatre in the 1920s. Programmatically speaking, the CEIP figured prominently as a harbinger of legal internationalism, meant to secure US governance of the post-First World War world by resolving interstate disputes with the aid of legalist strategies for conflict resolution. Its most prominent American leaders, such as James Brown Scott and Nicholas M. Butler, wanted to promote the internationalist rapprochement of Europeans based on intellectual exchange and (legal) knowledge transfers across the Atlantic. Their expectations bore witness to the contemporary faith, promulgated within elite circles, in the regulating potential of academic discourse and scientific knowledge, and more explicitly in the potential of international law for appeasement. At a time when post-war Republican administrations were backing away from associating with the League of Nations, the CEIP establishment advocated Wilsonian internationalism to fight anti-democratic ideologies. This would become the overriding mission of the Carnegie Endowment in the light of the withdrawal of the US Government from foreign entanglements.

The CEIP's inter-war activities reveal two important features of foundations' behaviour. First, outcomes could fall far short of expectations. The CEIP's strategy to provide allegedly neutral knowledge to investigate the cause of bellicose power politics ultimately failed to contribute significantly to the post-war political settlement. Tempers were still raw after the experience of 1914–18. The Paris Peace Conference also provoked persistent interstate conflicts and political instabilities.[16] To gain momentum in such unfa-

---

14 See Berman, *Influence*.
15 See Engerman/Unger, "Global History of Modernization"; Raphael, "Ordnungs-muster".
16 See Mazower, *No Enchanted Palace*.

vourable conditions – and almost in a move of defensive reaction – CEIP representatives resorted to strategies of adjustment.[17] They embarked on multilingual publications to secure the broadest possible reach for their activities; they gave up exclusive coalitions with European pacifists and reached out to the reinvigorated nationalist forces instead; and they became sensitive to European fears of being dominated by a mighty American player and therefore acted more discreetly, even if they were still as power-oriented as before. Once they encountered a politically charged situation in post-war Europe, philanthropists shifted to making practical arrangements that were responsive to the precarious morale of their European counterparts. In that sense, the CEIP leaders allowed European interests to modify philanthropic practice while they clearly insisted on American precedence.

If, in the inter-war period, the Carnegie agenda remained somewhat limited to issues of "international understanding", the programmatic goals and funding activities of the Rockefeller Foundation were more widespread. One of the most important pioneering efforts of the Rockefeller Foundation was to transfer the practices of the natural sciences to the field of biological knowledge, deemed to be trapped in metaphysical speculation.[18] The attempt to reconfigure French biomedicine as part of its global involvement proved to be a rather smooth undertaking. The foundation's engagement was facilitated by the basic congruency between philanthropist expectations and the aims of the majority of French researchers, who spoke out in favour of a more coherent science policy and who could easily be mobilised for multidisciplinary large-scale projects since they shared the philanthropists' positivist faith in the progressive potential of fundamental research. It may well be that, in the period after 1945,[19] the Rockefeller Foundation's preference for fundamental research resulted from the fact that it was conceived of as enriching the French research landscape while also generating action-oriented knowledge that could be useful for the United States as well.

The Rockefeller Foundation's funding of anthropology in inter-war Europe suggests that philanthropic ambitions were partially inspired by the officers' expectation that Europe and its overseas territories could serve as laboratory spaces.[20] While the American foundation, in line with the official foreign policy communiqués of the US administrations at the time, avoided taking a clear anti-colonial stance, Rockefeller observers were attracted by the idea of engaging in the production of anthropological expert knowledge that would potentially enrich American strategies for dealing with their do-

17 See Wegener in this volume.
18 See Abir-Am, "Rise of Molecular Biology".
19 See Krige, *American Hegemony*, 12–13.
20 See Tilley, *Africa as a Living Laboratory*.

mestic and contemporary multi-ethnic society. There was no explicit philanthropic attempt to back up European colonial policies; rather, these were
deemed objectionable as they were based on special and privileged economic relations between the metropolitan powers and their respective colonial possessions.[21] In view of its role as a global philanthropist, the Rockefeller Foundation's anthropology programme in inter-war Britain and
France essentially testified to the technocratic vision of its representatives,
who believed that such engagements would foster modern politics as well as
social and political stability. Funding for both anthropology and biomedical
research in France and Britain in the inter-war period illustrates the Rockefeller Foundation's outstanding position as a key player in what was conceived of as progress-oriented and politically adaptable research to foster social stability.

With the advent of the Cold War, the animating spirit behind philanthropic policies and engagement on a global scale, and more explicitly in Europe, became more combative.[22] Each of the major philanthropic players –
the Rockefeller and Ford Foundations – approached the new situation in its
own way. Skilfully combining inter-war attitudes with an international engagement that bore witness to the exigencies of the early Cold War, the Rockefeller Foundation consolidated its extensive involvement abroad in the
1950s and early 1960s. One of the hallmarks of its funding operations in Europe became support for research targeted at deciphering the ideological
enemy. Some projects bore explicit witness to confrontational Cold-War
thinking, like the Rockefeller patronage of Secret Service analyses of the Soviet Union by European emigrants and American social and humanities
scholars. Others were less ideologically charged: Rockefeller representatives
emphatically avoided aligning their grant-giving activities with the sort of
politically desirable knowledge production that was deliberately financed by
the State Department. For example, foundation officers gave ample scope to
leftist thinking that was co-produced by former German-Jewish immigrants, such as Herbert Marcuse, and American intellectuals shaped by New
Deal liberalism, notably Barrington Moore – and this at the very moment
when the domestic politics of the Eisenhower Administration were obsessed
by McCarthy's witch-hunt on Communism. In this respect, the Rockefeller
Foundation became a vector of modernisation in a ground-breaking new
sense of the notion: Its funding strategy lent weight to a kind of Cold-War
social science and knowledge that included critical reflections on the self-
confident expectations of a Western linear, teleological notion of modernisation that converged on the American social model. This does not mean

---

21 See Louis, "American Anti-Colonialism".
22 See Krige, *American Hegemony* and Berghahn, *Intellectual Cold Wars*.

that the Rockefeller Foundation was willing to dilute its clear alignment with the West. Quite the contrary, Rockefeller officers ostentatiously conceded intellectual latitude to their leftist grantees exactly because they were convinced that supporting cutting-edge research even at the systemic margins of Western science would further confirm the hegemonic potential of a vastly superior Western knowledge culture. In the long run, the Rockefeller Foundation basically patronised Western leftish critiques of Communism, which proved to be much more enduring than the McCarthyist hysteria of the 1950s that was quickly discredited.

While much philanthropic energy was directed towards Europe, the Rockefeller Foundation also became active in a wide area of non-Western countries, funding an enormously broad range of what was defined as modernisation expertise.[23] The Rockefeller International Health Board proved to be a pioneer arm of Rockefeller philanthropy, initiating pilot programmes mainly targeted at hookworm, yellow fever and malaria eradication. Beginning in the inter-war years, it sought to bring modern Western medicine and especially American tropical medicine to the Southern hemisphere. Yet such top-down techno-politics of health could not prevent local agents from asserting their own views of how health policies could best be realised.[24] In addition to the self-declared humanitarianism, anxieties about regional instability as a result of poverty and social unrest in the areas of intervention engaged philanthropic concerns. All the same, in 1951 the Rockefeller Foundation unexpectedly closed down its International Health Division. This structural disruption of inter-war practices has been the subject of diverse scholarly interpretations, and it reveals the myriad internal and external exigencies and pressures upon philanthropic elites which had accumulated at the outset of the Cold War. It is argued here that the restructuring was less an indication of the unreserved positive appraisal of a successfully completed programme than a sign of internal institutional weaknesses in the division's approach to medical intervention along with a widespread disillusionment with international health activities. The alarmist tone of the neo-Malthusian narrative in the early 1950s, pointing to imminent global decline as a result of cataclysmic population growth,[25] figured prominently in marginalising philanthropic interest in what was now conceived of as an outdated approach to public health. Some even insisted that it was irresponsible to save lives if one could not properly contain population expansion and feed the

---

23 See Berman, "Educational Colonialism in Africa".
24 See Amrith, *Decolonizing International Health*; Solomon/Murard/Zylberman, *Shifting Boundaries*. On the issue of local agency in Rockefeller Foundation health policies, see also Borowy, *World Health*.
25 See Connelly, *Fatal Misconception*.

teeming (saved) millions. Thus, the competing claims of newly emerging experts communities from both within and without traditional philanthropic domains of intervention catalysed major adjustments of the Rockefeller Foundation's agenda.

The combative spirit of Cold-War philanthropy was especially present in the positioning of the Ford Foundation, which emerged as one of the staunchest strongholds of American Cold-Warriors, while not necessarily being congruent with each and every move of US foreign policy of the day.[26] We must be careful not to take the self-proclaimed agendas of the foundations at face value: They could engage other domestic actors who had their own motives for supporting a particular initiative. The foundations did not act alone during the Cold War, particularly when the projects they supported could be understood as contributing in important ways to the anti-Communist struggle. In this case, their grant-giving activities catalysed the interest of other arms of the Administration, and their motives for making awards had to be combined with the quite different and sometimes contradictory demands placed on them by the administration in Washington. Indeed, the Ford Foundation could not act autonomously when promoting international exchange with two major Western European physics research laboratories in the 1950s. The knowledge that would circulate through these nodes was at first deemed too sensitive by the State Department and the CIA to allow scientists from the Communist bloc to become part of the programme. The Ford Foundation adjusted the meaning of "international" accordingly, as did the directors of the two laboratories in question. Later this position was reversed, and the promotion of the noble ideal of international scientific co-operation was subverted by the opportunities it provided for informal intelligence gathering through American encounters with Soviet and Chinese physicists. In cases like these foundation rhetoric, while not empty, certainly served as a smoke-screen for the performance of typical Cold-War rivalry and the pursuit of American scientific and technological pre-eminence. The promotion of international peace and mutual understanding that provided the major public rationale for the Ford Foundation's intervention went hand in glove with the informal circulation of insights into Soviet and Chinese physics back to the CIA and the FBI – apparently with the willing consent not only of the officers and the President of Ford, but also of much of the American physics community.

The Ford Foundation's activities in the Netherlands described in this volume were part of their effort to promote the practices of American law as a universal model of organising and regulating Western democratic societies. Their choice of partners only testified to the philanthropists' intimate

---

26 See Berghahn, *Intellectual Cold Wars*; Krige, *American Hegemony*.

knowledge of the European terrain, which made the Netherlands appear as an exceptionally appropriate stage for such endeavours. Thus, the Ford Foundation targeted a joint law summer school at Leiden and Amsterdam universities as well as Dutch legal institutions such as the Hague Academy of International Law as strategic "beachheads" into Western Europe. By introducing legal expertise at critical nodes of knowledge formation, the foundation hoped to increase the possibilities of transferring an American awareness of problems and models for conflict resolution to the very heart of European political practice. In addition, by training emerging administrative, political and economic elites from Africa and Asia at privileged Dutch law institutions, the foundation also hoped to sponsor "beachheads" to the "Third World", which was emerging as fertile ground for enthusiastic philanthropic modernisation campaigns.

Though American philanthropy was already engaged in the Southern hemisphere during the inter-war years,[27] the struggle for allegiance and the competing social models for "development" that emerged during the Cold War – and the fear of political blowback if the Administration intervened too conspicuously – encouraged the foundations to redirect their resources. They scaled down expenditures on Western regions while dramatically increasing investments in the Southern hemisphere beginning in the late 1950s. In doing so, they were not simply arms of the US foreign policy establishment, determined to cut the ground from under Communism. For the Rockefeller and Ford Foundations, the invention of, and intervention in, the "Third World" was undoubtedly a matter of securing an American presence and influence in the region. The mutually reinforcing politicisation and scientisation of discourses on population, poverty and hunger that had begun to take root in the mid-1940s dovetailed with the emergence of the Southern hemisphere as a new laboratory where philanthropists could experiment with technocratic social engineering utopias and extraordinary large-scale projects that would transfer supposedly modernising knowledge from the advanced US metropole to the "backward" periphery.[28]

Excessive rates of population growth against the backdrop of increasing poverty and hunger – and the threat posed by Mao Zedong's model of development – turned democratic India into a major crisis region in the view of the self-proclaimed development experts of the day. It was thus also an attractive theatre for philanthropic and especially Ford Foundation commitment. Although the market-driven Green Revolution enthusiastically pro-

27 See Bell, "American Philanthropy".
28 See Speich/Nützenadel, *Global Inequality*; Cullather, *Hungry World*; Frey, *Asian Experiences of Development*; Connelly, *Fatal Misconception*; Escobar, "Worlds and Knowledges Otherwise"; Amrith, *Decolonizing International Health.*

moted by the Rockefeller Foundation in India in the 1960s brought no long-lasting relief from rural poverty, philanthropic strategies on the ground revealed a remarkable responsiveness to intricate local conditions. The Ford Foundation representative in Delhi, Douglas Ensminger, was adept at engaging with the Indian elites' decision-making beginning in the early 1950s. He was careful to distance himself from US government policies by couching his office's highly political choices in a language of technocracy and humanitarianism. This rhetorical tactic was indispensable for the Ford Foundation to gain access to a highly complex field of minor and major political players in Indian domestic politics in the 1950s and 1960s. When the foundation's Indian counterparts associated with Jawaharlal Nehru picked up on the same language, the strategy seemed to work at least temporarily. The Delhi field office acted not only as a facilitator to ensure philanthropic influence, however; it was of immense importance when it came to diverting initiatives emerging from Ford headquarters in New York that Ensminger deemed controversial or unenforceable in the light of the opposition that he expected them to produce if they were implemented. The New Delhi office became a filter preventing exuberant planning utopias by metropolitan foundation elites from being rejected outright by sceptical Indian actors, with the associated de-legitimation of the foundation's activities that that would entail.

In sum, the following articles convey the notion that, while the big three perceived themselves as vectors of stabilisation and modernisation, their claims of transferring understanding and modernisation abroad for the benefit of all mankind involved a precarious balancing act. Their programmatic self-assessments were more than simply declarations of intent: The increasingly asymmetrical power relationships between US grant-makers and European and Asian grantees enabled the foundations to leverage resources for producing knowledge in domains of their choosing. Their self-perception drew a veil over the many political and academic, infrastructural, institutional and individual, as well as local, regional and national preconditions that were necessary to co-define and consolidate their role as vectors of enlightened modernisation.

3. Local Grantees Beyond "Receiving-End" Logics: Interest Constellations, Tactics and Potentials

Throughout the twentieth-century history of international philanthropy, agency was not confined to the United States, but also performed by prospective and actual grantees in different regions of the world. US philanthropy never worked as a mere one-way street, a mechanism for spreading neat modernisation knowledge packages unilaterally from US philanthropists to passive, receptive actors in Europe – and the world for that matter. Rather, US modernisers were often put to the test in a series of local encounters with scientists, intellectuals, expert advisors and knowledge brokers in their respective civil societies. Identifying professional interests and individual characters, political, economic, social and cultural backgrounds and particular knowledge "demands" on the "receiving end" of the historical encounter is vital to completing our focus on agency and to exploring the possible dimensions of knowledge co-production.

In the case of the CEIP activities in post-First Word War Europe, the political situation and discursive atmosphere hardly nurtured the sort of transnational understanding envisioned by the programme's elites. Instead, the national antagonisms of the war years in Europe largely undermined philanthropic ambitions. International and more explicitly European power structures that characterised the First World War and persisted well into the 1930s seemed to work to the detriment of philanthropically induced knowledge circulation. Lacking a shared language, prone to conflictual nationalist divisions and concerned about being patronised by the United States, European infrastructures and actors were not quick to embrace the solicitations of Carnegie representatives. On the contrary, such factors served as barriers that could easily stifle American-led initiatives – as when the European members of the Comité d'Administration of the CEIP withheld approval of a pioneer project in the Balkans on the grounds that it was politically impossible.

The impact that local internal dynamics could have on philanthropic action is especially visible in the case of anthropology funding in inter-war Britain and France, where the interventions brought the Rockefeller Foundation to the limits of its ambitions when it came to financially supporting knowledge production in Europe that would fit into US expectations about colonial planning expertise. Of course, inter-war anthropology had been a core discipline among the sciences advanced by European colonial powers to consolidate core parts of their empires at the high noon of late colonial emergencies.[29] Thus, the Rockefeller Foundation encountered both political and academic, institutional and individual situations on the spot that partially facilitated, but also partially thwarted, its goals. Most notably, it met with intricate networks both in political and scientific *milieux* in London and Paris that complicated the dynamics of US patronage. Actors in both localities competed for recognition as experts on a field of knowledge that was just then taking disciplinary shape as academically institutionalised "anthropology" or "ethnology": Both pursued their own specific interest agendas. Colonial administration elites, claiming that there was a crisis of colonial

29 For more general contexts see Stuchtey, *Science*.

government, called out for anthropologically informed expertise that would prevent imperial decline. British and French social anthropologists tried to establish themselves as expert advisers to scientifically informed colonial governments. Thus, the driving force behind allegedly politically adaptable anthropological knowledge was in fact the demand from within European political and academic circles – not the intervention of the United States. This tended to reduce the big project of knowledge circulation to instances of funding that bore the signs of local conditions and relationships rather than the imprint of some philanthropic programme. The foundations could not, nor did they want to, impose an agenda on the "receiving end"; on the contrary, the polycentric network of local actors transformed the philanthropic offer to fit into their own respective agendas.

In a similar vein, the funding activities of the Rockefeller Foundation in France during the 1920s and up to the 1940s in the field of biomedicine suggest that US philanthropy did not leave more traces on the shape of the field than French scientists and scientific managers found acceptable at the time. Local dynamics clearly pre-structured the foundation's options to engage in the field. Their French counterparts were actively professionalising their fields: They spoke out in favour of concentrating biomedical research in multidisciplinary institutions and, maintained a close relationship both with French political elites and private patrons of biomedical science such as the Deutsch de la Meurthe family. To that extent the soon-to-be grantees were already equipped with considerable experience in collaboration and negotiation at a national level before they established closer contacts with the Rockefeller Foundation. Genetics, research on nervous diseases and on radioactivity proved to be the most prominent fields of Rockefeller funding – all knowledge sectors carefully chosen by the foundation in accordance with contemporary French research trends in the 1920s and 1930s, and thus funded in order to secure rapid progress by expeditiously generating new, co-produced expert knowledge.

If the Rockefeller Foundation was able to leave its imprint on the construction of the Caisse Nationale des Sciences, the newly emerging centre co-ordinating French science policy, it was only to the extent that it was expressly asked to do so by leading organisers of science in France who oriented themselves towards the foundation's divisional structure as a model to compartmentalise academic research on a national level. The major impetus for this (mainly French-inspired) transfer was the perception (commonly shared with many contemporaries in Europe and the United States) that the institutional streamlining of science policies was, both in war time and beyond, a matter of mobilising national strength and – more explicitly in the French case – of gearing up to enter into intense national(istic) competition with the much-mistrusted German science world in particular.[30] Thus, when turning to the Rockefeller divisional model, the French, determined to get ahead in their fierce competition with their menacing German neighbour, appealed to what they believed to be the most modern version of science policy organisation in the United States at the time.

With the advent of the Cold War, power relationships between philanthropists and – in this volume mainly Western European – grantees became more pertinent compared to the inter-war period. If Europeans lacked resources after the First World War and therefore turned for support to the United States as world creditor, fiscal and power imbalances were even more distinct after 1945.[31] Moreover, the wide-ranging task of reconstruction to compensate for political, economic and moral devastation (above all in Germany, but also in neighbouring countries affected by National Socialism) created widespread European demand for US support. While it would be hard to identify an overall pattern of grantees' inclusion into philanthropic activism, there is every indication that the Rockefeller philanthropy of the early Cold-War period and up until the mid-1950s tolerated a diverse range of prospective grantees' political leanings. This happened notwithstanding the constraints imposed by the Cox Congressional Committee and successive reports in the early 1950s that chided the foundations for being lax in supporting Communists and left-leaning grantees, threatening to remove their tax-exempt status as a result. A significant case in point is the Rockefeller Foundation's international Marxism-Leninism project and its programme on legal and political philosophy during these years. These offered massive intellectual space to non-conformist émigré scholars and Leftist grantees such as Herbert Marcuse. Marcuse, who had been recruited to work for the Office of Strategic Services when he came to the United States in 1941, and who was transferred to the State Department after the war, eventually became embedded in informal transnational networks.[32] Against the tide of McCarthyist anti-Communist paranoia, the Rockefeller Foundation sought to provide a sheltered sphere for research that allowed these grantees to reorient and adjust their analytical approaches – previously directed towards the critique of National Socialist rule – towards Communism and Marxism in order to better know the Cold-War enemy.[33] Eschewing the simplifications of current theories of totalitarianism that collapsed Communism into National Socialism, they insisted upon the modernity of the Soviet Union and found the humanistic ideals of Marxism attractive. Moreover,

---

30 See Rausch, "Scientific Philanthropy".
31 See Leffler/Westad, *Cambridge History of the Cold War*.
32 See Wheatland, *Frankfurt School in Exile*; Krohn/Schildt, *Zwischen den Stühlen*.
33 See Engerman, *Know Your Enemy*.

they provided justifications for the policy of détente rather than of containment towards what was considered to be a defensive Soviet Union. The room they had to manoeuvre intellectually resulted from the fact that early Cold-War philanthropists at the Rockefeller Foundation clearly sided with foreign policy elites on issues of national interest and security while being convinced of the value of a liberal social model that prized openness and intellectual flexibility as defining marks of Western liberal capitalism (as opposed to the closed world of state-driven socialism). That said, in the mid-1960s this period of ostentatious openness of mind towards alternative modes of reasoning was stretched to its limits as an embattled US elite came increasingly under assault from the Left for its engagement in Vietnam.

If only as a result of fierce inter-European factionalism, possible foundation grantees tried to use their prospective and actual entitlement to enhance their international position. It comes as no surprise that this was particularly true for smaller countries like the Netherlands, whose elites were eager to invite the Ford Foundation into their networks and thus showcase their attractiveness especially to their German and French neighbours. Accordingly, a majority of Dutch intellectuals at the Hague Academy of International Law and the Institute of Social Studies were anything but fearful of an attempted takeover if they received substantial grants – on the contrary, they argued strongly for major philanthropic engagement. If the level of resistance remained low, this was as much a sign of the Ford Foundation's strategy to widen the purview of US legal thought and practice as it was a consequence of the strategic openness of these Dutch academics. The symbolic capital the Dutch hoped to gain from their closeness to the Ford Foundation swamped other concerns. It is also plausible to argue that advancing the professionalisation of Dutch experts by adopting American models was expected to help deal with the challenges posed by European integration, enabling Dutch legal authorities to better position themselves and the Netherlands in a supranational community, a "United States of Europe".

Ford Foundation support for physics was also warmly welcomed at major research centres in Copenhagen and Geneva. No matter how it was justified at foundation headquarters in New York – or configured to meet the demands of the national security state in Washington – the grantees made sure that their interests were respected.[34] What they sought above all were the resources to invite leading American physicists for extended in-house sojourns, thus benefitting from their deep experience and cutting-edge knowledge. Ford could make sense of this programme in terms of its transformative ambitions and its desire to strengthen Western science with an injection of American ideas and practices, and it found the perfect partner in

34 See Krige, "Die Führungsrolle der USA".

two established laboratories in Europe, which already defined themselves as nodes for international scientific exchange and sought exactly what Ford wanted to give (even if that meant accepting unpalatable terms). And if the marriage ran so smoothly, it was also because of a complicity between the directors on both sides of the Atlantic, a complicity that accepted that international collaboration was also a strategy for enhancing national pre-eminence, and that the pursuit of mutual understanding went hand in glove with national rivalry, above all in a sensitive field of research like physics.

The determination that grantees had to profit from their status and use their closeness to American foundations as a trump card in internal local power struggles was by no means confined to the European setting. All the same, their tactics on extra-European terrain had very specific characteristics. In the field of international health campaigns, the official programmatic wording saw the Rockefeller Foundation's stimulating the general advancement of humankind as an ongoing project that had already led to its engagement in non-Western regions in the inter-war period. Philanthropic practice on the ground was messier. The endeavour was often characterised by bringing top-down, donor-driven, Western knowledge transfers to what were treated as backward peripheries.[35] Local medical professionals had, however, started mapping and treating some diseases long before the philanthropies became involved, so that the Rockefeller public health work could build on already available local awareness and knowledge potentials. This occasionally compelled philanthropists to negotiate their prerogatives on the spot.[36] If, under these auspices, the foundation managed to operate as a flexible vector of modernisation processes, this was due more to its remarkable responsiveness to local exigencies and prevailing claims *in situ* that obliged it to refashion a top-down approach to health reform policies.

The Ford Foundation's commitment in India in the 1950s and 1960s confirms that "peripheral" grantees could hope to reconfigure the philanthropic agenda. Development plans legitimised through rhetoric based on scientific and technological knowledge had been mobilised in Indian political debates since late colonial times. This was even more relevant after 1947, when decolonisation was no longer anticipated but formally enacted, and it provoked a new sense of urgency. Although fighting unchecked population growth and blatant poverty by central planning schemes and industrialisation figured prominently in development debates, Indian anxieties about securing an "indigenous" presence in domestic politics and avoiding foreign

---

35 See Page/Valone, *Globalization of Scientific Medicine*; Anderson, *Colonial Pathologies*; Birn, *Marriage of Convenience*; Farley, *To Cast Out Disease*; Cueto, *Missionaries of Science*.

36 See Palmer, *Launching Global Health*; Amrith, *Decolonizing International Health*.

tutelage also loomed large.[37] Thus, when Jawaharlal Nehru, having assumed office as India's first Prime Minister in 1947, addressed the Ford Foundation four years later to bargain for a "village-level 'community development'" plan "aimed at raising agricultural production and village conditions" (according to Nicole Sackley), he found the foundation field office strategically useful to circumventing a host of obstacles and opposition forces from within. These included sceptical or downright hostile actors among powerful state-level politicians and in the Indian civil service. Adopting the programmatic rhetoric of the Ford Foundation, Nehru's government presented its alliance with the US philanthropists as an effectively non-political, technocratic coalition fully in line with his party's reform ambitions. There was no guarantee that this strategy would work. Both Nehru's political allies and his fierce Communist opponents were disgusted by what they saw to be a much-too-close allegiance between the Ford Foundation and the US Government. Nehru's attempt at extracting the invited intervention of the Ford Foundation from obvious larger Cold-War logics (all the while pleading non-alignment) could work only for a while and could not hope to be durable in the long run.

A systematic reflexion on the interests and tactics of local grantees when negotiating knowledge transfers with philanthropists suggests that there were – either within or outside Europe – no easily identifiable groups of actors to be captured in neat country- or region-wide typologies. International as much as internal distributions of political power, along with institutional and financial infrastructure and diversity among the main actors, coalesced in complex matrices producing highly specific dynamics in each and every case. What we can say is that grantee reactions went far beyond mere "receiving-end" logics and resulted in various degrees of absorption, interference, retardation or even hindrance of philanthropic agendas. Ultimately, the grantees' respective environments, far from being mere *tabulae rasae* on which US-led transformations could be inscribed, were also substantial arsenals of knowledge in their own right, and resources upon which philanthropists could draw.[38] While there is no need to essentialise "indigenous" knowledge in non-American sites of US philanthropic activity, the capacity of the foundations' counterparts to shape the modes of knowledge circulation was always discernible; none of the contributors to this volume adopts a model in which the knowledge–power vector is unidirectional and points outwards, towards "backward" regions and populations at the mercy of philanthropy. Admittedly, US knowledge was produced in and circulated

37 See Zachariah, *Developing India*; Amrith, *Decolonizing International Health*; Gupta, *Postcolonial Developments*.
38 See Krige, "Building the Arsenal of Knowledge".

through an asymmetric field of force defined by the strong power position of US actors vis-à-vis Europe and Asia both in the inter-war and early Cold-War periods. But any diffusionist notion of an almost unchallenged philanthropic centre from which prescribed knowledge norms and practices trickled into, or were imposed upon, the wider world arena would gravely underrate the much more complicated logics of knowledge circulation explored here.[39]

4. Time and Dynamics: A *Longue-Durée* Perspective on Philanthropy

One of the still widely unexplored issues concerning US philanthropy is its long-term development over the course of the twentieth century. While it is obvious that the philanthropic endeavour was deeply entrenched in the progressivist and New Deal thinking of the early twentieth century in the United States, ideals, agendas and strategies kept changing over time from the inter-war years onwards – and even more so as the twentieth century progressed. When and how such change came about more exactly is still difficult to trace. Based on the evidence contained in this volume, we sense that the crucial question of what connects pre- and post-Second World War philanthropy remains open at this point. Taken together, nevertheless, the contributions allow for a set of preliminary conclusions that will need further refinement in ongoing studies.

As most research has been done on the Cold-War period, the answer to how we launch a *longue-durée* perspective on twentieth-century US philanthropy depends crucially on a comprehensive and sophisticated understanding of Cold-War philanthropy. Contributions in this volume's Cold-War section offer a complex reading of the post-1945 scene. They identify two intricately interwoven dimensions of philanthropic rationalities and effects: On the one hand, philanthropy as a political endeavour eventually became a core part of international power relations during the Cold War. In particular, the relationships of the Ford Foundation with the respective US administrations ranged from intimate collaboration to formal autonomy, depending on the pertinence of the project to American global interests. While cultural diplomacy – understood as propagating American values as well as the benefits of Western science and of anti-Communist ideals throughout the world – mattered a great deal,[40] the Ford Foundation brand of philanthropy was ultimately about "knowledge and power" defined in the American interest.

---

39 See esp. Berman, *Influence*.
40 See Berghahn, *Intellectual Cold Wars*.

Thus, funding physics in Denmark and Switzerland was clearly a Cold-War proposition, geared to further the production of strategically critical knowledge and thereby protect national security and strengthen "America's competitive scientific and technological advantage" (John Krige). In that sense, US philanthropy after 1945 tends to merge into the East–West dialectics that underpinned major segments of international power politics after 1945. Against this background, it seems obvious to start from the premise that the Second World War and the immediately subsequent years entailed a decisive cut: More often than not, US philanthropy after 1945 became an arm of American foreign policy, mobilised to consolidate American hegemony and build a world order based on (sometimes informal) domination and (sometimes consensual) subordination that cohered with American aims. This involved a significant rupture with the dynamic of the previous inter-war period when US philanthropy worked as merely one of many other signs and occasions of transnational internationalism and increasingly global network-building under much less asymmetrical political and economic power conditions. But then this was also a response to the perceived Communist threat to American global leadership, be that in Europe or Asia, Latin America or Africa.

That said, the contributions in this volume also demand that we should not exaggerate the rupture in 1945 and recognise that the break between the inter-war and post-war periods was not that clear-cut. A closer look at the intellectual makeup of inner Rockefeller circles in the early Cold War testifies instead to a specific mindset of foundation officers that does not so much corroborate the notion of a substantial break between inter- and post-war philanthropic ideologies as point to strong intellectual continuities between the two time periods. In fact, the Rockefeller Foundation's Cold-War programme choices and tactics were always infused with a revitalised New Deal liberalism that after 1945 prompted foundation elites even to adhere to the idea that scientific knowledge and rationality (funded by the Rockefeller Foundation) would by themselves ultimately be congenial to further social progress. As a result, funding cutting-edge knowledge, even if unconventional or possibly non-conformist, was deemed to coexist easily with the philanthropists' mission to advance an at times contradictory, unpolished modernity. If the Rockefeller Foundation proudly insisted on intellectual pluralism and diversity, such openness was strategically motivated as a means to promote Western liberal modernity in fierce competition with the utterly rejected counterproject of Soviet modernity. Seen from this angle, the early Cold-War philanthropy of the Rockefeller Foundation, while clearly differing from that of the pre-war period, also testifies to a consistent continuity with inter-war philanthropic creeds and practices. We must avoid reductionism. Rockefeller philanthropic programmes after 1945 drew together a variety of threads in their texture of thought, weaving anti-Soviet Cold-War attitudes into the more pluralist attitudes of New Dealers in the rank and file of the inter-war Rockefeller Foundation.

Contributions to the inter-war section of this volume can be seen as converging with such a perspective from the opposite end of the timescale we cover. From this angle as well, they illustrate aspects of both continuity and of discontinuity between inter- and post-war activities. Another look at the Rockefeller Foundation's anthropology initiatives in inter-war Britain and France points to the fact that US philanthropy in the inter-war years was driven by two overarching agendas: bringing modern and potentially modernising knowledge to the outside world, and promoting knowledge that would facilitate social engineering practices to control and to legitimise such control of non-Western societies.[41] These aims were thus by no means reserved for Cold-War American actors and the foundations after 1945 in particular. Instead, foundations responded to diverse claims of political and scientific actors especially in inter-war Europe. In fact, some interest groups within inter-war British and French colonial administrations, much as within the ranks of British and French social scientists, had already developed a strong interest in generating and using anthropology as a form of knowledge that could legitimate and help keep their eroding empires under control. In other words, the idea of producing useful knowledge in *milieux* where politics and science intersected did not wait on the intervention of US philanthropy. The inter-war anthropology funding of the Rockefeller Foundation ultimately marked the encounter of two parallel modernisation projects on both sides of the Atlantic. As a corollary, the Foundation was far from having a carte blanche for promoting major research agendas. It found itself relegated to just one (foreign) benefactor alongside several other, and at times potentially competing, (domestic) actor groups. The Foundation's scope of action depended more on its ability to capitalise on local preconditions than on its appearing as a staunch defender of modernisation knowledge *à l'américaine*.

The foundations were not monolithic agencies, and their strategies changed over time. Philanthropic programmes responded creatively to the dynamic of international power arrangements. While the pre-war agenda of the Carnegie Endowment, for instance, had been cautiously non-offensive, Butler's post-war CEIP was more intrusive. With its academic exchange programmes and publication activities, it became ensnared in built-up tensions especially between the former Central Powers and their many neighbouring rivals.[42] Moreover, CEIP representatives preferred to shy away from distribu-

---

41 See also Hochgeschwender, "Noblest Philosophy"; Jordan, *Machine-Age Ideology*.
42 See Winn, "Nicholas Murray Butler".

ting grants more widely under increasingly confusing political circumstances – the emergence of dictatorial regimes and then another world war. Closing down the European Comité d'Administration and finally the Centre Européen in 1939–40 essentially turned out to be an inevitable reaction to the inhospitable situation in Europe. If we look beyond the inter-war period, this scenario changes again, now showing the Carnegie Endowment after the Second World War as rather inconspicuous when measured against the newly emerging transnational infrastructure for a peace settlement in Europe, but highly active in the newly discovered "Third World", the emerging laboratory for the modernisation fantasies of Western philanthropies, and not only of those from the Carnegie stable.

The years prior to and shortly after the Second World War constituted a transition period – if not a caesura – when not only the Carnegie but also the Rockefeller Foundation activities underwent serious revision. The closing down of Rockefeller's International Health Division is significant here as it illustrated a major "political shift" of foundation elites in the early 1950s. "Cold-War realism" prompted a new generation of trustees to establish structural conformity within and scale down international health issues in favour of competing new fields of strategic knowledge such as population studies, believed to allow for even more visibility of the Rockefeller Foundation as a powerful exponent of regulative knowledge.[43]

One of the reasons why the philanthropic impact is so difficult to measure lies in its remaining in force even after the official withdrawal of the endowment or the foundation from the terrain. Network-building with international elites – one of the most widely used philanthropic strategies to exert lasting influence on the hearts and minds of their grantees – did of course not collapse straightaway with such withdrawal; it could outlast temporary periods of philanthropic absence only to be reactivated under more favourable conditions, like those that emerged after the end of the Second World War. In this sense, the example of the Rockefeller Foundation's funding of French biomedical science is another case in point, as it opens up a wide panorama of dense inter-war network-building that could be capitalised on after 1945. Pre-war experiences of co-operation could provide useful nodes of communication and exchange that were ready to be revitalised. Earlier ties between French biomedical researchers and Rockefeller Foundation representatives obviously facilitated the French view that they could continue to benefit from foundation largesse, if only reluctantly, under still more asymmetrical power relationships after 1945.

More research is needed to account for such long-term developments as indicators of mutations or changes of earlier philanthropic ambitions. In

---

43 See Cullather, *Hungry World*; Etzemüller, *Ein ewigwährender Untergang*.

any event, it is obvious that substantial reconfigurations of the international order, including co-constructed new transnational actor groups and newly emerging power and interest constellations following the two world wars, like other major epochal transformations, left their marks on philanthropic activities.

5. What's Next?

Given the broad scope of the subject, the set of articles collected here clearly does not exhaustively explore the vast field of US philanthropies and knowledge circulation on a global scale. What we offer is a reading of foundation activities through the lens of the co-production of knowledge and of an American-led regime of world order, a theme we consider to be both important and understudied. By way of conclusion, and building on the comments at the end of each section, we want to place this work in the broader perspective of transnational history and point to the kinds of research questions and desiderata that are pertinent to embedding the philanthropic phenomenon into a broader historical view of multilayered processes of global entanglements and knowledge circulations.

First, while this volume focuses on knowledge circulation that gave paramount importance to foundations and their respective grantees, the array of historically relevant actors is far greater. In order not to inflate the foundations' importance, particularly after the Second Word War, when so many other political and economic bodies became engaged in efforts to improve the human condition, international histories of US philanthropy will have to define more carefully the foundations' relationship to these other arms of the US administration and international organisations that intervened in the global arena.[44] Were they essential catalysts for action, partners in a major transformative project, legitimators for later state-sponsored interventions or just rather minor players? How can we measure their impact and how does this vary over time and between countries, regions and fields of action? While none of the articles deals with these questions in detail, comparing them already suggests the immense variety and dynamics of additional agencies that will need further exploration. In the inter-war period, for instance, the Carnegie Endowment was far from acting in a vacuum, but came, amongst many others, upon European pacifist organisations in the immediate period following the First World War. The latter maintained ambivalent relations with US philanthropy, as they appreciated its financial support, while at the same time being suspicious of the unsolicited intrusive efforts of

---

44 See Iriye, "Internationalizing International History".

CEIP representatives. When myriads of additional actors populated the international stage after 1945, the Ford Foundation representatives saw themselves, amongst many others, in a strategic alliance with the United States Information Agency (USIA), the CIA and the State Department, even though such interconnections could prove incriminating. While all stakeholders were promoting cultural diplomacy by grant-making to academics abroad, the Ford Foundation was at times less closely intertwined with the US Administration than with the USIA.

Philanthropists operated on terrain filled with a multitude of intergovernmental organisations such as the League of Nations or the United Nations as well as many other agencies working for a sustainable world order. These had mushroomed at the end of the nineteenth century, but mostly tended to perpetuate Western dominance by structuring internal participation to exclude undesirable others.[45] While we do not see US philanthropists maintaining relations with proponents of alternative modes of internationalism such as the pan-African nationalist movement[46] (which was ignored by the Rockefeller Foundation in the inter-war years), it will be important to measure to what extent such internationally competing or coalition forces may have modified the foundations' self-perceptions. Their rhetoric of political and economic entitlement (to citizenship and prosperity) within or possibly even beyond "the West", and their increasing concern with worldwide inequality and its underlying causes, certainly left their marks on philanthropic self-perceptions and strategies to a degree yet to be established.[47] In this regard, Madeleine Herren's comment on the first three articles reminds us that, if localities mattered a great deal, philanthropic competition (not the least for public acknowledgement) with national governments and with an ever-increasing bulk of international organisations on the one hand, and philanthropic co-operation with international organisations on the other, still need more a systematic reflection to evaluate their role.

In their comments on the other two sections of this volume, both Kiran Patel and Volker Berghahn emphasise the need to pay close attention to the complex dynamics of foundation activities in the Cold War, when their traditional commitment to humanitarian ideals became entangled with superpower rivalry and the promotion of the American model of liberal democracy. Patel particularly stresses the need for careful analyses of the role

---

45 See Laqua, "Transnational Intellectual Cooperation"; Herren, *Internationale Organisationen seit 1865*; eadem, Networks in Times of Transition; Clavin, *Bread and Butter Internationalism*; Amrith/Sluga, "New Histories"; Kott, "Une 'communauté épistémique'"; Iriye, "Role of International Organisations" and "Internationalism".

46 On the issue of competing non-Western sorts of internationalism and world order visions see Conrad/Sachsenmaier, *Competing Visions*.

47 See Maier, "Alternative Narratives".

of foundations in the expansion of the Cold War beyond the East–West confrontation and their capacity to respond to competing and parallel global dynamics that transcended bipolar logics. Berghahn insists, above all, on the need for an even clearer definition of how US Cold-War philanthropy could combine highly asymmetrical power constellations – which privileged US actors – with seemingly "softer" strategies of mutually negotiated bilateral blending and circulating of knowledge.

Second, further research is needed to address more specifically the activities of US foundations during the post-1970s and 1980s period (not to speak of the post-Cold War period).[48] In any event, there are clear signs that both the Rockefeller and Ford Foundations drastically cut back their global commitment especially in so-called Third World countries such as India after the late 1960s.[49] Their doing so was both symptomatic of the détente reached with the Soviet Union and of a growing sense of disillusionment with the soaring philanthropic ideals of the earlier post-war years. By the early 1970s, political enthusiasm was clearly waning for modernisation and planning as some sort of ready-made universal tools for alleviating poverty and overcrowding. Planning prophecies were falsified by the persistence of all sorts of inequalities. The appalling inconsistency between reality and the American concept of development, together with the democratic and pluralist aspirations that it was supposed to promote, further discredited the foundations' transformative agenda. That said, the disenchantment with so-called development policies and the general critique of modernisation and planning visions so widespread in the 1970s were by no means unique to US philanthropy, but were rather in line with an epochal sea-change of Western and international (development) policies more broadly understood.[50] At the same time, by the late 1960s the economic surge in many countries of (Western) Europe led both the Rockefeller and Ford Foundations to withdraw their attention from what had previously been a site for resource-intensive American reconstruction endeavours. Many more parallel, and at times competing, state and non-state actors (as well as private, economic and political institutions of all sorts) also became involved in transnational science policy at this time, thereby curtailing the former prominence of US philanthropy as a major "external" co-producer of knowledge in the European theatre.

Third, interesting work also remains to be done in comparing the role of foundations as nodes in the circulation of knowledge and the co-production

48 For the effects of the end of the post-war economic boom in Europe see Wirsching, "1970s and 1980s".

49 See Gordon, "Wealth Equals Wisdom?".

50 See Ekbladh, *Great American Mission*; Engerman et al., *Staging Growth*; Gilman, *Mandarins of the Future*; Ferguson, *Anti-Politics Machine*; Ferguson et al., *Shock of the Global*; Doering-Manteuffel/Raphael, *Nach dem Boom*.

of world order in different regions of the globe. American hegemony was not of one piece. On the one hand, the United States could deploy its scientific and technological preponderance, enhanced by the wealth and international prestige of the foundations, as an instrument to reshape practices in both Europe and a country like India. On the other hand, the fields of intervention were obviously different, reflecting the differing priorities in advanced industrialised countries and in a developing world shaking off the shackles of colonialism. And if the strategy was the same – enrolling educated elites in the American-led modernisation project – and if local resistance was always to be expected, the very different structures of power in different regions of the globe had marked effects on how knowledge was fused with practice. The modernisation of post-war Europe was facilitated by a general rise in the standard of living after the mid-1950s, the entrenchment of democracy and the routing of Communism: Europe became an essential node in the co-production of knowledge to strengthen the "free world". The modernisation of the Third World was in thrall to the structural problems of poverty, over-population and famine, which called forth sometimes violent responses by the American government and by domestic national elites that often came to serve as "gateways" and essential points of passage between the North and the South.[51] The liberal humanitarian rhetoric of the foundations was hollow besides the Johnson Administration's determination to transform Indian agriculture by denying food aid at a time of famine. Forced sterilisation in the Indian country-side was not the kind of education the foundations had in mind when they promoted family planning. The relationship between the foundations' transformative goals and local political cultures, and their capacity to reject, appropriate or absorb and apply new forms of knowledge as tools of change, is at the core of the articles in this book, and will remain so in any analysis that seeks to push its arguments further.

---

51 See Cooper/Stoler, *Tensions of Empire.*

1. Interwar Philanthropy –
Internationalism and Power Politics

Jens Wegener

"An Organisation, European in Character"

European Agency and American Control at the Centre Européen,
1925–40

When James Brown Scott, a director of the Carnegie Endowment for Inter-national Peace (CEIP) and distinguished professor of international law, went to Heidelberg in June 1928, he expected to give a lecture on the judicial foundations of state authority. Instead the president of the university, Rektor Karl Heinsheimer, took to the podium at the scheduled hour. Addressing the crowd of students and faculty, Rektor Heinsheimer announced that, in a backstage meeting, Professor Scott had failed to give him assurances that he would not reiterate his position on Germany's guilt for the Great War. Thus, the event was cancelled, and the audience was asked to go home. For the American professor the event must have felt twice as hurtful since it was not only a snub from a fellow distinguished colleague, it also challenged the very ideas that he, an officer of the Carnegie Endowment, had been working to establish for almost two decades, in particular the idea that open and rea-soned debate, overcoming national biases and understanding other points of view could help transform Europe into a more peaceful continent. Rektor Heinsheimer probably disagreed; he viewed the American professor as someone who dresses up politics as academic discourse, perpetuating foreign domination under the pretence of open debate.[1]

American foundations in the interwar period had to contend with the in-evitable – and often uncomfortable – relationship between academic knowl-edge and political discourse. The notion that the exchange of ideas and the intellectual rigour of academia could assuage the nationalist passions that had manifested themselves in the First World War was widespread among American intellectuals – especially in the offices of the American foun-

---

1 "Un incident à l'Université de Heidelberg", *Journal des débats politiques et littéraires* (22 June 1928), 2. In 1919, acting on behalf of the US government, Scott had signed the Report of the Commission on the Responsibility of the Authors of the War and on En-forcement of Penalties, which declared Germany culpable for the war. "Report of the Commission", 125.

dations of the 1920s and early 1930s. Marshalling the forces of modern scientific inquiry for the cause of international peace held special appeal at a time when the potential of scientific knowledge to advance "civilisation" was rarely questioned. Yet, during this time American foundations were to discover the limits of this approach. Far from establishing a dispassionate sphere of academic debate, these foundations were forced to contend with political considerations, nationalist resistance and language boundaries in promoting their agendas to European audiences. That Americans could encounter anxiety and resistance upon becoming active in Europe was plainly visible at the time. American technological achievements were often admired, but fears of cultural imposition and foreign interference were never far off. One strategy pursued by American foundations to avoid contentious debates was to attempt to conceal the source of the money and exert their influence covertly.[2] The Carnegie Endowment for International Peace, however, opted for a more interactive model, inviting a group of Europeans to join in its work in an effort to gain legitimacy and local knowledge. In 1925, it created an administrative body for all programs run out of its Centre Européen in Paris. The members of this group – known as the Comité d'Administration – were closely involved in most decisions that concerned the endowment's operations on the Continent. In discussing the European activities of the Carnegie Endowment during the interwar years, this article seeks to highlight the extent to which the foundation relied on local partners to navigate Europe's complex political and cultural landscape.[3]

Although the well-established rubric of "Americanisation" is still a prevalent shorthand for the study of the process by which the United States came to exert an outsized cultural influence on Europe, recent research has eschewed unidirectional interpretations and emphasised instead a more mutual exchange of goods and ideas.[4] Although a number of different models have been suggested to replace the traditional sender–receiver model, as Volker Berghahn has pointed out imbalances in power relationships still need to be taken into account.[5] Locating the work of American foundations in this context poses the challenge of recognising the extent to which philanthropic forums opened the door to European agency while acknowledging

2 See the Rockefeller Foundation's efforts to conceal the American ties of its subsidiary Abraham-Lincoln-Stiftung in Germany. Richardson, *Weimars transatlantischer Mäzen*.

3 In recent years there has been renewed scholarly interest in the Carnegie Endowment. See, for example, Winn, "Nicholas Murray Butler"; Tournès, "La Dotation Carnegie"; Rietzler, "Philanthropy, Peace Research, and Revisionist Politics"; idem, "Before the Cultural Cold Wars".

4 Recent literature that has highlighted the interactive nature of transatlantic transfer processes includes Rodgers, *Atlantic Crossings*; de Grazia, *Irresistible Empire*.

5 Berghahn, "Debate on 'Americanisation'", 120.

the power dynamics that shaped these transatlantic relationships. Ultimately, American foundations, represented by their field officers and directors, held the power of the purse over their European recipients. But to overemphasise their superior financial position affords only a limited view of the web of interests that shaped American philanthropic policies in Europe. Not every financial transaction can be reduced to an attempt at influence peddling; not every European recipient could be assumed to be susceptible to monetary inducements. American foundations at the time were aware of the fact that simply throwing money at the problem was a solution unlikely to lead to the desired results.[6]

And yet, money did matter. When the Carnegie Endowment was founded in 1910 with $10,000,000 backed in U.S. Steel bonds, this sum supported a moderate staff of eighteen employees at its headquarters in Washington, DC.[7] In the decades that followed the organisation's funds stagnated and were insufficient to expand its programmes or even to make up for the inevitable decline in purchasing power brought about by inflation. As the endowment's third decade drew to a close, in 1939, it reported assets of just over $12,000,000.[8] The Carnegie Endowment was quickly surpassed by other major American philanthropies such as the Rockefeller and Ford foundations in terms of financial capacity, and by 1960 it had fallen from the list of the twenty-five wealthiest American foundations.[9]

Under these circumstances the endowment could not rely on its financial largesse to the extent that other philanthropies did. Different means were required, and starting in the mid-1920s the Carnegie Endowment sought to promote what it called an "international mind" in Europe and throughout the world. Through its European centre, the endowment sponsored educational programmes and sought to create transnational connections among European educational, political and economic elites. The combination of knowledge transfer and personal connections was seen as a promising approach to overcoming Europe's divisions.

6 For works that highlight the economic interests behind the domestic and foreign policies of US foundations, including the Carnegie Endowment, see Berman, *Influence of the Carnegie, Ford, and Rockefeller Foundations*; Parmar, "Engineering Consent".

7 Pay Roll for August 1 to 15, 1912, Box 28, Folder 7, CEIP Records, Rare Book & Manuscript Library, Columbia University (hereinafter RBML).

8 *Carnegie Endowment for International Peace Year Book* 28 (1939), 172.

9 Cf. Berghahn, *Intellectual Cold Wars*, 299.

1. The Carnegie Endowment's Early Presence in Europe

Within the first year of its establishment, the Carnegie Endowment determined to take its campaign to Europe. Initially, the idea was to establish two
bureaus in Europe – one in Paris and one in London. However, following a
study of conditions in Europe, a move to England was deemed inadvisable:
The situation of the pacifist movement in Great Britain was regarded as too
complex to permit the endowment's easy entry.[10] To gain a foothold, the
Carnegie Endowment tapped into internationalist pacifist networks that
had developed since the mid-nineteenth century. The two peace conferences
at The Hague in 1899 and 1907 had galvanised the movement and elevated
its concerns to the level of international diplomacy. Peace activists, publicists
and experts in international law either became part of national delegations
or participated in efforts to lobby their foreign ministries to support arbitration measures and armament reductions.[11] It was precisely at this inter-
section between transnational peace activism and international politics that
the Carnegie Endowment recruited its first European partners. Eminent
French peace activists Paul-Henri-Benjamin d'Estournelles de Constant and
Jules-Jean Prudhommeaux were brought on board to open the endowment's
Centre Européen, located in an apartment on rue Pierre Curie in Paris.

The Carnegie Endowment's conception of what constituted Europe for the
purposes of the foundation's work was fluid and was shaped as much by
world events as by practical considerations such as the availability of funds.
Although questions regarding the extent of the European centre's ambit were
rarely discussed in detail, actions that effectively defined Europe were part of
the everyday decision-making process. One way of reconstructing this evol-
ving process of the endowment's mapping of Europe is to track the selection
of its partners on the continent, which clearly took geographical priorities
into account. One of the first major recruitment drives of the Carnegie
Endowment was the creation of a European Advisory Council in 1911. The
roster featured many well-known personalities from internationalist circles,
among others diplomats such as foreign ministers Edvard Beneš and Paul
Hyman as well as prominent academics such as Paul Appell and Charles
Richet. In a sign that the foundation perceived "European" as synonymous
with "international" rather than as indicating a self-contained spatial cat-
egory, the group also included representatives from China and Japan.[12] With

10 The CEIP continued to keep its distance from British pacifism for some time, focussing its resources on Continental Europe instead. This came as a disappointment to the
London Peace Society, which had hoped for financial relief. Ceadel, *Semi-Detached Idealists*, 171.

11 Cf. Cooper, *Patriotic Pacifism*, esp. 60–87.

12 *Carnegie Endowment for International Peace Year Book* 12 (1923), vi–x.

approximately thirty members dispersed throughout the world, the Advisory Council could not be expected to assemble regularly to conduct business on behalf of the endowment. In reality, the work assigned to the Advisory Council was carried out by a smaller Executive Committee comprised of those half-dozen members who resided in Paris. Some of the cosmopolitanism suggested by the council's membership was in effect more a matter of appearance than of substance. It was, as the endowment's Board of Trustees knew, "an organisation international in character, but essentially French in function".[13]

With the entry of the United States into the First World War, the Carnegie Endowment's affinity for Western Europe – France, particularly – continued as it participated in a broader effort to rebuild internationalist structures without a German presence.[14] In 1917, the names of all Germans and Austro-Hungarians were struck from the list of collaborators, and immediately after the war fourteen of the twenty-one members of the Advisory Council lived in either French- or English-speaking countries.[15] When the Centre Européen made grants in the early 1920s, the recipients were almost always French peace groups such as La Paix par le Droit or Franco-American friendship associations such as the Comité France-Amérique.[16]

During the mid-1920s the scope of the Carnegie Endowment's European activities began to expand again. The death of the French chairman of the Centre Européen d'Estournelles de Constant in 1924 momentarily disrupted activities but also created an opening for reform. De Constant's long experience in internationalist organisation and his deep familiarity with the landscape of French pacifism (and that of Western Europe in general) had made him the dominant figure in the endowment's European activities. By the mid-1920s he had, in fact, become so central that his death presented the endowment with a true dilemma, as de Constant "had practically been the entire organisation" in Paris.[17] Yet, the reorganisation of the Paris bureau was more than a bureaucratic necessity. It reflected a broader desire on the part of the Carnegie Endowment's leadership under the direction of its new President, Nicholas Murray Butler, President of Columbia University, to intensify its international outreach. As European governments appeared to be moving towards rapprochement, new opportunities for fostering European co-operation would present themselves.

---

13 Board of Trustees Annual Meeting, 4 December 1925, pp. 35–40, Box 14, Folder 3, CEIP Records, RBML.

14 Cf. Fuchs, "Wissenschaftsinternationalismus".

15 Prudhommeaux, *Le Centre Européen*, 71; *Carnegie Endowment for International Peace Year Book* 9 (1920), viii–x.

16 *Carnegie Endowment for International Peace Year Book* 11 (1922), 59.

17 Nicholas M. Butler to Andrew J. Montague, 6 June 1924, Box 20, Folder 11, CEIP Records, RBML.

The foundation had also recently made a sizeable investment towards its new headquarters, an eighteenth-century townhouse on Paris's boulevard Saint-Germain. This five-storey property was to be the Carnegie Endowment's new centre of influence in Europe and to be used "in spreading the knowledge of America and American points of view and American methods in other things than the specific work of this Endowment and its several divisions".[18] By what specific means these goals were to be achieved was still ill-defined at the time of de Constant's death. The Board sent one of its Trustees, a Congressman from Virginia named Andrew J. Montague, on a fact-finding mission to rethink its presence in Europe and to draw up recommendations on reorganising the Centre Européen.[19] After observing the situation in Paris, Montague recommended placing an American in charge, to be assisted by an all-European executive committee. He stressed the importance of regional diversity on the new Board, stating that it would be "unfortunate for France at this particular time to constitute a majority of the committee".[20] Characteristically, the reform process proceeded in dialogue with European leaders and activists, whose input was clearly sought. Again, concerns regarding French overrepresentation were voiced, this time by the Norwegian internationalist and Carnegie correspondent Christian L. Lange, who called for a more truly "European" committee: "It is called a European organisation, but it comprises representatives of a good many non-European countries, – China, Japan, Latin-American countries, for instance. On the other hand, there are several European countries which are not represented, or at any rate are poorly represented."[21] The original twelve members of the new Comité d'Administration were mostly drawn from academia or from the world of international politics. Most of them had already been connected to other internationalist organisations, either by working for or with institutions of international law and arbitration, or by actively participating in internationalist friendship societies. Former Greek Foreign Minister Nikolaos Politis had been a member of the Permanent Court of Arbitration at The Hague and Vice-President of the Institut de Droit International. The latter institution was also familiar to Belgian professor of international law Alfred Nerincx, who served as its Secretary General. Swiss member and banker Guillaume Fatio was an active participant in the World Alliance for Peace Through the Churches and the Geneva-based Union Internationale

18 Report by Nicholas M. Butler, Board of Trustees Annual Meeting, 8 December 1922, pp. 18–21, Box 14, Folder 2, CEIP Records, RBML.
19 Butler to Montague, 6 June 1924, Box 20, Folder 11, CEIP Records, RBML.
20 Montague to Butler, 17 October 1924, Box 20, Folder 11, CEIP Records, RBML.
21 Christian L. Lange to Montague, 5 November 1924, Box 20, Folder 11, CEIP Records, RBML.

des Étudiants.[22] Politically, almost all of the founding members identified themselves as liberals in their countries, and many of them, such as British classicist Gilbert Murray, French politician André Honnorat or former Italian Foreign Minister Carlo Sforza, had been active in liberal democratic politics. Finally, it is evident that the Carnegie Endowment preferred partners who already had prior experience in dealing with Americans, often in the course of their professional work. Journalist Georges Lechartier had worked as the Washington correspondent for several French newspapers, while Austrian legal scholar Josef Redlich and German economist Moritz Julius Bonn both taught at American universities. In fact, certain members, Bonn and Lechartier included, had established reputations in their home countries as experts on American culture and politics.[23]

For all the effort invested in bringing European perspectives into the work of the Paris office, the endowment also sought to strengthen direct American control over the Centre Européen. Incoming endowment President Nicholas Murray Butler had wondered from the outset whether the question could not be "tactfully" brought up that an American should play an "important part" in the work of the Paris bureau. Andrew Montague agreed, and he returned from his fact-finding mission convinced that securing the presence of a permanent American resident in Paris as chief administrator was indispensable to the success of the whole enterprise.[24] As Butler explained to the Board of Trustees, it was essential to "have an American secretary or administrator, one who understood our standards, our psychology, and who would introduce our methods of financial control and general dealing with these problems".[25] Yet the Americans were keenly aware of the importance of recognising, respecting and, if necessary, circumventing European apprehensions of American domination. In recounting the first meeting of the Comité d'Administration to the Trustees, Butler described the nomination of the new director as a clever manipulation of the Comité. Having already decided on Earle B. Babcock, a professor of Romance languages at New York University and the Dean of its graduate school, he purportedly tricked the Europeans into accepting his choice:

When I got there, sat them down around a table like this, I said: "Now, gentlemen, our first step must be to find an executive officer for our newly constituted body. How should we do that?" Well, to my delight, they all said: "You must do it. You must be our executive of-

22 Curricula vitae André Honnorat, Nicolaos Politis, Alfred Nerincx, Guillaume Fatio, Box 108, Folder 5, CEIP Centre Européen Records, RBML.
23 On Bonn see Clavin, "Wandering Scholar", 30; Hacke, "Moritz Julius Bonn".
24 Butler to Montague, 6 June 1924, Box 20, Folder 11, CEIP Records, RBML; Montague to Butler, 2 December 1924, Box 20, Folder 11, CEIP Records, RBML.
25 Board of Trustees Annual Meeting, 4 December 1925, p. 21, Box 14, Folder 3, CEIP Records, RBML.

ficer." I said: "Splendid." I had no modesty about it at all, because they opened the way for me to appoint somebody, and that is what we want. … We thought this out in advance ourselves. But it was so worked that it appeared to come from our French friends.[26]

This anecdote, even if apocryphal, demonstrates the desire of the Carnegie Endowment's officers to occasionally steer their European partners in a preferred direction, while attempting not to appear to be undermining their independence.

Nevertheless, the Carnegie Endowment remained aware that consultation of and co-operation with their European partners was a precondition for successful work on the continent. According to Butler, no money was to be spent by the Division of Intercourse and Education without first soliciting the recommendations of the Centre Européen. Furthermore, grants and subsidies to outside organisations were to be scaled back, leaving more resources for the centre to develop its own initiatives. To contribute to a more regular attendance of Comité meetings than had been the case with the former Advisory Council, the Carnegie Endowment significantly increased the budget of the European centre from $10,000 in 1925 to $35,000 in 1927 and $60,000 in 1929.[27] The role of the Comité d'Administration was conceived as analogous to that of the Executive Committee of the Board of Trustees that supervised the work of the Carnegie Endowment's headquarters in New York and made most decisions on the allocation of funds. Butler's rather idealistic plan for a harmonious co-operation between the two sides called for "an organisation, European in character but in close touch with our Executive Committee as well as in sympathy with it and under its general control".[28] A strong European identity and American control were not perceived as contradictory goals, but rather the result of a shared internationalist purpose to advance the agenda of the foundation.

The means by which the Carnegie Endowment attempted to advance its agenda were diverse, but two distinct strands may be discerned. On the one hand, the foundation participated in a broader trend of American scientific philanthropy, seeking to advance American achievements in the natural and social sciences abroad.[29] In particular, the endowment espoused a systematic, scientific approach to foreign relations, in which the participants assessed national interests rationally and dispassionately, and perceived this to

26 Board of Trustees Annual Meeting, 4 December 1925, p. 21, Box 14, Folder 3, CEIP Records, RBML.

27 *Carnegie Endowment for International Peace Year Book* 15 (1926), 139; *Carnegie Endowment for International Peace Year Book* 17 (1928), 179; *Carnegie Endowment for International Peace Year Book* 19 (1930), 151.

28 Butler to Montague, 6 June 1924, Box 20, Folder 11, CEIP Records, RBML.

29 Cf. Rausch, "Scientific Philanthropy"; Gemelli, "Permanent Connections"; Gemelli and MacLeod, *American Foundations in Europe*.

be an antidote to nationalistic stereotypes and warmongering. The Centre Européen sought to promote this approach by supporting efforts of European institutions of higher learning to introduce international relations courses.[30]

The second strand of the CEIP's programmes was concerned with fostering cultural exchange between nations.[31] This approach, which appealed particularly to Butler's professional background as an educator, rested on the assumption that personal contacts between representatives from different countries and personal experiences in foreign countries created a sympathy and understanding that would lessen the likelihood of another large-scale conflict. The Carnegie Endowment addressed its programmes specifically to those individuals who held positions of leadership in society and who could be expected to exert some level of influence on their compatriots. Starting in 1926, the endowment organised regular trips to bring European academics, journalists and lawyers to the United States and vice versa. The endowment carefully structured these trips to not only give travellers a first-person view of the other continent, but also to cultivate social interaction among the participants themselves and with local elites.

2. Working Towards an "International Mind"

Despite its deep investment in transatlantic relations, the Carnegie Endowment took a reserved stance toward the foremost foreign policy issue that gripped American politics and the internationalist community after the war: the debate on the League of Nations. Far from becoming an outspoken supporter of American membership, the endowment held an ambivalent position in these discussions. Indeed, its officers supported the notion that some form of international organisation was needed to help prevent future warfare; but even as they considered the stonewalling by some politicians unconstructive – most notably the so-called Irreconcilables in the United States Senate who were stalling the peace treaty – they nevertheless shared some of their concerns over the League Covenant. Both the endowment's first President Elihu Root and his successor Nicholas Murray Butler felt that the United States could only ratify the treaty following changes that addressed vital concerns regarding America's national interests. The validity of the Monroe Doctrine was not to be called into question, and there could be no

---

30 Rietzler, "Philanthropy, Peace Research, and Revisionist Politics", 68 ff.

31 See the literature on philanthropic diplomacy and on the philanthropic roots of (particularly US) cultural diplomacy, e.g., Ninkovich, *Diplomacy of Ideas*; Rietzler, "Before the Cultural Cold Wars"; Tournès, "La Dotation Carnegie".

enforcement mechanisms that would obligate America to take up arms in retaliation against an aggressor nation.[32] In later years, the endowment did co-
operate with the League of Nations on specific issues, for example through
its support for the League-sponsored Institute of Intellectual Co-operation.[33] Cognisant of the potential volatility of the issue in domestic politics,
the Carnegie Endowment never became a forceful champion of American
membership in the League.

For President Butler at least the entire debate on treaty mechanisms and
compulsory military intervention missed the point: International law could
only function on the basis of an international public consensus to solve
problems in a peaceful manner. Without this support, no legal structures or
international police forces would be able to keep the peace.[34] Butler had already made this argument before the end of the war, and he would use it
again to argue for a non-aggression treaty between France and the United
States in 1927: "But why between France and the United States? There is no
danger of war between them. That is precisely the reason. Such a treaty is as
useless as a resolution out-lawing war, unless it rests upon public conviction
that its aim and purpose are supported by public opinion."[35] There was a certain amount of tension between the emphasis Butler placed on the importance of public opinion and the narrow socio-economic group that supported the Carnegie Endowment's brand of internationalism. As Inderjeet
Parmar showed in a prosopographical survey of the thirty-five Trustees who
served during the years 1939–45, the endowment's Board was a remarkably
homogeneous group that represented a narrow East Coast elite. Most of its
members were born in post-Civil War America, educated in a select handful
of prestigious American universities and either worked in business management or as corporate lawyers.[36] Although the divisional directors in charge
of running the day-to-day administration of the endowment were mostly
academics, by virtue of their elevated status as prominent professors they
participated in the same socio-cultural field as the members of the Board.

Few people represented this social group better than Nicholas Murray
Butler. The son of a small-scale businessman from New Jersey, he attended
Columbia University and afterwards embarked on a career in academia, cul-
minating in his election as the President of Columbia in 1901. He became an
avid member of Manhattan's elite social clubs; the *Social Register* for 1930

32 Rosenthal, *Nicholas Miraculous*, 303–304; Dubin, "Elihu Root", 454–455.
33 Rietzler, "Before the Cultural Cold Wars", 162.
34 Rosenthal, *Nicholas Miraculous*, 223.
35 Address of Nicholas M. Butler to the American Club in Paris, 16 June 1927, p. 5, Box
220, Folder 220.2, CEIP Centre Européen Records, RBML.
36 Parmar, "Engineering Consent", 37–38.

lists Butler as a member of no less than eleven clubs.[37] To his supporters, Butler was one of the foremost public intellectuals of his time. His trifecta of achievements – long-serving President of Columbia University, Republican Party politician and vice-presidential candidate in 1912, and President of the Carnegie Endowment – made Butler one of the most frequently quoted public commentators on international affairs. His detractors saw him as a conservative, if not reactionary, promoter of the status quo; Upton Sinclair called him the "intellectual leader of American plutocracy".[38] It would be hard to argue that the foundation's President was a truly imaginative thinker.[39] He did, however, command unusual access to opinionmakers and to the mass media. A man who rarely walked past a reporter without giving a comment, Butler was one of the more visible public figures in the American press of the time.

The organising theme of Butler's internationalism was the advancement of what he called the "international mind". The term derived from the title of his opening address to the Lake Mohonk Conference on International Arbitration in 1912. For the sake of consistency, Butler continued to use the exact same definition of the term throughout the interwar years: "The international mind is nothing else than that habit of thinking of foreign relations and business, and that habit of dealing with them, which regard the several nations of the civilised world as friendly and co-operating equals in aiding the progress of civilisation, in developing commerce and industry, and in spreading enlightenment and culture throughout the world."[40] It was not a particularly succinct way of expressing his internationalist creed, but it captured the teleological interpretation of historical development toward a more civilised and peaceful world that characterised Butler's public pronouncements. To Butler, this progression was best illustrated by the American model of economic liberalism. He had come of age politically as part of the progressive, reformist wing of the Republican Party centred around the charismatic figure of Theodore Roosevelt, and he was convinced both of the efficiency of the American capitalist economy and the need for government regulation in certain sectors, such as public health. He condemned the excesses of laissez-faire capitalism, perceiving the exploitation of man by his fellow man as antithetical to liberty. Yet he saw economic opportunity – and consequentially inequality – as indispensable to economic and social devel-

37 *New York Social Register* 44 (1929) 23, 115.

38 Sinclair, *The Goose Step*, 29–30.

39 Butler was originally a professor of education, but distinguished himself through his administrative skills rather than through his scholarship. As Albert Marrin notes: "In the sense that a book is an extensive and sustained treatment of a limited theme, Butler never wrote a book." Marrin, *Nicholas Murray Butler*, 29.

40 Butler, *The International Mind*, 102.

opment. As a staunch anti-communist, Butler saw the idea of eliminating in-equality as a vision of the past rather than the future: "Mankind got away from communism somewhere between 5,000 and 6,000 years ago because there was no progress possible except by getting away from it, no achiev-ement, no satisfaction, no happiness, no growth, no development, no dis-covery, no new movement of life or thought."[41] The economic system in the United States, on the other hand, allowed inequality to exist, though it worked to improve the standard of living for the entire population. Con-trasting America with Europe, Butler espoused what he regarded as the im-permanence of socio-economic classes in the United States owing to the continuous social mobility that guaranteed a steady exchange between the different strata.[42]

A striking aspect of Butler's endorsement of free-trade policies is the way in which he applied his observations of America's historical economic devel-opment to the world and in particular to Europe. In a 1926 article written for the journal *Foreign Trade*, Butler suggested that, but for constitutional provi-sions prohibiting the imposition of tariffs by individual states against goods imported from other states, economic growth in America would have been stymied. Transposing this experience to Europe, he then called for smaller and larger nations to join together in economic federations. While this was most urgently needed in the successor states of the former Habsburg Empire and in the Balkans, the principle was not to stop there: "That Western Euro-pean nations will find themselves tempted or driven into similar economic understandings and arrangements seems evident, although it may take years for statesmen and for peoples, who are accustomed to the phrases and party cries of the extreme nationalism that is passing, to understand this fact or to admit it."[43] The American model of a vast internal market behind a common and deliberately low protective scheme was thus presented for European imitation. American-style federalism as the solution for Europe's economic and political woes had already been the subject of a book Butler had pub-lished during the First World War, when, harking back to a phrase used by Victor Hugo, he had suggested the creation of the "United States of Eu-rope".[44] Speaking in London in 1930, he affirmed his conviction that the existing system of nation-states in Europe had proved unworkable and failed to "adjust to the growth of civilisation". Sensing a further shift of public opinion in favour of a European federation, he again called for a United

41 Address of Nicholas M. Butler to the American Club in Paris, 16 June 1927, Box 220, Folder 2, CEIP Centre Européen Records, RBML.
42 Butler, "Les attaques contre le libéralisme", 503.
43 Butler, "National Boundaries", 16–17.
44 Butler, *A World in Ferment*, 27 ff.

States of Europe "not in order that the nations constituent of such a federation may be lessened in authority or in influence, but for the purpose of
establishing free, helpful and profitable economic cooperation with neighbours".[45]

3. Navigating Europe's Political Landscape

In its European endeavours the Carnegie Endowment could count on a general interest in America. As Moritz Julius Bonn observed dryly on the success
of his lectures on the American economy: "If you talk about America, every-
one shows up" (*Quand on parle de l'Amérique chez nous, tout le monde
vient*).[46] But general interest did not necessarily correlate with an enthusiastic reception of the endowment's plans. One of the first major expenditures made by the Carnegie Endowment in Europe had been a $20,000 sub-
sidy to the group Bureau International de la Paix. But instead of celebrating
the sudden influx of cash, the European activists were irritated by the Americans' suggestion that the Bureau's office should be moved from Berne to
Brussels to increase efficiency. The prospect that American money could
open the door to foreign domination of their groups provoked resistance
in European pacifists, and in particular many French activists came to see
the Americans as arrogant.[47] As a result of these past pitfalls and critique,
the Comité d'Administration was established as an administrative body
composed entirely of Europeans who took part in the endowment's decision-making process and served to help deflect such criticism. In addition,
the members of the Comité were to serve as surrogates for the endowment in
Europe. Many of them had been in government service at some point during
their professional lives or had otherwise established connections to their
countries' foreign policy elites. There can be little doubt that, by selecting its
partners in this way, the Carnegie Endowment hoped to gain both timely information on international politics and opportunities to more effectively
deliver its message to foreign policy elites.

This strategy is evident in the case of German member Erich von Prittwitz
und Gaffron, whose standing rose considerably after his brother Friedrich-
Wilhelm was appointed German Ambassador to the United States in 1927.
Two years later, in June 1929, Friedrich-Wilhelm came to Syracuse Univer-

45 Nicholas M. Butler: The Richard Cobden Lecture. Nation Building and Beyond,
7 May 1930, Box 220, Folder 5, CEIP Centre Européen Records, RBML.
46 Meeting of the Comité d'Administration, Centre Européen, Carnegie Endowment
for International Peace, 20 December 1930, p. 31, Box 120, Folder 6, CEIP Centre Européen Records, RBML.
47 Cooper, *Patriotic Pacifism*, 82–83.

sity to receive an honorary doctorate in law alongside former American Ambassador to Germany Alanson B. Houghton. In an address that was discussed the following week in a *New York Times* editorial, the German diplomat praised Henri Lichtenberger's concept of "international citizenship", for which he saw the "development in all countries of an international mind" as an essential precondition. No reader of the event's newspaper coverage would have suspected the extent to which the appearance of the German Ambassador bore the imprint of an American foundation. And yet the entire event was a successful demonstration of the ability of the Carnegie Endowment to place its message in diplomatic circles and to translate it into public diplomacy: Here was a high-ranking diplomat, the brother of a member of the Comité d'Administration, extolling two internationalist concepts developed, respectively, by Henri Lichtenberger – another member of the Comité – and the endowment's President Nicholas Murray Butler. Ambassador Houghton – the man who shared the stage with Prittwitz – would become a member of the endowment's Board of Trustees the following year.[48] Finally, media coverage of the event was essential to broadening the reach of the endowment's message beyond those in the audience in Syracuse that day. Given President Butler's close association with the editorial board of the *New York Times*, the increased attention the paper devoted to this event was likely no accident either.[49]

The aspiration of the Carnegie Endowment to become an arbiter of objective information in Europe and thus to help undermine national biases and prejudices proved a much greater challenge. Time and again the endowment discovered – as in James Brown Scott's ill-fated visit to Heidelberg – the challenges of separating academic inquiry from international politics. The Comité d'Administration was often instrumental in highlighting potential areas of conflict, as in the case of a Europe-wide study of schoolbooks started in 1922. The project had originally been intended to draw attention to national biases that could instigate hatred between national and ethnic groups, but it soon became an intractable public relations problem for the endowment. The production of the individual studies on textbooks in specific countries or regions was assigned to a single author from the respective nation, and then bound into volumes. This arrangement made it difficult for the endowment to exert any editorial control. When one German contributor supplied a manuscript that was patently anti-French, the Comité faced

---

48 Address of Friedrich-Wilhelm von Prittwitz und Gaffron at Syracuse University, 10 June 1929, Friedrich-Wilhelm von Prittwitz und Gaffron Papers, Archiv für Christlich-Demokratische Politik Konrad-Adenauer-Stiftung, Sankt Augustin, I 138, no. 002; Editorial "International Citizenship", *New York Times* (16 June 1929).

49 Cf. Rosenthal, *Nicholas Miraculous*, 15–16.

the unpleasant choice of suppressing the manuscript or publishing a document that could not help but exacerbate Franco-German animosity. Although the Comité decided to preface the second volume with a declaration distancing the Carnegie Endowment from any conclusions drawn by the individual authors, this episode effectively signalled the failure of the project. At the Comité's next meeting the programme was unceremoniously aborted.[50]

The Comité's deliberations mostly progressed in a calm, constructive atmosphere, and the members were generally deferential to the wishes of their American partners. But as they gained experience and confidence, members started to question the instructions or indications of preference they were given. As the 1920s drew to a close, the Comité had reached a point where it challenged the Carnegie Endowment's officers on some of their favourite projects. Since the late summer of 1929, President Butler had become more and more enthusiastic about a plan to help solve the tense political situation in the Balkans by sending a group of independent experts to study economic and social conditions as well as the ethnic composition of the region. The commission would then issue an authoritative report that could form the basis for a more rational approach to political differences: "Thoroughly scientific and objective treatment of these subjects, prepared without any political end in view and free from any political motive, might well provide the public opinion of the world with the material that we need in order to understand the Balkan problem and, therefore, to aid in its peaceful and orderly solution."[51] Butler was so convinced of the efficacy of this approach that he claimed to have already cleared the plan with Aristide Briand, Benito Mussolini and the Hungarian elder statesman Albert Apponyi. But when it was presented to the Comité, the reaction was overwhelmingly negative: "absolutely disastrous" (*tout à fait malheureuse*), "like adding fuel to the fire" (*jeter de l'huile sur le feu*). The Europeans were convinced that, rather than calming the debate, such a report would itself become an object of contention and expose the Carnegie Endowment to sharp criticism from all sides. The plan did not get the desired approval.[52]

Both the aborted schoolbook study and the cancelled Balkan inquiry are telling examples of the failure of the Carnegie Endowment to act as an ar-

50 Meeting of the Comité d'Administration, Centre Européen, Carnegie Endowment for International Peace, 1st sess., 28 March 1927, p. 55, Box 117, Folder 2, CEIP Centre Européen Records, RBML; Prudhommeaux, *Enquête*.

51 Butler to Earle B. Babcock, 22 April 1930, Box 120, Folder 5, CEIP Centre Européen Records, RBML.

52 Meeting of the Comité d'Administration, Centre Européen, Carnegie Endowment for International Peace, 30 May 1930, p. 48–50, Box 120, Folder 5, CEIP Centre Européen Records, RBML.

biter of objective information in European disputes. The European members of the Comité d'Administration knew that the results of scientific research or thorough academic study could not be expected to transcend political, ethnic or national divisions and boundaries. Even the stamp of approval by an American, and hence putatively independent, organisation would not shield the results from charges of bias and favouritism.

One persistent problem the endowment faced in its European endeavours was the need to take Europe's multitudinous language boundaries into account. The lack of a lingua franca among European intellectuals posed a major problem for any efforts to bring about an open and frank exchange of ideas. Essentially, the use of language determined which audiences the Carnegie Endowment could hope to reach and how far its message could travel. Starting in 1927, the Centré Européen published the journal *L'Esprit International*, a collection of articles on international affairs, book reviews and reports on current events. The journal was monolingual, meaning that articles submitted in any other language than French were translated. Immediately after the publication of the first issue there were plans to translate the contributions into additional languages such as English and German. It is illustrative of Butler's keen sense for public relations that he promptly directed the European bureau to pay attention to the exact wording of the title. *L'Esprit International* was of course the direct translation of his "international mind" concept, and if there was to be a German edition, he advised Babcock to make "sure they use the same translation Die Internationale Gesinnung that we have statedly used heretofore. I send you the German version of the phrase and its definition."[53] The Comité d'Administration was aware of the possibilities for a wider dissemination of the endowment's themes and ideas. This applied both to the geographical distribution of its readers – a Spanish version could have put the South American market within reach – as well as their social composition. As some members of the committee noted, while there was an interested, educated core group of Europeans with a thorough command of French, translations into more languages could help broaden the audience.[54] It is perhaps indicative of the endowment's geographic priorities as well as of its preferred target audience that these proposed translations never came to fruition.

The problem of language was not confined to publications, but extended to the endowment's cultural exchange programmes. One of the cornerstones of

53 Butler to Babcock, 6 January 1927, Box 108, Folder 2, CEIP Records, RBML.
54 Meeting of the Comité d'Administration, Centre Européen, Carnegie Endowment for International Peace, 30 December 1930, p. 14, Box 120, Folder 6, CEIP Centre Européen Records, RBML; Meeting of the Comité d'Administration, Centre Européen, Carnegie Endowment for International Peace, 28 March 1927, p. 22–3, Box 117, Folder 2, CEIP Centre Européen Records, RBML.

the Centre Européen's activities was internationalist instruction through public lectures. Courses on international relations were organised in co-operation with the Institut des Hautes Études Internationales at the University of Paris, and the endowment sponsored permanent Carnegie Professors of International Relations in Paris and Berlin.[55] In addition, lecture series and individual presentations were held at the lecture hall of the Centre Européen both in Paris and in other European cities. To Butler, the exchange of speakers among European countries was one of the most promising means for furthering international understanding. Bringing European audiences in contact with foreign speakers would enable them to better understand the interests and mentalities of foreign nations, while the pleasing personality of the speaker could help eliminate or pre-empt negative stereotypes. To show that exchange on this level could bridge even the widest chasms in Europe, the German Comité member Moritz Julius Bonn was sent on a lecture tour to France, Thomas Mann read at the endowment's bureau in Paris, and French and Polish speakers were sent to the German capital to address audiences there.[56] Throughout the late 1920s and early 1930s, via his representative Babcock, Butler urged the Comité to expand on these activities and to encourage more border crossings by European academics and other persons of elevated social status. The lecture programme was to become truly international.[57]

The members of the Comité, however, struggled to fulfil Butler's wishes. Granting the necessary funds proved relatively simple, but finding the appropriate speaker turned out to be more demanding. No single language was universally understood across Europe's scattered linguistic landscape, even by educated audiences. French was widely understood but was gradually losing its dominant position as the language of international communication. German, which had enjoyed wide dissemination as a language of science, was in retreat after Germany's defeat in the war and the country's concomitant decline as a point of reference for international academia. English was ascendant but did not yet have anywhere near the currency it would gain after 1945. Even the meetings of the Comité d'Administration were held in French and not in English. While the world grew ever more interconnected,

55 The two professors were André Tibal, formerly of the Institut Français in Prague, and Hajo Holborn at the Deutsche Hochschule für Politik. *Carnegie Endowment for International Peace Year Book* 16 (1927), 60; *Carnegie Endowment for International Peace Year Book* 22 (1933), 101.

56 Before the introduction of a permanent professorship, French sociologist André Siegfried and Polish classicist Tadeusz Stefan Zielinski gave lectures at the Carnegie-Lehrstuhl in Berlin. Missiroli, *Die Deutsche Hochschule für Politik*, 209.

57 Meeting of the Comité d'Administration, Centre Européen, Carnegie Endowment for International Peace, 30 May 1930, p. 54, Box 120, Folder 5, CEIP Centre Européen Records, RBML.

communication across boundaries remained difficult. The growth of the Esperanto movement during the 1920s was partly the reflection of the need to correct this imbalance between increased opportunity for international and transnational interaction and deficient language capacities.[58]

For the Comité this meant that, when identifying possible lecturers, they not only had to look for candidates with suitable personalities and competencies, but also ones who possessed the necessary language skills. Debates over language and speaker compatibility thus figured prominently in the deliberations of the Comité. Even where the preconditions for communication between speaker and audience were met, the ramifications of using a particular language needed to be taken into account. While the Comité agreed that Hungarians could probably understand a German speaker, Alfred Nerincx gently reminded his colleagues that German was "not very popular at the moment" (*l'allemand n'est pas en ce moment très populaire*). Moritz Julius Bonn was more emphatic and argued that Hungarians might be prepared to accept internationalist arguments from a Frenchman or an Englishman, but would reject them if they were presented by a German.[59]

Few were more aware of the challenges of Europe's linguistic landscape than the endowment officer and language specialist Earle Babcock. Since 1924, the professor of Romance languages had headed the International Auxiliary Language Association, which had been founded to promote the use of synthetic languages such as Esperanto. Modern means of communication were to be matched by a "linguistic medium adequate for the utilisation of the possibilities of these devices for the diffusion of knowledge and the promotion of human understanding".[60] As the Carnegie Endowment prepared to extend its activities beyond the Anglo- and Francophone parts of Western Europe, Babcock was uniquely positioned to fully understand this challenge. Educated partially at the Sorbonne and originally married to a French woman, the endowment had found in Babcock an ideal choice to allay French fears of an estrangement of the foundation from its traditional French partners. When, starting in 1927, the foundation attempted to aid Germany's return into the internationalist fold by expanding its presence there, it lacked officers with the necessary language skills. Instead, it placed more responsibility on the shoulders of its German partners, whom it relied on to act as surrogates. In practice, increased responsibility also meant more influence on the endowment's work.

58 Forster, *The Esperanto Movement*, 171.
59 Meeting of the Comité d'Administration, Centre Européen, Carnegie Endowment for International Peace, 28 March 1927, p. 37–9, Box 117, Folder 2, CEIP Centre Européen Records, RBML.
60 International Auxiliary Language Association in the United States, *Outline of Program*, 5.

The first signs of rapprochement between the European adversaries of the First World War in the 1920s promised new opportunities for an American foundation dedicated to furthering contacts between peoples. The treaties of Locarno from 1925 seemed to herald a new era of peace in Europe which the Carnegie Endowment wanted to be part of. These new prospects, however, also created new challenges: As peace and internationalism became acceptable issues in the political centre, Nicholas Murray Butler grew eager to engage the establishment, the mainstream of power. In these endeavours, the pacifist individuals and organisations that the foundation had formerly co-operated with came to be seen as a historical burden that could paint the Carnegie Endowment with the taint of political extremism. The conclusion was that if the Carnegie Endowment wanted to have any impact in Europe, it needed to address as broad an audience as possible to help create the desired support for peaceful internationalism.

This concern had already driven the reorganisation process of the Centre Européen. The reason that, following the death of de Constant, he had not been succeeded by his Vice-President Justin Godart was that the latter, in Butler's words, was "more of a pacifist in the technical sense of the word". The Carnegie Endowment, he explained, should try to work with nationalist forces in Europe and not against them. While limited co-operation with pacifist organisations was desired, the endowment should attempt to "keep [itself] free of entanglements with the ordinary pacifist agitators and agitations" so as not to appear to be in conflict with nationalists.[61] The members of the Comité largely agreed with the premise that the endowment should keep its distance from any groups that were publicly associated with left-wing causes for fear of losing its non-partisan appeal. At the very first official meeting of the newly constituted body, Henri Lichtenberger, speaking on the French situation, urged looking beyond the usual circle of Leftist pacifists since their voices only reached one political camp. Instead, he called for creative ways of making inroads into the French Right by engaging what he saw as an incipient internationalist wing of the Action Française or by working with Catholic royalists receptive to a restoration of medieval peace ideals.[62]

In Germany, the endowment had long relied on two so-called Special Correspondents to speak and act on its behalf: publicists and peace activists Hellmut von Gerlach and Friedrich Wilhelm Foerster. Their connection to the Carnegie Endowment was the legacy of d'Estournelles de Constant's first post-war attempts to integrate Germany into the work of the Centre Euro-

---

61 Butler to Montague, 6 June 1924, Box 20, Folder 11, CEIP Records, RBML.
62 Meeting of the Comité d'Administration, Centre Européen, Carnegie Endowment for International Peace, 2nd session, 25 October 1925, p. 68–69, Box 115, Folder 1, CEIP Centre Européen Records, RBML.

péen. After attending a conference in Paris just after the war, they received yearly stipends to write confidential reports to the endowment's Trustees on conditions in Germany, and to collect and pre-evaluate grant requests by German entities. When the Comité d'Administration added first one and then two German members to its ranks, the role of Foerster and von Gerlach receded further and further into the background. When Nicholas Murray Butler sought closer relations to official German circles, the two pacifists had fallen out of favour.[63]

Especially Erich von Prittwitz und Gaffron played an influential role in reorienting the endowment's activities in Germany. At the Comité's meeting in March 1926 he began to argue that the foundation was needlessly limiting its audience in Germany by relying only on pacifist leaders and publications. Instead, he suggested entering into a co-operative arrangement with the Deutsche Hochschule für Politik, a privately run academy in Berlin dedicated to political education. Success for Prittwitz's initiative came quickly. That summer he received Butler and Babcock in the German capital where he arranged for meetings with the academy's leadership. Butler was enthusiastic and promised to quickly realise the plan, indicating that Prittwitz's suggestions would be "acted upon favourably at least in principle and probably in every detail". In late October the Comité d'Administration voted unanimously to institute a Carnegie professorship at the Deutsche Hochschule für Politik, a decision that was ratified by the Executive Committee of the Board of Trustees in New York only a few days later.[64]

While negotiations on the Deutsche Hochschule für Politik came to a quick and successful conclusion, the question of the fate of the endowment's existing German Special Correspondents, especially of Friedrich Wilhelm Foerster, proved more contentious. The outspoken Foerster was a controversial figure in his home country, and his publicly stated support for a German admission of war-guilt placed him at odds with the policy of the German Government. When, in 1925, Foerster wrote to the Carnegie Endowment a confidential report highly critical of his Government's policies which ended up in the German Foreign Ministry, the controversy threatened to strain the foundation's relationship with Berlin.[65]

---

63 Winn, "Nicholas Murray Butler", 568–569.

64 Meeting of the Comité d'Administration, Centre Européen, Carnegie Endowment for International Peace, 1st sess., 22 March 1926, p. 46, Box 115, Folder 5; Meeting of the Comité d'Administration, Centre Européen, Carnegie Endowment for International Peace, 1st session, 25 October 1926, pp. 41–3, Box 117, Folder 1; Butler to Babcock, 4 November 1926, Box 116, Folder 5; Butler to Erich von Prittwitz und Gaffron, 23 July 1926, Box 182, Folder 6, CEIP Centre Européen Records, RBML.

65 Winn, "Nicholas Murray Butler", 569; Rietzler, "Before the Cultural Cold Wars", 162.

It is unclear whether the Americans realised to what extent they were entering the realm of European politics – and how deeply its divisions ran through their European committee. Besides Prittwitz, the Comité's second German member Moritz Julius Bonn was also highly critical of Foerster. A firm believer in hard-headed national interests, Bonn found Foerster's emphasis on the moral dimension of foreign policy dangerously naive. With respect to the pacifist position on the war-guilt question, Bonn later suggested that Foerster was part of a group of "neurotics" for whom "self-inflicted suffering was a source of joy".[66] On the other side of the issue was Austrian member Josef Redlich, who disagreed with the notion that the funding of pacifists could present an obstacle to further co-operation with Germany; he warned that German intellectuals who were working to push Germany into a more democratic and peaceful direction could be demoralised. Calling Foerster "une figure européenne", Redlich disputed that the publicist could be seen as a political actor and maintained that his work was a central pillar to the German peace movement.[67] He finally took his case directly to President Butler while travelling in the United States as a Visiting Carnegie Professor. Apparently hoping that the Comité's policy could be overruled by New York, he enthusiastically praised Friedrich Wilhelm Foerster's work. Butler remained unimpressed:

I gathered the impression, though entirely by inference, that either he had gained his slant from Professor Foerster or else was himself in agreement with Professor Foerster's ultra-pacifist opinions. … If we are to work with the new Germany, we must work with her spokesmen and representatives [e.g. foreign minister Gustav Stresemann and Prussian minister of education Carl Heinrich Becker] and should make no progress if we tried to work only with the Foersters.[68]

Ever careful not to cause negative publicity, the foundation did not immediately sever all ties with Foerster and von Gerlach, but rather quietly kept interaction with them to a bare minimum. It took almost four years until the endowment finally decided to cease funding for all Special Correspondents, thereby ending their official association with the two German pacifists.[69]

---

66 Bonn, *So macht man Geschichte*, 200 (transl. J.W.).

67 Meeting of the Comité d'Administration, Centre Européen, Carnegie Endowment for International Peace, 1st sess., 22 March 1926, pp. 57–60, Box 115, Folder 5, CEIP Centre Européen Records, RBML.

68 Butler to Babcock, 21 December 1926, Box 108, Folder 1, CEIP Records, RBML.

69 Winn, "Nicholas Murray Butler", 571.

4. Epilogue

The years 1928–30 were the high point of both the Centre Européen's and the Comité d'Administration's influence on foundation policy. The morale of the internationalists was boosted by recent progress in international co-operation and an environment that seemed ever more amenable to their goals. The Carnegie Endowment had plans to greatly expand its presence in Europe in the coming years. An additional Carnegie professorship was to be founded in Vienna, and the Centre Européen was to open offices in all major European capitals. Then, the effects of the economic crisis that soon began to grip the world put these ambitious plans out of reach. With money in short supply, the Comité's main activity and source of authority – approving or declining requests for subsidies – lost much of its significance. What little money there was left was often tied up in long-term projects, giving the Europeans hardly any opportunity to participate in major decisions. In the late 1930s, as conflict and war were approaching, the Carnegie Endowment began to reorient its activities away from solving the intractable problems of mainland Europe and towards bolstering solidarity among English-speaking countries. Signifying this shift, a new Carnegie office was opened in London in 1937.[70]

The end of the Comité came on 5 May 1939, when the Carnegie Endowment's Board of Trustees officially dissolved the body. The rationale Butler cited for this move was that recent events had caused so many members of the Comité to relocate or change citizenship that they could no longer be said to represent the countries for which they had been selected. This statement contrasted with the long-standing policy that members of the Comité would not be chosen to represent any one country. What had, however, always mattered to the cautious Carnegie Endowment officers was that all persons the foundation worked with had the backing of their national Governments. Despite the endowment's vocal appeal to world public opinion, its main interlocutors remained the leading political classes in Europe – and they were not to be alienated. By the late 1930s many members of the committee had clearly become dissidents in their home countries. Calling a meeting of these *personae non gratae* in the tense political environment of 1939 could have been politically inconvenient for the Carnegie Endowment. The Board approved Butler's recommendation without discussion, and only a few days later the members of the European committee received letters from Butler thanking them for their service to the cause of international

---

70 The London office consisted, however, only of the endowment's representative in Britain, Hubert J. Howard. *Carnegie Endowment for International Peace Year Book* 27 (1938), 105.

peace and declaring the Comité d'Administration dissolved.[71] The Centre
Européen itself continued to operate for another year, until the invasion of
France by German troops in May 1940.[72]

The activities of the Carnegie Endowment in Europe from 1925 to the late
1930s provide a case study of the interplay between American control and
European agency in the work of American philanthropy. The reform of the
Centre Européen in 1925 was a unique attempt to both Europeanise and
Americanise the foundation's presence in Europe. The solution offered by
the introduction of an American director checked by a European executive
committee rested on the assumption that a common purpose – a shared belief in liberal internationalism – would make for a harmonious co-operation. In an ideal scenario, the American side would provide the financial
means and programmatic guidance, while the Europeans would use their
local expertise and their influence in their home countries to implement
projects. Nevertheless, President Butler made it clear from the very beginning that he was willing to influence decision-making and work around the
Europeans when he saw the necessity.

Over the course of fifteen years the Carnegie Endowment's lectures, trips
and publications reached thousands of Europeans. During this time the
foundation contributed to the creation of international relations studies in,
among other places, Paris, Berlin and Geneva. It published hundreds of
books, pamphlets, speech manuscripts and journal issues. Yet, it is also safe
to assume that the endowment's publications were more widely distributed
than they were read. The back issues of *L'Esprit International* may still be
found in many major European libraries. In January 1930 the journal had a
circulation of 3,987 though only 213 of those copies had actually been sold;
the rest had been distributed to libraries and individuals free of charge.[73]
When we look for the impact of the Carnegie Endowment's "international
mind" campaign, it is instructive to consider the long-term impact of the
networks created. Two former members of the Comité d'Administration, Bo
Östen Undén and Carlo Sforza, later became Foreign Ministers and played
key roles in moving their respective countries into the Western bloc after
1945. That the effects of co-operation did not point in only one direction is
shown by the migration of a sizeable number of CEIP collaborators to the
United States after 1933. This included the Carnegie professor in Berlin Hajo

71 Board of Trustees, Annual Meeting, 5 May 1939, pp. 11–13, Box 15, Folder 4, CEIP
Records, RBML; Erich von Prittwitz und Gaffron to Butler, 24 May 1939, Box 316, Nicholas Murray Butler Papers, RBML.

72 *Carnegie Endowment for International Peace Year Book* 34 (1945), 67.

73 Meeting of the Comité d'Administration, Centre Européen, Carnegie Endowment
for International Peace, 30 May 1930, p. 2, Box 120, Folder 5, CEIP Centre Européen Records, RBML.

Holborn, who stayed permanently, integrated into American society and eventually became a US citizen. The Carnegie Endowment had successfully lobbied the Emergency Committee in Aid of Displaced Foreign Scholars to fund a position at Yale University. In 1967 he became the first foreign-born President of the American Historical Association.[74]

As the Carnegie Endowment navigated the pitfalls of international and European domestic politics, it learned to adjust its working methods to the local requirements. Foundation officers remained convinced that American economic and political achievements provided at least part of the solution to Europe's seemingly intractable problems. Free-market liberalism, modern business practices, a robust federal system of government and scientific approaches to social problems, they believed, could bring economic progress and political stability to the continent. But experiences of failure, such as James Brown Scott's ill-fated speech at Heidelberg or the controversial study of European schoolbooks, made them cautious of proceeding without European advice and political cover. The creation of transnational networks of academic, economic and political elites to advance their goals was one of the most consequential legacies of their work.

---

74 Emergency Committee in Aid of Displaced Foreign Scholars Records, 1927–49, MssCol 922, New York Public Library, Box 171, Folder 8 – Carnegie Endowment for International Peace, Box 15, Folder 10–11 – Holborn, Hajo.

Ludovic Tournès

L'américanisation de la science française?

La fondation Rockefeller et la construction d'une politique
de recherche en biomédecine (1918–1939)

Il n'est pas exagéré de dire que la présence de la fondation Rockefeller dans la recherche scientifique française de l'entre-deux-guerres a été massive, en particulier dans le domaine de la biologie et de la médecine. L'organisation américaine a en effet financé à des degrés divers presque toutes les institutions impliquées dans ce secteur alors en plein développement: entre 1925 et 1939, ce sont cinq universités (Paris, Lyon, Marseille, Strasbourg, Toulouse) et sept institutions dédiées à la recherche (l'Institut Pasteur, le Collège de France, l'Institut de biologie physico-chimique, l'École Pratique des Hautes Études, l'Institut du Radium, l'Institut Henri Poincaré, le Muséum d'histoire naturelle), pour un total de 41 laboratoires, qui ont reçu des crédits américains. Il faut y ajouter 101 *fellowships* (bourses), dont les bénéficiaires iront le plus souvent étudier aux États-Unis. Au total, on peut estimer le montant du financement de la recherche par la fondation Rockefeller à environ deux millions de dollars entre 1925 et 1939. Encore ces chiffres ne représentent-ils que la partie la plus visible du processus, car le rôle de la fondation ne se limite pas à l'aspect financier: elle contribue également à l'élaboration de nouvelles procédures d'administration de la recherche ainsi qu'à la conception de plusieurs programmes. De sorte qu'elle est un partenaire important dans le processus d'organisation et de centralisation de la recherche française, qui mènera en octobre 1939 à la création du Centre national de la recherche scientifique (CNRS).

Cette participation massive, qui se poursuivra après 1945, pose des questions aux historiens des sciences ainsi qu'aux historiens de l'américanisation. Les premiers ont analysé l'établissement de l'hégémonie américaine sur la science européenne après 1945, mais se sont peu penchés sur l'entre-deux-guerres, traditionnellement considérée comme une période pendant laquelle les relations géoscientifiques entre l'Europe et les États-Unis sont équilibrées, par opposition à l'asymétrie post-1945 marquée par la domination de la superpuissance américaine. Les seconds ont étudié la place majeure prise par les États-Unis dans le monde contemporain et l'établissement de leur hégémonie dans de nombreux domaines, mais, le plus souvent, ils ont analysé les rapports États-Unis/monde de manière schématique, les réduisant au processus de diffusion unilatérale d'un modèle américain naturalisé. L'analyse de la politique internationale de la philanthropie américaine au XXe siècle permet d'apporter des éléments de réponse sur ces deux points (la chronologie de l'hégémonie et ses modalités), et de jeter un pont entre les historiens des sciences et ceux de l'américanisation, qui dialoguent assez peu, alors que leurs terrains respectifs se recoupent en bien des endroits. L'analyse de la politique scientifique des fondations, et en particulier de la fondation Rockefeller, permet d'abord de mettre en avant l'importance de l'entre-deux-guerres dans l'établissement de l'hégémonie américaine[1], et ensuite de discuter les modalités concrètes de l'établissement de cette hégémonie qui restent mal connues, car les historiens de l'américanisation s'y sont peu intéressés. Cet article vise donc à la fois à contribuer à l'étude de la chronologie de l'établissement de l'hégémonie américaine, comme à approfondir la discussion heuristique sur le concept d'américanisation, qui reste à bien des égards flou et problématique et dont la clarification est indispensable pour mieux comprendre la nature et l'évolution des rapports entre les États-Unis et le monde et enfin à définir la place qu'y occupent les fondations américaines.

En effet, en analysant la politique scientifique de la philanthropie américaine en France à long terme, et en observant la densité des interventions de celle-ci (dont le cas de la biomédecine, traité ici, n'est qu'un exemple parmi d'autres), il est tentant d'y voir un phénomène d'américanisation. Mais en regardent de plus près, la situation est bien plus complexe, de sorte qu'il faut expliquer la pertinence de cette notion d'américanisation telle qu'elle a été entendue par la grande majorité des historiens. La plupart des travaux sur cette question depuis les années 1970 ont adopté explicitement ou – plus souvent – implicitement une grille de lecture issue de l'anthropologie, plus particulièrement des travaux sur l'acculturation, grille que l'on pourrait résumer par le triptyque diffusion/réception/réinterprétation[2]. Or, cette grille de lecture pose de nombreux problèmes que les historiens n'ont pas toujours pris à bras-le-corps. D'une part, cette perspective va de pair avec une naturalisation de la culture américaine conçue comme une totalité cohérente préalablement constituée à l'intérieur des frontières des États-Unis avant d'être exportée dans le reste du monde; d'autre part, le processus d'américa-

---

1 Tournès, «Le réseau des boursiers Rockefeller»; Id., «Comment devenir une superpuissance intellectuelle?»

2 Voir par exemple Bosscher/Kroes/Rydell, *Cultural Transmissions*; Kuisel, *Seducing the French*; Ory, «L'américanisation»; Pells, *Not Like US*; Barjot/Reveillard, *L'américanisation de l'Europe*; Pour une bibliographie plus complète et une discussion plus développée sur l'américanisation, voir Tournès, *Sciences de l'homme*, 10–19.

nisation est le plus souvent analysé dans une perspective unidirectionnelle, comme si la culture américaine était intrinsèquement exportatrice et peu ou prou imperméable aux influences extérieures, tandis que les cultures, qui lui sont confrontées, seraient intrinsèquement importatrices; enfin, les études existantes se focalisent le plus souvent sur la réception par des cultures nationales d'objets venus des États-Unis, sans étudier le processus d'exportation ni le contact en train de se faire. Cette triple aporie épistémologique ne permet pas de saisir dans toute sa complexité le phénomène de mondialisation de la culture américaine au XXe siècle.

Pour mieux comprendre celui-ci, il est important de réviser cette perspective diffusionniste et d'adopter une approche circulatoire qui envisage dans une même analyse les différents partenaires de la relation et leurs interactions[3], plutôt que de postuler un émetteur qui exporte et un récepteur qui se contente de réagir. Dans le cas précis qui nous occupe dans cet article, la participation de la fondation Rockefeller à la construction de la politique scientifique française dans l'entre-deux-guerres ne peut pas être interprétée comme un phénomène d'importation culturelle. Il faut l'envisager plutôt comme la cristallisation locale d'un processus transnational qui voit émerger des politiques scientifiques dans un certain nombre de pays au cours de cette période. Au lieu d'américanisation, on parlera de coproduction *in situ,* une notion qui sera discutée au cours de cet article à partir de trois problèmes que les historiens de l'américanisation, tout comme les historiens de la philanthropie, n'ont que très partiellement résolus. Le premier est celui de la pertinence de la notion de «modèle» américain, que l'on discutera dans la première partie de l'article en replaçant l'histoire des politiques scientifiques dans une perspective transnationale. Le deuxième est celui du rôle des dynamiques locales dans le processus d'américanisation, illustré ici par le fait que l'intervention de la fondation Rockefeller ne fait que se greffer sur des initiatives locales antérieures, tout en leur donnant une impulsion parfois décisive. Enfin, le troisième problème concerne l'interaction entre les partenaires de la relation, représentés ici par les donateurs et les bénéficiaires de l'aide philanthropique; l'analyse de cette interaction montre comment la fondation Rockefeller, tout en déployant une stratégie internationale, est capable de se «localiser» et de se faire reconnaître par ses interlocuteurs français comme un partenaire à part entière du processus d'organisation de la science, si bien que son influence est à la fois indéniablement forte et difficile à qualifier «d'américaine».

---

3 Parmi les ouvrages récents qui adoptent cette perspective, voir en particulier de Grazia, *Irresistible Empire*; Rydell/Kroes, *Buffalo Bill in Bologna*.

1. Modèle américain ou exemple rockefellerien?

La participation rockefellerienne à l'organisation de la recherche française en biomédecine pose d'emblée plusieurs problèmes d'interprétation. Dans le domaine de l'histoire des politiques scientifiques tout d'abord: si l'histoire des sciences en général est habituée à travailler sur la dimension transnationale des savoirs et des pratiques, l'histoire des politiques scientifiques fait partie des secteurs qui restent largement prisonniers de la perspective nationale. C'est le cas notamment en France, où la littérature scientifique a majoritairement traité le phénomène dans une perspective internaliste et institutionnelle[4]. Or, l'intervention de la fondation Rockefeller témoigne de la limitation de cette perspective. L'autre problème consiste à se demander s'il existe un modèle américain d'organisation de la recherche qui se serait appliqué en France au cours de la période considérée; comme on le verra plus loin, il n'en est rien.

Cette double impasse invite à déplacer la perspective et à ne plus considérer l'organisation de la recherche française comme un processus national mais comme la déclinaison locale d'un processus transnational dans lequel les modèles circulent en tous sens et donnent lieu à des appropriations diverses. *In fine*, cette perspective amène également à élargir le cadre d'analyse de l'américanisation, alors que la plupart des études existantes ont jusqu'à une date récente privilégié une perspective diffusionniste et bilatérale qui ne dit pas toute la complexité du processus. On ne compte plus les études de cas concernant l'américanisation de la France[5], de l'Australie[6], de l'Autriche[7], de la Suède[8], de l'Allemagne[9], du Canada[10], etc. Les travaux à l'échelle continentale, notamment européenne, sont dans la majorité des cas des synthèses comparatives d'études bilatérales[11], et les études avec une perspective globale à l'échelle proprement européenne sont rares[12]. Si la pertinence du point de vue bilatéral n'est pas discutable en soi, celui-ci a ses limites, car les sociétés européennes confrontées au processus d'américanisation sont des sociétés

---

4 Voir par exemple Picard, *La république des savants*; Chatriot/Duclert, *Le gouvernement de la recherche*; ou encore la série des Cahiers pour l'histoire du CNRS.

5 Kuisel, *Seducing the French*.

6 Bell/Bell, *Americanization and Australia*.

7 Wagnleitner, *Coca-Colonization*; Bischof/Pelinka, *Americanization/Westernization*.

8 Lunden/Asard, *Networks of Americanization*.

9 Stephan, *Americanization and Anti-Americanism*.

10 Moffett, *The Americanization of Canada*.

11 C'est le cas en particulier des nombreux et excellents travaux menés par l'équipe rassemblée autour de l'historien hollandais Rob Kroes depuis 1991.

12 Voir notamment Pells, *Not Like US*; et les travaux consacrés au Wild West Show: Sears, «Bierstadt», 3–14; Bieder, «Marketing the American Indian», 15–23; Rydell & Kroes, *Buffalo Bill in Bologna*, 97–119.

ouvertes à des multiples influences, les hommes, comme les idées ou les pratiques, effectuant souvent des circuits complexes qui engagent plus de deux partenaires. Analyser l'américanisation dans le cadre d'un face à face entre deux cultures nationales aboutit à une vision trop schématique; il est donc préférable d'adopter une perspective plus vaste, que l'on qualifiera de circulatoire et multilatérale.

Dans cette perspective, l'histoire des politiques scientifiques est sans doute une contribution intéressante, à la fois thématique et épistémologique, à l'histoire de l'américanisation. La construction de ces politiques apparaît en effet comme un processus transnational, la question de l'organisation de la recherche scientifique se posant avec acuité dans tous les grands pays industrialisés à partir du début du XXe siècle: ainsi en France la Caisse des recherches scientifiques (CRS) est-elle créée en 1901, tandis qu'en Allemagne, la Kaiser Wilhelm Gesellschaft est fondée en 1911. Mais c'est la Première guerre mondiale qui donne à cette question son caractère d'urgence et d'enjeu national qu'elle va garder jusqu'à nos jours[13]. Tous les pays belligérants se lancent en effet dans la mobilisation scientifique et tout au long du conflit, les scientifiques sont mobilisés pour participer à l'effort de guerre organisé par l'État. Au lendemain de la Grande Guerre, l'organisation de la recherche scientifique est un problème politique dans les pays européens insatisfaits du traité de Versailles en raison de la probabilité d'une nouvelle guerre à plus ou moins longue échéance. Il en résulte dans plusieurs pays la création d'organismes nationaux d'administration de la recherche: le Consiglio Nazionale delle Ricerche italien en 1923, le Fonds National pour la Recherche Scientifique belge (FNRS) en 1928[14], la Caisse nationale des sciences française en 1930; la Fondation nationale de recherches scientifiques espagnole en 1931. En Grande Bretagne, si le Medical Research Council créé en avril 1920 n'est pas un organisme public, une partie de son financement vient de l'État. C'est le cas également de la Notgemeinschaft der Deutschen Wissenschaft créée en 1920 en Allemagne; devenue Deutsche Forschungsgemeinschaft en 1929, elle passe totalement sous contrôle gouvernemental lors de l'arrivée de Hitler au pouvoir en 1933. Pendant ce temps, aux États-Unis, on assiste à un processus différent: passé la mobilisation dans le cadre de la guerre[15], l'État fédéral se désengage après la fin du conflit et la recherche y restera presque exclusivement privée pendant tout l'entre-deux-guerres. Jusqu'à la fin des années 1930, la mise en place d'une politique de recherche publique, y compris pendant le *New Deal*, se heurtera à de fortes réticences de la part des industriels partisans de l'exclusivité de l'initiative privée dans ce

---

13 Pestre, «Le nouvel univers», 18; Id., «Science», 67 sq.
14 Bertrams, «Le Fonds National», 36–39.
15 Geiger, *To Advance Knowledge*, 97.

domaine, et aux structures même du champ universitaire américain qui
concentre l'essentiel de la recherche scientifique, et reçoit l'essentiel de son
financement des industriels et des fondations[16].

Parmi ces fondations, la Rockefeller élabore un projet qui parvient à maturité à partir de la fin des années 1920 au lendemain de l'épisode, bien
connu des historiens de la philanthropie, de sa réorganisation qui se dé-
roule entre 1926 et 1928[17]. Au sortir de celle-ci, elle offre l'exemple, encore
rarissime dans le monde, d'une véritable politique scientifique articulée autour de grands thèmes correspondant à ses *divisions* (Natural Science, Medical Science, Social Science, Humanities, Public Health) et mise en œuvre à
l'aide d'une gamme de financements qui lui permet d'intervenir aux différents étages de la production du savoir scientifique: *fellowships* (bourses
d'étude de longue durée) et *travel grants* (bourses de voyage de quelques se-
maines) pour les chercheurs individuels, financement de laboratoires, financement d'équipes associant plusieurs laboratoires, soutien au développement de la documentation scientifique, financement de publications, etc.
Mais la réorganisation de la fondation n'est que le reflet des mutations du
monde de l'enseignement et de la recherche scientifique, tant aux États-Unis
que dans le reste du monde[18]; l'appareil philanthropique est de ce point de
vue une chambre d'écho d'un mouvement de structuration de la recherche
qui s'observe un peu partout dans les pays industrialisés. Il reste, qu'à partir
de sa réorganisation, la Rockefeller va servir, sinon de modèle, du moins
d'exemple aux Français qui sont au même moment à la recherche de solutions organisationnelles pour mettre en place une politique scientifique à
l'échelle nationale.

C'est en particulier le cas du physicien Jean Perrin et du biologiste André
Mayer, qui sont en contact permanent avec les Américains depuis le milieu
des années 1920. Au début de l'année 1930, les deux hommes présentent au
gouvernement français un avant-projet de loi proposant la mise en place
d'un Service national de la recherche scientifique dans lequel ils évoquent
«l'admirable organisation de la Rockefeller et celle du Fonds National de la
Recherche Scientifique belge[19]» qui leur ont servi de source d'inspiration. En
avril 1930, le gouvernement crée une Caisse nationale des sciences (CNS)
qui reprend en grande partie leurs propositions, et en particulier l'organi-
gramme disciplinaire qu'ils ont imaginé. Celui-ci se fonde sur le principe de
la division en grands champs disciplinaires, également adopté par la Rockefeller. La CNS comprend deux comités, l'un consacré aux «sciences mathé-

16 Masseys-Bertonèche, *Philanthropie*, 131–134.
17 Kohler, «A policy for the Advancement of Science», 480–515.
18 Tournès, «La fondation Rockefeller».
19 Picard/Pradoura, «La longue marche», 19 sq.

matiques et expérimentales», l'autre aux «sciences humaines». Le premier
est lui-même divisé en cinq sections: «sciences mathématiques», «sciences
physiques», «sciences chimiques», «sciences naturelles» et «sciences biologiques[20]», cette dernière intégrant les recherches menées à la croisée de la biologie et de la médecine. Cette organisation sera reconduite lors de la création
de la Caisse nationale des recherches scientifiques (CNRS) au printemps
1935, dont l'existence est pérennisée par la victoire du Front populaire aux
élections législatives de 1936. Le nouveau gouvernement marque en effet sa
volonté d'aller plus loin dans la constitution d'une véritable politique scientifique en créant un secrétariat d'État à la Recherche[21]. Au cours des années
1936–1939, le budget consacré à la recherche ne cessera d'augmenter. La
création du Centre national de la recherche scientifique (CNRS) en octobre
1939 marquera l'aboutissement de ce processus.

2. Les dynamiques locales

Pour aller plus loin dans la discussion, il est important d'analyser la nature
du terrain local sur lequel la politique rockefellerienne se déploie. Cette
question renvoie à un problème épistémologique important dans l'étude des
phénomènes d'américanisation. En effet, la problématique diffusion/récep-
tion adoptée par la plupart des études ne rend pas pleinement compte de la
dynamique des partenaires, en particulier parce que les travaux se concen-
trent essentiellement sur la réception. Ils analysent les réponses, les adapta-
tions et les réinterprétations du récepteur, mais abordent peu l'étude des
situations locales préalables à l'arrivée des Américains. De sorte que les
conclusions qui ressortent de ces études insistent, selon les cas, soit sur la
manière dont l'action américaine aurait promu un processus de modernisation face à des acteurs locaux implicitement considérés comme immobilistes
ou conservateurs, soit sur le refus opposé aux initiatives américaines. Dans le
cas qui nous occupe ici, l'analyse des dynamiques préalables à l'arrivée de la
fondation Rockefeller permet d'éviter cet écueil qui consiste à considérer le
partenaire uniquement comme un réactif dépourvu d'initiative propre antérieure à la sollicitation américaine ou, pire, comme une force d'opposition
à la modernisation. Si l'on peut incontestablement analyser certains aspects
de l'américanisation sous l'angle de la modernisation, les deux termes sont
loin d'être systématiquement synonymes, ne serait-ce que parce qu'existent
des forces modernisatrices locales, mais aussi parce que la modernisation

---

20 Caisse Nationale des Sciences, Rapport annuel 1932, Archives Nationales françaises,
sous-série F17, carton 17 458 (ci-après AN F 17/17 458).
21 Ory, *La belle illusion*, 471.

proposée par l'Amérique est parfois décalée par rapport aux contextes locaux, comme le montre par exemple l'échec de certaines campagnes d'éra-
dication de maladies menées en Amérique latine à l'aide de dispositifs techniques inadaptés aux réalités des pays où les fondations interviennent[22].
Dans le domaine biomédical comme dans d'autres secteurs d'intervention
de la philanthropie en France (santé publique, enseignement médical, sciences sociales), des projets préexistent à l'arrivée des fondations. L'une des
conclusions qui s'en dégage est le fait que les fondations n'interviennent
nulle part *ex nihilo*, mais s'intègrent systématiquement dans des processus
déjà enclenchés avant leur arrivée et dont elles ont repéré l'état d'avance-
ment suffisant pour que leur intervention apparaisse comme décisive. Le cas
de la biomédecine illustre bien les différentes facettes de la dynamique locale, qui est à la fois une dynamique institutionnelle, une dynamique intellectuelle et une dynamique sociale.

Dynamique institutionnelle

Du point de vue institutionnel, la politique de recherche française est déjà
bien engagée avant l'intervention de la fondation Rockefeller. À ce sujet, il
faut noter que si l'histoire de la politique scientifique française est bien
connue pour l'après 1945, la période antérieure a beaucoup moins retenu
l'attention des historiens. Pourtant, c'est dès avant 1914 que l'organisation de
la science est devenue un enjeu national, sur fond de rivalité avec l'Allemagne.
La création de la Caisse des recherches scientifiques (CRS) en 1901 avait mar-
qué une première étape, limitée à la recherche médicale. Après 1918, non seulement la question de l'organisation et du financement de la recherche
concerne toutes les sciences, mais, compte tenu de l'affrontement qui vient
d'avoir lieu avec l'ennemi héréditaire, elle devient «une question politique à
part entière[23]». La confrontation avec la politique mise en place par l'Allemagne au même moment n'est pas pour rien dans cette promotion. C'est d'ailleurs l'écrivain Maurice Barrès, l'un des ténors de la majorité nationaliste élue
au parlement en 1919, qui lance le pavé dans la mare et donne un retentisse-
ment national à cette question en dénonçant à la Chambre des députés, le
11 juin 1920, la situation misérable de la recherche française[24]: face à une Allemagne qui a démontré pendant le conflit une capacité d'organisation de la
science supérieure à la France, celle-ci doit se ressaisir et utiliser toutes les res-

22 Farley, *To Cast Out Disease.*
23 Pinault, *La science au Parlement*, 134.
24 *Revue des deux mondes*, série VI-55, 1920, pp. 244–260; Barrès, *Pour la haute intelligence française*, iii.

sources de ses scientifiques pour être prête à affronter un conflit futur. Mais Barrès n'est que la chambre d'écho d'un mouvement plus profond initié par les scientifiques eux-mêmes, et dont l'animateur principal est le chimiste Charles Moureu (1863–1929). Membre de l'Académie des sciences et professeur au Collège de France depuis 1917, Moureu s'intéresse à l'organisation de la recherche depuis l'avant-guerre; en 1920, il suscite la création d'une Fédération des sociétés de chimie et favorise la création d'une Fédération des sociétés de sciences naturelles dont la cheville ouvrière est le biologiste André Mayer (1875–1956), qui a participé comme Moureu à la mobilisation scientifique pendant la guerre et qui devient professeur au Collège de France en 1922. En 1920, les deux fédérations produisent en commun un rapport rédigé par Mayer, où il est noté que «l'ancien type d'organisation [de la recherche] ne suffit plus. [...] Elle ne peut plus seulement être l'apanage de quelques chercheurs isolés ou de professeurs entourés d'élèves, il lui faut des moyens plus larges, une organisation plus étendue[25]», et en particulier une politique de financement des laboratoires et des chercheurs. La mobilisation scientifique qui s'exprime à partir du début des années 1920 est donc l'expression d'un mouvement de fond qui traverse les spécialités scientifiques.

Dans cette mobilisation, la synergie entre recherche fondamentale et recherche appliquée est intime dès le début: pour la stimuler, le gouvernement sépare depuis le commencement des années 1920 une partie des activités de recherche auparavant placées sous la direction du ministère de la Guerre, pour les placer sous la direction du ministère de l'Instruction publique. Cette organisation est confirmée par l'instruction ministérielle du 18 novembre 1925 sur la mobilisation scientifique, qui va progressivement faire de l'État un acteur majeur de l'organisation de la recherche. Par ailleurs, afin de développer la recherche à l'université, les pouvoirs publics prennent deux types de mesures. Des mesures juridiques tout d'abord, avec le décret Honnorat du 31 juillet 1920 qui crée les instituts d'université. Des mesures foncières ensuite: Pour agrandir les facultés de médecine et de sciences, des acquisitions de terrains sont envisagées dès 1920. Alors que plusieurs organismes de recherche tels que l'Institut océanographique, l'Institut de chimie appliquée ou l'Institut du radium sont déjà installés sur la Montagne Sainte-Geneviève (dans le quartier latin), des locaux pour de nouveaux instituts y seront construits à partir de 1925, en particulier le Laboratoire de chimie physique de Jean Perrin, l'Institut Henri Poincaré et l'Institut de biologie physico-chimique dont il sera question plus loin. En 1926, ces grandes manœuvres immobilières sont déjà bien avancées, et les doyens des facultés sont optimistes

---

25 *Sur quelques questions relatives à l'organisation des recherches scientifiques, rapport présenté aux comités nationaux de recherches par les fédérations des sociétés de chimie et des sociétés de sciences naturelles. Rapporteur: André Mayer, 1920.*

devant la construction en cours de cette «cité nouvelle[26]» qui permettra de créer au centre de la capitale un grand pôle scientifique.

Dynamique intellectuelle

La dynamique proprement intellectuelle est aussi présente avant l'arrivée de la Rockefeller, sous la forme d'un rapprochement entre la médecine clinique, la biologie, la chimie ou encore la physique. Certes, les facultés de médecine et les facultés des sciences sont alors deux mondes séparés physiquement et institutionnellement. Mais depuis les années 1910, les voix s'élèvent de plus en plus nombreuses pour réclamer le rapprochement des démarches des chercheurs appartenant à ces différentes disciplines. Parmi de nombreux signes, on relèvera la création en 1914 de la Société française de chimie biologique, la réclamation en 1918 par le doyen de la faculté de médecine de Paris, Henri Roger, de fonder un institut de biologie médicale sur le modèle de celui qu'ont créé les Allemands à Charlottenbourg en 1916[27], ou encore l'intégration en 1925 à l'université de Lyon d'un enseignement de sciences dans le cursus des étudiants de médecine dès la première année. Ce mouvement ne se fait pas facilement, car l'articulation de ces disciplines différentes provoque à la fois des controverses intellectuelles et des enjeux de pouvoirs entre universitaires, ainsi qu'entre facultés de médecine et facultés des sciences. L'enjeu que représente l'organisation de la recherche scientifique vient donc bousculer des équilibres complexes, en particulier la délimitation des frontières disciplinaires, mais aussi les patriotismes d'institutions hérités de sédimentations historiques diverses. Cette situation explique que les croisements disciplinaires s'opèrent prioritairement en dehors de l'université. C'est le cas de la génétique, domaine pionnier qui émerge du croisement de l'embryologie, de la chimie, de la biologie et de la physique, en particulier au sein du laboratoire d'embryogénie comparée du Collège de France, dirigé par Emmanuel Fauré-Frémiet à partir de 1923, puis au sein de l'Institut de biologie physico-chimique, dit aussi Institut Rothschild, créé en 1927. C'est aussi le cas des neurosciences: le pionnier de la neurochirurgie en France, Clovis Vincent, commence à opérer les tumeurs du cerveau dans une clinique privée à partir de 1928, l'Assistance publique et la faculté de médecine ayant refusé de créer un enseignement spécifique dans un grand hôpital public; de son côté, Alfred Fessard, qui commence à explorer le domaine de la physiologie cérébrale à partir de 1931, effectue ses travaux sous la direction d'Henri Piéron au Col-

26 *Annales de l'Université de Paris*, n°2, mai 1926, p. 117.

27 Université de Paris. Faculté de médecine. *Rapports sur la réorganisation de la faculté*, 7 février et 20 juin 1918.

lège de France et à l'Institut Marey. Les applications biologiques et médicales de la radioactivité sont un autre exemple: elles ont trouvé un lieu privilégié avec l'Institut du radium (dit aussi Institut Curie) achevé en 1919, et où officie à partir de 1925 le jeune Frédéric Joliot-Curie; lorsqu'il sera élu au Collège de France en 1936, la collaboration entre les deux institutions se poursuivra, comme nous le verrons plus loin. Ces exemples, qui ne sont pas limitatifs, montrent qu'une dynamique de transversalité et d'interdisciplinarité existe bel et bien à la charnière de la médecine, de la biologie, de la chimie et de la physique, et ce avant l'arrivée de la fondation Rockefeller. Celle-ci ne fera que donner une impulsion, parfois décisive, au processus.

Dynamique sociale

Aux dynamiques institutionnelle et intellectuelle s'ajoute une dynamique sociale, qui s'exprime à travers les contacts constants entre les universitaires, les hommes politiques et les mécènes français qui interviennent dans le financement de la recherche. C'est cette dynamique, préexistante à l'arrivée de la Rockefeller, qui permet au processus impulsé au plus haut niveau de l'État de prendre corps sur le terrain, ce qui est fondamental. L'analyse de ce type de dynamique est rarement menée par les historiens de la philanthropie, qui se focalisent souvent sur la mise en place financière, administrative et technique des projets, en négligeant le tissu de relations sociales dans lequel ils se déploient. Ce manque d'intérêt est sans doute l'une des plus grandes lacunes de l'historiographie des activités internationales de la philanthropie américaine, car la dimension sociale est essentielle pour comprendre l'implantation locale des actions des fondations. Dans le cas de la recherche biomédicale, il est clair que cette dynamique sociale préexistante a favorisé le processus de «localisation» de la politique rockefellerienne.

    La connexion entre les milieux universitaires et les mécènes privés est l'un des éléments de cette dynamique. Au lendemain de la première guerre mondiale, l'insuffisance du financement des pouvoirs publics constitue un des obstacles majeurs à la mise en œuvre d'une politique de recherche, les priorités budgétaires de l'État étant ailleurs: reconstruire le pays, payer les pensions des anciens combattants, rembourser les dettes de guerre aux États-Unis, etc. C'est pourquoi les universitaires vont se tourner vers les financements privés. Charles Moureu suscite au lendemain de la guerre la création d'un Comité national d'aide à la recherche scientifique, qui organise des manifestations pour rendre visible son action et lever des fonds[28]. En 1926 le

---

28 *L'art français au service de la science française. Exposition d'œuvres d'art des XVIIIe, XIXe et XXe siècles au profit du Comité national d'aide à la recherche scientifique*, Paris, 1923.

recteur de l'université de Paris, Paul Lapie, créé la Société des amis de l'université de Paris, habilitée à recevoir dons et legs; ceux-ci proviennent en particulier de mécènes tels que le banquier Albert Kahn (également trésorier de la Société), mais aussi des fondations Edmond de Rothschild, Singer-Polignac ou Deutsch de la Meurthe. Ces mécènes financent également des instituts de recherche privés ou semi-privés tels que l'Institut du radium ou l'Institut de biologie physico-chimique. De sorte que tout au long de l'entre-deux-guerres, le monde de la recherche sera largement financé par des organisations privées. La fondation Rockefeller n'est donc que l'une d'entre elles, même si elle est l'une des plus importantes, et même très probablement la plus importante. Mais son intervention ne détonne pas dans un contexte où les grands mandarins universitaires de la Sorbonne et du Collège de France sont habitués à solliciter les mécènes privés, et où la connexion entre les universitaires et les philanthropes est déjà une réalité.

L'autre élément de la dynamique sociale est l'interconnexion entre les universitaires et le monde politico-administratif. Celle-ci est capitale pour comprendre le processus de construction de la politique scientifique, en raison du rôle important joué par certaines personnalités dont l'autorité scientifique se double de qualités organisationnelles, et qui sont bien introduites chez les décideurs, ce qui va leur permettre de plaider la cause de l'organisation de la science. C'est le cas de Charles Moureu, qui a joué un grand rôle dès avant 1914 dans l'émergence de la politique scientifique en faisant sortir le débat des cercles de chercheurs pour le porter devant le Parlement; après 1918, il continue à agir dans ce sens en cherchant à regrouper les associations de chercheurs pour créer un groupe de pression susceptible de convaincre les pouvoirs publics d'investir dans la recherche. C'est le cas aussi d'André Mayer et de Jean Perrin (prix Nobel de physique 1926), qui vont mettre toute leur autorité scientifique dans la balance pour obtenir l'engagement des pouvoirs publics en présentant en 1930 leur plan d'organisation (parfois désigné sous le nom de «Plan Perrin») qui va aboutir à la création de la Caisse nationale des sciences. C'est enfin le cas d'Émile Borel, qui cumule les distinctions scientifiques et les fonctions politiques et constitue le parfait exemple de relais entre le milieu universitaire et le monde politique: professeur au Collège de France et membre de l'Académie des sciences, il a également été pendant la Grande Guerre sous-directeur des Inventions au secrétariat d'État à la Guerre puis secrétaire général à la présidence du Conseil; en 1924, il a été élu député et le restera jusqu'en 1939. En 1926, c'est lui qui fait voter par le Parlement la première vraie attribution de crédits pour la recherche scientifique, qu'on appellera «le sou du laboratoire». Une fois arrivés en France, les *officers* rockefelleriens se mettront immédiatement en contact avec tous ces personnages qui les feront bénéficier de la synergie déjà bien établie entre universitaires, philanthropes locaux et décideurs politiques.

3. La coproduction franco-rockefellerienne

La fondation Rockefeller: un partenaire local

L'importance et la précocité de cette dynamique locale interdit d'interpréter l'action rockefellerienne comme l'exportation d'un modèle, tout comme elle interdit d'opposer une fondation représentant la modernité et la réforme à un milieu universitaire français immobiliste et conservateur. L'image est plus subtile: si la Rockefeller a joué un rôle important dans la construction de la politique scientifique, ce n'est pas en exportant un modèle américain, mais en s'imposant comme une actrice locale qui participe à l'élaboration des projets. Le succès de ce processus de «localisation» est dû à la capacité des *officers* à aller sur le terrain et à y multiplier les contacts personnels avec les acteurs français pour acquérir une vision claire de la situation et élaborer des projets en adéquation avec le contexte local. Cet activisme relationnel a été peu étudié par les historiens de la philanthropie, qui, jusqu'à une date récente, se sont peu intéressés au processus de négociations entre les donateurs et leurs bénéficiaires qui précède l'attribution de subventions. Or, en France, ces négociations peuvent s'étendre sur plusieurs années. Mais au-delà du cas français, l'art de la négociation fait partie de la *Rockefeller touch*, car c'est à force de discuter avec les partenaires locaux que les *officers* se font une idée précise des actions à entreprendre; il est même clair que les projets rockefelleriens, dans bien des cas, se construisent au fur et à mesure de ces négociations. Enfin, ces négociations permettent à la fondation de s'insérer dans les réseaux locaux et de s'y faire reconnaître comme une partenaire à part entière, et non pas simplement comme une organisation américaine. Cette dimension est une constante de l'action de la Rockefeller en France et en Europe pendant l'entre-deux-guerres. La notion de coproduction *in situ*, que l'on utilise ici pour caractériser ce phénomène, s'inscrit dans la ligne droite des renouvellements récents de l'historiographie de la philanthropie qui s'attachent à repenser les rapports entre donateur et bénéficiaire en mettant l'accent sur les circulations croisées et la dimension à double sens de leur relation[29].

Du côté des historiens de l'américanisation, l'analyse des interactions entre les partenaires du processus est également souvent absente: c'est sans doute sur ce point que les historiens de l'américanisation sont restés, paradoxalement, les plus allusifs, tant ils se sont focalisés sur un processus à sens unique et sur les conséquences du contact plutôt que sur l'étude du contact *en train de se faire*. Influence, impact, réception, réaction, adaptation, réin-

---

29 Voir par exemple Birn, *Marriage of Convenience* ; Amrith, Decolonizing International Health; Saunier/Tournès, *Philanthropies croisées*.

terprétation: tous ces termes renvoient le plus souvent à ce qui se passe *après* le contact, mais peinent à cerner le contact lui-même. C'est ici que les apports de la *global history* et de la *transnational history* permettent de renouveler la perspective sur l'américanisation, en montrant que les savoirs et les pratiques n'ont pas forcément leur origine dans les États-nations, mais aussi «dans le monde qui existe entre eux[30]», c'est-à-dire dans les connexions qui se tissent au gré des circulations transnationales. De ce point de vue, l'un des éléments majeurs qui ressort de l'analyse du rôle des fondations en France est un tissu extrêmement serré de contacts interpersonnels multidirectionnels qui rendent impossible le raisonnement fondé sur le triptyque diffusion/réception/réinterprétation qui sous-tend la plupart des études d'américanisation. L'hypothèse d'un projet international philanthropique élaboré à l'intérieur des frontières américaines et mis en œuvre aux États-Unis avant d'être exporté ne résiste en effet pas à l'analyse: la densité des contacts qui s'établit entre les représentants de la fondation Rockefeller et leurs interlocuteurs français montre à quel point ces projets sont négociés et coproduits *in situ*, et non exportés «clés en main» puis réinterprétés par le récepteur. Cette proximité établie dès l'entre-deux-guerres permet de mieux comprendre le phénomène de coproduction d'hégémonie qui intervient après 1945[31], dans un contexte de forte asymétrie entre les États-Unis et l'Europe: l'impérialisme américain est d'autant mieux accepté que la proximité intellectuelle remonte à la période précédente, où le déséquilibre entre les deux partenaires, s'il existait déjà, n'était pas aussi visible. On notera que dans la coproduction d'après 1945, la marge de manœuvre des Français, et des Européens en général, sera plus faible qu'avant 1939.

L'insertion dans les réseaux français

Il est intéressant de suivre le processus d'implantation de la Rockefeller dans les réseaux français car il montre qu'elle ne diffuse pas un projet achevé mais configure et reconfigure son projet en fonction du terrain local.

Dans un premier temps, au cours des années 1920, l'action menée par la fondation Rockefeller et l'International Education Board (IEB) en matière biomédicale n'est pas sous-tendue par une politique cohérente. Elle fonctionne plutôt selon une logique opportuniste dont l'objectif principal est manifestement d'acquérir une bonne connaissance de ce terrain complexe qu'est le paysage universitaire français, d'en identifier les personnages importants et de préciser les projets que la fondation pourrait y mettre en œu-

---

30 Rodgers, *Atlantic Crossings*, 5.
31 Krige, *American Hegemony*, ch 1.

vre, afin d'être en position de participer à la vaste réorganisation de la recherche qui est à l'ordre du jour et dont les Américains sont informés grâce à
leur carnet d'adresses très fourni. Par ailleurs, au cours des années 1920, le
projet international de la philanthropie rockefellerienne est en pleine élaboration et ne suit pas un fil conducteur bien identifié, comme ce sera le cas
dans les années 1930. Les années 1924–1930 doivent donc avant tout être in-
terprétées comme une phase de reconnaissance.

À partir de 1924, et surtout de 1926–27, le représentant de l'IEB en
France, Augustus Trowbridge, physicien à Princeton, multiplie les contacts
avec les acteurs du processus d'organisation de la recherche, par exemple le
doyen de la faculté de sciences Charles Maurain, mais aussi Émile Borel[32],
Jean Perrin, ou encore le nouveau recteur de l'université de Paris Sébastien
Charléty. En 1926, les premiers financements se concrétisent: l'IEB aide le laboratoire de chimie physique de Jean Perrin en voie d'achèvement mais dont
la construction a dépassé le budget prévu[33]; et surtout il décide de financer
l'Institut Henri Poincaré dédié aux mathématiques et à la physique théorique. L'initiateur de cet institut n'est autre qu'Émile Borel, que Trowbridge
rencontre en mai 1926 pour discuter de l'opportunité d'un financement
américain[34]. Celui-ci intervient à la fin de l'année: sur les trois millions de
francs nécessaires pour construire le bâtiment et payer les salaires des professeurs, deux seront fournis par l'IEB et un par l'université de Paris[35]; les
Américains ont, comme d'habitude, mis comme condition à leur soutien la
nécessité de trouver un financement local qui permettra de prendre le relais
du soutien américain après quelques années. Borel les assure que le gouvernement français débloquera les fonds nécessaires. À partir de là, les choses
iront très vite: en décembre 1926, l'IEB débloque la première partie de la
subvention pour construire le bâtiment, et l'Institut sera inauguré en novembre 1928. Sa création permet de donner une impulsion importante au
développement de la physique théorique, alors extrêmement marginale
puisqu'il n'existait avant cette création que quatre postes de cette spécialité
dans les établissements d'enseignement supérieur et de recherche français[36].

---

32 Augustus Trowbridge, Memorandum of conversation with professor C. Maurain,
Dean of the Faculty of Science, Sorbonne, and The university architect in the latter's of-
fice, 1 avril 1927, International Education Board, series 1.2, box 33, folder 470 (ci-après
IEB 1.2/33/470).

33 IEB Minutes, 19 novembre 1926, IEB 1.2/34/473.

34 Augustus Trowbrigde, Memorandum of conference in office with Emile Borel,
29 mai 1926, IEB 1.2/33/470.

35 Projet de création d'un institut de mathématiques et de physique mathématique,
séance du conseil de l'université, 28 juin 1926, Archives Nationales françaises-Centre des
Archives Contemporaines, versement 20010498, carton 130 (ci-après CAC 20010498/130).

36 Pestre, *Physique et physiciens*, 105.

L'autre financement important durant les années 1920 est celui accordé au Muséum d'Histoire naturelle. Celui-ci est alors indépendant de l'université de Paris, mais le directeur de l'enseignement supérieur Jacques Cavalier a profité du décès d'un des membres de son conseil d'administration au printemps 1927 pour y faire entrer Sébastien Charléty et amorcer ainsi un rapprochement avec l'université de Paris[37], dans la perspective de créer un grand pôle scientifique regroupant les deux institutions. L'initiative n'échappe pas aux Américains qui apprennent rapidement que, comme bien d'autres établissements parisiens, le Muséum est alors en proie à la pénurie financière[38], qui affecte une partie non négligeable de ses bâtiments, en particulier son herbier dont les collections sont uniques au monde. Au printemps 1928, l'IEB accorde 200000 dollars (cinq millions de francs)[39] pour construire un nouveau bâtiment, à condition que le gouvernement français s'engage pour un montant identique. La construction de l'édifice commencera en 1929 et s'achèvera en 1935. Dans cette affaire, la contribution de l'IEB a été avant tout une occasion pour les Américains de s'insérer dans le processus de réorganisation globale de la recherche scientifique alors en gestation. En effet, ce n'est pas tant le financement de l'herbier *per se* qui intéresse l'IEB, mais l'opportunité offerte aux Américains de devenir des acteurs du processus et de participer aux étapes futures de la réorganisation.

Après la période 1926–1928 qui voit la fusion des différents *boards* rockefelleriens, c'est une fondation Rockefeller transformée qui reprend pied en France à partir du printemps 1929. La recherche scientifique a été substituée à l'amélioration de la santé comme principe unificateur du projet philanthropique. L'objectif central de la fondation est désormais «le progrès des connaissances[40]» à travers la recherche scientifique, afin de réaliser la «rationalisation de la vie[41]» et la régulation (*control*) des conduites humaines (*human behaviour*). Cet objectif ambitieux doit être atteint à l'aide de la mobilisation de l'ensemble des savoirs scientifiques, parmi lesquels la biologie et la médecine occupent une place centrale. Au début des années trente, la philosophie rockefellerienne se présente ainsi sous la forme d'un projet hyperscientiste à forte dimension eugéniste, visant à créer un homme nouveau et une nouvelle société régulée par la science[42]. Ce projet explique l'intérêt

37 Cavalier à Herriot, 21 mai 1927, AN F17/13 559.
38 Aperçu sur le budget du Museum, Assemblée des professeurs du 4 juillet 1935, Archives Museum d'Histoire Naturelle, carton 51.
39 IEB Minutes, 25 mai 1928, IEB 1.2/34/479.
40 Rockefeller foundation program and policy. Advancement of knowledge, 3 janvier 1929, Rockefeller Foundation Archives, Record Group 3, series 900, box 22, folder 166 (ci-après RF 3/900/22/166).
41 RF Minutes, 11–12 avril 1933, RF 3/900/B21/158a.
42 Kay, *The Molecular Vision*.

porté par la fondation à un ensemble de disciplines situées à la croisée de la médecine et des sciences de la nature: embryologie, génétique, neurologie, physiologie, biochimie, etc. Cette culture scientiste désormais pleinement assumée met la fondation un peu plus en phase avec les acteurs français de l'organisation de la recherche, qui partagent avec les Américains une foi sans faille dans le pouvoir de la science d'assurer le progrès de l'humanité. Il est d'ailleurs à noter qu'une partie d'entre eux participent en 1930 à la création de l'Union rationaliste, un groupe de pression intellectuel qui joue un rôle important dans l'institutionnalisation de la politique scientifique, dans lequel on retrouve notamment Perrin, Borel, Maurain, mais aussi le doyen de la faculté de médecine Henri Roger. Cette culture scientiste partagée est indéniablement un terrain de rencontre qui favorise le dialogue entre les *officers* américains et les universitaires français. Autrement dit, au début des années 1930, les positions des deux protagonistes sont plus ajustées que dans les années 1920, ce qui va faciliter la mise en œuvre de projets communs.

La coproduction des projets

De nombreux projets entrepris dans le domaine biomédical au cours des années 1930 sont construits conjointement par le gouvernement français et la Rockefeller, comme l'attestent les contacts constants, les échanges de documents, les discussions relatives à la mise en place des projets, mais aussi les financements communs. Ces projets se caractérisent non seulement par la diversité des dispositifs technico-administratifs utilisés (financement de laboratoires, achat de matériel, bourses individuelles et collectives de durée ajustée aux projets, etc.), mais aussi par la dimension pluriannuelle des financements, la transversalité disciplinaire, le travail collectif, ainsi que la forte ouverture internationale. Ils témoignent non seulement de la naissance d'une politique scientifique cohérente, mais aussi de recompositions disciplinaires qui vont profondément transformer le champ de la production du savoir scientifique et commencer à faire émerger le domaine de la biomédecine qui arrivera à maturité après 1945. Dans cette politique comme dans ces recompositions, la Rockefeller s'impose comme un partenaire incontournable, dont on examinera le rôle à partir de trois exemples: la génétique, les maladies du système nerveux et les applications biologiques de la radioactivité.

Embryologie et génétique: l'hérédité
La génétique est en plein essor dans l'entre-deux-guerres. En France, son développement se fait avant tout au sein de deux institutions. La première est le Collège de France, où enseignent l'embryologiste Emmanuel Fauré-Frémiet et le biologiste André Mayer. L'IEB, qui prend contact avec eux dès 1922, ac-

corde ses premières *fellowships* à plusieurs de leurs élèves: le chimiste René
Wurmser, préparateur au laboratoire de Mayer[43], en 1924; le biologiste Louis
Rapkine en 1925; l'embryologiste Boris Ephrussi, assistant au laboratoire de
Fauré-Frémiet, en 1926; le chimiste Albert Kirrmann en 1928. L'autre lieu
phare de développement de la génétique est l'Institut de biologie physico-
chimique (Institut Rothschild), où les personnages susmentionnés travail-
lent également. À partir de 1930, les subventions de la Caisse nationale des
sciences viennent compléter le financement Rothschild, et en 1936 la fondation Rockefeller apportera également son soutien pour financer un projet
collectif dont la gestation s'étend sur plus d'un an et qui se traduit par la fusion de trois projets initialement séparés: le premier, conçu par Fauré-Frémiet pour son laboratoire d'embryogénie comparée; le deuxième par
Wurmser pour l'Institut Rothschild; le troisième par Ephrussi, qui, après sa
fellowship de 1926, en a obtenu une deuxième en 1934 pour aller travailler
avec son collègue George Beadle dans le laboratoire de T.H. Morgan au California Institute of Technology, et envisage au printemps 1935 d'en demander une troisième pour achever ses recherches. La Rockefeller et la Caisse nationale des sciences, toutes deux désireuses de soutenir ces projets, vont
s'efforcer de les fusionner, à la fois en raison de leur proximité scientifique et
pour des motifs financiers, les ressources de la fondation tout comme celles
du gouvernement français étant en diminution depuis la crise de 1929. Pendant un an, le projet va s'affiner intellectuellement au gré des discussions entre les chercheurs, André Mayer (qui occupe des fonctions à la CNS) et les *officers*. Pour leur permettre de continuer leur travail pendant ce temps, la
Rockefeller accorde au printemps 1935 un financement d'urgence à Fauré-
Frémiet et une *travel grant* qui permet à George Beadle de venir à Paris pour
poursuivre son travail avec Ephrussi, dont les premières publications interviennent à la fin de l'année[44]. C'est au vu de ces résultats intermédiaires que
la fondation accorde une troisième *fellowship* à Ephrussi qui retourne au
Caltech au début de 1936, accompagné de son assistant Jacques Monod qui
bénéficie également d'une bourse[45]. Pendant ce temps, Warren Weaver, le directeur de la Natural Science Division et son assistant Wilbur Tisdale achè-
vent de déterminer les contours du projet collectif avec Fauré-Frémiet,
Wurmser et Mayer; une fois les discussions terminées, Mayer effectue une
demande officielle de financement auprès de la fondation, qui est acceptée
au mois de mars 1936, pour un montant de 50000 dollars étalés sur cinq ans.
Au cours de ces années, le groupe réalise des progrès importants dans le do-

---

43 *Notice sur les travaux scientifiques de René Wurmser*, Paris, PUF, 1931.
44 Boris Ephrussi & George W. Beadle, «La transplantation des ovaires chez la drosophile», *Bulletin biologique de la France et de la Belgique*, LXIX, 1935, fascicule 4.
45 Tournès, «Le réseau des boursiers Rockefeller».

maine de la génétique, publiés dans des revues françaises et américaines[46], à la grande satisfaction des *officers* qui voient dans ce projet l'une de leurs grandes réussites. À la fin des années trente existe en France un petit noyau de chercheurs spécialisés sur les questions de génétique (Fauré-Frémiet, Wurmser, Eprhussi, Monod, Rapkine) et dont les travaux sont reconnus par leurs collègues étrangers.

Les neurosciences: système nerveux et maladies mentales

On observe le même processus avec les neurosciences, dont la Rockefeller s'efforce également de favoriser le développement en France. Dès 1929, Alan Gregg, directeur de la Medical Science Division, a rencontré plusieurs professeurs de la faculté de médecine de Paris, en particulier Antonin Gosset et Georges Guillain, afin d'évaluer les possibilités de financement qui peuvent s'offrir à la Rockefeller. Il faut cependant attendre 1936 pour qu'une vraie opportunité se fasse jour, année où il est décidé de fonder un institut de neurobiologie à la faculté de médecine. L'objectif est de «créer un centre de recherches biologiques concernant le système nerveux» et surtout de fédérer l'étude des «problèmes de neuro-histologie, de neuro-physiologie [et] de neurochirurgie[47]». La Rockefeller, qui voit dans cette création «un pas important vers la concentration dans un seul centre de toutes les recherches dans le champ de la neurobiologie à Paris[48]», lui accorde une subvention qui semble se monter à 230000 francs sur quatre ans. En 1937, la fondation contribue 50000 francs au budget de l'institut, une somme plus grande que les subventions de l'université (20000 francs), de la Caisse nationale des sciences (20000), et de l'hôpital de la Salpêtrière (5000) prises ensemble. L'Institut reçoit par ailleurs d'autres financements privés tels que celui de la famille Deutsch de la Meurthe. Grâce à toutes ces dotations, il pourra acheter du matériel et créer en 1938 le premier laboratoire d'électroencéphalographie dans un hôpital parisien[49].

Dans le même temps, Alan Gregg suit également le projet de développement d'un service de neurochirurgie destiné à opérer les tumeurs du cerveau à l'hôpital de la Salpêtrière. Le pionnier de cette spécialité est Clovis Vincent, qui s'est initié aux États-Unis dans le service du professeur Harvey Cushing, à l'hôpital de Boston. En 1937, la faculté de médecine décide d'officialiser la naissance de cette spécialité en votant la création d'une chaire de neurochirurgie. Le coût total étant estimé à trois millions de francs, le ministère accepte d'en donner la moitié à condition que la faculté

46 Gayon, «Génétique», 191 sq.
47 Statuts de l'institut de neuro-biologie, 3 juin 1936, CAC 20010498/165.
48 Formulaire de bourse, 29 juin 1937, RF 1.1/500A/6/63.
49 Bertrand/Delay/Guillain, *L'électro-encéphalogramme normal et pathologique*, 1.

de médecine trouve une autre source de financement. Le projet est active-
ment soutenu par le ministre de l'Instruction publique, Jean Zay, et par le
recteur de l'université, Gustave Roussy. Compte tenu de ces soutiens, la
Rockefeller accepte en décembre 1937 de donner l'autre moitié, exigeant
que la chaire soit créée au cours de l'année 1938[50]. Trois mois plus tard, la
nouvelle est rendue publique: «Rockefeller offre une chaire de neurochirurgie à la France», titre *L'Intransigeant* le 6 mars. Le titulaire en est, sans
surprise, Clovis Vincent, qui inaugure son enseignement à la rentrée universitaire 1938.

La Rockefeller s'intéresse enfin à la neurophysiologie, en particulier aux
recherches menées par Henri Piéron, professeur de physiologie des sensa-
tions au Collège de France depuis 1923, et par son élève Alfred Fessard. À la
charnière de plusieurs disciplines (psychologie, psychiatrie, neurologie, physiologie), Fessard s'intéresse à la physiologie cérébrale et fait partie des premiers scientifiques en France dont la carrière commence d'emblée sous le signe de la recherche *full-time*, puisqu'il est nommé chargé de recherches par
la Caisse nationale des sciences en 1931 puis, en 1936, promu maître de recherches par la Caisse nationale des recherches scientifiques. Cette promotion, sans doute exceptionnelle à l'époque, tient à l'originalité de sa recherche, mais aussi à la protection de son mentor Henri Laugier qui est un des
dirigeants de la CNRS. La même année 1936, alors qu'il soutient sa thèse, la
Rockefeller lui accorde une *fellowship* qui lui permettra d'aller confronter ses
travaux à ceux de ses collègues anglais. À l'issue de ce séjour de six mois, la
fondation accorde en 1937 un financement de 50 000 francs au nouveau laboratoire de neurophysiologie qu'il vient de créer à l'École Pratique des
Hautes Études avec le soutien d'Henri Laugier, qui lui a obtenu également
un financement de la CNRS[51]. Ce financement est renouvelé en 1938 et permet à Fessard d'expérimenter des installations d'électroencéphalographie,
un domaine dans lequel il fait bénéficier de ses connaissances l'Institut de
neurobiologie de la faculté de médecine, où, au même moment, est mise au
point une installation d'électroencéphalographie destinée aux opérations
neurochirurgicales menées par Clovis Vincent. En 1939, Fessard retourne en
Angleterre avec une deuxième *fellowship* ; il est alors considéré par ses pairs
comme un scientifique de premier plan et ses collègues anglais font son
éloge aux *officers* rockefelleriens. Cet exemple témoigne de la complémentarité qui s'établit *de facto* entre les financements publics français et ceux de la
Rockefeller.

50 RF Minutes, 12 décembre 1937, RF 1.1/500A/6/65.
51 Alfred Fessard Fellowship card, RF 10.

Radioactivité et biologie: le traitement du cancer

Le troisième domaine où les conséquences concrètes de l'action de Rockefeller sont particulièrement visibles est celui des applications biologiques de la radioactivité, notamment dans le traitement du cancer. Les recherches dans ce sens sont menées principalement à l'Institut du radium, créé pour mettre en synergie «les sciences physiques et chimiques avec les sciences biologiques pour l'étude des corps radioactifs et de leurs applications à la biologie et à la médecine[52]». En 1932, la Rockefeller marque un coup réussi en lui accorde un financement de 120000 dollars étalé sur dix ans, soit 240000 francs annuels pour salarier quatre chercheurs à temps plein pendant cette période[53]. Il s'agit du premier financement de chercheurs sur une durée aussi longue jamais effectué par la Rockefeller en France, et jamais réalisé par un organisme français: même les financements de la Caisse nationale des sciences n'excèdent alors jamais cinq ans, et les salaires qu'elle verse sont bien moins élevés. Entre 1932 et 1938, ce financement aura servi à salarier six chercheurs par an en moyenne; au total, ce sont huit des dix-neuf postes de chercheurs des divisions «Physique-chimie» et «Applications thérapeutiques» de l'Institut qui ont fonctionné grâce à lui. La plupart pourront ainsi consacrer l'intégralité de leur temps à la recherche, et certains bénéficieront du financement pendant cinq ans[54]. Au moins six d'entre eux vont consacrer la majorité de leurs travaux au cancer: c'est le cas d'Antoine Lacassagne, François Baclesse, Octave Monod, Henri Coutard, Georges Gricouroff et Jacques Lavedan[55]. Ces travaux contribuent à installer la radiobiologie comme un des domaines d'étude majeurs dans la lutte contre la maladie, reconnaissance consacrée par l'élection en 1941 d'Antoine Lacassagne au Collège de France, sur une chaire d'histophysiologie transformée à son intention en chaire de radiobiologie expérimentale[56].

L'autre lieu où se développent des recherches sur les implications biologiques de la radioactivité est le laboratoire de synthèse atomique du Collège de France dirigé par Frédéric Joliot-Curie. En automne 1935, alors que celui-ci est pratiquement certain de recevoir le prix Nobel de chimie (il sera officiel-

---

52 Les départements biologique et médical de l'Institut du Radium: organisation, moyens d'action, activités, besoins, 1935, RF 1.1/500/8/82.

53 RF Minutes, 3 juin 1932, RF 1.1/500A/8/79.

54 Institut du radium, rapport sur les travaux et les publications fait par les travailleurs du laboratoire de radiophysiologie de l'institut du radium et des services de la fondation Curie avec l'aide de la fondation Rockefeller, de 1932 à 1937, RF 1.1/500A/8/82.

55 Institut du radium, rapport sur les travaux et les publications fait par les travailleurs du laboratoire de radiophysiologie de l'institut du radium et des services de la fondation Curie avec l'aide de la fondation Rockefeller, de 1932 à 1937, RF 1.1/500/8/82.

56 Antoine Lacassagne, *Leçon inaugurale de la chaire de radiobiologie expérimentale au Collège de France*, 19 décembre 1941, p. 3.

lement décerné en décembre), il présente une demande de subvention à la Rockefeller. Elle lui accorde en novembre une *grant-in-aid* qui lui permet d'engager un jeune physicien autrichien en tant qu'assistant dans son laboratoire; l'année suivante, ce dernier se voit également accorder une *travel grant* par la fondation pour étudier la physique théorique dans le laboratoire de Niels Bohr à Copenhague. En automne 1936, Joliot-Curie est élu professeur au Collège de France où il crée un laboratoire de synthèse atomique qui sera abondamment doté par la Caisse nationale des recherches scientifiques. Mais le financement porte essentiellement sur la partie physique des recherches, et la Rockefeller accorde en octobre 1937 une subvention complémentaire de 15000 dollars étalée sur cinq ans pour en développer la partie biologique, utilisée pour payer le salaire d'un assistant[57], Charles-Philippe Leblond. Celui-ci a déjà bénéficié d'une *fellowship* en 1934 pour aller à l'université de Yale. À son retour en 1937, il obtient une bourse de la CNRS et est affecté à l'Institut du radium pour assister Antoine Lacassagne. La subvention accordée en octobre 1937 par la Rockefeller permet notamment, comme dans le cas de Fessard et d'autres, de compléter le maigre salaire donné par la CNRS. À partir de la fin 1937, Leblond effectue des recherches sur le cancer de la glande thyroïde[58] pour lesquelles il travaille à la fois dans le laboratoire de Joliot-Curie et celui de Lacassagne. Il se développe ainsi dès la deuxième moitié des années trente une complémentarité entre les travaux de Joliot-Curie et ceux de Lacassagne, qui s'approfondira pendant et après la deuxième guerre mondiale[59], et dans laquelle la Rockefeller joue un rôle non négligeable.

Au terme de cette plongée dans les milieux scientifiques, il apparaît clair qu'au cours de l'entre-deux-guerres, l'International Education Board et la nouvelle fondation Rockefeller réorganisée après 1929, se sont imposés comme des partenaires importants du processus d'organisation de la recherche dans le domaine biomédical. Ce partenariat se manifeste à travers des contacts constants et une insertion des hommes de la fondation dans les réseaux universitaires hexagonaux, eux-mêmes liés aux réseaux administratifs et politiques par l'entremise de certains hommes tels que Borel ou Perrin. De son côté, la Rockefeller apporte à ces scientifiques des financements importants, mais fait également bénéficier les jeunes chercheurs du vaste réseau international de laboratoires et de scientifiques qu'elle a tissé dans le monde entier, jouant un rôle indéniable dans l'ouverture internationale de cette gé-

57 RF Minutes, 15 octobre 1937, RF 1.1/500D/10/111.
58 Frédéric Joliot, «La radioactivité artificielle et ses applications en biologie», Ligue nationale contre le cancer, *Assemblée générale du 8 juin 1943*.
59 Chamak, «Un scientifique pendant l'Occupation».

nération de scientifiques français; dès son arrivée à la tête de la Natural
Science Division en 1932, Warren Weaver a insisté sur ce point et c'est également dans cette perspective que la Rockefeller contribuera en 1945 au re-
démarrage du CNRS[60] puis, dans les années suivantes, au financement de
nombreux laboratoires[61]. Le partenariat de la fondation avec les organisa-
teurs de la science se manifeste aussi à travers le financement d'institutions et
de chercheurs, conjoint à celui de la Caisse nationale des sciences puis Caisse
nationale des recherches scientifiques. Pour autant, malgré sa présence
constante dans le paysage scientifique de l'entre-deux-guerres, la Rockefeller
ne joue en aucun cas un rôle démiurgique dans le processus d'organisation
de la recherche française, déjà bien amorcé avant son arrivée. Elle n'est pas
non plus l'importatrice d'un modèle américain d'organisation de la recherche dont nous avons vu qu'il reste alors presqu'entièrement appuyé sur le
secteur privé, aux antipodes du système de financement public qui se met en
place en France au cours de la même période. Alors que la recherche américaine se conduit essentiellement dans les universités, la recherche française
se construit largement, si ce n'est contre, du moins en dehors de l'université,
au grand dam de nombreux universitaires qui voient les crédits dont ils ont
tant besoin aboutir dans le giron de la CNS puis de la CNRS. L'inanité de la
problématique du «modèle» n'empêche pas cependant de conclure à l'importance du rôle joué par la Rockefeller dans la recherche française de l'entre-deux-guerres, et ce, à trois niveaux. Dans son organisation générale
d'abord, où il est indéniable que la fondation offre une source d'inspiration
aux scientifiques, Perrin et Mayer en tête, qui font le siège des gouvernants à
partir de la fin des années 1920 pour obtenir la mise en place d'une administration de la recherche. Dans les modes de financement ensuite: du fait de sa
pratique précoce du financement pluriannuel, la fondation fournit aux
Français un exemple d'administration de la recherche cohérente et montre
comment la politique financière peut être au diapason du projet scientifique, en particulier par sa gamme de financements variés qui permettent de
coller au plus près les besoins des chercheurs. Enfin, le troisième secteur
dans lequel le rôle de la Rockefeller est visible est celui des recompositions
disciplinaires en cours dans les années trente, et notamment l'apparition de
nouvelles spécialités qui viennent modifier l'architecture et la hiérarchie des
disciplines scientifiques. L'intervention de la fondation Rockefeller dans la
recherche n'est qu'un des multiples facteurs de ces évolutions, mais elle y
joue un rôle d'aiguillon significatif, comme le montrent les exemples cités en
génétique, neurobiologie, neurochirurgie, neurophysiologie ou radiobiologie. Ceux-ci montrent également que l'action de la fondation ne saurait être

---

60 Krige, *American Hegemony*, ch. 1.
61 Tournès, *Sciences de l'homme*, ch. 7.

limitée à la dimension financière, celle-ci étant inextricablement liée à la dimension intellectuelle, mais aussi à la dimension institutionnelle. En ce sens, la fondation Rockefeller est bien l'un des éléments incontournables du paysage scientifique français de l'entre-deux-guerres. Mais est-elle uniquement un vecteur d'hégémonie américaine, avant 1939 comme après 1945? La réponse est ici plus complexe, car le tissu serré de relations transnationales dans lequel prend place la politique française de la Rockefeller aboutit aussi probablement à diluer l'influence proprement «américaine» dans un continuum d'expériences mises en place dans tous les pays où opère la fondation. Si les fondations sont incontestablement des organisations américaines, elles sont aussi des plaques tournantes, des *go-between* qui jouent un rôle de redistribution des savoirs et des pratiques à l'échelle internationale, depuis les États-Unis vers l'Europe et les autres continents, mais aussi depuis les pays d'Europe où elles interviennent vers d'autres pays européens, et, sans doute également, depuis l'Europe vers les États-Unis. Ce tissu de relations multidirectionnelles a été pour l'instant peu analysé en détail. Quel impact a-t-il sur la production de la science aux États-Unis mêmes? En quoi permettrait-il d'affiner la connaissance des phénomènes d'hégémonie scientifique? Voilà un vaste champ de recherche pour les historiens de la philanthropie.

Helke Rausch

Expertenkämpfe

Die Rockefeller Foundation im Interessendickicht
europäischer Anthropologie, 1925/26–1940

In die Geschichte der Internationalen Beziehungen in der zweiten Hälfte des
20. Jahrhunderts haben sich die amerikanischen Stiftungen weithin sichtbar
eingeschrieben. Eine wachsende Zahl von historischen Studien bescheinigt
den Philanthropen, an jener großen Modernisierungsmission federführend
beteiligt gewesen zu sein, die nach 1945 von den politischen, wirtschaftlichen und kulturellen Eliten der USA lanciert wurde, um den globalen Wett-
bewerb mit der Sowjetunion um Macht und Einfluss für sich zu entscheiden.
Teils im engen Schulterschluss mit den amerikanischen Nachkriegsregierun-
gen, teils in bemerkenswerter ideologieskeptischer Distanz zu ihnen, verstanden sich die Stiftungen immer auch als Makler eigener Interessen. Zu ihrem Weltbild gehörte freilich die Erwartung, dass keine zur Logik des Kalten
Krieges alternative Weltordnung denkbar sei.[1]

Inzwischen boomt die internationale Forschungsliteratur zu den Modernisierungsideologien und Entwicklungsutopien nach 1945,[2] die die
Kalten Krieger antrieb. In dieses Bild lässt sich zwar auch die US-amerikanische Philanthropie einschließlich der Rockefeller Foundation (künftig: RF)
einordnen.[3] Als starr monolithischen Block hartgesottener Cold Warriors
wird man sie aber inzwischen nicht mehr bezeichnen wollen.[4] Eine weitere
Schieflage des historischen Narrativs besteht allerdings weiterhin. Denn es
hat sich wenig geändert am Bild der RF als regelrecht triumphalem Player in
einer zunehmend asymmetrischen Weltordnung schon vor 1945, bis die ein-
schlägig neue Weltlage nach Kriegsende die RF nun ganz zum Profiteur ma-
terieller und machtpolitischer Überlegenheit der USA zu machen schien.
Nur so erklärt sich die zum Teil immer noch investigative Verve, mit der die

---

1 Vgl. Ekbladh, *The Great American Mission*; Krige, *American Hegemony*; Gilman,
Mandarins of the Future; Engerman, *Staging Growth*; Rausch, »Verordnetes Wissen?«.
2 Vgl. u.a. Cullather, *The Hungry World*; Amrith, *Decolonizing International Health*.
3 Vgl. neben der oben genannten Literatur u.a. Frey, »Experten, Stiftungen und Politik«.
4 Berghahn, *Transatlantische Kulturkriege*.

Vernetzungen der Stiftungs- mit anderen Eliten an sich schon als Nachweis
einer Verschwörung des Großmachtkapitalismus gegen unterlegene Gesellschaften nicht erst nach dem Zweiten Weltkrieg, sondern durchaus bereits
vor 1945 gedeutet wird.[5] Als Testfall für die These von der weltweiten Philanthropie als Oktroi gelten regelmäßig nicht nur Interventionen in der sogenannten Dritten Welt, sondern auch philanthropische Aktivitäten im
wohlhabenderen westlichen Europa, wo die Nachkriegsgesellschaften bereits
nach dem Ersten Weltkrieg dem Stiftungshandeln nachgerade ausgeliefert
schienen.[6] Dieser voreiligen Assoziation möchte der folgende Beitrag nicht
folgen: Er wird stattdessen das Axiom von der Allmacht der philanthropischen Macher infrage stellen und dezidiert nach den Grenzen philanthropischer Planungsambitionen fragen. Zudem bleibt er nicht auf die Ära des
Kalten Krieges fixiert, sondern greift zurück auf die Zwischenkriegsjahre,
also die Zeit des Aufstieges der US-amerikanischen Akteure. Schließlich
wird der Blick ausdrücklich vom philanthropischen Entscheidungszentrum
gelöst und stattdessen auf die europäischen Aushandlungspartner und deren
Interessen und Strategien sowie auf strukturelle Bedingungen am jeweiligen
Förderort gerichtet. Denn Akteure und Infrastrukturen vor Ort hatten am
Hauptgeschäft der Stiftung bereits vor 1945, der Planung von herrschaftssta-
bilisierendem Wissen, nicht nur einen genuinen Eigenanteil, sondern prägten die Parameter der Wissensproduktion oftmals mehr, als es den Philanthropen selbst je möglich gewesen wäre.

Fraglos hatte die RF seit ihrer Gründung 1911 maßgeblich an der Fiktion
von Omnipotenz mitgewirkt, indem sie sich notorisch als Beförderer eines
vordefinierbaren »well-being of mankind« und Protagonist eines universa-
len humanitären Aktivismus auswies. Die Grenzen philanthropischer Intervention, über die sich dieses Selbstbild freilich ausschwieg, bestanden aber
schon allein darin, dass die Stiftung insbesondere im westlichen Europa
bereits in den Zwischenkriegsjahren auf Projekte zur Produktion von »mo-
dernem« Planungswissen traf, die ihren eigenen Ambitionen ähnelten: Im
breiten Feld europäischer Sozialwissenschaften erwies sich das Fach der Anthropologie bzw. Ethnologie als kongenialer Partner. Deren Expertise für
das Koloniale war nutzbar und nützlich zum einen für die metropolitane
Politik und Verwaltung in London und Paris. Die Einbeziehung ins koloniale Projekt war zum anderen aber auch für die britischen und französischen *scientific communities* der Anthropologen und Ethnologen von kaum

---

5 Vgl. Berman, *The influence of the Carnegie, Ford and Rockefeller Foundations*, bes.
11–40; Arnove, *Philanthropy and Cultural Imperialism*; Parmar/Cox, *Soft Power and US
Foreign Policy*.

6 Vgl. für die Phase nach 1945 im Blick auf die Intervention in Deutschland Plé, *Wissenschaft und säkulare Mission*; zur vermeintlichen Suprematie der RF bereits vor 1945 v. a.
Fisher, »Rockefeller Philanthropy«.

zu überschätzendem Interesse, da sie mit ihrem vor allem afrikaspezifischen Fachwissen nicht nur professionelles Prestige gewinnen, sondern auch Fördergelder akquirieren konnten.[7]

Für die RF musste die Anthropologie als prekäre Wissensressource erscheinen. Diente sie doch einer europäischen Kolonialpraxis, die auf privilegierte Wirtschaftsbeziehungen mit den Kolonien abstellte und daher der außenpolitischen Maxime der US-Administrationen zuwiderlief, eine liberale Weltwirtschaftsordnung zu befördern.[8] Offenkundig sahen sich die Stiftungsvertreter hier aber nicht als Sprachrohr der politischen Eliten in den USA, sondern förderten anthropologische Forschung in Großbritannien und Frankreich in der Erwartung, dass sich aus dem europäischen Umgang mit anthropologischem Steuerungswissen taktische Lehren für die multiethnische *melting-pot society* ziehen ließen.[9] Insofern entstanden aus Stiftungssicht willkommene Anknüpfungspunkte und Initiativen, britische und französische anthropologische Forschungseinrichtungen zu fördern.

Anhand zweier Fördertranchen der RF für die *social anthropology* in London und die *ethnologie* in Paris zwischen den 1920er und 1940er Jahren lässt sich zweierlei zeigen: Zum einen stießen die amerikanischen Philanthropen in der europäischen Politik und Wissenschaft auf parallele Konzeptionen von anwendungsorientierter Wissenschaft als Inbegriff »moderner« Prävention gegen Entwicklungskrisen; zum anderen hing das philanthropische Engagement stark von lokalen Befindlichkeiten an den einzelnen europäischen Wissenschaftsstandorten ab. Denn die europäische Bedarfslage definierten an den beiden Förderorten neben der RF immer auch zahlreiche akademische und politisch-administrative Akteure, die, teils im Alleingang, teils in komplexen Interessenallianzen, eigene, vom Stiftungskalkül mitunter entfernt liegende Agenden verfolgten. Für die RF hatte dieser Umstand schwerwiegende Konsequenzen, engte er doch ihre Handlungsspielräume und Einwirkungsmöglichkeiten vor Ort deutlich ein. Das große Projekt, globale Wissenszirkulation über die Kontrollierbarkeit nicht-westlicher, sogenannter indigener Gesellschaften zu lancieren, reduzierte sich damit auf situative Interessenarrangements mit britischen und französischen Akademikern und Kolonialadministratoren, die häufig eher den lokalen Gegebenheiten als einem machtvollen Modernisierungsprojekt der Stiftung Rechnung trugen.

Die Philanthropen maßen der Anthropologie als Wissensressource in den Kolonialreichen Großbritannien und Frankreich eine Art experimentelle

---

7 Vgl. hier nur Hodge, »British Colonial Expertise«; Dimier, »Politique indigène en France et Grande-Bretagne«.

8 Vgl. Louis/Robinson, »The Imperialism of Decolonization«.

9 Die Philanthropen selber haben dieses Interesse selten explizit gemacht, artikuliert haben es aber u. a. ihre präferierten Förderkandidaten in den USA, so Boas, »The Aims of Anthropological Research«.

Bedeutung bei: Schließlich spezialisierte sich die Wissenschaft in beiden Ländern unter dem Label der Anthropologie auf einen dichotomisierenden Blick auf die Bevölkerungen in den kolonialen Besitzungen des britischen und französischen Empire. Für sich selbst reklamierten die Anthropologen in beiden Ländern nicht nur Fortschrittlichkeit und zivilisierte Modernität, sondern auch eine besondere Expertise dafür, die nicht-westlichen Gesellschaften zu beschreiben, zu klassifizieren und zuletzt als primitiv, rückständig, vormodern oder tribal auf ihren vermeintlichen Entwicklungsabstand zum industrialisierten Europa hin zu bewerten.[10] Dass der klassifizierende Blick der selbst ernannten Experten die Differenz zwischen zentralen und peripheren Gesellschaften bzw. Ethnien nicht wertneutral diagnostizierte, sondern entlang des langfristigen Machtgefälles zwischen kolonialen Metropolen und abhängigen kolonialen Bevölkerungen absichtsvoll mitbegründete, spielte bis weit nach dem Zweiten Weltkrieg weder im Selbstverständnis der Disziplinenvertreter noch in den Einschätzungen der Philanthropen eine Rolle.[11]

1. Die Rockefeller Foundation und die Londoner Sozialanthropologie

Als die RF – zu diesem Zeitpunkt vor der großen Fusion und Reorganisation der Stiftungsstrukturen 1928/29 zunächst noch als Laura Spelman Rockefeller Memorial aktiv – in den frühen 1920er Jahren in Großbritannien ihre Förderprogramme startete, traf sie gerade im Bereich der Sozialwissenschaften noch auf sehr dynamische Disziplinen. Der Markt akademischer Institutionen und wissenschaftlicher Projekte war ebenso wie die Finanzierungsmodi, Organisationsformen und forscherischen Tätigkeiten mit dem Weltkrieg in Bewegung geraten und stabilisierte sich erst langsam.[12] Als bevorzugte Förderkandidaten im Disziplinenfeld der britischen Anthropologie kristallisierten sich schnell die London School of Economics (LSE) und insbesondere das International Institute for African Languages and Cultures (IIALC) heraus. Das IIALC verdankte sich 1926 unabhängig von der amerikanischen Intervention einer Aggregation durchaus weit verzweigter britischer Interessen. Dafür stand schon die Gründertrias, bestehend aus dem Repräsentanten der protestantischen Missionsbewegung und Mitglied eines

---

10 L'Estoile/Neiburg/Sigaud, »Savoirs Anthropologiques«, 233.

11 Vgl. dazu grundsätzlich Cooper, »Development, Modernization, and the Social Sciences«.

12 Vgl. MacCurdy, »Extent of Instruction in Anthropology«; Temple, *Anthropology as a Practical Science.*

Educational Committee beim Colonial Office, Joseph H. Oldham, dem ehemaligen Gouverneur von Nigeria und *spiritus rector* britischer Kolonialherr-
schaft in Afrika, Lord Frederick Lugard, sowie Bronislaw Malinowski, jenem
Exponenten der Sozialanthropologie, die rasch den besonderen Zuspruch
der RF gewinnen sollte.[13] Gerade Malinowski war eine schillernde Mittler-
figur. Er verfolgte als transnationaler Routinier polnischen Ursprungs und
nach akademischen Zwischenstationen in Leipzig seit 1913 eine steile akademische Karriere an der LSE, die seit dem ersten *Readership* in *social anthropology* in den frühen 1920er Jahren und bis zu seiner Migration nach Yale
1939 philanthropisch unterstützt wurde.[14]

Die Stiftung ließ sich zeitig auf das Institut ein. Vor allem dessen ausge-
sprochene Erziehungsmission und Bildungsoffensive in Afrika, die systematisch europäisches Wissen in den verfügbaren afrikanischen Landessprachen
verbreiten sollte, weckte Interesse.[15] Aber erst nachdem Malinowski das Projekt immer mehr in Richtung einer etablierten westeuropäischen Afrikafor-
schung verschoben hatte, für die das IIALC Ende der 1920er Jahre mit seinen
über 900 individuellen und korporativen Mitgliedern schließlich stand, stiegen die Philanthropen enthusiastischer in das Unternehmen ein. Ab 1932
stockte die Stiftung das Fördervolumen deutlich auf und stand neben der
Carnegie Corporation bis 1937 für über die Hälfte des gesamten Institutsbudgets des IIACL ein.[16] In dieser Etappe wurde sie zum Hauptsponsor und
stellte dann vor allem Stipendien für die Feldforschung in Afrika zur Verfügung, die Kandidaten aus dem Umfeld von Malinowski regelrecht für sich
monopolisieren konnten.[17] Auch schulterte die Stiftung einen Großteil der
beträchtlichen Publikationskosten, die die umtriebige Feldforschung dieser

13 Vgl. Lugard, »The International Institute«.

14 Vgl. Stocking, Malinowski.

15 Vgl. Smith, »The Story of the Institute«, 1 und Davis, »The Christian Mission in
Africa«. Zu den Financiers des Instituts zählten neben der amerikanischen Stiftung im-
mer auch zahlreiche Missionsgesellschaften, Regierungsbehörden, wissenschaftliche Institute, Gesellschaften und Unternehmen vor allem aus Großbritannien, Frankreich und
Deutschland. Vgl. Stoecker, Afrikawissenschaften in Berlin, 176–215, hier bes. 192.
Nach Gründung des Instituts konnte man für die ersten fünf Jahre die RF für eine jähr-
liche Zuwendung von etwa 1000 GBP in das Boot der Mäzene holen. Vgl. »Report on
Progress of Work during the Period 1926-Oct. 1929«, 97. Vgl. auch Kuklick, The Savage
within, 198.

16 Vgl. »Summary of Proceedings of the Ninth Meeting of the Executive Council«,
484. Die RF bewilligte einen Fünfjahresplan mit einer jährlichen Grant-Summe von
5000 GBP und weiteren 5000 als matching funds, deren Auszahlung an die Einwerbung
weiterer Fördergelder bei Dritten gebunden blieb. Die Carnegie Corporation vereinbarte
u.a. 1931 einen Dreijahres-Förderplan mit einem Jahresvolumen von 15000 GBP, vgl. »A
Five-Year Plan of Research«.

17 Die Fellowship-Listen wurden regelmäßig im Bericht des Executive Council (*Report
of Meeting*) im Institutsjournal *Africa* veröffentlicht, so u.a. in: *Africa* 9, 1936, 536–543.

Institutsmitarbeiter in den britisch kontrollierten afrikanischen Territorien nach sich zog.[18]

Im Falle der LSE, wo die RF-Gelder unter anderem Malinowskis Forschung und Lehrtätigkeit zugute kamen, bildeten sie aber bei Weitem nicht das Rückgrat des Budgets. Denn seit ihrer Gründung vor der Jahrhundertwende engagierten sich für die LSE dank einer extrem erfolgreichen Finanzierungspolitik auch eine ganze Reihe britischer Mäzene.[19] In mancher Hinsicht erachteten die Beobachter der RF die LSE als einen akademischen Ort, an dem die Kombination aus theoretischer und empirischer Forschungsarbeit so erfolgreich gelang, dass sie selbst US-amerikanischen Einrichtungen weit überlegen schien.[20]

Philanthropische Interessen am britischen Planungswissen

Aus der Langzeitperspektive auf die anglo-amerikanische Konstellation lassen sich drei Gründe ausmachen, die die RF-*Officers* dazu bewogen, der *social anthropology* in der von Malinowski an der LSE und am IIALC vertretenen Variante vor zeitgleich verfügbaren Alternativen den Förderzuschlag zu geben. Erstens bewährte sich Malinowski – dies ist ein Symptom der hohen Bedeutung personaler Förderkriterien – als geschickter Verhandler in den Unterredungen mit der RF. Er verstand sich darauf, mit der Semantik des Stiftungsprogramms zu operieren, und stellte daher in seinen Anträgen vor allem auf den sozialtechnologischen Mehrwert der *social anthropology* für die britische Kolonialpolitik ab. Anthropologische Feldforschung, so Malinowski, verhindere spekulative Generalisierungen über die sogenannten kolonialen *natives* und sichere demgegenüber die empirische Basis einer erst auf diesem Wege verlässlichen Sozialwissenschaft. So würde sie in einem zweiten Schritt einen methodologischen Überbau und stärker theoretischen Reflex über die gesammelten Fakten und Daten entwickeln können.[21] Aus Sicht der RF löste Malinowski sein Postulat maximaler Nähe von anwen-

18 Vgl. Smith, »The Story of the Institute«, 1. Vgl. Zum Institut Kuper, »Alternative histories«, 52.

19 Vgl. »The London School of Economics 1895–1945«; LSE Archives, LSE Registry Files.

20 Vgl. Memorandum for Dr Ruml, 12. Nov. 1923, RAC LSRM III 6.1 Box 10 Folder 592. Die Beobachter der RF taxierten die LSE demzufolge als einen »very, very few places where the academic and the actual come together.«

21 Vgl. Malinowski, Memorandum for the Rockefeller Foundation (erstellt für Mr Embree im März 1926), LSE Archives Malinowski 36/80, Papers by Malinowski, 1912–1940s; Report on the conditions in the Rockefeller interest supplied confidentially to B. Malinowski by an American Observer. Memorandum, LSE Archives Malinowski 8/3.

dungsorientierter Wissenschaft und Politik vor allem im Rahmen seiner An-
thropologieseminare an der LSE ein, die nicht nur Studenten, sondern auch
Missionare, Kolonialbeamte und Geschäftsleute frequentierten.[22] Zugleich
sympathisierten die amerikanischen Beobachter damit, dass Malinowski die
evolutionistische Sichtweise traditionaler anthropologischer Paradigmen
aufgab, sich vom historisierenden, theoretischen *armchair-approach* des
19. Jahrhunderts definitiv verabschiedete und stattdessen darauf verlegte,
aktuelle Gesellschaften in den britischen Kolonien zu untersuchen.[23]

Zweitens honorierten die RF-Officers das Bekenntnis zum *scientific internationalism*, für das mit Lugard und den Ethnologen und Linguisten Henri
Labouret und Diedrich Westermann die Führungsriege am IIALC stand.[24]
Freilich klaffte zwischen programmatischer Vision und wissenschaftlicher
Praxis rasch eine große Lücke. Epistemologische Zwistigkeiten, vor allem
aber politische Verstimmungen und besonders das französische Unbehagen
an den vitalisierten kolonialwissenschaftlichen Aktivitäten Deutschlands
seit den 1930er Jahren mischten sich schließlich mit nationalistisch gefärb-
ter, spannungsgeladener Rhetorik, die das Bekenntnis zum Internationalismus auszuhebeln drohten.[25] Die Vision der US-Philanthropen, mit dem
Institut dem Wissenschaftsinternationalismus als dezenter Spielart amerikanischer Kulturdiplomatie in Europa zuzuarbeiten, scheiterte schließlich spätestens mit Beginn des Zweiten Weltkrieges, als Kontakt und Kooperation
mit den deutschen Institutsmitgliedern abbrachen und die britische Mit-
gliedschaft sich dominant auszuwirken begann.[26]

Drittens konnte der Eindruck entstehen, dass die Präferenz der RF für LSE
und IIALC von einem stillschweigenden politischen Konsens der US-Philanthropen zum Subtext von Malinowskis *social anthropology* herrührte. So wenig sich die RF, ähnlich wie die US-Administrationen der Zwischen- und
Nachkriegszeit, als Sympathisanten europäischer Kolonialpolitik erwiesen,
so attraktiv erschien ihnen die Option, dem britischen Empire zumindest
aus Sicht des sozialanthropologischen Paradigmas Stabilisierungs- und
Ordnungswissen zuzuarbeiten. Hier schloss die *social anthropolgy* aus US-
amerikanischer Sicht unmittelbar zur Idee des *social engineering* progressi-

22 Zur Feldforschung als zeitgenössisches catchword vgl. Kuklick, »Personal Equations«.
23 Vgl. Malinowski, Memorandum Concerning the Research Needs and Possibilities
in the Field of Social and Cultural Anthropology, LSE Archives Malinowski 16/6, Jane
Ellen Harrison Lecture, 1928–30.
24 Vgl. Westermann, »Das Internationale Institut«; programmatisch Labouret, »Ethnologie coloniale«.
25 Vgl. L'Estoile, »Internationalization and ›scientific nationalism‹«.
26 Vgl. »Notes and News«, 68–69. Vgl. zum Institut im Zweiten Weltkrieg Stoecker,
Afrikawissenschaften in Berlin, 211–215.

ver Machart auf, der man sich in den Reihen der Stiftung an zentraler Stelle verpflichtet fühlte.[27] Die Emphase der Stiftungsvertreter für die dezidiert empirische Ausrichtung der Gruppe um Malinowski trug demzufolge alle Züge einer rhetorischen Camouflage. Mit dem Lob der Empirie ließ sich das eigentliche amerikanische Interesse an der Produktion von Herrschafts- und Stabilisierungswissen für den Fortbestand des Britischen Empire allemal in Zeiten der Wirtschaftskrise seit den 1930er Jahren kaschieren.[28]

Mit ihren beträchtlichen Subventionen schrieb sich die RF zweifellos in die Geschichte der britischen Anthropologie ein. Sie verhalf langfristig einem Paradigma zum Durchbruch, das Malinowskis Seminare an der LSE und dem IIALC als Kaderschmieden künftiger Stelleninhaber in universitären *anthropology departments* vermittelten, bevor es allerdings spätestens in den 1970er Jahren im Kontext einer fundamentalen Neuaufstellung der Disziplin erodieren sollte.[29] Weitet sich allerdings die enge Perspektive, die zunächst nur auf Motivation und Verfahren der Stiftung zielte, um andere Akteure und Interessen auf diesem Wissensfeld, wird offenkundig, dass der philan-thropische Einfluss während der 1920er bis 1940er Jahre zwei fundamentale Voraussetzungen hatte, ohne die er nicht hätte zustande kommen und nach-haltig wirken können: ein massives Interesse der britischen Kolonialadmi-nistration an der Sozialanthropologie als Kontrollressource zum einen und intellektuelle Etablierungskämpfe auf der akademischen Bühne zum ande-ren, die die RF für rivalisierende Gruppen der Profession als ein finanzkräf-tiger Koalitionspartner zu einem hochattraktiven Verbündeten machten.

Empirie fürs Empire

Die zweite Akteursgruppe, die nicht nur über die Institutionalisierung-schancen und das Prestige anthropologischen Wissens, sondern auch über die Finanzierung entsprechender Forschung mitentschied, stammte aus der britischen Kolonialverwaltung. Von dieser Seite her wurde vehementer

27 Vgl. Malinowski, »The Present State of Studies in Culture Contact 36: »The more fully the problems of administration are studied both from the European technical side and in their anthropological perspective, the clearer it becomes that knowledge here does not affect any political principles or moral issues, but that it is a technical help in the car-rying out of social engineering in a task where the mutuality of interests cannot be ques-tioned.«

28 Vgl. Tracy B. Kittredge (RF) to Bronislaw Malinowski (o.J., vermutlich um 1931), LSE Archives Malinowski 8/5 Rockefeller Papers, 1931–1934.

29 Vgl. Kuper, »Alternative Histories«. In den 1940er und 50er Jahren erschienen das Rhodes-Livingstone Institute unter Godfrey Wilson bzw. Max Gluckman und das East African Institute of Social Research unter Audrey Richards als eine Art afrikanische Aus-gründungen der Malinowski-Schule, vgl. Wilson, »Anthropology as a Public Service«.

Bedarf an einer empiriebasierten, anwendungsbezogenen Anthropologie angemeldet. Dabei erkannte man der *social anthropology* aus einer ganzen Reihe von Gründen einen hohen Ressourcenwert zu: Die Lage des British Empire hatte sich seit Ende des Ersten Weltkrieges drastisch verschlechtert. Infolgedessen wurde die Kolonialpolitik in den 1920er und 1930er Jahren grundlegend neu ausgerichtet. Das Empire erschien nach dem Krieg als an vielen Stellen im Niedergang begriffenes und von Auflösungserscheinungen gezeichnetes, dysfunktionales Machtgebilde.[30] Zugleich waren die deutlich vergrößerte Wählerschaft und die erstarkte Gewerkschaftsbewegung in der Metropole nur noch dann für koloniales Engagement zu gewinnen, wenn gewährleistet war, dass unter dem dafür erforderlichen materiellen und personellen Ressourcenaufwand nicht das große Projekt einer umfassenden Sozialreform im Mutterland in Mitleidenschaft gezogen würde.[31]

Vor diesem Hintergrund wurde aus Sicht des Colonial and Dominion und des Foreign Office in Whitehall der Bedarf an administrativer Effizienz besonders dringlich. Diese Einschätzung leitete schon lange zu der kritischen Selbstdiagnose an, die britische Kolonialverwaltung leide unter schlecht ausgebildetem Personal, das unbedingt professionalisiert werden müsse, um zur Kontrolle kolonialer Bevölkerungen in der Lage zu sein und um besonders die neuen Funktionserfordernisse des strauchelnden Empire erfüllen zu können.[32] Abhilfe versprach als Summe längst vorher geäußerter Reformbegehren Lugards 1920 propagierte Strategie der *Indirect Rule*, wonach die kolonialpolitische Neuaufstellung nur glücken könne, wenn autochthone Autoritäten systematischer in die Wahrnehmung kolonialer Aufsicht einbezogen und traditionale Infrastrukturen gestärkt würden, um Stabilität vor Ort zu gewährleisten. Unter diesen Bedingungen schienen britische Herrschaftsabsichten und das aus britischer Sicht definierte Interesse kolonialer Gesellschaften an ihrem umfassenden politisch-sozialen und moralischen Fortschritt fusionierbar.[33]

Für die Legitimationspotenziale, die die *social anthropology* speziell für die Strategie indirekter Herrschaft zu bergen schien, interessierte sich die britische Kolonialverwaltung auch aus zwei anderen Gründen: Zum einen suchte man entsprechenden Rückhalt besonders für die Wahrnehmung

---

30 Vgl. Hyam, *Britain's Declining Empire*, 1–15.

31 Vgl. Lawrence, »The transformation of British Public Politics«, 203–212.

32 Vgl. zur in dieser Hinsicht symptomatischen Gründungsinitiative für ein britisches Bureau of Anthropology bereits kurz nach der Jahrhundertwende: *The Journal of the Royal Anthropological Institute of Great Britain and Ireland* 38, 1908, 489–90. Vgl. auch Temple, *Anthropology as a Practical Science*, 25.

33 Lugard, *The Dual Mandate in Tropical Africa*. Vgl. Flint, »Frederick Lugard«.

kolonialer Herrschaftsrechte Großbritanniens in den Mandatsgebieten, die
man wie Tanganyika/Deutschostafrika aus der Abwicklung des ehemaligen Kolonialbesitzes des Deutschen Reiches nach 1918 hinzugewonnen
hatte. Britische Kontrolle ließ sich dort, so die offizielle Einschätzung, mit
dem Verweis auf eine wissensbasierte, an indigenen Strukturen orientierte
Machtpolitik im Sinne eines anthropologisch hergeleiteten *Indirect Rule*-
Konzepts plausibler rechtfertigen.[34] Zum anderen steigerten mehrere Aufstände an der sogenannten kolonialen Peripherie den Bedarf der britischen
Kolonialverwaltung an anthropologischem Herrschaftswissen: Seit der
drohenden Bürgerkriegsgefahr in Kenia 1923 hatte die britische Regierung
wiederholt einen notorischen Bedarf an empirischem Wissen über indigene
Interessenlagen in Afrika angemeldet. Entsprechende Stellungnahmen verdichteten sich im Umfeld der Aba Riots in Nigeria im Dezember 1929, in
denen lokaler Protest gegen ein britisch implantiertes Rechtssystem zum
Ausdruck gekommen war, das, wie jetzt diagnostiziert wurde, ohne Verbindung mit traditionalen Autoritäten jeder Glaubwürdigkeit entbehre. In diesem Zusammenhang wurde der Bedarf an Anthropologen als Experten für
eine Optimierung kolonialer Verwaltungsstrategien noch einmal gebündelt
geäußert.[35]

Die in diesem Sinne dreifach begründete Interessenfusion zwischen britischer Kolonialadministration und *social anthropologists* schlug sich Ende der
1930er Jahre nieder, als eine ganze Reihe von Fellows des IIALC zum von
Lord Hailey herausgegebenen und von Lugard unterstützten *African Survey*
beitrug.[36] Dieser Survey sollte als sozialanthropologisch informierte Handreichung im Dienst einer reformorientierten Kolonialpolitik im Geiste der
Indirect Rule wirken, als Urtext reformistischer Kolonialpolitik in den 1940er
Jahren.[37]

Freilich war die Koproduktion reformorientierten Kolonialwissens zwischen *social anthropologists* und britischen Kolonialeliten kein Selbstläufer.
Im Gegenteil hatte gegenüber der akademischen Anthropologie lange ein
hartnäckiges Misstrauen der Kolonialbeamten bestanden. Feldforschung

---

34 Vgl. »The Hilton-Young and Wilson Reports«; Mair, »Colonial Administration as a
Science«; Baker, »An Experiment in Applied Anthropology«, 310–311. Vgl. dazu auch
L'Estoile, »The ›natural preserve of anthropologists‹«, 350.

35 Vgl. Perham, *Native Administration*, 218–220; vgl. auch die Besprechung von Lucy
Mair im Institutsorgan des RAI: Mair, »Review«. Vgl. dazu auch Kuklick, *The savage
within*, 214.

36 Vgl. Melland/Lugard/Harlech u. a., »Lord Hailey's African Survey«; Hailey, »The
Role of Anthropology in Colonial Development«. Vgl. dazu auch Cell, »Lord Hailey and
the Making of the African Survey«.

37 Mair, »Chieftainship in Modern Africa«. Vgl. zum Survey ausführlicher Mills, »British Anthropology at the End of Empire«, 164.

und empirische Bestandsaufnahmen vor Ort fielen ihnen zufolge ohnedies ganz in den Kompetenzbereich der Administration.[38] In diesem Sinne sahen sich die höherrangigen britischen Kolonialbeamten selbst als kenntnisreiche »practical men« und dezidierte Experten kolonialer Praxis.[39] Folglich erhielten über weite Strecken der 1920er und 1930er Jahre hinweg weder die *social sciences* allgemein noch die sozialwissenschaftliche Forschung in den Kolonien nennenswerte finanzielle Unterstützung vonseiten der britischen Kolonialadministration.[40] Vor diesem Hintergrund erwiesen sich die Rockefeller-Gelder für das IIALC bzw. den *African Survey*, den darüber hinaus auch die Carnegie Foundation und der Rhodes Trust subventionierten, als wichtiges Elixier für eine enge Kooperation mit der Kolonialadministration.[41]

Die zunächst geballten amerikanischen Investitionen in die enge Koproduktion kolonialpolitisch verwendbarer sozialanthropologischer Expertise wurden allerdings spätestens ab 1940 rückläufig, als die britische Kolonialadministration mit dem Colonial Development and Welfare Act eine Art technokratische Wende vollzog und nun auch zunehmend staatliche Gelder in die kolonialwissenschaftliche Forschung flossen.[42] Die Interessenkoalition zwischen britischen Anthropologen der Malinowski-Schule und britischer Kolonialverwaltung blieb unterdessen in den Folgejahren stabil.[43] Im 1944 gegründeten Social Science Research Council übernahmen namentlich mit Raymond Firth und Audrey Richards namhafte Vertreter der Malinowski-Schule führende Positionen.[44] Im Vorfeld und während des Zweiten Weltkrieges schwang offenbar bei den britischen Kolonialeliten um Hailey auch die Einschätzung mit, dass der britische Kolonialismus eine umso geringere Belastung der anglo-amerikanischen Kriegskoalition darstellte, je überzeugender es der britischen Kolonialverwaltung gelingen würde, ihre Strategien als wohldurchdachtes Ergebnis einer auf Fachwissen basierten Politik auszuweisen.[45] Auch nach 1945 blieben Malinowski-Schüler wie Lucy Mair als Vertreter einer dezidiert anwendungsorientierten Colonial Administration

---

38 »Colonial Office Minutes, 3. 1. 1931«.

39 Vgl. Mitchell, »The Anthropologist and the Practical Man«.

40 Eine Ausnahme bildete das Colonial Research Committee (1919), vgl. Jeffries, *A Review of Colonial Research*.

41 Vgl. Plant, »An African Survey«.

42 Vgl. Clarke, »A Technocratic Imperial State?«, hier u. a. 455 und Mills, »British Anthropology at the End of Empire«, 165. Mit 5 500 000 GBP auf 10 Jahre war das Fördervolumen mitten im Krieg enorm.

43 Vgl. Wilson, »Anthropology as a Public Service«.

44 Vgl. Mills, »British Anthropology at the End of Empire«, 163–164; ders., »Professionalizing or Popularizing Anthropology«.

45 Vgl. Hyam, »Bureaucracy and ›Trusteeship‹«.

im Fächerspektrum der LSE präsent, die sie Mitte der 1950er Jahre schließlich dezidiert zu einer anwendungsorientierten »Entwicklungs«-Expertise
ausbauten.[46]

Behauptungskämpfe der britischen Sozialanthropologen

Eine besondere Prägekraft für das Fördergeschehen in Großbritannien entfaltete schließlich die Anthropologie selbst, die zwar in den 1920er Jahren
noch kaum profiliert war, aber rasch einen klaren Kompetenzvorsprung vor
anderen Spielarten der Sozialwissenschaften beanspruchte. Denn die *social
anthropologists* traten mit dem Anspruch an, grundlegendes Expertenwissen
zum Modus des Kulturkontakts zwischen weißen Europäern und farbigen
indigenen Nichteuropäern zu liefern.[47] Und sie betraten zu einem Zeitpunkt
die Bühne, als es gerade einmal vier Lehrstühle für Anthropologie (an der
LSE, am University Colege London (UCL) sowie in Oxford und Cambridge)
gab und die Zunft untereinander über der Frage zerstritten war, was als stan-
dardisiertes anthropologisches Wissen zu gelten habe. Das waren entscheidende formative Prozesse.[48] Um sich vor diesem Hintergrund zum einen
gegenüber angrenzenden Fächern und zum anderen innerhalb des noch dynamischen, unstrukturierten Feldes der Anthropologie zu positionieren,
verfolgte vor allem Malinowski in dreifacher Hinsicht eine erfolgreiche rhetorische und forschungsprogrammatische Strategie.

Erstens entwarf er einen an Émile Durkheim erinnernden expansiven Zu-
ständigkeitskatalog der *social anthropology*, die als regelrechte Königsdiszip-
lin nachrangigere Wissensformate überlagern sollte. In diesem Sinne deckte
die *social anthropology* Malinowski zu Folge »the problem of population
(…) the study of social organizations and educational agencies (…), law,
economics and politics (…), sociological and cultural linguistics« ab.[49] Breiter und inklusiver ließ sich die disziplinäre Tagesordnung wohl kaum definieren. Grenzen zog Malinowski demgegenüber mit besonderem Nachdruck gegenüber der Geschichtswissenschaft und der Philosophie, die er als

46   Die Malinowski-Koalitionärin Lucy Mair, ebenfalls in Haileys African Survey involviert, unterrichtete »Colonial Administration« und ab Mitte der 1950er Jahre »Applied
Anthropology« an der LSE; vgl. Mair, »Colonial Administration as a Science«; Mair, »Applied Anthropology«.
47   Vgl. Malinowski, »Practical Anthropology«, 22; ders., *Methods of Study*; ders., »The
Rationalization of Anthropology«.
48   Vgl. Keith, »Presidential Address«, 28.
49   Vgl. Malinowski, »Practical Anthropology«, 37 und ders., The Teaching of Practical
Anthropology in Connection with Colonial Studies, LSE Archives, Malinowski 36/80, 4.

rückwärtsgewandt und archäologisch disqualifizierte, um sie als potenzielle Beratungsressource auszuschließen.[50]

Zweitens verfolgte Malinowski auch gegenüber konkurrierenden Zuschnitten auf dem engeren Feld der britischen Anthropologie handfeste Verdrängungsstrategien. Zu diesem Zweck scheute er unter anderem nicht davor zurück, andere Einrichtungen gerade gegenüber den amerikanischen Geldgebern systematisch zu diskreditieren und etwa das prestigereiche, allerdings museologischen Praktiken verpflichtete Royal Anthropological Institute (RAI) als Relikt einer veralteten Disziplin abzutun.[51] Symptomatisch für die Selektionsfreiheiten, die sich die Philanthropen auch gegenüber präferierten Förderkandidaten wie Malinowski sicherten, fruchtete dieser Versuch, Bewerber abzudrängen, allerdings nur sehr bedingt. Die Stiftungsvertreter ließen sich nicht davon abhalten, auch das RAI als etablierte akademische Institution mit Fördergeldern auszustatten.[52]

Drittens positionierte Malinowski sich besonders klug gegenüber der britischen Kolonialverwaltung. Dabei kalkulierte er sowohl deren Misstrauen gegenüber der akademischen Anthropologie als randständiges Theorieunternehmen als auch deren Anspruch mit ein, Feldforschung und empirische Bestandsaufnahmen autochthoner Gesellschaften selbst am besten leisten zu können.[53] Gegen diese schematische Aufgabenverteilung, die der *social anthropology* ihre politikberatende Funktion abzuerkennen drohte, setzte sich Malinowski energisch zur Wehr. Wohl auch, weil er auf das ungebrochene bzw. wachsende Interesse der Kolonialadministration an einer Expertise besonders für den afrikanischen Kolonialraum spekulierte, verlagerte Malinowski bis Ende der 1920er Jahre seinen eigenen Forschungsschwerpunkt weg von den südpazifischen Inseln auf ein breiteres, nicht-westliches Terrain, dem er Afrika dezidiert zurechnete.[54] Die topografische Neuorientierung gab Malinowski als Abkehr von einem früheren Wissenschaftseskapismus aus, dessen er die Forschung zum Südpazifik jetzt bezichtigte.[55] Stattdessen wandte er sich demonstrativ dem afrikanischen Kulturraum zu, wo die funktionalistische Anthropologie substanzielle Bedeutung für jeden

50 Vgl. Malinowski, Memorandum for the Rockefeller Foundation, 7.

51 Vgl. Malinowski, »The Rationalization of Anthropology«, 428–429, Vgl. dazu auch L'Estoile, »The ›natural preserve of anthropologists«, 361–362.

52 Vgl. Royal Anthropological Institute, Oct. 1 1931 to Sept. 30 1937, RAC RG 1.1 Series 401 S Box 77 Folder 1001; sowie »Report of the Council for the year 1928«, 3; »Report of the Council for the year 1930«; »Report of the Council for the year 1931«.

53 Vgl. Malinowski, »Ethnology and the Study of Society«, 208.

54 Vgl. ders., »The Primitive Economics«; ders., »The Rationalization of Anthropology«, 407.

55 Vgl. ders., »The Rationalization of Anthropology«, 406: »Anthropology, to me at least, was a romantic escape from our overstandardized culture.«

»colonial practitioner« gewinne.[56] Den strategischen Afrikaschwerpunkt machte Malinowski nicht zuletzt dadurch plausibel, dass er Rockefeller-Gelder primär für Feldarbeit in Afrika einwarb.[57]

Bei alledem legte Malinowski Wert darauf, dass sein Paradigma gerade keiner politischen Akkreditierung seitens der kolonialen Eliten bedurfte, sondern als Kooperationsofferte auf Augenhöhe unterbreitet wurde.[58] Auch um dieser Strategie willen definierten die Sozialanthropologen um Malinowski den Kompetenz- und Gegenstandsbereich der *social anthropology* ausladend weit von der empirischen Feldforschung bis hin zur Datenauswertung und versierten Theoriebildung an universitären Institutionen. Je expansiver sie ihre eigene Expertise deuteten, umso mehr verweigerten sie sich einer funktionalen Unterordnung unter die kolonialpolitischen Eliten.[59] Kritik an einer problematischen Zulieferfunktion der Wissenschaft gegenüber der Politik wies Malinowski bezeichnenderweise mit dem Bekenntnis zum Ideal des *social engineering* zurück, das anthropologisches Wissen weder politisiere noch moralisch diskreditiere, sondern darauf abziele, seinen technologischen Mehrwert abzuschöpfen.[60] Die Fiktion von der zwar unmittelbar politisch wirksamen, aber normativ apolitischen, anthropologischen Wissenschaft gehörte zu den fast schon ideologischen Prämissen der *social anthropology*.

Damit trat Malinowski der RF gegenüber erfolgreich mit einer wissenschaftspolitischen Strategie auf, die die *social anthropology* zum alternativlos zeitgemäßen Ansatz anthropologischer Forschung erklärte. Mit diesem Konzept verband er den Anspruch, einer Wissenschaftspraxis Geltung zu verschaffen, die empirische Fakten- und Datensicherung eng mit theoretischer Reflexion verband. Langfristig gelang es ihm auf diesem Weg, zum einen die *social anthropology* als sozialtechnologisches Instrument für die Mitarbeiter im britischen Kolonialbeamtenapparat anzubieten, sie zum anderen aber auch als akademisches Projekt eigenen Rechts auszuweisen, das sich gerade nicht darin erschöpfte, der britischen Kolonialpolitik Handlungsanleitungen anzubieten.

Von einem Export amerikanischer Anthropologiemuster nach Großbritannien konnte unter den genannten Umständen keine Rede sein. Wohl aber von einem höchst dynamischen Prozess der Verteidigung professioneller Ansprüche. Wissenschaftspolitische und konzeptuelle Anwartschaften machten die Positionierung auf dem Wissensgebiet der Anthropologie zu

---

56 Vgl. ebd., ab 424.
57 Vgl. »Annual Report«, 101–102.
58 Vgl. Malinowski, »The Rationalization of Anthropology«, 429 u. ö.
59 Ders., Some Practical Problems of Administration, LSE Archives Malinowski 36/80.
60 Vgl. Ders., »The Present State of Studies in Culture Contact«, 36.

einem umkämpften Ereignis an der Schnittstelle zwischen Philanthropie, britischer Politik und Wissenschaft. Die RF begünstigte mit ihrer Selektionsentscheidung die sich gerade etablierenden Sozialanthropologen an der LSE statt der evolutionistisch und museal orientierten Anthropologie des RAI oder der naturwissenschaftlich-biologistischen Ansätze am UCL. Allerdings traten ihr mit den kolonialpolitischen Eliten und den britischen Akademikern nicht minder prägungsbeflissene Akteure zur Seite, die nicht weniger Willens waren, ihre Interessen mit Nachdruck zu verfolgen. An der Legitimationsrhetorik und am vitalen Planungseifer der britischen Akteure und Institutionen vor Ort war auch für eine noch so zahlungskräftige Stiftung nicht vorbeizukommen.

2. Die Rockefeller-Allianz mit dem Pariser Institut d'ethnologie

Begaben sich die US-amerikanischen Philanthropen in Großbritannien in eine enge Interessenallianz mit Verfechtern einer wissensbasierten Kolonialpolitik, so gestalteten sich die Rahmenbedingungen zeitgleicher Intervention in die anthropologische Expertise in Frankreich trotz mancher Verwandtschaften anders. Der britischen Situation in den Zwischenkriegsjahren durchaus ähnlich war in Frankreich gleichwohl der zeitgenössische Krisendiskurs in Politik und Wissenschaft, in dessen Folge das französische Empire nach dem Ersten Weltkrieg zum Gegenstand erhitzter Debatten wurde. Entsprechende Voten reichten weit, von der Forderung, die metropolitanen Ausbeutungsinteressen im Stile einer engen *assimilation* an die französische Zivilisation kompromisslos durchzusetzen, über das Postulat einer an indigenen Kulturen orientierten Assoziations-Politik bis hin zum pessimistischen Blick auf die abgewirtschafteten Kolonialterritorien als Ballast einer Nation im Niedergang.[61] Mit der britischen Situation vergleichbar war zudem der Umstand, dass die französische *ethnologie* ähnlich wie die *social anthropology* als gleichermaßen akademisch ambitionierte wie auf kolonialpolitische Verwertung ausgerichtete Wissensressource während der 1920er und 1930er Jahre noch tief in ihrer mühsamen Etablierungsphase steckte, sodass ihre Vertreter schon von daher ein besonderes Interesse an einer Allianz mit den Philanthropen hegten.

Eine ganze Reihe spezifischer Befindlichkeiten schuf allerdings eigene Bedingungen für die US-amerikanische Wissenschaftsförderung in Frankreich und zeitigte andere Effekte als in Großbritannien. Als besonders prägender Faktor erwies sich hier erstens die britischen Verhältnissen ganz fremde politische Umbruchsituation der metropolitanen Gesellschaft Frankreichs

---

61 Zum Spektrum zeitgenössischer Debatten vgl. Thomas, *The French Empire*.

seit den 1930er Jahren, die die amerikanische Stiftung mit einem diffuseren Meinungsklima zur Frage einer wissenschaftsgeleiteten Kolonialpolitik konfrontierte und ihr zugleich massiv engere Interventionsspielräume beließ. Zweitens traf die RF in Frankreich auf eine im Vergleich mit den USA und Großbritannien spezifisch eigene Beschaffenheit und Gemengelage des akademischen Feldes und disziplinärer Traditionen, die der französischen *ethnologie* eingeschrieben waren. Solche spezifischen Konstellationen und Interessenkoalitionen vor Ort verhinderten eine einseitige Wissensinfiltration von amerikanischer Seite. Der genauere Blick auf zeitgenössische Diskurse sowie auf Akteure und ihre Verbünde macht vielmehr deutlich, dass der Handlungsspielraum der Philanthropen auch hier durchaus eng ausfiel, sodass die frankoamerikanischen Aushandlungen zugunsten der geförderten *ethnologie* eher die Handschrift französischer als amerikanischer Protagonisten trugen.

Philanthropische Erwartungen an die Pariser Ethnologie

Das amerikanische Hauptaugenmerk in Frankreich galt dem Institut d'ethnologie an der Universität Paris, das seit seiner Gründung 1925 erheblich subventioniert wurde.[62] Ausschlaggebend für diese Wahl war erstens, ähnlich wie im Londoner Raum, die Affinität der Stiftungsvertreter zu dessen wichtigsten Initiatoren und ihren programmatischen Erklärungen zur *ethnologie* als ordnungspolitisch relevanter Wissenschaft. Hier bekannte sich aus Sicht der amerikanischen Beobachter eine Gruppe etablierter Akademiker zu einer empirisch basierten, auf die koloniale Gegenwart Frankreichs zielenden Anwendungswissenschaft. Dies galt insbesondere für Lucien Lévy-Bruhl, einen der wichtigsten Mitgründer des Instituts, der als ehemaliger Attaché der französischen Regierung und international renommierter Inhaber eines Philosophielehrstuhls an der Sorbonne umtriebiges Wissenschaftsmanagement betrieb. Ebenso traf dies auf den Soziologen und Ethnologen Marcel Mauss zu, der sich aus Stiftungsperspektive verdienstvoll dafür einsetzte, die bisherige, auf Feldforschung fixierte koloniale Ethnografie in das Profil einer soziologisch informierten, akademischen Disziplin einzubinden. Lévy-Bruhl und Mauss befreiten damit aus Sicht der RF die *ethno-*

---

62 Vgl. Lévy-Bruhl, »L'Institut d'ethnologie pendant l'année scolaire 1928–29«. – Hier ist kein systematischer Vergleich zwischen IIALC und dem Institut d'ethnologie beabsichtigt bzw. möglich, da beide im Blick auf investierte Fördersummen sowie auf ihre jeweilige Bedeutung für die Disziplinenentwicklung ganz unterschiedlich gelagert waren. Vergleichbar sind allerdings die – symptomatischen – Grundzüge der anglo-amerikanischen und französisch-amerikanischen Förderkonstellationen einschließlich der zeitgenössischen Rhetoriken beiderseits des Atlantiks.

logie dauerhaft vom Vorwurf, eine Disziplin zu sein, in der die Theorie eine zu große Rolle spiele. Freilich taten sich die US-Philanthropen nun im französischen anders als im britischen Fall nicht immer leicht mit den politischen Affinitäten ihrer bevorzugten Kooperationspartner. Aus diesem Grund begegneten sie vor allem Mauss regelmäßig reserviert, auch wenn er zum Zeitpunkt der Institutsgründung anders als noch knapp zehn Jahre zuvor kaum mehr dezidiert sozialistische Voten veröffentlichte.[63]

Bei aller Distanz zur französischen Kolonialpolitik faszinierte die amerikanischen Beobachter das Wissenschaftsverständnis der französischen Ethnografen und wissenschaftsnahen Kolonialeliten. Diese schienen angetreten, die Kolonialpolitik zu verwissenschaftlichen, und sahen in dieser Zielvorgabe den ultimativen Ausweis zivilisatorischer Fortschrittlichkeit. Zugleich musste aus Stiftungssicht die große Rationalisierungsidee attraktiv wirken, wie sie die kolonialpolitischen Reformdenker vom Schlage des am Institut weithin sichtbaren Maurice Delafosse vertraten und sich gegen jede Form des Inkrementalismus und stattdessen für eine großflächig-rational geplante koloniale Strategie aussprachen.[64]

Zweitens beeindruckte die RF am Institut d'ethnologie, dass es, wenn auch zunächst ohne eigenen universitären Lehrstuhl, ganz im Sinne philanthropischer Wissensplanung als erste akademisch zertifizierte und staatlich anerkannte Ausbildungsstätte für Ethnologen im französischen Bildungssystem fungierte.[65] Tatsächlich konnte vor allem auf Betreiben von Mauss eine neue Generation auch in praktischer Feldforschung geschulter Ethnologen am Institut ausgebildet werden (zu denen etwa Jacques Soustelle und Claude Lévi-Strauss zählen sollten), die, so die philanthropische Erwartung, einen Beitrag zum Erhalt indigener Kulturen würden leisten können.[66] Lévy-Bruhl plädierte dafür, Mitglieder des Instituts an ethnografischen Forschungsmissionen zu beteiligen oder qualifizierte Kolonialbeamte mit entsprechenden Studien und mit der Sammlung und Klassifizierung von Daten und Objekten zu beauftragen, die in kolonialen und metropolitanen Museen Frankreichs ausgestellt werden sollten. Er strich damit die von der RF für substanziell erachtete empirische Wissensbasis der französischen *ethnologie* heraus.[67]

---

63 Vgl. Moebius, »Intellektuelle Kritik und Soziologie«.

64 Delafosse verstarb allerdings bereits 1926. Zum Konzept der wissenschaftsnahen Kolonialpolitik vgl. Delafosse, »Sur l'orientation nouvelle«.

65 Vgl. Lévy-Bruhl, »L'Institut d'ethnologie de l'université de Paris«, 235. Freilich hielten sich die Absolventenzahlen in einem bescheidenen Rahmen und stiegen nur langsam von 67 (1927–8) auf 89 (1928–9). Vgl. u. a. Lévy-Bruhl, »L'Institut d'ethnologie pendant l'année scolaire 1925–26«; Fournier, *Marcel Mauss*, 511–512.

66 Vgl. Lévy-Bruhl, »L'Institut d'ethnologie de l'université de Paris«, 235.

67 Ebd., 236

Schließlich – und drittens – gewährleistete für die RF-*Officers* die besondere Nähe zur direkt dem Kolonialministerium zugeordneten École coloniale, an der künftige Kolonialbeamte ausgebildet wurden, dass man sich am Institut d'ethnologie nicht in Lippenbekenntnissen erging, sondern im institutionellen Austausch mit der École und somit an der Schnittstelle von akademischer und kolonialpolitischer Berufswelt über eine auf ethnologischem Wissen basierende Planungspolitik diskutierte.[68] Von dieser Grundidee rührte tatsächlich die selbst erklärte Mission der École her, die Kolonialverwaltung und ihre Mitarbeiter durch gezielte, nicht zuletzt sozialwissenschaftlich ausgerichtete Schulung zu professionalisieren.[69]

Anders als im britischen Fall brachten allerdings die politischen Umbrüche im Frankreich der 1930er Jahre die Vertreter der RF zum Institut d'ethnologie auf Distanz. Zwar sammelten sich dort kaum Sympathisanten des autoritären Vichy-Regimes und behielt die Stiftung auch nach dem Systemwechsel hinreichend viele Gestaltungs- und Vernetzungsspielräume, um weiter aktiv zu sein, während die offizielle Politik der USA sich zunächst neutral verhielt.[70] Dass ausgerechnet diejenigen Intellektuellen ausgebremst wurden, die das Institut aus philanthropischer Sicht interessant gemacht hatten, ließ die RF in den 1940er Jahren aber von weiteren Subventionen absehen.

Insgesamt schlug sich in der amerikanischen Präferenz für das Institut weniger der Wille nieder, Wissenschaftspraktiken einzuführen, die es in Frankreich und der Wissenschaftshochburg Paris so noch nicht gab, sondern willkommene Paradigmen und Kooperationen im Grenzbereich von französischer *ethnologie* und kolonialpolitischer Praxis zu unterstützen. Im dichten Interessengeflecht von akademisch ambitionierten *éthnologues* und kolonialpolitischen Eliten trafen die Philanthropen damit durchaus eine politische Richtungsentscheidung: Zwar mieden sie jede politische Aussage zur französischen Kolonialpolitik, allerdings interessierten sie sich nicht erkennbar für kolonialpolitische Ordnungsentwürfe jenseits derjenigen, die Pariser Wissenschaftler und Kolonialbeamte mit einem klaren Schwergewicht auf einer steuerungsbeflissenen Metropole produzierten. Es waren auch die ungenutzten Optionen, die diese Tendenz offenbarten. Denn auf die zwar diffuse, aber dezidiert antikoloniale *négritude*-Bewegung, die sich in den 1930er Jahren gerade in Pariser Intellektuellenzirkeln und Diasporagruppen zusammenfand,[71] gingen die Stiftungsvertreter nicht erkennbar zu. Umgekehrt unterstützten die Philanthropen – ähnlich wie im britischen

---

68 Zur École vgl. Dimier, »Le Commandant«.
69 Vgl. dazu Brahm, *Wissenschaft und Dekolonisation*, 40–41.
70 Vgl. Schneider, »War, Philanthropy, and the National Institute«, 2.
71 Vgl. Eckert, »Afrikanische Intellektuelle«, 252–260.

Fall – eine anthropologische Expertise, die sich nicht auf Superioritäts-floskeln beschränkte, sondern zumindest die Absicht verfolgte, indigene Gesellschaften und Kulturen nicht nur um der besseren Beherrschbarkeit willen methodisch reflektiert zu untersuchen.

La condition coloniale

So wichtig sich die amerikanischen Gelder für die Forschungsarbeit erwiesen, so wenig war die RF der einzige Interessent und Mäzen einer kolonial-politisch verwertbaren Anthropologie. Erheblicher Zuspruch für das Pariser Institut kam aus den Reihen der französischen Kolonialeliten, sodass die regelmäßigen jährlichen *subventions coloniales* der zuständigen Kommission beim Kolonialministerium bis 1933 den Löwenanteil des Institutsbudgets abdeckten.[72] Das Interesse der kolonialen Eliten wusste vor allem Lucien Lévy-Bruhl zu sichern. Zumal der Sieg des Linkskartells bei den Wahlen der Abgeordnetenkammer 1924 dafür zusätzlich günstige Rahmenbedingungen geschaffen hatte: Gemeinsam mit Mauss mobilisierte Lévy-Bruhl dann seine politischen Netzwerke aus der Zeit seiner Tätigkeit als Regierungsattaché und als international umtriebiger Wissenschaftsmanager.[73] Auf diesem Wege konnte er den neuen radikal-sozialistischen Kolonialminister Édouard Daladier sowie namentlich Alexandre Varenne, Mitte der 1920er Jahre Generalgouverneur Indochinas und sozialistischer Verfechter einer moderni-sierenden Sozialpolitik, für die Institutspläne gewinnen.[74]

Im Zuspruch der kolonialen Eliten zum Institut d'ethnologie spiegelte sich nicht nur die republikanische Emphase für das französische Empire-projekt, sondern auch eine (selbst-)kritische Reformerwartung des Estab-lishments im Kolonialministerium und an renommierten Ausbildungsor-ten wie der École Coloniale wider. Zu dieser politischen Stimmungslage schloss Lévy-Bruhl auf, wenn er die Gründung des Instituts 1925 zum Anlass nahm, die französische Ethnologie als Wissensressource für die Inwertset-zung der Kolonien zu definieren, die möglichst genaue Erkenntnisse über die kulturellen und sozialen Befindlichkeiten indigener Bevölkerungen lie-

---

72 Vgl. Lévy-Bruhl, »Rapport«, 421 (166 000 Francs); *Annales de l'université de Paris 1931*, 250 (170 000 Francs). Offenbar erodierte diese Finanzquelle ab 1933, als die Commission nur noch 10 000 Francs bereitstellte und einige Kolonien wie Marokko, Algerien und Tunesien keine Subventionszahlungen mehr leisteten, vgl. *Annales de l'Université de Paris 1934*, 167–168. Mit etwa 5000 Francs blieb demgegenüber das finanzielle Engage-ment der Universität Paris eher symbolisch.

73 Vgl. Plé, »Lucien Lévy-Bruhl«.

74 Zu Varenne vgl. Thomas, *The French Empire*, 65 und 116, 132–133. Vgl. auch Sibeud, *Une science impériale pour l'Afrique?*, 261 ff. und 365; Fournier, *Marcel Mauss*.

fern würde.[75] Mit der *mise en valeur* griff Lévy-Bruhl das Herzstück der Kolonialreformpläne Albert Sarrauts auf, die allerdings, 1921 lanciert, bereits 1924 bis zur Unkenntlichkeit verwässert worden waren.[76] Denn zum einen hatte die *mise en valeur*-Idee an den ökonomischen Realitäten der französischen Regierung weit vorbeigezielt, da die Währungskrise Mitte der 1920er Jahre den Investitionsspielraum des Staates so eng begrenzte, dass ein massives Wirtschaftsengagement in den Kolonien nicht mehr opportun erschien.[77] Zum anderen widersprach das Plädoyer für eine langfristige Investition in die Infrastruktur der Kolonien klar der Mehrheitsmeinung konservativer Imperialisten in Paris, die von Sarrauts Plänen zu viel Dynamik und folglich den Kontrollverlust einer dominanten Metropole befürchtet hatten.[78] Insofern griff Lévy-Bruhl als Leitfigur des neuen Institut d'ethnologie die eigentlich schon abgeschmetterte Reformidee noch einmal auf und konnte damit den finanzierungswilligen Gouverneuren offensichtlich signalisieren, dass am Institut eine Sorte ethnologischen Wissens produziert würde, die Reformpotenzial für die französische Administration bereithalte.

Darüber hinaus lieferte Lévy-Bruhl zwei zusätzliche attraktive Anreize für die Kolonialadministration: Zum einen meldete er Nachholbedarf gegenüber der Wissensinfrastruktur des kolonialen Konkurrenten Großbritannien an, wo den britischen Kolonialbeamten ein eigens eingerichteter anthropologischer Service zur Verfügung stehe, um anhand dichter Datensammlung praktische Verwaltungsprobleme vor Ort wirksam zu lösen – so, wie es nun auch das Pariser Institut zu tun versprach.[79] Zum anderen wies Lévy-Bruhl das Institut als Ausbildungsstätte und Ort der Professionalisierung kolonialer Beamter aus. Diesen Anspruch brachte er sorgsam mit parallelen Profilen traditionaler Einrichtungen gleichen Zwecks wie der École Coloniale in Einklang, indem er das Institut d'ethnologie – anders als diese – zum ergänzenden Ort von Forschung, Lehre und technischer Ausbildung erklärte.[80] Eine Konkurrenz mit den etablierten Einrichtungen, die die Chance auf Subventionen seitens der Kolonialverwaltung hätte mindern können, ließ sich so umgehen. In den Mittelpunkt des Institutsprofils rückte Lévy-Bruhl stattdessen eine neue Vermittlerfunktion zwischen administrativer und wissenschaftlicher Expertise. Aus dem Institut sollte die Kolonialverwaltung akademisch geschultes Personal rekrutieren können, während die Kolonialeliten auf die Standardisierung des Expertenwissens Einfluss würden nehmen können, indem sie dort regelmäßig Lehraufträge erhielten.

75 Vgl. Lévy-Bruhl, »L'Institut d'ethnologie de l'université de Paris«, 234.
76 Vgl. Sarraut, *La mise en valeur*.
77 Vgl. Wilder, *The French Imperial Nation-State*, 82–90.
78 Vgl. Thomas, »French Empire Elites«, 996–997.
79 Vgl. Lévy-Bruhl, »L'Institut d'ethnologie de l'université de Paris«, 233.
80 Ebd., 235.

Lévy-Bruhls Strategie verfing so sehr, dass die Kolonialgouverneure das Institut selbst dann noch mitfinanzierten, als sich abzuzeichnen begann, dass dessen Hauptaugenmerk weniger auf der Ausbildung kolonialer Beamter als auf der akademischen Standardisierung der *ethnologie* als universitärer Disziplin lag. Offenbar trafen die Institutsgründer mit ihrer Programmatik aber auch dann noch den Nerv des kolonialen Establishments.

Dieses seit Mitte der 1920er Jahre steigende Interesse der kolonialen Eliten an der *ethnologie* als Wissensressource erklärt sich erstens langfristig aus dem spannungsreichen Zusammenhang von metropolitaner und kolonialer Entwicklung der Dritten Republik und aus einem in den 1920er und bis Ende der 1930er Jahren zunehmenden Krisen- und Reformdiskurs über die Kolonien: Auf der einen Seite erhoffte sich die Metropole nach Kriegsende 1919 Prestigezugewinne und Erneuerungsimpulse aus dem kolonialen Raum,[81] der nach dem massiven militärischen Einsatz der Kolonialtruppen im Krieg einmal mehr als integraler Bestandteil der französischen Staatsnation galt.[82] Auf der anderen Seite verstärkten sich seit den frühen 1930er Jahren die kolonialpolitischen Krisendiagnosen, als deutlich wurde, dass die Große Depression den Druck nicht nur auf das metropolitane Frankreich, sondern auch auf die von den Turbulenzen besonders hart betroffenen Kolonien dramatisch erhöhte.[83] Anders als in Großbritannien sah sich die französische Kolonialadministration darüber hinaus infolge rasch wechselnder Parteikoalitionen und einer wachsenden antirepublikanischen Opposition in der Metropole in der Defensive.[84] Entsprechende Entwicklungen nährten die Sorge, dass sich die Krisenentwicklung in den Kolonien zu einer nationalen Gefährdung auswachsen könne. In den Jahren des Front Populaire (1936–1939) verstärkten die politischen Eliten Frankreichs daher die Reformrhetorik und wollten die *mise en valeur* mithilfe sachkundig ausgebildeter Kolonialexperten weiter rationalisieren, wiewohl sich faktisch mangels Ressourcen an den kolonialpolitischen Gepflogenheiten der Vorgängerregierungen der 1920er und frühen 1930er Jahre wenig änderte.[85] Es war dieser eher angefachte als abflauende Krisen- und Reformdiskurs, der die Chancen der Gründer des Institut d'ethnologie massiv verbesserte, Subventionen aus der Kolonialadministration einzuwerben, vor allem deshalb, weil er die Attraktivität der Anthropologie als Wissensressource deutlich steigerte. Denn ihre Vertreter am Institut d'ethnologie warben doch ähnlich wie am Londoner IIALC damit, zu einer exakten, datengestützten und zugleich theoretisch

81 Vgl. u.a. *L'Algérie en 1928*, 7; Michelet, »L'empire français«.
82 Vgl. Wilder, »Framing Greater France«, 203 ff.
83 Vgl. Coquery-Vidrovitch, »The Popular Front«.
84 Vgl. Margairaz, *Le Front populaire*.
85 Vgl. Thomas, »French Empire Elites«.

reflektierten Kenntnis des Indigenen verhelfen zu können, die als Voraussetzung für die Regierbarkeit der Kolonien galt.[86]

Zweitens gab es ähnliche Gründe wie im britischen Fall für das gesteigerte Interesse der französischen Kolonialeliten an der anthropologischen
Wissensproduktion am Institut d'ethnologie. Zum permanenten Legitimationsbedarf kolonialer Politik durch anthropologische Expertise kam eine
Serie von Aufständen: Schon in den 1920er Jahren gefährdete der Rifkrieg
(1921–1925) den marokkanischen Kolonialbesitz und schließlich schufen
im Gefolge der Wirtschaftskrise drastische Ausgabenkürzungen zusätzliches
Potenzial für Konflikte an der Peripherie, als etwa in Yên Bay in Indochina
1930 die deklassierte Kolonialbevölkerung gegen weitere Zusatzlasten aufbegehrte.[87] Entsprechende kontingente Außenfaktoren machten die Vertreter
der französischen Kolonialverwaltung hellhörig für die Erosionseffekte an
den Rändern des Empire und für das Wissenspotenzial der *ethnologie*, die zu
effizienteren Herrschaftspraktiken vor Ort anzuleiten versprach.[88]

Mit der deutschen Besatzung und der Kollaboration in Vichy spitzte sich
der kolonialpolitische Diskurs Frankreichs zu, was die Mäzene des Institut
d'ethnologie nicht unberührt ließ. An die Stelle einer Rhetorik, die auf die
Assoziation der kolonialen Ländern abhob und von der republikanischen
und der Volksfrontregierung getragen worden waren (die freilich das massive Machtgefälle zwischen Indigenen und Kolonialisten nur verbrämt
hatte), traten nun eine unverhüllt rassistische Sichtweise auf das koloniale
Terrain und eine deutlich aggressivere Ausbeutungspolitik in den Kolonien.[89] Zwar wertete das Vichy-Regime die ethnologische Forschung als kolonialpolitisches Wissensinstrument deutlich auf. Zur Kollaboration boten
sich aber vor allem Vertreter einer physischen Anthropologie wie George
Montandon an, der nach 1941 bereitwillig dem Commissariat Général aux
Questions Juives zuarbeitete.[90] Darüber hinaus wurde ein regierungsoffizieller Steuerungsehrgeiz sichtbar, der die Ethnologie im Sinne rassistischer
Positionen des Regimes dienstbar machen sollte.

Für das Institut d'ethnologie allerdings, das sich die neue tagespolitische
Agenda von Vichy nicht zu eigen machte, war von den neuen kolonialpolitischen Eliten keine Unterstützung mehr zu erwarten. Anders als im britischen Fall, wo das amerikanisch geförderte IIALC im Zuge der technokratischen Wende britischer Kolonialpolitik seit den 1940er Jahren zunehmend

---

86 Vgl. dazu oben.
87 Vgl. Levy, »Indo-China«. Zu Kontext und kolonialpolitischen Folgen vgl. Rettig,
»French military policies«.
88 Vgl. Sasse, *Franzosen, Briten und Deutsche im Rifkrieg*.
89 Vgl. Ginio, *French Colonialism Unmasked*.
90 Vgl. Maigron, »Résistance et collaboration«, 135; Paligot, »L'émergence de l'antisemitisme«.

staatliche Subventionen erhielt, sahen sich die Mitarbeiter des Institut d'ethnologie in Paris vom politische Umbruch nach 1940 stark marginalisiert,
weil die Prämissen republikanischen Reformdenkens jetzt entfielen, denen
das anthropologische Wissensformat am Institut eigentlich entsprochen
hatte.

Primat des Akademischen

Das strategische Interesse französischer *ethnologues* an den amerikanischen
Fördergeldern wies sowohl Ähnlichkeiten als auch Unterschiede mit dem
Londoner Umfeld auf. In jedem Fall trug die Institutsgründung langfristig
vor allem deren Handschrift, während konkurrierende Interessen auf dem
dicht besiedelten Akteurfeld die Vertreter der RF eher marginalisierte. Erstens und vor allem versuchten die Gründer und Mitarbeiter des Instituts, die
bis dahin kaum universitär verankerte *ethnologie* zu etablieren. Unter den
Bedingungen einer seit Mauss sprichwörtlichen, heillosen Zerrissenheit des
erst im Entstehen begriffenen disziplinären Feldes[91] verfolgten die französischen *ethnologues* ihre Institutionalisierungsstrategien ähnlich wie die britischen *social anthropologists* schon lange vor ihren ersten Kontakten mit der
RF: Weit vor der amerikanischen Förderofferte betrieb eine seit den frühen
1920er Jahren aktive Allianz das Institutsprojekt: An erster Stelle engagierten
sich hier die Vertreter einer soziologisch fundierten akademischen *ethnologie* wie namentlich Mauss aus dem Umfeld des Institut français d'anthropologie (seit 1910/11).[92] Hinzu kam eine Gruppe von Ethnografen, die sich bis
dahin in Delafosses' Institut d'ethnographie auf Sprachforschung und empirische Ethnografie konzentriert hatten. Beide Gruppen verfolgten durchaus das Ziel, akademische Theoriebildung und empirische Feldforschung
und Datensammlung zu verbinden und damit das Projekt einer universitär verankerten *ethnologie* zum Abschluss zu bringen.[93] Nicht anders als im
britischen Fall scharte man sich hier hinter dem französischen *fieldwork*-
Äquivalent der *études* oder *recherches sur le terrain*, die dem zeitgenössischen
Ehrgeiz entsprach, der Anthropologie die Weihen eines quasi naturwissen-
schaftlich-experimentellen und damit validen Wissensformats zu geben.[94]
Was allerdings der RF im filigranen Pariser Interessendickicht kaum hätte
gelingen können, nämlich ein solches Institut in der Pariser Universität zu

---

91 Vgl. Mauss, »L'ethnographie en France«.
92 Vgl. L'Estoile, »›Africanisme‹ & ›Africansim‹«, 28–30.
93 Vgl. Febvre, »Quelques aspects d'une ethnographie«.
94 Zum Teil handelte es dabei auch um eine intra-europäische Wissenszirkulation, vgl.
Malinowski, »Ethnologie Pratique«.

verankern, bewerkstelligte diese Gruppe längst selbst.[95] Die Institutsgründer machten es dem Conseil de l'Université de Paris leicht, ohne lange Beratungen einer Initiative stattzugeben, für die letztlich nicht die Universität, sondern diverse französische Generalgouverneure vor Ort aufzukommen hatten.[96]

Mit dem Institutsprojekt verbanden sich auch handfeste professionelle Karriereziele einzelner französischer Akademiker. Allen voran hatte Mauss lange Jahre vor seinen ersten Kontakten mit Vertretern der RF beim Ministre de l'instruction publique vergeblich um Unterstützung für ein universitäres Institut geworben, das es ihm erlaubt hätte, als staatlich sanktionierte, intellektuelle Leitfigur auf die Binnendifferenzierung der Disziplin noch prägender einzuwirken.[97] Dieses Verlangen nach Prestige veränderte allerdings nicht das anthropologische Konzept, für das Mauss am Institut stand. Denn sein ausgeprägtes Interesse an einer soziologisch informierten und rassismuskritischen *ethnologie*, um derentwillen er unter anderem auch das Interesse der RF auf sich zog, war nicht das Ergebnis opportunistischer Anlehnung an amerikanische Förderbedingungen. Spielten hier Anklänge an die Boassche Anthropologie in den USA eine Rolle, die die RF dort intensiv förderte, so stammte Mauss' Orientierung in dieselbe Richtung aus einer Zeit umtriebiger transatlantischer Kontakte und Austauscherfahrungen, die er noch vor dem Ersten Weltkrieg gesammelt hatte und die mit dem späteren Mäzenatentum der Stiftung nicht ursächlich zusammenhingen.[98]

Zweitens war – anders als im britischen Fall – das Interesse der *ethnologues* am Institut letztlich ein akademisches. Am ehesten teilten sie noch den Ehrgeiz der Malinowski-Schule, strukturell unabhängig von der Kolonialpolitik zu erscheinen. Im Unterschied zu den *social anthropologists* unternahmen sie allerdings, anders als gegenüber den amerikanischen Philanthropen und der französischen Kolonialadministration angekündigt, kaum Anstrengungen, vordringlich kolonialpolitisch verwertbares Planungswissen zu generieren. In dieser Distanznahme klangen, ganz anders als im britischen Fall, politische Vorbehalte nach, die die dezidiert linksrepublikanisch aufgestellten französischen Wissenschaftler wie namentlich Mauss in den Vorkriegsjahren noch dazu veranlasst hatten, sich politischer Voten zum zeitgenössischen Kolonialismus eher zu enthalten.[99] Mit der zumindest auf programmatischer Ebene vollzogenen reformistischen Wende in der französischen Kolonialpolitik in den Nachkriegsjahren seit Sarraut schwand dieser Vorbehalt

---

95 Vgl. Lévy-Bruhl, »L'Institut d'ethnologie de l'université de Paris«, 235.
96 Vgl. Conklin, »The new ›ethnology‹«, 34.
97 Vgl. als Quelle ediert von Sibeud, »Marcel Mauss«.
98 Vgl. Mauss, »L'ethnographie en France«, passim; Fournier, »Marcel Mauss, l'ethnologie et la politique«; vgl. Därmann/Mahlke, *Marcel Mauss*.
99 Vgl. Copans, »Œuvre secrète ou œuvre publique«, 219.

linksrepublikanischer Intellektueller vom Schlage Mauss' gegenüber der Kolonialpolitik. Zumindest schien in dieser Phase eine strategische Allianz der
ethnologues mit der Kolonialadministration als Financier des Institut d'ethnologie denkbar. Freilich kehrte die intellektuelle Skepsis zurück, als sich im
Laufe der 1930er Jahre die Reformrhetorik der Volksfront als vordergründig
erwies und schließlich seit 1940 autokratische Töne dominierten. Zu ihnen
blieben die linksrepublikanischen Akteure des Instituts auf Abstand.[100]

Insgesamt kam mit der Gründung des Institut d'ethnologie eine institutionelle Unterteilung des ethnologischen Feldes in Frankreich zum Abschluss, die in dieser Form nicht die RF, sondern die französischen Institutsgründer aus Gründen professionellen Eigeninteresses angestrebt hatten.
Denn im Ergebnis grenzten sich am Institut Ethnologen und Ethnografen
gemeinsam demonstrativ von den zahlreichen Einrichtungen ab, die die kolonialpolitischen Eliten seit dem frühen 20. Jahrhundert gegründet hatten,
um die Forschung über die Kolonien staatlich alimentieren zu lassen.[101]
Demgegenüber legten die Institutsmitarbeiter großen Wert darauf, Expertenwissen nicht nur für koloniale, sondern auch für nicht-koloniale Gesellschaften produzieren zu können.[102]

In diesem Sinne verband sich die Institutsgründung faktisch mit einer
emanzipatorischen Geste gegenüber der Kolonialadministration. Dass sie
mit der beträchtlichen Förderung just von dieser Seite her kollidierte, war offensichtlich. Versprach Lévy-Bruhl, am Institut politisch verwertbares Wissen über die indigenen Gesellschaften zu generieren, so entsprach dieser An-
kündigung nicht erkennbar die Taktik, Forschungsprojekte oder -themen
mit der Kolonialverwaltung abzusprechen oder gezielt Absolventen des Instituts in der Kolonialverwaltung unterzubringen. Ganz im Gegensatz dazu
ließ die neu lancierte institutseigene Publikationsreihe der *Travaux et Mémoires* eher den gesteigerten Ehrgeiz der Institutsgründer erkennen, mit den
renommierten akademischen Einrichtungen in der Metropole auf Augenhöhe zu kommen.[103] Von der ausdrücklich akademischen Agenda zeugte
auch die Rekrutierung der Institutsgremien. Dort hatten zwar Delegierte der
Generalgouverneure aus den Kolonien (Indochina, Afrique Occidentale
Française, Afrique Equatoriale Française, Madagaskar) sowie die Gouver-
neure von Algerien, Marokko und Tunesien Zutritt zu einem größeren Ver-

100 Zur diesen Etappen kolonialpolitischer Praxis vgl. weiter oben.
101 Vgl. Picard, La République des savants, 43–49; Charle, La République des universitaires, 331–340.
102 Vgl. Sibeud, »The Elusive Bureau«, 63.
103 Als erste Bände der institutseigenen Reihe Travaux et Mémoires de l'Institut d'Ethnologie erschienen u. a. Em. G. Waterlot, Les Bas-Reliefs des Bâtiments Royaux d'Abomey
(Dahomey), Paris 1926 (Bd. 1), G. H. Luquet, L'art néo-calédonien, Paris 1926 (Bd. 2);
vgl. dazu u. a. die Rezension von Werner: »Rezension«.

waltungsrat, nicht aber zum engeren Kreis der Institutsdirektoren, der sich
mit Ausnahme des ehemaligen Kolonialbeamten Maurice Delafosse aus-
schließlich aus wenigen Akademikern metropolitaner Einrichtungen rekrutierte.[104] Damit blieb das Institut d'ethnologie, durchaus entgegen anders
gearteter Verlautbarungen gegenüber seinen wichtigsten Geldgebern französischer wie amerikanischer Provenienz, vorrangig ein Ort akademischer
Produktion ethnologischen Wissens. Kaum erkennbar war dagegen im For-
schungs- und Lehrprofil, dass es den Institutsvertretern vordringlich um
jene Produktion anwendungsorientierten, kolonialpolitisch nutzbaren Mo-
dernisierungswissens gegangen wäre, um derentwillen das Institut aus beiden Quellen seine Förderung erhielt.[105]

Geriet das Institut Ende der 1930er Jahre in schweres Fahrwasser, so nicht
deshalb, weil die RF die mangelnde politische Verwendbarkeit ethnologi-
scher Forschung am Institut geahndet hätte, sondern eher als Konsequenz
der politischen Zeitläufte. So zwang die antisemitische Personalpolitik während der deutschen Okkupation Mauss 1939/40 zum Rückzug aus dem Institut wie auch aus der Ecole Pratique des Hautes Etudes und dem Collège,
drangsalierte oder relegierte zahlreiche jüdischstämmige Forscher und trieb
den Institutsmitbegründer Paul Rivet 1941 ins kolumbianische Exil.[106] Bis
dahin allerdings war es dem Institut bemerkenswerterweise gelungen, in
loyaler Nähe zu den kolonialpolitischen Eliten zu bleiben, ohne sich durch
diese Allianz auf eine rein utilitaristische Zulieferfunktion gegenüber der
Kolonialpolitik reduzieren zu lassen oder als eine Art Dépendance der École
Coloniale zur Ausbildung künftiger Kolonialeliten zu wirken.

Finanzierte also die RF das Institut d'ethnologie, so verwirklichte sie damit vor allem die genuinen Interessen französischer Ethnografen und Ethnologen, das Institut als eine Art Expertengremium eigenen Rechts von der
Kolonialadministration zu trennen. Von einem Oktroi amerikanischer Wissensformen und -praktiken konnte mithin keine Rede sein. Die eigentliche
Bedeutung der philanthropischen Intervention lag dann auch nicht darin,
diese Klärung des disziplinären Feldes der französischen Ethnologie erst
eigentlich provoziert zu haben. Vielmehr unterstützte die RF diese Art der
Neukartierung des anthropologischen Wissensfeldes in Paris, die französische Exponenten wie Mauss und Delafosse schon seit Jahren mit erfolglo-
sem Werben um staatliche Fördergelder betrieben hatten.[107]

---

104 Vgl. Conklin, »The new ›ethnology‹«, 36.
105 Vgl. dazu u. a. Lévy-Bruhl, »Institut d'Ethnologie«.
106 Vgl. Fournier, *Marcel Mauss*, 733; Gaillard, *Cadres institutionnels et activités*, 7.
107 Vgl. Sibeud, »The elusive bureau«, passim und Wartelle, »La Société d'anthropologie«.

3. Die Rockefeller-Stiftung als Koproduzent kolonialen Planungswissens in Europa

Wo die RF in London und Paris anthropologische Forschungsinstitute und
-gruppen förderte, traf sie ihre Wahl nicht aus Mangel an konzeptionellen
Alternativen auf dem intellektuellen Markt.[108] Ebenso wenig sollten die För-
derbeziehungen aber dazu führen, dass die Philanthropen auf pekuniärem
Wege eine neue Disziplin oder zumindest eine neue Ausrichtung eines Fa-
ches aus der Taufe gehoben hätten, die es so vorher noch nicht gegeben
hatte. Stattdessen wählten die Stiftungsvertreter aus einer hinreichend vor-
handenen kritischen Masse von Ansätzen in der anthropologischen Forschung mit der *social anthropology* am IIALC bzw. der LSE und mit der
neuen *ethnologie* am Institut d'ethnologie diejenigen Wissensformate aus,
die dem planungstechnologischen Denken aus US-amerikanischer Sicht
am ehesten zu entsprechen schienen. So sichtbar sich die Philanthropen damit in die anthropologische Wissensproduktion in der britischen und
französischen Metropole einmischten, so wenig stifteten sie in beiden Fällen
gänzlich neue Forschungsansätze, sondern verstärkten bereits bestehende
strukturelle und intellektuelle Schwerpunkte. Hier hatten die Philanthropen
einen gewichtigen Anteil am großen Paradigmenwechsel hin zu einer theoretisch reflektierten empirischen Feldforschung, indem sie sich an den neu-
ralgischen institutionellen und personalen Knotenpunkten zu positionieren
wussten, an denen sich die Agenten der neuen Paradigmen zusammenfan-
den. Die RF wirkte unter diesen Umständen nicht als genuiner Impulsgeber,
sondern als Katalysator, indem sie zeitgenössische Verfechter einer strate-
gisch wissensgeleiteten und wissenschaftlich induzierten Kolonialpolitik zu
begünstigen versuchte.

Weitet sich also die historische Perspektive so, dass nicht nur die Förder-
agenda der Stiftung, sondern vor allem Interessen und Kalkül kolonialpolitischer und akademischer Akteure in den Blick genommen werden, erscheint
die RF nur noch als eine – und nicht einmal dominante – neben zahlreichen
anderen Antriebskräften für die Produktion anthropologischen Planungs-
wissens. Besondere Prägekraft entfalteten fernab vom Stiftungsengagement
im britischen wie im französischen Fall sowohl die Kolonialadministratio-
nen als auch die Professionalisierungsstrategien europäischer Akademiker.
In beiden europäischen Fällen spielte eine entscheidende Rolle, dass die Ko-
lonialmächte im Anschluss an den Ersten Weltkrieg in eine schwere Krise geraten waren. Diese Krisendiagnose der 1920er und 1930er Jahre brachte

---

108 Vgl. In diesem Sinne z.B. ausdrücklich der Leiter der social sciences-Division der
RF, John van Sickle Diary, Paris 6 Oct. 1930, Rockefeller Archive Center [RAC] Laura
Spelman Rockefeller Memorial [LSRM] Series III 6.1 Folder 664.

nicht nur den Fortbestand des jeweiligen Empire, sondern die politische Legitimation kolonialer Machtausübung schlechthin auf die Tagesordnung.

Zum einen fanden sich unter diesen Bedingungen in London und Paris europäische Koalitionäre für die Idee, anthropologisches Planungswissen zu produzieren, die sich nicht erst vom amerikanischen Förderangebot anwerben ließen, sondern längst selbst von der Anthropologie Regulierungseffekte erwarteten. Gleichzeitig wuchs dort die Nachfrage nach anthropologischem Wissen, um angesichts nationalistischer Unruhen an der »Peripherie« über Kenntnisse des »Indigenen« zu verfügen, die geeignet schienen, mögliche Konflikte frühzeitig zu erkennen und dabei demokratische Forderungen kolonialer Gesellschaften abzuwehren. Den Leitgedanken, anthropologische Expertise zur Herrschaftskontrolle und -legitimation zu nutzen, brachten jedenfalls keineswegs erst die Philanthropen nach Europa. Er stand vielmehr längst im strategischen Mittelpunkt zeitgenössischer Diskurse britischer und französischer Wissenschaftler, Administratoren und Politiker und bestimmte vielerorts längst die administrative Praxis in den französischen und britischen Kolonialterritorien. Dies gilt besonders für die 1920–1940er Jahre, die sich im Rückblick als eine ganz entscheidende Vorphase der dritten Dekolonisierungswelle erwiesen, die schließlich nach 1945 einsetzen sollte.[109]

Zum anderen begünstigte die sprunghaft gestiegene kolonialpolitische Nachfrage nach anthropologischer Expertise die langfristigen Professionalisierungsbemühungen britischer und französischer Forschergruppen, von denen sich die *social anthropologists* und die *ethnologues* als besonders geschickt erwiesen, wenn es darum ging, mindestens rhetorische Interessenkoalitionen mit der Kolonialpolitik nicht anders als mit den amerikanischen Förderern herzustellen, indem sie sich als Lieferanten von krisentauglichem Regulierungswissen auswiesen. Dieser Anspruch diente zugleich dazu, intellektuelle Mitbewerber im akademischen Umfeld zu marginalisieren und nicht-akademischen Amateuren den Expertenstatus abzusprechen. Wo die RF also als mächtiger Sponsor anthropologischen Wissens auftrat, verdankte sie ihren Handlungsspielraum ganz wesentlich solchen Strategien vor Ort.

Im Blick auf diese Akteursgruppe der Sozialwissenschaftler und auf ihre kolonialpolitischen Präferenzen wichen schließlich die beiden europäischen Konstellationen am stärksten voneinander ab: Im britischen Kontext begünstigte die Politik der Indirect Rule die Fiktion, dass die *social anthropology* eine Sorte Expertise darstellte, die mit indigenen Traditionen kompatibel sei; im französischen Fall schufen die politischen Friktionen vor allem der späten 1930er und ab den 1940er Jahren einen unversöhnlicheren Ab-

---

109 Vgl. u.a. Stockwell, *The British Empire;* Chafer, *The End of Empire.*

stand zwischen (links-)republikanisch gesinnten *ethnologues* und einer zunehmend autoritär und rigide definierten kolonialen Ausbeutungspolitik. Unter diesen Umständen entschieden die politischen Umbrüche mehr als der amerikanische Förderwille darüber, wie lange sich die transatlantischen Planungsallianzen halten konnten.

Jenseits aller Unterschiede anthropologischer Forschungskonzepte im Detail verdankte sich die transatlantische Allianz der 1920er bis 1940er Jahre in beiden Fällen schließlich auch einem epistemologischem Zirkelschluss: Bei den »indigenen Gesellschaften« vornehmlich in Westafrika handelte es sich gerade nicht um vorfindliche Entitäten, sondern um Objekte zeitgenössischer Diskussion und politischen Handelns, die die anthropologische Forschung und ihrer Förderer nicht anders als die Kolonialpolitik in wechselseitiger Abhängigkeit voneinander konstituierten.[110] Weder die US-Philanthropen noch Wissenschaftler und Politiker in Großbritannien und Frankreich waren allerdings damit befasst, diese Verzahnung von Wissensproduktion und politischem Kalkül zu hinterfragen. Welche absichtsvollen Vorannahmen über das »Indigene« (als nicht-westliche, nicht »progressive«, ausbeutbare und beherrschbare soziale Formation) von den anthropologischen Experten ebenso wie von der kolonialen Verwaltung produziert wurden, war nicht Teil des transatlantischen Wissenskanons.

Die Verve, mit der die Vertreter der RF und mit ihnen zahlreiche Verfechter der *social anthropology* wie der *ethnologie* für eine anwendungsorientierte Anthropologie einstanden, verpuffte nach 1945 rasch. Stattdessen zeichnete sich ab, dass die sozialtechnologischen Regelungsimpulse, die von der *social anthropology* oder der *ethnologie* zur Aufrechterhaltung der imperialen Ordnungen ausgehen sollten, auf einer Serie unzutreffender kategorialer Vorannahmen beruhten. Nach 1945 wurde deutlich, dass beide Interpretationen ihrer Disziplinen über weite Strecken ihrer eigenen Paradigmenbildung erlagen, die die kolonialen Gesellschaften statischer, tribaler oder traditionaler fasste, als sie faktisch waren.[111] Das dynamische Potenzial kolonialer Gesellschaften, das nicht zuletzt im Zuge der Dekolonisierung zutage trat, ging jedenfalls mit solchen sozialanthropologischen Vorannahmen der Zwischenkriegsjahre kaum zusammen. Zum neuen Modernisierungswissen der Nachkriegsära geriet demgegenüber das *development knowledge* – auch dies dann erneut vehement unterstützt von den US-Stiftungen, bis zu seiner allmählichen Entzauberung in den 1970er Jahren.[112]

---

110 Vgl. Cooper, »Writing the History of Development«; Ash, »Wissenschaft und Politik«.

111 Cohen, *British Policy in Changing Africa*.

112 Ferguson, »Anthropology and Its Evil Twin«; Escobar, *Encountering Development*.

Madeleine Herren

Kommentar – Ambivalente Akteure in grenzübergreifenden Netzwerken der Zwischenkriegszeit

Interferenzen zwischen nationaler Deutungsmacht und Durchsetzung grenzübergreifender Ordnungsvorstellungen beschreiben ein Forschungsfeld von wachsender Bedeutung für eine Gegenwart, die von *multiple modernities* ausgeht. Carolyn Bynum hat bereits 2009 konzise die neuen Forschungsperspektiven benannt, die in der Fokussierung auf Verflechtungsgeschichten, Diversität und Durchlässigkeit von Grenzen liegen und sich gegen die Konstruktion und Essenzialisierung von Entitäten wie Nation, Imperium, Region richten.[1] Dabei ist es dank breiter postkolonialer Diskurse und einer transdisziplinären Öffnung keineswegs der für die Geschichtswissenschaft sprichwörtliche und auch immer wieder zitierte Theoriemangel, der limitierende Konsequenzen zeitigt. Vielmehr ist die Konzeptualisierung einer transkulturellen und globalen Verflechtungsgeschichte nach wie vor erst in Ansätzen geschehen. Selbst die Suche nach paradigmatischen Themen ist noch im Anfangsstadium. Die Erforschung der Rockefeller- und der Carnegie-Stiftung kann aus der Perspektive wechselnder Ordnungsvorstellungen für diesen Bereich der historiografischen Reflexion in der Tat einen wesentlichen Beitrag leisten. Jens Wegener, Ludovic Tournès und Helke Rausch kommen dabei allesamt zu dem Schluss, dass die Analyse des europäischen Engagements der beiden großen amerikanischen Stiftungen in der Zwischenkriegszeit keineswegs eindeutige Thesen liefert – die institutionellen wie die politischen Beziehungen der Stiftungen in Frankreich wie in Großbritannien sind nur ambivalent zu beschreiben. Alle drei Autoren halten fest, dass ein Sender-Empfänger-Modell die vielschichtigen Verflechtungen keineswegs adäquat abbilden kann. Die aus dem Kalten Krieg stammende Logik einer Vereinnahmung Europas durch die reichen amerikanischen Stiftungen trifft dabei ebenso wenig zu, wie sich die Frage, ob und wann die Stiftungen eine amerikanische oder vornehmlich internationale Initiative entwickelten, eindeutig beantworten ließe. Die Darstellung von Tournès

---

1 Bynum, »Perspectives, Connections and Objects«.

zeigt allerdings, dass die Stiftungen auch nicht unterschätzt werden sollten. Das finanzielle Potenzial der Rockefeller Foundation war in der Tat für die Zwischenkriegszeit bemerkenswert. Die ökonomischen Möglichkeiten der Stiftung erlaubten die gezielte Lancierung von diversen Forschungsfeldern, die im Bereich von Biologie und Medizin deutlich nachzuweisen ist. Aus diesem Spannungsverhältnis zwischen einer sehr bedeutenden internationalen Agency-Funktion einerseits und einer nicht minder starken nationalen und gelegentlich auch antiamerikanischen Abgrenzung in den europäischen Empfängerländern andererseits entwickeln die drei Autoren unterschiedliche Vorschläge, wie sich grenzübergreifende Ordnungsvorstellungen am Beispiel der amerikanischen Stiftungen rekonstruieren lassen.

Die Frage, ob Rockefeller und Carnegie beispielgebende Modelle entwarfen oder eher transnationale *soft power* entwickelten, öffnet den Blick auf unterschiedliche Dynamiken, Entwicklungsprozesse und Konzepte. In der Tat dürfte der intellektuelle Mehrwert der Auseinandersetzung mit Rockefeller und Carnegie nicht zuletzt darin liegen, dass diese die Funktionen von Netzwerken sichtbar machen und die Grauzone zwischen nationaler Politik, transnational organisierten *scientific communities* und deren Finanzierung aufdecken. Dabei stellt sich bei allen drei Autoren heraus, dass die lokale Verankerung der jeweiligen Wissenschaftspolitik trotz Wirtschaftskrise stark war. Die Vorstellung einer amerikanischen Vereinnahmung der nach dem Ersten Weltkrieg darniederliegenden wissenschaftlichen Institutionen Europas lässt sich demnach nicht halten. Vielmehr ist von einer komplexen Beziehung zwischen Akteuren der Stiftungen einerseits und den wissenschaftlichen Institutionen andererseits auszugehen.

Polyzentrische Ordnung

In der derzeitigen Wissenslandschaft bieten sich meines Erachtens drei große Felder an, die zur Diskussion wandelnder Ordnungsvorstellungen geeignet sind und dabei ein grundsätzlich polyzentrisches Konzept anbieten. Erstens sind es kultur- und sozialwissenschaftliche Debatten, die statt Themen und Territorien funktionalen Wandel in den Vordergrund rücken. Relationale Soziologie setzt sich mit Beziehungsmustern statt abgrenzbaren Einheiten wie Staaten, Parteien, Organisationen auseinander, kulturwissenschaftliche Ansätze überwinden im Konzept der Transkulturalität die Vorstellung kultureller Authentizität.[2] Ein weiteres Feld bieten zweitens Netzwerktheorien, die mit einem polysemantischen Verständnis von Grenzen

2 Donati, *Relational Sociology*; Benessaieh, »Multiculturalism, Interculturality, Transculturality«.

arbeiten.[3] Ein drittes Feld öffnet sich an der Schnittstelle von *Empire building* und medienorientierter *Public Diplomacy*.[4] In allen drei Fällen spielen die USA eine zentrale Rolle. Am Beispiel der amerikanischen Stiftungen lassen sich Funktionsverschiebungen mitsamt demokratischem Begründungsbedarf in einer transkulturellen Wissenschaftsgemeinschaft nachweisen. Die jüngere Forschung hat begonnen, auch die amerikanische Nationalgeschichte zusehends im Lichte durchlässiger Grenzen darzustellen. Der Philanthropie kommt bei der Transformation der Vereinigten Staaten zu einem »Moral Empire« eine besondere Bedeutung zu.[5] Mit der Neupositionierung der USA und der Umdeutung von religiösen Netzwerken in säkulare, pazifistisch und wissenschaftlich begründete Kontakte ging eine nicht zu unterschätzende *Invention of tradition* einher. Die von Wegener angemerkte frühe Präsenz der Carnegie Stiftung in Europa in der Vorkriegszeit wurde in den 1920er und 1930er Jahren Teil eines globalen Narrativs.

Edward T. Devine, Gründer der New York School of Social Work, lässt sich als überzeugendes Beispiel dafür heranziehen, wie Philanthropie 1928 in soziale Kategorien übersetzt und als eine in das 19. Jahrhundert zurückreichende Form des amerikanischen Internationalismus präsentiert werden konnte.[6] In Devines Argumentation bewies das amerikanische Rote Kreuz die frühe amerikanische Beteiligung am europäischen Vorkriegsinternationalismus, während noch die 1872 gegründete American Public Health Association mit lateinamerikanischer Beteiligung die Deutungsmacht über den Kontinent betonte. Die amerikanische Präsenz beim internationalen Tuberkulosekongress 1905 in Paris war für Devine deshalb besonders erwähnenswert, da diese Konferenz der amerikanischen Delegation die Möglichkeit bot, zum nächsten internationalen Treffen in die USA einzuladen. Damit relativierte sich der eurozentrische Fokus des Vorkriegsinternationalismus und öffnete für die Zwischenkriegszeit ein Narrativ der Kontinuität. Devine verstand den Ersten Weltkrieg nicht als Zäsur, ja nicht einmal als Unterbrechung, sondern als Fortschreibung des amerikanischen Internationalismus, der in seiner charakteristischen Zusammensetzung aus privater Philanthropie, Wissenschaft und Politik in der Nachkriegszeit seine Fortsetzung fand. In diesem Narrativ nahm die Rockefeller-Stiftung eine Scharnierfunktion ein. Devine betonte allerdings deren pragmatischen Charakter: Sie erschien als Teil eines historischen Entwicklungsmodells und nicht als exklusives amerikanisches Alleinstellungsmerkmal. Mit der Einbindung der Stiftungen

---

3 Castells/Cardoso, *The Network Society*; Balibar, *Politics and the other Scene*.
4 Gilboa, »Theory of Public Diplomacy«.
5 Tyrrell, *Reforming the World*; ders., *Transnational Nation*; Herren, *Hintertüren zur Macht*.
6 Devine, »International Implications of Social Work«.

in den amerikanischen Vorkriegsinternationalismus wird zum einen deren
semioffizielle Bedeutung klarer und zum anderen die Konkurrenzsituation
deutlicher, in der sich auch die bedeutenden und ökonomisch handlungsfä-
higen Stiftungen befanden. Wenn Rausch die Frage nach den Grenzen der
Netzwerke aufwirft sowie Wegener und Tournès die Grenzen der Durchlässigkeit in der nationalen Selbstdarstellung betonen, so ist jeweils dieses Moment der Konkurrenz mitzudenken. Für die Zwischenkriegszeit kann nicht
genug betont werden, dass Philanthropie einen hart umkämpften internationalen Markt darstellte, wie das im Beitrag von Tournès aufgeführte Fi-
nanzvolumen der Rockefeller Foundation in aller Deutlichkeit zeigt. Erfolg
war zum einen von der Durchsetzung politischer Ordnungsvorstellungen
und zum anderen von deren Akzeptanz in einer Öffentlichkeit abhängig, die
sowohl international wie auch national und lokal den Handlungsspielraum
abgrenzte. Dennoch bleibt die Frage, ob die Stiftungen als verlängerter Arm
der amerikanischen Politik nicht fehlinterpretiert werden. Wäre es sinnvoll,
stattdessen den eigenständigen Charakter der Stiftungen und deren Bedeutung als internationale Organisationen stärker zu betonen? Obwohl die
historische Forschung zur Geschichte der internationalen Organisationen
formale Kriterien eher überwindet und sich Debatten zur Definition internationaler Organisationen als unergiebig erwiesen haben, so ist dennoch auf
deren fragilen Rechtsstatus in der Zwischenkriegszeit zu verweisen. Selbst
für internationale Regierungsorganisationen ist in der Zwischenkriegszeit
der Rechtsstatus weitgehend ungeklärt. Nur der Völkerbund und dessen Organisationen sowie die Bank für Internationalen Zahlungsausgleich hatten
einen exterritorialen Status – die Büros aller anderen Organisationen unter-
standen der Oberaufsicht des Stammlandes und genossen unterschiedliche
Privilegien. Für private Organisationen sah die Situation noch anders aus –
ein privates Vereinsrecht, das internationale Vereinigungen einschloss, exis-
tierte in Europa nur in Belgien. Selbst Organisationen vom Format der
Rockefeller- und der Carnegie-Stiftung taten daher gut daran, ein Arrangement mit den jeweiligen Regierungen zu finden und sich der öffentlichen
Unterstützung zu versichern. Öffentlichkeit ist denn auch ein wesentliches
Merkmal des internationalen Handelns in der Zwischenkriegszeit, in verschiedenen Bereichen nachzuweisen und nicht zuletzt in der deutlichen
Konkurrenz philanthropischer Stiftungen greifbar.

Die Bedeutung von Öffentlichkeit

Am Beispiel der Hungerhilfe für Russland in der unmittelbaren Nachkriegszeit wurde dieser Aspekt besonders deutlich. Der Auftritt amerikanischer
Akteure in einem von der zaristischen Herrschaft zum bolschewistischen

Staat übergehenden Land steht dabei in einem bemerkenswerten Gegensatz zu jenen Darstellungen, in denen die Nichtbeteiligung der USA am Völkerbund betont wird. Das Beispiel der russischen Hungerhilfe lässt klare Gegensätze erkennen. In der Konfrontation zwischen dem Hochkommissar für Flüchtlingsfragen Fridtjof Nansen und dem US-Präsidenten Herbert Hoover, der American Relief Administration (ARA) und der für die ARA tätigen Laura Spelman Rockefeller Memorial wurde auch deutlich, wer diesen Wettlauf der Wohltätigkeit für sich entscheiden sollte.[7] Die russische Hungerhilfe sollte nicht das einzige Beispiel bleiben, bei dem sich Stiftungen, Politiker und Staaten einen philanthropischen Wettlauf lieferten. Selbst in den späten 1930er Jahren führte der Aufruf des Völkerbundes, Cholera-Impfstoffe nach China zu liefern, zu mehr Zuwendungen, als die chinesische Regierung vernünftigerweise gebrauchen konnte.

Die Bedeutung von Öffentlichkeit offenbart sich zudem, wenn man die Unterstützung öffentlichkeitswirksamer Bereiche als eine politische Strategie begreift, derer sich internationale Organisationen bedienen konnten. Die im Beitrag von Tournès hervorgehobenen Aktivitäten zogen, wie die Radiumforschung, mediale Aufmerksamkeit auf sich, und Ähnliches lässt sich auch für deren Vertreter feststellen. Neben Albert Einstein gehörten die Curies zu den internationalen Medienstars der Zwischenkriegszeit. Ihre Geschichte schloss zwei nobelpreisgekrönte Generationen ein und wies mit dem kurzen Eintritt von Irène Joliot-Curie in die französische Volksfrontregierung einen dezidiert politischen Kontext auf. Jean Perrin gehörte mit dem Palais de la Découverte zu den wichtigen Vertretern einer öffentlichkeitsbezogenen Wissenschaftspolitik und hatte ebenfalls eine hohe Medienpräsenz. Justin Godart führte die internationale Vereinigung für die Krebsbekämpfung an, saß im ständigen Ausschuss der internationalen Konferenz für soziale Arbeit und in der internationalen Vereinigung für sozialen Fortschritt. Ähnliches lässt sich für Bronislaw Malinowski sagen. Der Anthropologe nutzte seinerseits seine internationale Bekanntheit und verwies dabei auf den Kubaner Fernando Ortiz,[8] einen der bis heute prägenden Vordenker transkultureller Verflechtung und überdies eine Persönlichkeit, welche die

---

7 Wie die Netzwerke der beteiligten Organisationen verflochten waren und wer dabei die Deutungsmacht übernahm, lässt sich aus Fishers 1927 publizierter Monografie ersehen. Der Autor erklärte die Beziehungen zwischen amerikanischem Rotem Kreuz und der ARA: das Rote Kreuz hätte nur einen Vertreter in Russland gehabt »nominated by the Red Cross, but was, of course, an official of the A.R.A. Russian unit.« Fisher, *The Famine in Soviet Russia*, 167. Für eine Übersicht zur Konfrontation von Völkerbundhilfe und amerikanischer Philanthropie vgl. Daniel R. Maul, »Appell an das Gewissen Europas – Fridtjof Nansen und die russische Hungerhilfe 1921–23«, in: Themenportal Europäische Geschichte (2011), URL: http://www.europa.clio-online.de/2011/article=519.

8 Malinowski, »Pan-African Problem«, 650.

unterschiedlichen Formen internationaler Präsenz in seiner eigenen Biografie verband: Ortiz trat als Anthropologe im wissenschaftlichen Diskurs auf, vertrat Kuba als Diplomat und prägte als Politiker die kubanische Zivilgesellschaft.

Beides, Konkurrenz und Öffentlichkeit, prägten die Geschichte der großen Stiftungen. Beide Elemente konnten für einander widersprechende Ziele instrumentalisiert werden. Öffentlichkeitswirksame Auftritte sorgten für sichtbare Alleinstellungsmerkmale und Abgrenzung gegenüber anderen forschungsfördernden Initiativen. Gleichzeitig beteiligten sich die großen Stiftungen in nahezu allen, auch nur ansatzweise bedeutenden internationalen Organisationen. Das vom Völkerbund herausgegebene *Handbook of International Organisations* vermittelt in seiner Auflage von 1938[9] eine Ahnung von der allumfassenden Präsenz philanthropischer Stiftungen – und von deren deutlicher Nähe zu Organisationen mit staatlicher oder semistaatlicher Beteiligung. Dabei lassen sich aus dem Handbuch nur formelle Mitgliedschaften herauslesen. Temporäre Engagements, persönliche Verbindungen und Kooperationen – etwa mit der mächtigen YMCA – gehen noch wesentlich weiter: Carnegie finanzierte die Haager Academie de droit international, die semioffizielle Union juridique internationale in Paris, die panamerikanische Union, war Mitglied des Joint commitee of the major international organizations, einer dem Institut de coopération internationale zugeordneten Institution. Das Endowment for Peace finanzierte Organisationen zur Unterstützung von Migranten, Museen, Völkerbundorganisationen. Die Rockefeller Stiftung hatte überdies einen deutlich globalen Fokus. Die Stiftung hatte einen lokalen Schwerpunkt in China und engagierte sich – zusammen mit der Carnegie Foundation – am Londoner Institute of African Languages and Cultures. Beide große Stiftungen waren regelmäßig bei Konferenzen des Institute of Pacific Relations vertreten. Dieser amerikanische Thinktank, der die Positionierung der USA im pazifischen Raum markierte, kann als Referenzbeispiel für die enge Kooperation zwischen den großen Organisationen und den bedeutenden amerikanischen Stiftungen zitiert werden. Noch 1943 waren bei der in Kanada abgehaltenen Konferenz des Instituts sowohl die Carnegie- als auch die Rockefeller-Stiftung neben der Internationalen Arbeitsorganisation und dem Völkerbund vertreten.[10]

9 League of Nations, *Handbook of International Organisations*.
10 The Conference of the Institute of Pacific Relations, Zum Internationalismus des Institute vgl. Akami, *Internationalizing the Pacific*.

Grenzen der Philanthropie

Ungeachtet der Medienpräsenz, des politischen Supports und ökonomischen Potenzials betonen alle drei Beiträge die mannigfaltigen Schwierigkeiten der großen Stiftungen. In Frankreich stieß die Rockefeller-Stiftung an die Grenzen der nationalen Profilierung der Wissenschaftspolitik. Auf dem europäischen Feld entfalteten zudem der europäische Antiamerikanismus und die Sprachenproblematik eine nicht zu unterschätzende Wirksamkeit. Die feine und entscheidende Balance zwischen dem Auftritt der Stiftungen als genuin amerikanische Kräfte und die Nation als Ordnungsvorstellung überwölbende, grenzübergreifende Institutionen umreißt eine Problematik, die in den Beiträgen auf verschiedenen Ebenen diagnostiziert wird. Rausch stellt die Frage nach Handlungsmacht und Ordnungskompetenz ins Zentrum ihrer Darstellung und kommt zu dem Ergebnis, dass eine wissenschaftliche Umdeutung von kolonialem Planungswissen entscheidend zum Erfolg der Rockefeller-Stiftung in der Zwischenkriegszeit beigetragen habe. Die These ist überzeugend und gewinnt nochmals an analytischer Schärfe, wenn die Zwischenkriegszeit trotz – oder besser: wegen – der nationalen Fragmentierung Europas als Phase einer intensiven Suche nach universellen Narrativen verstanden wird. Eine solche gemeinsame Basis bot zumindest in den 1920er Jahren die Zielformulierung des Völkerbundes – Friedenssicherung durch Abrüstung. Es bleibt allerdings festzuhalten, dass es sich dabei um eines von zahlreichen zeitgenössischen Narrativen handelte, das Nationalstaaten in einen von grenzübergreifenden persönlichen und institutionellen Beziehungen wohl präparierten grenzübergreifenden Kontext einzubinden versuchte. Zu sehr machten nicht zuletzt die verheerenden Folgen der Weltwirtschaftskrise auf die Gleichzeitigkeit von internationaler Durchlässigkeit und nationaler Begrenzung aufmerksam. Grenzübergreifende Plattformen waren demnach in der hier diskutierten Zeitspanne in besonderem Maße in einem Prozess des dynamischen Wandels begriffen. Die im Beitrag von Wegener ausgeführten Vorstellungen europäischer, respektive westlicher Identitätsfindung (*international mind*) wären demnach gegen neu konzipierte Imperialismen totalitärer Staaten abzugrenzen. Zwar müssen quellengesättigte Arbeiten zu diesem Thema noch geschrieben werden. Zumindest sei die These gewagt, dass die imperialen Vorstellungen an der Deutungsmacht des alten Internationalismus nicht spurlos vorüberzogen und diesen auch nicht einfach eliminierten. Vielmehr lässt sich in den 1930er Jahren eine Territorialisierung grenzübergreifender Vorstellungen nachweisen. Spezialisten für diese Form der Vernetzung kamen dabei zusehends nicht mehr aus den wohlbekannten Milieus der internationalen Juristen, der wissenschaftlichen Verbände und den Organisationen einer pazifistisch orientierten Zivilgesellschaft. Ebenso war die neu entstandene Klasse internationaler Beamter zu schwach ausgeprägt, als dass diese Gruppe ein tragfähiges Paradigma hätte entwickeln können. Imperiale Expansionspläne begünstigten in den 1930er Jahren jene, deren Erfahrungen eher auf der territorialen denn auf der ideellen Seite zu suchen waren. Die Renaissance der Kolonialbeamten in diesem Jahrzehnt ist ein interessantes Phänomen, das weiteren Überlegungen zugeführt werden sollte. Die von Rausch festgestellte professionelle Verschiebung von den Kolonialwissenschaften zur (amerikanischen) Anthropologie lässt sich im politischen Umfeld des Völkerbundes nicht minder gut dokumentieren. Die Lytton-Kommission, 1931 nach dem Einmarsch der japanischen Truppen in China vom Völkerbund mit einer Untersuchung vor Ort beauftragt, hatte in erster Linie koloniales Wissen zu bieten: Lord Lytton war über das India Office zum Vizekönig von Indien aufgestiegen, der französische Vertreter in der Kommission, Henri-Edmond Claudel, hatte Kolonialtruppen befehligt, Heinrich Schnee war als vormaliger Gouverneur in Deutsch Ost-Afrika in die Völkerbundkommission berufen worden, selbst der amerikanische Vertreter Frank Ross McCoy hatte seine militärische Karriere seiner Zeit in den Philippinen zu verdanken.[11] Der Völkerbund sollte den Richtungswechsel auch intern nachvollziehen – »the non-political achievements of the League«[12] gehörten fortan zum viel zitierten neuen Profil der Organisation, die sich vornehmlich in Bereichen der sozial-medizinischen und wirtschaftlichen Kooperation platzierte und damit in einem Bereich, den auch die großen amerikanischen Stiftungen bedienten. Planungswissen mit kolonialem Kern sollte insbesondere geeignet sein, den Übergang in die Nachkriegszeit vorzubereiten, und beweist überdies, dass die amerikanischen Stiftungen als Testfälle für die Verschiebungen grenzübergreifender Ordnungsvorstellungen überaus geeignet sind.

11 Zur Zusammensetzung der Lytton Kommission vgl. Global Politics on Screen, http://kjc-fs2.kjc.uni-heidelberg.de/omeka/the-lytton-commission---composition
12 Sweetser, »Non-Political Achievements«.

2. Constructing World Order in the Cold War

Redefining the Mission

Paul Weindling

From Disease Prevention to Population Control

The Realignment of Rockefeller Foundation Policies
in the 1920s to 1950s

The Rockefeller Foundation pioneered model schemes of disease control, prevention and surveillance in the first half of the twentieth century. The institutional basis was its International Sanitary Commission, later renamed and reorganised as its International Health Division (IHD). In 1951 the foundation abruptly closed down this division. The closure came unexpectedly and remained unexplained at the time. Those involved puzzled over the causes. Did the closure signify the foundation's disillusionment with international health activities or its disenchantment with conventional preventive medical strategies? Was this perhaps simply a successfully completed programme, meaning that it was time for the Rockefeller Foundation to move on to new challenges? The IHD had achieved much as an international sanitary organisation; it had shown what could be done through scientifically organised fieldwork and the application of laboratory-based discoveries. Governments and the new World Health Organisation (WHO) could now take over from the philanthropic pump-priming activities.[1] A new direction was needed, and population control appeared to be a field ripe for intervention. Perhaps, again, the disengagement stemmed primarily from political reasons. This was a time when the Cold War caused not just a reappraisal of foundation activities, but a realignment with US strategic and political aims. Does this dramatic internal restructuring reveal, in the final analysis, that a foundation whose inception was surrounded by political controversy was primarily driven by political goals? This article addresses these issues from a historical perspective and argues that the closure of the IHD was in fact a response to a set of internal and external factors, of which US Cold-War priorities and a new, more intimate relation with the American Administration were an important, if not decisive, consideration in the Trustees' thinking.

1 On the process of state appropriation see Picard, *La fondation Rockefeller*, 216.

1. The History of the International Health Division

The activities of corporate philanthropies in international health during
the first half of the twentieth century went against the aspirations of a liberal era of free population movement and of states concerned with minimal protection of law and order. Instead of free migration and notions of
individual opportunity, the prevalent policy became one of assistance at
the point of disease epicentres and social deprivation. The emergent welfare systems crystallising in Europe in the decade before the First World
War were a major factor in the imposing of immigration restrictions. Entitlement to benefits within a nation-state meant excluding all "aliens".
While domestically the new breed of US corporate foundations like the
Rockefeller Foundation and the smaller but innovative Milbank Memorial
Fund focused on community health, internationally foundations took a
crucial role in the framing and delivery of targeted assistance at the point
of need.

This helps to explain the paradox of an isolationist United States in the
inter-war period being notably active in the international health arena. The
social and philanthropic agendas of corporate philanthropies compensated
for sometimes fragmentary public welfare systems. Despite a weak social security provision in the United States, Federal state-imposed immigration
quotas, selection of immigrants and exclusion by means of immigration
controls and quotas intensified. These policies of exclusion reached their
culmination during the era of Nazi persecution and the Holocaust.

Foundations operated at a number of strategic levels. They provided assistance to the distressed with delivery of food and grain as well as medical
relief – notably Herbert Hoover's American Relief Administration in the Soviet famine, 1919–21. Other examples include medical and food relief in
First World War and post-First World War Europe (for example, assistance
for Serbian child welfare, an initiative closely linked to the Milbank Memorial Fund). They also worked to build up administrative capacity (for
example, the Rockefeller Foundation in Central European health departments developing public health systems). And they built research capacity
(for example, vaccines, pharmacology and neurophysiology).

The Rockefeller Foundation and the Milbank Memorial Fund were
rapidly drawn into Central and then Eastern Europe after the First World
War, remaining active until 1939. This can be seen as a state-building exer-
cise at a time when the stabilisation of Central Europe was deemed a bulwark
to containing both Germany and the Soviet Union. State public health became an area of intensive activity, initially in fledgling Czechoslovakia and
insecure Poland, but then throughout East-Central Europe from the Baltic
to the Black Sea. Hungary, although a First World War opponent, became a

favoured location for the Rockefeller Foundation.[2] Policies of relief and structural solutions to poverty and disease were accompanied by transformative socio-political agendas. The hope was that an enlightened elite of professional experts would discover solutions to poverty and disease, and if this was not forthcoming, then at least put into place effective public health systems.

The situation remained complex with the Rockefeller Foundation pursuing dual policies. On the one hand, the foundation supported a younger generation of researchers in the 1920s and major institutions for research in areas like cell biology in the 1930s. On the other hand, the International Health Board (later Division) was highly active in inter-war Central Europe but virtually absent from Germany. The IHD disliked German approaches to hygiene as being overly based on experimental medicine, contrasting a far more synthetic US idea of "public health". The low number of public health fellowships in Germany compared to Poland illustrates this.

Instead of establishing controls at borders to prevent the spread of infectious diseases, the new aim was to improve the health of total populations and to use a range of medical and social measures to promote the health of families and communities from the village to the metropolis. The founding of welfare states and health ministries at a national level coincided with a shift of international concern away from epidemics like the plague and cholera to endemic and chronic diseases with domestic and environmental implications such as malaria, tuberculosis and sexually transmitted diseases. Central hygiene institutes and peripheral health centres would constitute a scientifically more rational form of health provision. The hope was that improving overall health would contribute to social stability and international peace, as national self-determination became the basis of international relations. The new system was a means to secure a more equitable provision of health care and to improve overall levels of health for populations.

A further dimension of foundation involvement came with the Rockefeller Foundation's support for the League of Nations Health Organisation (LNHO), compensating for the American failure to join the League of Nations. By 1930, half the LNHO staff was being paid by the Rockefeller Foundation. The LNHO was directed by the dynamic Ludwik Rajchman (himself Polish), who saw opportunities for developing professional elites and public health infrastructure in Central Europe while establishing links with the US foundation. The Rockefeller Foundation was also influenced by new thinking on primary health care by the Croatian health reformer Andrija Štampar, whose organisational model called for a central state hygiene institute to oversee peripheral clinics staffed by public health nurses. Simi-

2 Weindling, "American Foundations".

larly, the Serbian co-operative policlinic or *zadruga* shaped the Milbank Memorial Fund's agenda of improving primary health care. American foundations derived much from European models of primary health care, while offering funding and innovative public health and health education models.

The Rockefeller Foundation tried to replace German medical influence in countries like Bulgaria and Greece with an American style of public health oriented more toward the community and less toward experimental biology. The International Health Board helped establish schools of public health in Czechoslovakia (1920), Poland (1921) and Hungary (1925). The foundations in turn guided and supported the LNHO programmes for interchanges, conferences and medical statistics.[3] LNHO and Rockefeller Foundation officers shared the progressive view that private medical practice was a barrier to improving health care.[4] In this sense, the foundations took a markedly different socio-political view to prevalent free-market notions of unregulated professionals.

The LNHO worked primarily at an expert level, seeking to disseminate knowledge among public health professionals on methods for raising standards and spreading best practice. This placed public health in the hands of a technocratic elite, many (but not all) of whom were left-leaning and impatient of political restrictions from national public health administrations. As a consequence, new states and medical reformers looked to the LNHO for guidelines on public health provision. The result was a dynamic system of interchanges among public health personnel from 1922 onwards, statistical monitoring of morbidity and mortality to enable comparisons between countries, as well as a steady flow of publications on health services.

It was not simply a question of dollars paying for public health initiatives in the economically fragile successor states: US public health reformers toyed with the idea of adapting European health care and social security in homespun American terms. We see this with figures like Charles Winslow, professor of public health at Yale who visited Russia in 1917, where he was impressed with the *zemstvo* community-based health care. Similarly, Alan Gregg of the Rockefeller Foundation struck up a fruitful dialogue with Štampar while undertaking surveys of European health starting in 1921. Such contacts reinforced optimistic views on the community-building role of public health and the preventive value of health education, providing American resources for European schemes. Europeans and Americans established health demonstration units. The idea was to show how policlinics and socialised health care could reduce the rates of social diseases like tuberculosis. As a re-

3 Weindling, "Philanthropy and World Health"; idem, "Public Health and Political Stabilisation".
4 Fee, *Disease and Discovery*, 228.

sult, ideas on primary health care were dynamic, and significant initiatives were undertaken on rural health, housing and nutrition. The Rockefeller Foundation additionally supported medical research, schools of hygiene as well as public health nursing in Central Europe.

The Rockefeller Foundation supported LNHO interchanges of public health personnel to visit model sanitary and medical schemes. Interchanges covered – for example – visits to Piraeus and Salonika in December 1925 as part of a study of Mediterranean port hygiene. Additionally, the foundation gave funds for public health and nurse training fellowships; again, Greek public health personnel were the beneficiaries. The model was based on regional institutes, each the focus of a network of dispensaries and staffed by public health nurses. In 1931, the Rockefeller Foundation financed the School of Public Health Nursing within the Athens School of Hygiene.

Despite the deteriorating economic and political situation in the 1930s, the Rockefeller Foundation and the LNHO undertook important initiatives in social medicine. A conference was held on malnutrition due to the Depression. The Milbank Memorial Fund defrayed the costs of American delegates to the conference, which was held in Berlin in a last democratic gasp in December 1932.[5] The LNHO sought to lay down minimal dietary requirements as well as optimal standards for different age groups and occupations. The circumstances of the Depression revealed the social potential of international standards at a time of malnutrition due to unemployment. Biochemists calculated nutritional standards by which the individual food factors that make up a healthy diet were identified as well as the quantity in which they were required. Conferences on vitamin standards, held in London during June 1931 and June 1934, publicised standard units for vitamins A, B_1, C and D.[6] By the early 1930s Rajchman was sponsoring programmes on a broad range of social factors affecting health, such as diet, occupation, unemployment and housing.[7]

"Positive health" and ideas of economic determinants of health now shaped an innovative agenda. The emphasis was on health indices, housing, unemployment and nutrition. Support continued from the Rockefeller Foundation, which gave the LNHO autonomy from the politically fragile

5 Library of Congress, Kingsbury Papers II: 23 Welch to Kingsbury, 21 November 1932.

6 "Report of the Inter-governmental Conference on Biological Standardisation", *Bulletin of the Health Organisation of the League of Nations* IV (1935). LN Archives, Geneva, R 6078–9 concerning standardisation of vitamins.

7 Research Publications LN Documents, Spool 3:9, Work of the Health Committee at its 19th Session, Geneva, 10–15 October 1932. ILO Hy 200, Hy 200/2/2 Collaboration of the ILO and League of Nations.

League of Nations. A wide range of social contexts were an object of concern: industrial cities, ports as well as rural areas and villages, and there was a new endeavour to measure health within the community.

Beginning in 1928, the Greek Government invited the LNHO to conduct a morbidity survey and to advise on the training of health personnel. The LNHO recommended a total reorganisation of Greek public health and a new permanent Hellenic health service. As a start, surveys were carried out in Athens and Salonika. By 1930 the Rockefeller Foundation was assisting the Greek government with the development of a division of malariology. In the same year Greece invited the LNHO to submit plans for the reorganisation of public health services. Julius Tandler, politically radical and as such dismissed as director of the municipal health administration of Vienna, was commissioned by the LNHO to draw up a plan for the health services of the Athens–Piraeus area. The League of Nations gave scholarships to five Greek medical officers to study health administration, and the Rockefeller Foundation supported a scheme for a model health centre.[8] Other displaced public health officials such as Gustavo Pittaluga and Marcelino Pascua from Spain also worked for the LNHO. The Rockefeller grants enabled an ambitious programme on the social bases of disease. The culmination of the internationalisation of the health demonstrations came in 1935–36 with the scheme of "health indices" (a term coined by Rajchman) as a simplified form of the "health appraisal" system used in US health demonstrations and in City and Rural Health Conservation Contests first held in 1929. The aim of the health indices was to measure community health and the associated environmental and administrative factors.[9] The eleven headings ran from population to examinations of physical fitness. After an initial trial in New Haven (CT), the indices were applied in a rural district of eastern Hungary in 1937 and in Poland. In October 1938 a group of experts endorsed the value of indices as an international standard. The idea was that, after careful measurement of the epidemiological and demographic conditions as well as an understanding of human psychology, radical health reform was achievable. The new ideal of social medicine was based on nutrition and sanitary housing. In 1935, the Rockefeller Foundation supported local health departments in Albania, Hungary, Romania, Spain, Greece and Turkey. The Ambelokipi Health Centre opened in 1935 with funding from the Rockefeller Foundation supplementing municipal and state support. It was a model scheme designed by Tandler, with clinics for prenatal, infant, pre-school and dental hygiene, tuberculosis, syphilis and vaccination, while it also served as

8 Cf. Giannuli, "Repeated Disappointment".
9 Stouman/Falk, "Health Indices".

a training school.[10] The scheme shows efforts to transfer best practice from one location to another.

US foundations continued to fund academic initiatives in Germany after 1933, albeit at a reduced level. The ethos remained that of aid *in situ*, as advice to persecuted academics was to stay in place. The amount eventually granted to displaced scholars was less than that for major schemes under National Socialism (there was large-scale funding for racial research from 1930 to 1935, and for the Kaiser Wilhelm Institutes).

The late entry of the United States into the Second World War allowed the Rockefeller Foundation to keep its Paris office open even under German occupation. The IHD mounted an expedition to Vichy France with the ultimate aim of contacting public health officials in Berlin. These initiatives were eventually curtailed by the political realism of the foundation director late in 1941, but they indicate a sense that the foundation was willing to hedge its bets on the eventual victorious power in Europe. At the same time, the foundations supported dynamic disease control measures on the Allied side with DDT and penicillin.

There was a brief phase of Rockefeller Foundation activity in Eastern Europe immediately after the Second World War which was concerned with distribution of medicines and supplies of DDT for epidemic prevention. The Rockefeller Foundation Director still had a "one world" mentality with the notion of a world government by experts. At the same time, foundation officers, notably Medical Sciences Programme Officer Alan Gregg and Physical Sciences Officer Warren Weaver, blocked and prevaricated over any funding in Germany. Despite John D. Rockefeller III's pressing for such an initiative, Gregg preferred funding for critical dissidents like the advocate of psychosomatic medicine (and observer at the Nuremberg Medical Trial) Alexander Mitscherlich. UNESCO favoured support for the returned sociologist Max Horkheimer and the Frankfurt Institute for Social Research – something the academic traditionalists subverted. Analyses of international initiatives in the Federal Republic, for example, the UNESCO institutes for youth, education and social research in the early 1950s, show traditionally minded German elites resisting any challenges to professorial power and biologistic thinking from the pre-1945 era.[11] Adjustment to Cold-War realities was slow, as US occupation authorities found the Rockefeller Foundation cautious over renewing its German funding.

10 *The Rockefeller Foundation Annual Report* (1936), 118–119.
11 See my case study of the UNESCO institutes, Weindling, *John Thompson*, Chapters 12–13.

2. Structure and Function

The reasons for terminating the IHD provide a means of examining the structure, social interests and organisational components of the Rockefeller Foundation. Given that its historiography has long been dominated by such issues as whether it was shaped by monopoly capitalism, US strategic interests or strategies of social modernisation, examining a major policy change at a time of political change reveals much about the historical factors that shaped organisation and policy. There are several possible explanations for the ending of the IHD. John Farley, in his history of the IHD, points to post-Second World War concerns with the rigidity of the division's organisation, its heavy financial cost and its lack of innovative policies.[12] Others saw the IHD as successful in the past but now superfluous. The IHD had adopted a disease-specific approach: from the campaign against hookworm to ambitious programmes against yellow fever and malaria it had targeted individual diseases. In the late 1940s there was a growing sense of unease that the disease-specific model was naive and itself antiquated.[13] Novel approaches such as population control appeared more attractive. The IHD was taking on innovative roles by aiding state and local health services as well as professional public health education. These tasks could be viewed as pump-priming, and they were being taken over by state and public bodies. But the IHD had remained innovative, not least during the Second World War when new disease eradication strategies (peculiarly with DDT) were being tested. In its final phase the IHD was examining the organisation and costs of medical care.[14] At a time of socialisation of health services and incipient Communism, this socio-economic approach appeared too radical. Could the IHD have been a casualty of the Cold War?

It is certainly possible to interpret the closure in terms of the inner administrative momentum of the foundation. John D. Rockefeller, Sen.'s early interest in the Rockefeller Sanitary Commission preceded the formal organisation of the foundation in 1913. At first, there was an International Health Board, which formed a coherent administrative division for international sanitary interventions. In 1927, the Rockefeller Foundation organised administrative divisions on a subject basis: for the natural sciences, social sciences, humanities and medical sciences. The Rockefeller Foundation reorganised its haphazard portfolio of philanthropic initiatives (such as the General Education Board) into a subject-oriented and project-driven

---

12 Farley, *To Cast Out Disease*, 278–280.
13 Rockefeller Archive Center (RAC) RF RG3/SER 908/BOX 15 Series of files on past IHD/IHB policies and programmes – disease specific since inception.
14 RAC RF 3/920/1/3 Andrew Warren, The Program in Medicine and Public Health.

agency. Its move from endowments (as for the Schools of Public Health) to projects represented a switch to a more managed approach. At this point the International Health Board became the International Health Division, though it retained substantive autonomy.

Medicine fell into two organisational structures: the IHD, oriented to fieldwork, and the laboratory-based Medical Sciences Programme under the mercurial Programme Officer Alan Gregg. In fact, the IHD vacillated between laboratory-based research with its central laboratory in metropolitan New York and sanitary measures on the global peripheries, while the Rockefeller Foundation's Medical Sciences Division had an interest in clinical research, best practice in the organisation of health care and virology. These overlapping interests meant that the division between field and laboratory was never immutable.

Why then was the administrative division between the IHD and the Medical Sciences Division allowed to continue on into the 1940s? The Rockefeller Foundation found that its staff of field officers were an immensely valuable asset. They knew the local public health circumstances, the health problems and the governmental agencies of each geographical theatre of application – such as the Far East, Brazil and India. The Second World War had demonstrated the importance of new discoveries like penicillin, and the Rockefeller Foundation had taken a hand in supporting war-time emergency projects. Another new factor was that the US Federal Government increasingly recognised a responsibility for public health research and implementation. It was always implicit in the foundation's aims that widespread success could render the international health programme redundant.[15]

During the inter-war period the Rockefeller Foundation's global interventions stood in marked contrast to American isolationism. The foundation always denied that it was in any way tied to US government policies. After all, it had pursued global philanthropy in the 1920s and 1930s at a time of US isolationism, notably subsidising the League of Nations Health Organisation for an imaginative international health programme when the United States was not even a member of the League.[16] When the Second World War ended, there were expectations of a return to the inter-war political arrangements of an isolationist United States and an inward-looking Soviet Union. This would have allowed the Rockefeller Foundation to operate in what was in effect a politically neutral sphere of world health. Yet post-war reactions to the aftermath of war and the incipient Soviet menace meant that it was unrealistic to revert to the inter-war "one world" aspirations. Rockefeller Foun-

15 RAC RF 3/908/12/127 W. A. Sawyer, Program of the International Health Division, 1 December 1943.
16 Weindling, "Philanthropy and World Health".

dation Programme Officers like Gregg and Weaver had a distaste for the German scientists they had once backed with such confidence.[17] The war record showed how human lives had been brutally exploited by German medical and physical scientists.[18]

The war had also seen a massive transfusion of economic, military and medical assistance for the Soviet Union. The Rockefeller Foundation had sponsored tours by Soviet medical experts on infectious diseases.[19] There had always been an element of reserve and suspicion on both sides[20], and Soviet scientists had to be circumspect given Stalin's murdering of scientists like the plant geneticist Nikolai Vavilov. Nonetheless, in 1945 the venerable Rockefeller Foundation President Raymond Fosdick still nurtured visions of "world government"; he thought in terms of a benign regime of academic visionaries and experts solving problems around the world while providing intellectual and moral leadership.[21] But Fosdick was close to retirement, and the "one world" rapidly fragmented into two irreconcilable political camps with antagonistic values and political agendas. The political exigencies of an increasingly polarised world order meant that intellectuals had to develop agendas within the ideological parameters of one or the other camp. No sphere of academic or intellectual activity was immune to political mobilisation, and international health became subject to new orthodoxies. It meant that the Rockefeller Foundation, in the space of a few years, would fundamentally reappraise, restructure and reduce its international health programme. Even so, these seismic political shifts took the international public health community, which saw rational arguments for some form of collective organisation, by surprise.

The Second World War had already precipitated profound shifts in American policy. Medical scientists were divided over American entry into the war. While physiologists with strong British ties such as John Fulton of Yale lobbied for the United States to enter the war, others supported the America First movement. During the 1930s, the Rockefeller Foundation had responded weakly to Nazism and the refugee crisis by only gradually reducing funding to Nazi Germany and offering all too limited assistance for displaced scholars.[22] The IHD retained Eugen Haagen, seconded from the Reich Health Office to learn techniques in virology from 1930 to 1934, al-

17 Idem, "The Rockefeller Foundation and German Biomedical Science".
18 Idem, "Out of the Ghetto".
19 Idem, *Epidemics and Genocide in Eastern Europe*.
20 Solomon/Krementsov, "Giving and Taking across Borders".
21 RAC RF 1.1/10/22/185 TBK to SHW, 8 May 1939, on the League of Nations as an experiment in world government.
22 Weindling, "An Overloaded Ark?".

though Haagen fulsomely expressed his Nazi sympathies.[23] At the outbreak of war in 1939 the Rockefeller Foundation still appeared to be keeping its options open in the event of a possible Axis victory. The foundation retained its office in German-occupied Paris, closing it only upon the United States' entry into the war in November 1941. Rockefeller Foundation officers like Daniel O'Brien appeared disengaged, if not antipathetic, toward refugee medical scientists, and for a time the IHD retained links to Vichy France and extraordinarily contemplated a programme in German-occupied Europe.[24] This reluctance to become embroiled in global conflict in 1941 was abandoned after the war as policies of international reconstruction rapidly became caught up in the emerging Cold-War agendas in defence of Western liberties. For administrative, legal and ideological reasons, the Rockefeller Foundation conformed to Cold-War exigencies. It became uneasy about having funded left-wing scientists like the crystallographer John Desmond Bernal. But this applied to the level of small-scale projects; the question is whether the terminating of the IHD was in any way a response to the Cold War. Just as the Rockefeller Foundation did not conform to the dictates of isolationism in the inter-war period, after the Second World War it did not fall in with incipient anti-Communism. It is necessary to read post-Second World War history rather differently than the political analysts; intellectuals could be seen as a Third Force of dispassionate world leaders.

3. The Immediate Post-Second World War Period

During the Second World War there was every reason to believe that the foundation's pre-war concerns with public health and preventive medicine would soon be resumed with renewed vigour. In 1944, the IHD official John B. Grant was commissioned to study the provision of medical care on a universal basis. He secured the agreement that the IHD had neglected socio-economic factors in public health. He reported to the Scientific Directors of the Rockefeller Foundation Divisions in September 1946, taking a judicious social-scientific approach to the politically controversial issue of medical care. In 1946, the Rockefeller Foundation declared its interest in promoting an analysis of the costs of health care – an initiative pointing towards some form of welfare state. In September 1948, Grant continued to see major opportunities for the foundation to fund social and community medicine in Europe while urging that programmes on specific diseases be terminated. He recommended major assistance to the Iron-Curtain countries by suppor-

---

23 Idem, "The Extraordinary Career of the Virologist Eugen Haagen".
24 Schneider, "War, Philanthropy, and the Creation".

ting schools of public health, developing public-health engineering and continuing the training of public health nurses.[25] The IHD officer Johannes
Bauer also favoured funding from the Rockefeller Foundation in Eastern Europe and – especially for maternal and child health – in the Soviet Union in
July 1948.[26] The response from the IHD Director George Strode was that the
programme was too "far-reaching".[27] Grant's progressive initiatives thus ar-
oused opposition from within the IHD, as well as opposition for political
reasons, given the fact that the American medical leaders equated socialised
medicine with socialism.

The foundation contemplated pilot experiments analogous to its support
for inter-war health demonstrations. These were model projects to evaluate
community health and the costs of medical care.[28] Grant pressed the urgency
of the issue of modernising the current haphazard arrangements for financ-
ing health care on into the 1950s. The invasion of Korea by Red China
prompted him to raise the implications of Rockefeller Foundation policy:
"Has the action of the Chinese communists influenced our [the Rockefeller
Foundation's] conscious thinking and planning …?" He saw that government had to shift from welfare to military expenditure, and that the political
stability was no longer present for a major new initiative on the costs of
medical care.[29] He nonetheless remained convinced that integrating preventive and curative medical services was required in some form.[30] It no longer
looked feasible to transform the IHD's disease-specific policies wholesale
into one focused on securing an extension of providing medical care. But
pilot schemes remained possible and ran counter to Farley's stress on administrative rigidity. One notable scheme, which also manifested a commitment to funding without racial bias, involved support for social medicine at
the Durban Department of Family Practice in South Africa. Grant continued to identify demonstration schemes for support until the mid-1950s.[31]

Before the United States' entry into the Second World War, Rockefeller
Foundation officers were generally welcomed, as they sought out innovative
thinking in public health the world over and financed ambitious disease-
control programmes. At times they even ventured into the Soviet Union,
where Alan Gregg noted the vigorous research and efforts to deliver a system

25 RAC RF 3/908/12/127 Grant to Strode, 8 September 1948 and Report. RAC
RF 3/900/25/193, 17 June 1946. IHD European Policy. Comments on Memorandum of Dr
Grant. Strode's diary has a final entry on 30 April 1951.
26 RAC RF 5/1/6/53 pp. 21–3.
27 RAC RF 3/908/12/127 Strode to Grant, 14 September 1948.
28 Weindling, "From Moral Exhortation to Socialised Primary Care".
29 RAC RF 3/900/25/194 Warren to Grant, 3 January 1951.
30 RAC RF 3/900/25/193.
31 Marks, "Doctors and the State".

of medical care to all sectors of society.[32] Yet the situation after the war was politically tense. In addition to McCarthyite witch-hunting for "un-American" thought, by August 1950 some foundation officers thought a new world war was immanent.[33] In the background was a changed mood among the Trustees. Whereas in the inter-war period the Rockefeller Foundation had pursued policies that were decisively at variance with the prevailing isolationism in foreign policy, after 1945 the Trustees sought to establish links with the US State Department. John Foster Dulles provided the key link, and his move from the State Department to becoming President of the Rockefeller Foundation was already a prospect when Chester Barnard was appointed foundation President in 1948.

Table: Rockefeller Foundation organisational Structures

Division/ Programme	Director	Length of Service	Period
International Health Division (IHD)	Russell/ Sawyer/ Strode	4/1/27–8/31/35	2/23/27–4/30/51
Medical Sciences	Pearce/ Gregg	1/3/29–2/16/30	1/3/29–4/30/51
Division of Medicine and Public Health	Strode/ Warren	5/1/51–5/31/51	5/1/51–4/5/55
Biological and Medical Research	Morison	4/6/55–3/31/59	4/6/55–3/31/59
Medical Education and Public Health	Bugher	4/6/55–3/31/59	4/6/55–3/31/59
Medical and Natural Sciences	Morison/ Weir	4/1/59–9/30/64	4/1/59–5/21/70
Biomedical Sciences	Weir	10/1/64–5/21/70	

4. The Arrival of Chester Barnard

The appointment of Barnard as Director of the Rockefeller Foundation to succeed Fosdick in July 1948 signalled a fundamental reappraisal of the foundation's substantial commitment to international health work. Barnard's experience at the New Jersey Bell Telephone Company and AT&T meant that he had a very different background and outlook than the one-world idealism

32 Solomon/Krementsov, "Giving and Taking across Borders"; Solomon, "Through a Glass Darkly".
33 RAC RF 3/908/12/127 Strode to K.C. Smithburn, 23 August 1950.

of Fosdick. Barnard had distinguished himself as a philosopher of corporate management, believing that organisations had to be fully integrated to sustain their viability.[34] He looked for programmes to sustain effective action while questioning the lack of impact of social science on social life.

By February 1949 the foundation was in the throes of a major evaluation of its policies, and the IHD came under close scrutiny. In March 1950, Barnard requested that scientific consultants and the Rockefeller Foundation Trustees make a fundamental review of the role of the IHD, a task completed by June 1951. He took the view that the previous system of the IHD receiving an annual block grant gave it too great an autonomy, and he scaled down its Board of Scientific Directors into a Board of Scientific Consultants.[35] Ironically, the expansion of public health beyond the prevention of specific diseases signalled the division's demise. Public health experts were asked to reconsider the IHD's potential for promoting improved health compared to other disciplines (notably nutrition and sciences concerned with human reproduction and population growth) and whether it was now an anomaly.

The Commission on Review of IHD was established on 26 April 1950 and first met on 19 May 1950. There were five IHD consultants (Fair, Halverson, Maxcy, Morgan and Parran) and four Rockefeller Foundation Trustees in addition to the Rockefeller Foundation Division Directors Gregg, Weaver and Willits. Barnard – significantly – added John D. Rockefeller III, who three years before had ignited enthusiasm on the Board for a general "ecological" approach – ecology being a euphemism for the sensitive issue of population control.[36] All commission members had previous IHD or Rockefeller Foundation experience with the exception of the Director of the Conservation Foundation Henry Fairfield Osborn Jr., who tellingly was a noted advocate of eugenics.[37] The idea gained currency that Medical Sciences and the International Health Division should be combined into a single organisation as best placed to promote "human ecology". The term bore the fingerprint of John D. Rockefeller III, indicating how radical agendas of population control were exploiting the issue of restructuring. The view that sanitary interventions were irresponsibly supporting excess population growth was a factor.[38]

In organisational terms the IHD was presented as an anomaly: It was an operating division rather than primarily a grant-dispersal agency, and it had

34 Barnard, *The Functions of the Executive*.
35 RAC RF 3/908/13/140 Chester Barnard, Memorandum to IHD Staff at Home and Abroad, 13 April 1950.
36 RAC RF 3/908/13/140 Barnard to Dean Fair, 25 April 1950.
37 RAC RF 3/908/13/140 Meeting on Review of IHD, 19 May 1950. Regal, *Henry Fairfield Osborn*.
38 RAC RF 3/920/1/3 Consideration of the Future, on Marston Bates of the IHD as Special Assistant to the Director to advise on human ecology.

its own board of directors.[39] The IHD was deemed costly at a time when Barnard saw the foundation as having diminishing resources, while state support for international health training, research and implementation was rising. The dropping of the atomic bomb had shown the strategic necessity of health monitoring work. What was not taken into account was that the IHD personnel exercised considerable influence and expertise in shaping policies in certain countries as well as taking the role of international advisors.

The Review Commission formed the opinion that a central IHD aim of initiating permanent government public health agencies could be regarded as largely fulfilled by 1949. Noting that a third of the IHD's budget was spent on its field offices, it was decided to retain only a small field staff resident in foreign countries. The commission recommended the fusion of the IHD and Medical Sciences in a unified Division of Medicine and Public Health. This retained support for medical education, medical care (to include field demonstrations) and the epidemiology of virus diseases. The division added to its agenda new initiatives in population control – here John D. Rockefeller III was again successful – as "human ecology". The expectation was of creating a new type of linkage between preventive and curative medicine. By way of contrast, IHD officials tended to take a retrospective view of restricting activities to areas of proven success. Henry Carr, based in the Dominican Republic, ventured to suggest that the Rockefeller Foundation should return to hookworm prevention.[40]

The Review Commission convened committees for policy, programme and finance. In April 1951, before the commission had delivered its final report, the Rockefeller Foundation Trustees summarily announced that they had decided to form a new Division of Medicine and Public Health. Robert S. Morison admitted that "very few of us really know what was in the Trustees' minds when they took the decision". Unfortunately, archival records at the level of the Trustees remain sparse. Morison decided to give the momentous decision a positive spin – as an opportunity to combine preventive and curative medicine.[41] Officers of the foundation hailed it as "the great rapprochement" and set to work considering the implications. Morison optimistically commented: "I think the new arrangement gives us all a chance to do something really original in the way of integrating preventive and curative medicine."[42] The linkage of research and practical outcomes accorded with Barnard's practically oriented outlook.

39 RAC RF 3/908/12/129 Edwin Wilson to Barnard 26 February 1950; 3/908/13/140 Barnard memo 13 April 1950.
40 RAC RF 3/908/14/148 Carr to Strode, 1 June 1950.
41 RAC RF 3/920/1/1 Morison note, 11 May 1951.
42 RAC RF 3/ 920/1/1 Morison, 6 April 1951.

A final session of the full commission took place on 29 June 1951, giving the commission's report a sense of retrospective legitimation: "The Commission arrived at the opinion that the International Health Division and Medical Sciences could be administered advantageously as a combined division, which is in accord with action by the Trustees in April 1951. The view is expressed that the medical interests of the Foundation should be redirected more adequately towards medical education." The report highlighted the urgency of population growth in relation to resources. The second section of the report, "Consideration of the Future", looked to a broader intellectual basis facilitated by combining the two divisions to allow for the funding of "human ecology".[43] On 1 November 1951 the commission transmitted its report to President Barnard.[44]

There were also incidental factors militating in favour of change, including financial constraints with a substantial fall in the value of the dollar as well as generational change among the Rockefeller Foundation's programme officers, who were now reaching the age of retirement. At the senior level came the retirement of the IHD Director, George K. Strode, who had been on the foundation staff from 1916 to 1951, and of Lewis Hackett, whose career with the foundation spanned the years 1914 to 1949. Alan Gregg, employed by the foundation since 1919 and the highly respected Director of the Medical Sciences Division since 1931, was elected Vice-President of the foundation until his retirement in 1956.

5. The New Emphasis on Population Control

The new Division of Medicine and Public Health came under the auspices of Andrew J. Warren, formerly an Associate Director of the IHD. Grant kept the community-based social medicine programme alive, but the costly IHD regional offices were dispensed with. The changes implemented before the final report of the review body suggest that Barnard, in association with the Trustees, had already decided on the restructuring. Rather than retaining its own staff for applying new innovations as in the IHD, the foundation's restructuring gave it a central role in what was considered a "free enterprise community" of academic grant holders.[45]

The momentum for change gathered force with a board of scientific consultants reappraising all of the foundation's programmes. Whereas in April

---

43 RAC RF 3/920/1/3 Gordon M. Fair to Barnard, 1 November 1951.
44 RAC RF 3/920/1/3 letter of transmittal, 1 November 1951 by G. M. Fair. Farley, *To Cast Out Disease*, 280.
45 RAC RF 3/900/25/198 Grant, Medical Care Program, 2 August 1952.

1949 Barnard had envisaged the restructuring to take several years, in fact major changes were accomplished in the space of a year the.[46] From the outset Barnard stressed population studies (along with communication and cooperation) as one of the three major sectors of foundation policy. He was attracted by the opportunity of subsuming public health into "human ecology". He regarded agriculture and population control as underdeveloped areas of immense significance for the welfare of mankind. He was responding in part to John D. Rockefeller III's personal interest in population control and in part to how the innovative Milbank Memorial Fund was moving out of public health work and concentrating on population and development. Cold-War concerns with population increase in areas of incipient Communism provided a political incentive for such a shift.

Warren canvassed suggestions from programme officers in December 1951. From within the division came internal criticism such as that from Robert R. Struthers, its Assistant Director.[47] Population was an area gaining increasing support, as indicated by John D. Rockefeller III's establishing the Population Council in 1952 as an independent non-profit organisation, presided over by the eugenicist Frederick Osborn.[48] The final report highlighted "Promotion of the Health Sciences", which meant population control measures. The idea was that existing programmes within Medical Sciences in the physiology of sex and in human genetics as well as within the IHD in human ecology would create expanded support for research on population problems.[49] Other areas that the new combined division was to cover included field and laboratory study of viruses, studies and experiments in medical care, human ecology, educational aspects of public health and preventive medicine.[50]

The Rockefeller Foundation was supposed to disengage from areas such as malaria control and the teaching of psychiatry. Instead, a programme was formulated around mental illness, human genetics and virology on the scientific side, and health care studies, professional education and population control on the applied side. The Division of Medicine and Public Health was again reappraised in 1955. The appointment of directors for Medical Education and Public Health and for Biological and Medical Research meant that the division was split once again. The brief life of the reconstituted division suggests that a single combined entity had been unwieldy.

46 RAC RF3/908/13/140 Barnard to IHD staff.
47 RAC RF 3/920/1/1 Struthers to Warren, 9 January 1952.
48 Connelly, *Fatal Misconception*; Weindling, "Modernising Eugenics".
49 RAC RF 3/920/1/1 memorandum, 11 April 1951.
50 RAC RF 3/920/1/1 Gregg to Esther E. Lape, 24 May 1951.

6. Cold-War Climate

The question arises as to the impact of the intensifying Cold War on the re-structuring. President Barnard stated explicitly in his memorandum of 13 April 1950 that the IHD enjoyed too great an autonomy in view of the uncertain economic and political conditions. His highlighting of the political significance of the Rockefeller Foundation's activities suggests a wish to impose conformity onto the reorganised division. He cited changed "political conditions especially as they affect the geographical scope of the work" as a major reason for terminating the autonomy of the IHD.[51] At the opening meeting of the Commission on Review, Barnard cited how "The world is undergoing radical changes, some of which result from the cold war; for example RF operations in China have terminated, our influence behind the curtain is largely curtailed, the office in Argentina has been closed."[52] The final report reiterated the requirement of responding to the "background of world conditions".[53] There was a shift away from economic to technically based programmes as Socrates Litsios has suggested for malaria.[54]

The Cold-War realism of Barnard as foundation President was strongly endorsed among the Trustees, since the previous Rockefeller Foundation President Fosdick's efforts to sustain funding in a war-ravaged Eastern Europe appeared hopelessly idealistic. National security was increasingly thrust onto the foundation's agenda: the President's *Report for 1949* opened with a statement on the Iron Curtain.

The Cold War saw a generation of Rockefeller Foundation Trustees involved in US foreign policy, notably the ambitious and politically malleable John McCloy (who returned as Trustee after serving as High Commissioner for Germany), Dean Rusk (a State Department official, Rockefeller Foundation Trustee from April 1950, then President of the foundation from July 1952) and John Foster Dulles (Secretary of State from 1953). All were noted Cold Warriors.[55] Following Barnard's considering the possibility of an ethics programme, Dulles strongly favoured a programme concerned with moral development in 1951. Ethics and international relations came onto the foundation's agenda.[56] International and intercultural studies, the strengthening of American national life and scientific research in human behaviour were new targets. In medical terms these were translated into problems of behav-

51 RAC RF 3/908/13/140 Chester Barnard, Memorandum to IHD Staff at Home and Abroad, 13 April 1950.
52 RAC RF 3/908/13/140 First Meeting of the Commission on Review of the IHD.
53 RAC RF 3/920/1/3 Letter of Transmittal.
54 Litsios, "Malaria Control".
55 Picard, *La fondation Rockefeller*, 212–3.
56 RAC RF 6.3.2/900/56/304.

iour, brain chemistry and human genetics.[57] The idea was to provide rationales for a free society.

In line with these shifts, John D. Rockefeller III combined with Rockefeller Foundation President Barnard and other Trustees to support an interdisciplinary agenda for population studies. Hitherto the Rockefeller Foundation's support for eugenics and birth control had existed only on a fragmented and sporadic basis.[58] John D. Rockefeller III had already campaigned for attention to the problem of population in the Far East. The outcome was a combined IHD and Social Sciences Division report on "Public Health and Demography in the Far East" in 1948. The *Annual Report of the Rockefeller Foundation for 1949* flagged up the centrality of population. By 1951 it was recognised that all divisions had a common potential focus on population growth.[59] By December 1953 the foundation was able to provide a coherent statement of its activities in the context of a world torn between totalitarianism and liberty.[60] The foundation identified its interests as food supply, population and reproduction, basic biomedical science and the provision of medical care, which it set within a Cold-War political discourse oriented towards drug research and population control and coming together in the contraceptive pill. One might see the foundation as generating a new form of "Cold-War medicine" with population control at its centre.

The Cold War elicited defensiveness among foundation officers, who were keen to demonstrate the rectitude of foundation principles concerning making grants without reference to race or politics. The foundation was indignant over accusations (as in the case of its funding in Greece) that it was an arm of US imperialism. There was the embarrassment that it might be subject to fiscal penalties for having violated federal legislation in funding Russian scientists as well as for supporting the research of celebrated political radicals like the left-wing British crystallographer John Desmond Bernal.[61]

The IHD reviewed its policy about Iron-Curtain countries in 1948, favouring caution. Between 1948 and 1958 the foundation had to draw up policies on how to deal with Communist scientists and countries. It was under some pressure to do so – the fiscal penalties imposed by Congress were much feared, and no officer wanted a particular programme to collapse because of one "injudicious" grant. By 1951 the Rockefeller Foundation had prioritised the issue of national security, believing that it faced an insidious

57 RAC RF 3/920/1/2 Notes on the Rockefeller Foundation Program, 1 December 1953.
58 Weindling, "Modernising Eugenics".
59 RAC RF 3/920/1/3 Consideration of the Future, p. 33.
60 RAC RF 3.1/920/1/2 Notes on RF Program, 1 December 1953.
61 RAC RF 3/900/25/201 Lindsley F. Kimball, The Rockefeller Foundation Vis A Vis National Security, 19 November 1951.

international enemy. The foundation was believed to be donating unwittingly to enemies of the country or "is itself fuzzy-minded, unrealistic, and even pinkishly inclined". The foundation officer Kimball feared Communist infiltration throughout American administrative and scholarly institutions. He pointed to the Rockefeller Foundation fellowships awarded in the past to known Communists and stated that this could not happen in the future. A major concern was that the Rockefeller Foundation could lose its tax-exempt status.[62]

Not only did the Rockefeller Foundation fear fiscal penalties, it also felt obliged to develop positive policies to underpin Western cultural values. The President and Trustees shared an interest in developing new programmes of morals and ethics as an antidote to Communism. The idea was that Western civilisation required a positive restatement of core values. This was something that had already been preoccupying a growing flock of academics and intellectuals, for example at UNESCO; one instance was the Rockefeller Foundation's support for the poet and cultural critic Stephen Spender at Sarah Lawrence College.[63] Seen in the light of these new political priorities, public health work appeared costly and out of step with the needs of the times.

7. Conclusions

The insightful Alan Gregg reflected on the fusion of the IHD and the Medical Sciences Division: "[T]he personal and adventitious seem to me to have entered into what foundations actually do rather more than historians realise. By so much as foundations try to keep up with change in society they are changeable and in some measure therefore unpredictable."[64] Gregg's analysis can be read as indicating a political shift among the Director and Trustees rather than any internal logic of administrative rationalisation or demonstrable scientific needs. The decision to wind up the IHD provides a revealing insight into foundation structures and the policy-making process. The one-year basis of staff appointments meant that the foundation always had the potential for radical change of policy, but it had rarely made use of this option. Traditionally, programme officers exercised considerable discretion, but always in the shadow of what the Trustees and Director might tolerate. The Trustees emerged as strongly interventive, overriding the programme

---

62 RAC RF 3/900/25/201 Kimball, National Security, 19 November 1951.
63 RAC RF 1.1/ 200/280/13337 Stephen Spender, J. Marshall memo, 25 November 1946. RG 3.2 Box 56 Morals and Ethics 1946–53.
64 RAC RF 3/920/1/1 Alan Gregg to Esther Everett Lape, 24 May 1951.

officers who had outlined and defended the achievements of the IHD. The Trustees became convinced of generational factors, a sense of a completed programme and increasing pressures for interventions in population and nutrition. Overall, the Trustees showed a new awareness for repositioning the foundation within a changed global political order.

The reorganisation marked a watershed in the history of the Rockefeller Foundation as a global force: While showing a new realism, the foundation arguably suffered a loss of significance in terms of its funding record in the second half of the twentieth century. In part, this was due to factors that lay outside the control of the President and Trustees, as new foundations like the Ford Foundation came to exert an enormous impact. Population control emerged as a political priority, and a long-term investment by the Milbank Memorial Fund, which also moved away from international health, coupled with a new wave of Rockefeller Foundation funding, achieved substantive influence. Links with the US State Department tightened. The CIA became notoriously involved in cultural politics and the developing ideas of academic and cultural freedom. At the same time there occurred increased US efforts to manipulate and control international agencies like the WHO and UNESCO. Whole departments within the US governmental machinery were devoted to monitoring the minutiae of such agencies and bringing expatriate US citizens to account before a Federal grand jury (as happened when Luther Evans became Director-General of UNESCO).

The Cold War era marked a shift away from foundation involvement in international health. Areas of public health activity by the Rockefeller Foundation between the wars – such as Eastern Europe and China – were now deemed inaccessible under Communism. The Cold War and post-atomic-bomb monitoring of radiation fallout meant that state support for medical research rendered Rockefeller Foundation support in the biological and medical sphere largely redundant. Foundations and US foreign policy were brought into alignment. No longer a compensatory (and perhaps conscience salving) mechanism for corporate wealth in an isolationist nation, US foundations promoted cultural policies of the "free world".

Acknowledgement
This article was researched with support from a Rockefeller Archive Center grant-in-aid to consult papers and archives.

Tim B. Müller

Die Macht der Menschenfreunde

Die Rockefeller Foundation, die Sozialwissenschaften und
die amerikanische Außenpolitik im Kalten Krieg

Die Frage nach der »Machtpolitik der Wissenszirkulation« im Kalten Krieg
führt zu den unterschiedlichsten lokalen Ausprägungen, zu unberechenba-
ren Verhandlungen, fragilen Kompromissen und innovativen Koproduktio-
nen. Die amerikanische Macht erfand sich in der Wissenschaftssphäre des
Kalten Krieges an Ort und Stelle immer wieder neu. Der Hegemon betrieb
keine lineare Machtpolitik: Die Ergebnisse waren nicht durch das Zentrum
determiniert, sondern von ihm in komplexer Weise dominiert und es wusste
die verschiedensten Potenziale für sich zu nutzen.[1] Allerdings sind heute
nicht nur die vielen Ausprägungen der lokalen Aushandlungs- und Aus-
tauschprozesse in aller Welt zu entdecken. Auch die Macht in den amerikanischen Zentralen war nicht monolithisch. Hegemonie wurde nach 1945
nicht nur vielgestaltig ausgeübt, sondern auch in den amerikanischen Schalt-
stellen der Wissensmacht bei allen Konvergenzen durchaus unterschiedlich
verstanden. Statt in die Peripherie blickt dieser Beitrag auf dieses Zentrum,
das so wenig von einer einzigen politischen Agenda determiniert war wie die
lokalen Praktiken der Wissenszirkulation. Am Beispiel der Rockefeller
Foundation soll ein komplexeres Bild der politischen Ziele amerikanischer
Stiftungen im frühen Kalten Krieg skizziert werden, als dies in vielen Darstellungen zu erkennen ist. Denn es kann nicht mehr genügen, auf prominente Kalten Krieger unter den Beiräten, Vorständen und Mitarbeitern einer
Stiftung zu verweisen; dafür ist unser Verständnis des Kalten Krieges, gerade
seiner ersten Jahrzehnte, viel zu differenziert geworden.[2]

Die Rockefeller Foundation (RF) gehörte zum amerikanischen »Establishment« im Kalten Krieg.[3] Doch was genau heißt das? Welche Erklärungs-

1 Vgl. Krige, »Die Führungsrolle der USA«; ders., American Hegemony.
2 Den Stand der Forschung spiegeln wider: Leffler/Westad, The Cambridge History of
the Cold War; Greiner u.a., Studien zum Kalten Krieg; exzellente Fallstudien zu den amerikanischen Sozialwissenschaften im Kalten Krieg sind Engerman, Know Your Enemy;
Gilman, *Mandarins of the Future*; Lowen, *Creating the Cold War University*.
3 So etwa schon vor Jahrzehnten Schlesinger, *A Thousand Days*, 128.

kraft kommt einer solchen Einordnung überhaupt zu? Für einen begrenzten
Zeitrahmen – die ersten beiden Jahrzehnte des Kalten Krieges – und für
einen Schwerpunkt der Stiftungsaktivitäten – die Förderung der Sozial- und
Geisteswissenschaften – soll hier eine genauere Bestimmung vorgenommen
werden. Zunächst wird das Problemfeld abgesteckt. Darauf folgen knappe
Anmerkungen zu dem für eine Modernisierungsagentur wie die RF bedeut-
samen Zusammenhang von Moderne und Kaltem Krieg. Anschließend geht
es einer ersten empirischen Skizze um die von der RF geförderte amerikanische Gegnerforschung, die sich zwischen politischen Erwartungen und
wissenschaftlicher Eigendynamik konstituierte. Abgeleitet aus diesem Fall,
werden danach die ambivalenten Leitkonzepte der Stiftung wie wissenschaftliche »Objektivität« und »Moderne« beleuchtet. Die politische Praxis
der RF im Zeitalter des McCarthyismus wird dann als konkreter Testfall für
die Vermittlung von wissenschaftlichen Leitbildern, politischem Druck von
außen und politischer Selbstmobilisierung herangezogen. Die Felder der
politischen Theorie und der Marxismusforschung bieten schließlich An-
schauungsmaterial für die zwischen Strategie und Wissenschaft austarierte
Förderpraxis der Stiftung – Gegensätze und Überlagerungen sind dabei gleichermaßen anzusprechen. Am Ende steht eine knappe Bilanz, die über den
untersuchten Zeitraum hinausreicht, um in die These zu münden, dass in
der Konstellation der 1940er bis späten 1960er Jahre die Konvergenz von
politischen und wissenschaftlichen Konzeptionen eine philanthropische
Praxis möglich machte, die zugleich im Dienste der amerikanischen Außenpolitik stand und dennoch nicht von ihr determiniert war.

Dass die Stellung der Stiftung zwischen akademischer und politischer
Welt Widersprüche und Rollenkonflikte zur Folge hatte, dessen waren sich
die Protagonisten innerhalb und außerhalb der RF bewusst. Nicht erst spätere Deutungen haben Spannungen herausgearbeitet und mitunter allzu di-
chotomisch vereinfacht. Doch nicht der Konflikt zwischen politischem und
wissenschaftlichem System verlangt nach einer Erklärung, sondern die
Selbstverständlichkeit, mit der die Verantwortlichen der Stiftung – die Trustees oder Beiräte, die Vorstände und die ihre Fachbereiche führenden »officers« – diese Gegensätze miteinander versöhnten. Im Umkreis der Stiftung
und in ihren höchsten Ämtern tauchten prominente Namen des frühen Kalten Krieges auf – Allen und John Foster Dulles, Dean Acheson, George F.
Kennan, John J. McCloy und Dean Rusk etwa. Die konzeptionelle und wis-
senschaftsstrategische Arbeit fiel jedoch den »officers« zu. Oft selbst ausge-
wiesene Wissenschaftler, legten sie auch immer wieder neue Entwürfe zu der
Frage vor, wie die RF ihre Aufgaben im Zeitalter von Antikommunismus
und Kaltem Krieg in ein Gleichgewicht bringen könnte. Die entscheidende,
weithin gebilligte (und doch für viele Auslegungen offene) Formel fand
schließlich der stellvertretende Direktor der geisteswissenschaftlichen Abtei-

lung, John Marshall, als er eine Kontinuität zwischen der internationalistischen Philanthropie der Zwischenkriegszeit und den strategischen Zwängen des Kalten Krieges feststellte. Die Stiftung blieb demnach dem »well-being of mankind« verpflichtet; so lautete ihr Motto. Der liberale Internationalismus operierte jedoch im Rahmen der amerikanischen Interessen: »obligations to American government and to American national interest are axiomatic for the Foundation and its officers. And it is within the limits they impose that the Foundation's reputation for disinterestedness in its international work has been established.«[4] Das klingt zunächst eindeutig; vom Internationalismus zur Strategie des Kalten Krieges war es nur ein kleiner Schritt. Wie sich diese Worte in der philanthropischen Praxis auflösen ließen, ist allerdings eine schwierigere Frage.

In der Diskussion über die Rolle der Wissenschaft – nach den Natur- nun zunehmend auch der Sozialwissenschaft – und der wissenschaftsfördernden Stiftungen im Kalten Krieg waren in jüngster Zeit binäre Deutungsmuster dominant. Demnach stand etwa Antikommunismus gegen akademische Freiheit oder der Staat gegen die Universität.[5] Diese Polarisierung trifft durchaus eine ideenpolitische Grundspannung der Epoche. Doch zur feineren Erfassung hat die Forschung seit kurzer Zeit zu Recht den Blick auf Nuancen und Ambivalenzen gerichtet: Im Bereich der staatlichen Auftragsforschung gab es Freiräume der wissenschaftlichen Innovation, während unabhängige Universitätsgelehrte sich politisch selbst mobilisieren und nur noch Legitimationswissenschaft betreiben konnten.[6] Ambivalenzen wie die im zuvor zitierten Dokument finden sich massenhaft in den Archiven des Kalten Krieges. Die Systeme Wissenschaft und Politik waren weder trennscharf voneinander getrennt, noch sollten sie es sein, und doch musste stets eine grundsätzliche Differenz aufrechterhalten werden. Die Praktiken der Vermittlung, die Techniken des Ausgleichs – darin verbergen sich die spannenden Fragen, die zu einem differenzierten Verständnis der Machtpolitik in der Wissenszirkulation im »hochmodernen« Kalten Krieg der 1940er bis 1960er Jahre beitragen.

---

4 Pro-51: Marshall, Relations of the Foundation with Governmental and Intergovernmental Agencies, 3. November 1950, S. 4, Rockefeller Archive Center, Sleepy Hollow, Rockefeller Foundation Archives (RFA), Record Group (RG) 3.2, Series 900, box (b.) 29, folder (f.) 159. Zur Diskussion in der RF vgl. Müller, *Krieger und Gelehrte*, 259–272.

5 Vgl. etwa Schrecker, *No Ivory Tower*; Diamond, *Compromised Campus*; Chomsky u.a., *The Cold War and the University*; Simpson, *Universities and Empire*; Wang, *American Science in an Age of Anxiety*. Einen Überblick bietet Unger, »Cold War Science«.

6 Vgl. Heyck/Kaiser, »New Perspectives on Science in the Cold War«; Engerman, »Social Science in the Cold War«; Isaac, »The Human Sciences in Cold War America«; Jureit, »Wissenschaft und Politik«.

1. Liberale Hochmoderne und Kalter Krieg

Dabei zeigt sich, dass die »Hochmoderne«, zu deren »Apotheose« Odd Arne Westad den Kalten Krieg erklärt, keineswegs notwendigerweise so autoritär zu verstehen ist, wie es im Gefolge von James Scott zumeist geschieht – und dass eine Abkehr von autoritären Modellen auch nicht unbedingt erst am Ende des langen Lernprozesses einsetzte, von dem Ulrich Herbert in seiner Skizze der Hochmoderne spricht. Er lässt die Hochmoderne bekanntlich in einen Prozess der Liberalisierung und Demokratisierung in den westlichen Gesellschaften der 1950er und 1960er Jahre münden. Am Ende stand der »specific balanced mix of the liberal and social market economy, of state concern for public welfare and private risk-taking, of parliamentary democracy and party-based structure, tradition and cultural modernity, of individualism and communal structures, national autonomy and supranational ties«. Mehr noch, ähnlich wie Eric Hobsbawm oder Tony Judt erkennt auch Herbert ein beinahe »goldenes Zeitalter«, einen erstaunlichen Grad der sozialen und politischen Stabilisierung: »It seemed that the really big problems, which had been in the flame of controversy since the century's turn, had now largely been solved – both the social question and the national one, the problem of what polity, what economic order and what cultural orientation.« In einigen dieser Gesellschaften waren diese Prozesse sogar bereits deutlich früher im Gang, diese Kompromissformeln bereits vor dem Krieg im Wesentlichen gefunden – und die ost(mittel)europäischen Gesellschaften befanden sich nach 1945 auf einer gar nicht so grundsätzlich abweichenden Suche (die freilich zu anderen Ergebnissen führte), wie die jüngere Forschung zum Kalten Krieg betont, dessen Kern Westad als einen »conflict between the two versions of Western modernity that socialism and liberal capitalism seemed to offer« deutet. Man kann also mit Scott die Staatszentrierung der Hochmoderne beklagen – oder ihren Fortschritts-, Wohlstands-, Planungs- und Ordnungswillen beobachten, aber nicht jede historische Erzählung der Epoche dystopisch in autoritärem *social engineering* und gewaltsamer Standardisierung enden lassen.[7]

In anderen Worten: Man kann mit guten Gründen genauso von einer demokratischen oder liberalen Hochmoderne sprechen, wie üblicherweise von einer autoritären Hochmoderne gesprochen wird. Statt einer zielgerichteten Entwicklung lässt sich der permanente Konflikt unterschiedlicher Lösungsstrategien beobachten. Sozialdemokratische und liberale – oder, wie es in Großbritannien schon zeitgenössisch formuliert wurde: sozial-liberale – Konzepte und Praktiken formierten sich in der Zwischenkriegszeit

---

7 Westad, »The Cold War and the international history of the twentieth century«, 10, 16–17; Herbert, »Europe in High Modernity«, 18; Scott, *Seeing Like a State*, 4–6.

genauso wie kommunistische und faschistische oder andere autoritäre Ordnungsmodelle. Die Geschichte der Hochmoderne ist voller Ambivalenzen; wenn man unbedingt nach einer Meistererzählung sucht, wäre eine ernüchterte, bescheidenere, für Widersprüche offene, selbstkritische Variante der Modernisierungstheorie jedenfalls plausibler als Scotts Eliten- und Staatsphobie. Natürlich lenkten staatliche und staatsnahe Eliten diese Modernisierungsprozesse, so eingeschränkt sie dazu in der Lage waren; doch zum Habitus dieser Eliten, wie sie etwa auch von den Wissenschaftsmanagern der RF verkörpert wurden, gehörten ideenpolitische Ressourcen, die man nur als liberal und – kulturell wie politisch – pluralistisch bezeichnen kann. Vielleicht ließe sich darum sogar völlig auf eine Teleologie des Lernens verzichten und an deren Stelle eine Abfolge von Konfliktkonstellationen analysieren, in der sich von Anfang an keineswegs immer die totalitären Kräfte durchsetzten oder die Gefahren des Totalitarismus abzeichneten.

Zugespitzt formuliert: Welche Epoche könnte wohl eher als Zeitalter der sozial-liberalen gesellschaftlichen Reform gelten als der Kalte Krieg (mit entscheidenden strukturellen Kontinuitäten zur Zwischenkriegszeit etwa im Amerika des »New Deal«, in Großbritannien oder in Schweden)? Systemdenken und integrative Sozialwissenschaften, die Suche nach Ordnung und Universaltheorien, die überragende Bedeutung sozialer Integration, die Betonung von bürokratischen Strukturen und Prozessen für die moderne Gesellschaft, Technokratie und »Expertenherrschaft«, die zunehmende, im »New Deal« und Zweiten Weltkrieg bereits ausgebildete Nähe von Staat und Wissenschaft gehörten zu den seit den 1970er Jahren standardmäßig kritisierten Grundzügen dieses Zeitabschnitts. Untrennbar mit diesen Merkmalen verbunden waren allerdings »korporatistische« soziale Kompromisse, die »keynesianische« Steuerung der Wirtschaft, der Ausbau des Wohlfahrtsstaats oder der zunehmende rechtliche und soziale Abbau von Klassen- und Rassenschranken. Es handelte sich um eine Vielfalt von Techniken und Strategien, die zwischen individuellen Rechten und gesellschaftlicher Umverteilung vermittelten und in der Überzeugung verwurzelt waren, die gegenwärtige Gesellschaft enthalte bereits die Möglichkeit einer besseren Gesellschaft – einer Gesellschaft ohne Klassen, die nicht dem Diktat der Konkurrenz unterworfen sei und ohne gewaltsame Umwälzungen, vielmehr durch kluge, auf Rationalität und Effizienz der liberalen Experten gestützte Reform herbeigeführt werden könne. Aufgrund ihrer Gemeinwohlverpflichtung und sozial-liberalen Normsetzung wurden bürokratische Experten mit einer demokratischen Legitimität ausgestattet, die der durch Wahlen nahezu gleichkam. Auch nach 1945 prägten der Sozial-Liberalismus und die sozialreformerische Tradition des »New Deal« die politische Kultur der USA und die westeuropäischen Eliten verpflichteten sich einer Modernisierungsmission, die als progressiv verstanden wurde.[8]

Ohne diesen sozial-liberalen Erwartungs- und Handlungshorizont lässt sich nicht begreifen, in welchem Sinne und zu welchem Zweck die Stiftungsstrategen die Machtpolitik der Wissenszirkulation betrieben, um diese Wendung der Herausgeber noch einmal aufzunehmen. Das zeigte sich auch auf dem Feld der Sozial- und Geisteswissenschaften – eine im Zeitalter der Sozialwissenschaften selbst bereits auffällige Verbindung. Die »New Deal«-liberale Gouvernementalität, in Erweiterung das System des zeitgenössischen westlichen Sozial-Liberalismus, hatte über die Stiftungen hinaus nicht nur aus strategischem Kalkül im Kalten Krieg Verwendung für unkonventionelle Wissenschaft – und auch nicht nur aufgrund des hochmodernen sozialwissenschaftlichen Selbstvertrauens, das von der Konvergenz von innovativer Wissenschaft und liberalen Werten überzeugt war. Von abweichendem Wissen, das möglicherweise eine nächste Stufe des wissenschaftlichen Fortschritts ankündigte, wollten sich die liberalen Eliten in Regierung, Stiftungen und Universitäten nicht abschneiden. Historische Komplexität hatte folglich in der wissenschaftspolitischen Praxis ihren Platz neben kontingenzinsensiblen makrotheoretischen Modellen, intellektuell riskante Projekte standen neben der Affirmation der westlichen Konsensmoderne; Geisteswissenschaften hatten ihre Bedeutung neben (und oft in Zusammenarbeit mit) den dominanten »modernen« Sozialwissenschaften, die gemeinhin das Leitbild der Epoche prägten – und die nicht zuletzt durch die Stiftungsarbeit sich auch in Europa durchsetzen sollten.[9]

2. Politische Gegnerforschung und wissenschaftliche Eigendynamik

Auch die RF gab sich in den späten 1940er und frühen 1950er Jahren zeitweilig der Attraktion durch den Behavioralismus als integrative Sozialwissenschaft hin[10] – doch niemals so vollständig, wie die Rhetorik der Jahre

8 Vgl. Bell, »Social Politics«; Brick, *Transcending Capitalism*; Doering-Manteuffel/Raphael, *Nach dem Boom*; Müller, »Reform und Rationalität«; Raphael, »Ordnungsmuster der ›Hochmoderne‹?«; Rosanvallon, *Demokratische Legitimität*, 45–77; Sejersted, *The Age of Social Democracy*; Sparrow, *Warfare State*; zu der aus einer späteren Konstellation hervorgegangenen, linke und rechte libertäre Argumente verbindenden Kritik an der sozialliberalen Ordnung seit den Siebzigern Rodgers, *Age of Fracture*.

9 Vgl. Ross, *The Origins of American Social Science*; Porter/Ross, *The Modern Social Sciences*; Wagner, *Sozialwissenschaften und Staat*; für die Nachkriegszeit in Deutschland zusammenfassend Raphael, »Die Verwissenschaftlichung des Sozialen«; als Fallstudie Unger, *Ostforschung in Westdeutschland*.

10 Siehe etwa die RF-Strategiedokumente Pro-40: Carl I. Hovland, Some Suggested Research Opportunities in Social Psychology, Sociology, and Anthropology, 13. Mai 1946;

glauben lassen könnte, ganz abgesehen davon, dass auch unter dem zeitgenössischen Schlagwort Behavioralismus keineswegs nur gleichförmig uni-
versalistische, quantitative, psychologisch-reduktive, unhistorische und den
politischen Konflikt ignorierende sozialwissenschaftliche Ansätze verfolgt
wurden.[11] Wie eng Sozial- und Geisteswissenschaften miteinander verwo-
ben waren, zeigt eines der Prestigeprojekte der Stiftung am Anfang des Kalten Krieges. Mit dem Russian Institute an der Columbia University wurden
1946 die Area Studies in Gestalt einer Leitwissenschaft des frühen Kalten
Krieges aus der Taufe gehoben, des interdisziplinären Konglomerats der
»Soviet Studies« oder Sowjetologie. Insgesamt flossen 1,4 Millionen US-
Dollar von der Stiftung an das Institut. Verantwortlich war die geisteswis-
senschaftliche Abteilung der RF, doch die Förderung wurde in enger Ab-
stimmung mit der sozialwissenschaftlichen Abteilung vorgenommen. Die
institutionelle Zuständigkeit zeigte jedoch an, dass Sprache, Geschichte und
Kultur, also nicht der behavioralistisch-sozialwissenschaftliche Ansatz, im
Zentrum dieser sowjetologischen Ausbildungsstätte stehen sollten. Das Institut rekrutierte viele seiner Mitarbeiter aus dem Office of Strategic Services
(OSS) und dem State Department, wo diese Experten während des Krieges
beschäftigt gewesen waren. Es hielt am politisch-strategisch begründeten
Area Studies-Ansatz der Kriegsjahre fest und wurde zum Modell für ähnliche Programme in den Vereinigten Staaten. Am Russian Institute trat allerdings die Forschung zugunsten der Lehre in den Hintergrund; es gab nur
wenige spätere akademische Sowjetforscher und kaum einen Regierungs-
oder Geheimdienstexperten, der nicht irgendeine Ausbildungsphase am
Russian Institute verbracht hätte. Die paradigmatische Bedeutung des Russian Institute zeigte sich nicht nur im permanenten und selbstverständlichen
Wechsel der Lehrenden zwischen den Rollen des akademischen Forschers
und des Regierungsberaters. Hier wurde auch erstmals die spezifische Konstellation sichtbar, der die »Soviet Studies« ihren rasanten Aufstieg zu verdanken hatten: Zu der im Zeichen des Kalten Krieges fortgeführten intellektuellen Mobilisierung des Zweiten Weltkrieges, die die bereits im »New Deal«
angebahnte Zusammenarbeit zwischen Wissenschaft und Politik intensi-

Pro-39: Willits, Social Sciences and Social Studies, 25. April 1952; Buchanan, Notes on Rockefeller Foundation Program in the Social Sciences, August 1955; RFA, RG 3.1, Series
910, b. 3, f. 19; Social Relations Conference, 1952–1953; RFA, RG 3.1, Series 910, b. 10,
f. 96–100; sowie die *Annual Reports* der RF.
   11 Zum RF-finanzierten Social Science Research Council als Bastion des Behavioralismus vgl. Fisher, *Fundamental Development of the Social Sciences*; Gilman, *Mandarins of the
Future*, 113–154; zur Bestimmung und sozialwissenschaftlichen Dominanz des Behavioralismus Herman, *The Romance of American Psychology*; dies., »The Career of Cold War
Psychology«; Robin, *The Making of the Cold War Enemy*; Schrecker, *Many Are the Crimes*,
404, 407–408; Seybold, »The Ford Foundation«.

viert hatte, traten der Ausbau der Universitäten und das Anwachsen der Studierendenzahlen nach dem Kriegsende. Angewiesen waren das Wachstum der akademischen Institutionen und die Formierung eines politisch-wissenschaftlichen Komplexes auf erhebliche Forschungsmittel. Eine entscheidende Funktion kam dabei in den ersten Jahren des Kalten Krieges den privaten Stiftungen zu, später stieg auch die staatliche Wissenschaftsförderung stark an. Neben der RF und der Carnegie Corporation weitete schließlich besonders die Ford Foundation ihr regionalwissenschaftliches Engagement aus. Die enge Verzahnung von Regierung, Philanthropie und Universität war der Ausgangspunkt der Russlandforschung. Doch schon diese Gründungskonstellation lässt sich nicht linear beschreiben – das Ziel einer Internationalisierung, einer »Kosmopolitisierung« von Kultur und Bildung in Amerika, getragen von einer Mischung aus liberalen Leitideen und der Absicht, isolationistische Tendenzen nachhaltig zurückzudrängen, gehörte ebenfalls zur Motivlage.

Das Russian Institute, schon in seiner Gründungskonstellation ein Modell der Wissensmobilisierung für den Kalten Krieg, war zwar eine Institution von Gegensätzen, diese ließen sich in der alltäglichen Praxis jedoch scheinbar leicht auflösen. Interkulturelles Verständnis sollte genauso auf dem Lehrplan stehen wie psychologische Kriegführung; das Institut bildete Offiziere und Regierungsexperten aus und zog zugleich den Zorn des organisierten Antikommunismus auf sich; linke Marxismuskenner wie Herbert Marcuse wurden beschäftigt, aber die Fäden hielten liberale Kalte Krieger in der Hand, ein »Cold War insider« wie Philip Mosely, RF-, Minister- und Geheimdienstberater, Direktor des Russian Institute und des Council on Foreign Relations.[12] In diesem Haus wurden viele Wohnungen eingerichtet, denn dahinter stand ein Geflecht aus strategischen, epistemologischen und institutionellen Gründen: der Kalte Krieg, die Vorstellung einer im Kern liberalen modernen Wissenschaft, das Eigeninteresse der Stiftung und die Eigendynamik der wissenschaftlichen Felder.[13] Typisch für dieses Geflecht war eine von Mosely herbeigeführte Entscheidung der RF Mitte der 1950er Jahre. Er hatte die Unterstützung der Stiftung für eine internationale Kooperation in der Marxismusforschung initiiert, deren Schwerpunkte in Berlin, Amsterdam und Fribourg angesiedelt waren und die auch lose mit dem Russian Institute verbunden war. Im Mittelpunkt standen dabei zunächst Überlegungen zu einer kritischen Edition der Werke von Marx und Engels. Nicht

---

12 RF Annual Report 1945, 13–15; vgl. Engerman, *Know Your Enemy*, 13–42 (zu Mosely ebd., 5, 14, 30); Unger, *Ostforschung in Westdeutschland*, 352–358, 369–379; Müller, *Krieger und Gelehrte*, 219–243; zum Typus des »Cold War insider« Suri, *Henry Kissinger*, 109–130.

13 Vgl. Müller, *Krieger und Gelehrte*, besonders Kapitel I, II, III und V.

länger sollten Marx und Engels allein der sowjetischen Seite überlassen werden, die deren Ideen »toward the justification of Communist ideology and action rather than toward a scholarly presentation of the actual documents« entstelle. Die Gründungskonferenz des internationalen Verbunds erhielt den Auftrag, »to consider what might be done by Western scholars to present the authentic version of what Marx, Engels and Lenin really said and to counteract the influence of Communist ideological propaganda«.[14]

Versteckt in diesen Sätzen waren zwei politisch-intellektuelle Implikationen von großer Tragweite. Das Marxismus-Leninismus-Projekt wurde in New York als eine mit wissenschaftlicher Objektivität durchgeführte Operation im Kalten Krieg der Ideen geplant. Wenn die Stiftungsstrategen aus dem liberalen Ostküstenestablishment sich aber eine »authentische Version« dessen erhofften, »was Marx, Engels und Lenin wirklich gesagt hatten«, um den ideologischen Einfluss Moskaus einzudämmen, dann teilten sie damit die sowohl unter unabhängigen Marxisten wie Marcuse als auch unter liberalen Denkern wie Isaiah Berlin verbreitete Prämisse, dass der Terror nicht bei Marx seinen Ausgang genommen hatte.[15] Marx galt als Korrektur, nicht als Schuldiger einer monströsen historischen Entgleisung. Zurück zu den Quellen hieß auch, ein humanistisches Ideal aus totalitären Trümmern zu retten. So wurde es denen entrissen, die es gewaltsam usurpiert hatten. Der Plan bestand darin, im Ideenkampf den Gegner mit seinen eigenen ideologischen Waffen zu schlagen. Die strategischen Notwendigkeiten des Kalten Krieges, das liberale Vertrauen in eine uneingeschränkte Wissenschaft, das Interesse der Stiftung an vernachlässigten Feldern und die disziplinäre Entwicklung von Marx-Philologie und Sowjetforschung trafen zusammen. Ihre Wirkung – etwa durch Stipendienprogramme, Forschungshilfen und Bibliotheksausstattungen – zielte besonders auf politische und ökonomische Schlüsselregionen, wo Arbeiterbewegung, Intellektuelle und Studenten eine Affinität zum Marxismus aufwiesen: in Westeuropa, in der Dritten Welt, besonders in Indien und Lateinamerika, und schließlich auch in Osteuropa, wo sich seit 1956 deutliche Anzeichen eines unorthodoxen und systemkritischen Marxismus entwickelten, dessen potenziell destabilisierende Folgen für die sowjetische Herrschaft von den Marxismusforschern ebenso wie von ihren politischen und philanthropischen Förderern deutlich erkannt wurden.

Mosely war bereits zuvor in der Stiftung für das Ziel eingetreten, durch wissenschaftliche Exzellenz – und keinesfalls durch politische Kompromisse der Wissenschaft – einen politischen Vorteil gegenüber der sowjetischen Deutung des Sozialismus zu erringen und damit auch die globale Anzie-

---

14 Bewilligung GH 56100, 7. September 1956, RFA, RG 1.2, Series 717, b. 7, f. 82.
15 Zu Marcuse und Berlin vgl. Müller, *Krieger und Gelehrte*, 448–489.

hungskraft des Staatssozialismus zu schmälern. Was Mosely vorschlug, wurde durch die Praxis der RF im Hinblick auf das Russian Institute oder den Marxismusforschungsverbund bekräftigt. Mosely zielte dennoch über die Wissenschaft hinaus, wenn er die Rückeroberung des »pathos of the labor movement for the democratic side« forderte. Moselys geopolitische Perspektive reichte dabei über Westeuropa hinaus, er dachte auch an ideenpolitische Verstärkung für den Kampf um »India and the Near East, where the Communists claim to be the only ones who have been interested for many years in the improvement of conditions generally«. Der Weg zu dieser erwünschten intellektuellen Revitalisierung eines antisowjetischen Sozialismus, zur Formierung eines westlichen intellektuellen Marxismus, führte über die historisch-philologische Grundlagenforschung hinaus. Und in der Tat waren es nicht zuletzt die in diesem Kontext bearbeiteten Marxschen Frühschriften und nichtsowjetischen, reformistischen, alternativen Traditionen des Sozialismus, die für die eigenständige Entwicklung des westlichen Marxismus durchaus eine besondere Bedeutung entfalteten.[16]

Allerdings ist damit keine politische Determiniertheit beschrieben – im Objektivitätskonzept der Wissensmanager konnte sich der strategische Erfolg nur aus der wissenschaftlichen Leistung speisen. Die Prinzipien einer interdisziplinären sozialwissenschaftlichen Forschungsorganisation, einer sich selbst korrigierenden Struktur, der permanenten Selbstkritik und der Abweichungstoleranz wurden von den Protagonisten selbst formuliert, in äußerster Klarheit vom Direktor des Nachrichtendienstes des State Department, Allan Evans, der nicht nur eng mit der RF zusammenarbeitete, sondern auch als Nachfolger der Forschungsabteilung des OSS Sowjetforscher lieferte und rekrutierte: »What is needed is a channel for informal ideas, for the posing of questions, for detecting the unexpected approach or element that might otherwise slip by.«[17] Politische Strategien, intellektuelle Diskurse, professioneller Habitus und Forschungspraktiken trafen sich in der Überzeugung, dass moderne, reformorientierte Sozialwissenschaften eine wesentliche Stärke der westlichen Moderne waren – ein entscheidendes Instrument ihrer Selbstreflexion, Selbstkritik, Selbstkorrektur und damit Selbsterhaltung.

16 Memo Edward F. D'Arms, 13 October 1954, RFA, RG 1.1, Series 200, b. 322, f. 3828. Vgl. zur begrenzten Reichweite und den dennoch nicht unerheblichen Ergebnissen und Wirkungen des Rockefeller-Projekts in der Marxismusforschung zwischen 1956 und 1964 Müller, *Krieger und Gelehrte*, 489–538; zum westlichen Marxismus die klassischen (und selbst in dieser Geschichte positionierten) Deutungen von Anderson, *Considerations on Western Marxism*; Jacoby, *Dialectics of Defeat*; sowie Jay, *Marxism and Totality*.

17 Memo Evans to Armstrong, Bissell Draft on Intelligence on Communism, 11, März 1955, S. 13, 15, NA, RG 59, E. 1561, b. 8, f. 4. Zur Arbeit dieses Nachrichtendienstes vgl. Müller, *Krieger und Gelehrte*, 89–186.

David Engerman hat über das Russian Institute hinaus Schritt für Schritt, Teildisziplin um Teildisziplin gezeigt, wie sich diese Heterogenität in den maßgeblich von der RF geförderten »Soviet Studies« auswirkte. Die amerikanische »Gegnerforschung« des Kalten Krieges schlechthin ging eben keineswegs in der politischen Funktion der Feindaufklärung oder auch der ideenpolitischen Hegemoniesicherung auf. Im Gegenteil, sie löste von Anfang an das Feindbild eher auf und war in jedem Fall in ihren Deutungen der Sowjetunion als moderne Gesellschaft viel differenzierter und moderater als die öffentliche Debatte über den Gegner im Kalten Krieg. Von wenigen konservativen Ausnahmen abgesehen, neigten die »Gegnerforscher«, soweit sie die politischen Implikationen ihrer Forschungen thematisierten, zu einer Politik der Entspannung. Vor allem waren es nicht politische Motive, die in erster Linie die amerikanischen Sowjetunion-Forscher antrieben, und weder Politiker noch Wissensstrategen schränkten ihre wissenschaftlichen Spielräume merklich ein. Disziplinäre Eigendynamiken und wissenschaftliche Traditionen rückten den politischen Auftrag nicht selten in den Hintergrund. Die Russlandforscher hatten weitgehend freie Hand. Vielfältige und selbst gegensätzliche Denkmodelle, Institutionen, Personen und Praktiken wurden im Dienste eines übergeordneten strategischen Ziels gekoppelt; die Vielfalt hing von diesem Ziel gerade ab. Vom politischen Kontext und den finanziellen Strukturen kann also keinesfalls auf das wissenschaftliche Resultat geschlossen werden – Linearität, Uniformität und Konventionalität der Forschung wären den Intentionen der meisten Geldgeber sogar zuwidergelaufen.[18]

3. Ambivalenz der Konzeptionen: Wissenschaft, Pluralität und Moderne

Im Zentrum der Wissensmachtpolitiker, in den Strategiediskussionen der Rockefeller-Programmverantwortlichen, finden sich also bereits – und zwar konstitutiv für ihre Aktivität – die komplexen und nicht von unmittelbaren Machtinteressen allein bestimmten Aushandlungsprozesse, die John Krige im Zusammentreffen von amerikanischer Hegemonie und lokalen Wissenschaftskulturen beobachtet und so treffend als »co-production of American hegemony« bezeichnet hat. Die globale amerikanische Hegemonie des Kalten Krieges stützte sich auch auf Vielfalt und freien Austausch von Wissen. Der Zugang zur (und die produktive Weiterentwicklung der) besten Wissenschaft überall auf der Welt war natürlich eine langfristige Strategie der Machterhaltung, doch darf das wissenschaftliche Eigeninteresse dabei nicht

18 Vgl. Engerman, *Know Your Enemy*, bes. 97–179.

völlig ignoriert werden.[19] Die zugleich politisch-strategische und epistemologische Objektivitätskonstruktion und das Selbstvertrauen in eine moderne, elitäre, aber uneingeschränkte Wissenschaft kamen auch in den Geisteswissenschaften zum Ausdruck. Der prominente Harvard-Historiker William Langer – auch er verkörperte die typischen Rollenwechsel, als Direktor der OSS-Forschungsabteilung im Weltkrieg und erster Leiter der CIA-Nachrichtenanalyse Anfang der 1950er Jahre – setzte sich gleich nach Kriegsende an eine groß angelegte Geschichte des Zweiten Weltkrieges, die mit enormen Beträgen von der RF finanziert wurde. Stiftung, außenpolitisches Establishment (so waren etwa der Council on Foreign Relations und die Dulles-Brüder involviert) und der Autor selbst verfolgten politische Absichten – vor allem eine endgültige Widerlegung des linken wie des rechten Isolationismus, außerdem eine Alternative zu den konkurrierenden sowjetisch-sozialistischen und britisch-imperialistischen Erzählungen über den Krieg. Ein »mature and experienced scholar« wie Langer könnte dieses Ziel allein durch seine gelehrte Meisterschaft in Quellendeutung und historischer Darstellung erreichen und eine »comprehensive, authoritative history of the United States during these years of turmoil« schreiben.[20] Das nationale Interesse der Vereinigten Staaten, wie es die liberalen (und moderat konservativen) Eliten definierten, und unanfechtbare, vorbildliche Wissenschaft gingen auch hier Hand in Hand. Auch die Stiftung war an der Konstruktion des »national security discourse« (Michael J. Hogan) beteiligt.[21] Doch waren diese Konzepte offener, als es den Anschein hat. Zahlreiche Beispiele dafür lassen sich finden.[22]

Die RF-Verantwortlichen sahen sich eben auch für wissenschaftliche Originalität und Innovation verantwortlich. Sie verbanden Staatsapparate und wissenschaftliche Forschung, Personal wurde wechselseitig ausgetauscht, wissenschaftliche Investitionen wurden auch im Dienste der amerikanischen Außenpolitik vorgenommen. Zugleich wurde die gerade nach dem Kriegsende beschworene philanthropische Tradition nicht abgebrochen: Die Rockefeller-Stiftung betonte philanthropische Kontinuität zur Zwischen-

---

19 Krige, *American Hegemony*, 1–14; ders., »Die Führungsrolle der USA«.
20 Langer, The United States in the Second World War, 1. Oktober 1945, S. 1–4; Memos Willits, 1. November 1945, 17. Dezember 1945; Langer, A Project for the Preparation of a History of American Foreign Relations during the War Period (For consideration of the Committee of Studies, Council on Foreign Relations), 8. Oktober 1945; Langer an Mallory, 8. Oktober 1945; Mallory an Langer, 23. Oktober 1945; Langer an Mallory, 29. Oktober 1945; CFR an Rockefeller Foundation, Proposal for a History of the United States in the Second World War, 21. Dezember 1945, S. 1–5; RFA, RG 1.2, Series 100 S, b. 58, f. 444.
21 Vgl. Hogan, *A Cross of Iron*, 1–22.
22 Vgl. etwa Müller, *Krieger und Gelehrte*, 189–403.

kriegszeit im Gegensatz zu einer vom Kalten Krieg bedingten politischen
Diskontinuität; in ihrem Selbstbild sah sie sich weiterhin den Prinzipien des
liberalen Internationalismus verpflichtet und förderte vor allem wissenschaftliche Leistung und nicht politisches Wohlverhalten. Das Spannungs-
potenzial, das aus diesen beiden unterschiedlichen Zielen resultieren konnte,
wurde durch die politische Epistemologie aufgelöst, auf deren Grundlage
die Stiftung operierte. Obwohl nach den Katastrophen des Zweiten Weltkrieges auch selbstkritische und wissenschaftsskeptische Reflexionen auf-
tauchten, bestimmte ein ungebrochenes, emphatisches Verhältnis zur Moderne und zum wissenschaftlichen Fortschritt das Denken und die Politik
der Stiftung. Gefördert wurden nur wissenschaftliche Spitzenleistungen; der
Fortschritt der Forschung maß sich allerdings am Wissenschaftsverständnis
einer amerikanisch-westlichen, liberalen Moderne. Wissenschaft als Arbeit,
als moderner, arbeitsteiliger Prozess, also moderne, professionelle, in Forschungsgruppen und Laboratorien kooperierende Natur- und Sozialwissenschaften, stellten das Leitbild dar. Die Attraktivität dieser Konzeptionen der
Moderne und der Wissenschaft war so groß, dass immer wieder die Zuver-
sicht bekundet wurde, die beste Forschung werde ganz natürlich diesem
Leitbild folgen – und wo sie politisches Terrain berührte, werde sie ebenso
natürlich zu einer politischen Bestätigung der amerikanisch-westlichen, liberalen Moderne führen. Die Förderungen sollten gezielt zur Verwestlichung der Wissenschaft beitragen, weil Verwestlichung mit der Wissenschaft und wissenschaftliche Avantgarde gleichgesetzt wurden.[23]

Bei näherer Betrachtung erweisen sich auch diese Konzeptionen als viel-
schichtiger. Die Stiftung beschränkte ihre Fördermittel keineswegs auf die
wissenschaftlichen Ansätze, die ihrer Konzeption von Moderne und Wissenschaft am nächsten kamen. Dem in den Sozialwissenschaften zeitweilig vor-
herrschenden Behavioralismus flossen zwar erhebliche Beträge zu, doch
pflegte die Rockefeller Foundation stets eine Diversifizierung ihrer wissenschaftlichen Investitionen – explizit mit dem Argument, dass man Vielfalt zu
fördern verpflichtet sei.[24] Die liberalen Stiftungsstrategen oder ihre Gesin-
nungsgenossen in den strategischen Staatsapparaten erkundeten viele Pfade,
die im Raum zwischen »Kommunismus« und »Amerikanisierung« verlie-
fen.[25]

23 Vgl. Hollinger, *Science, Jews, and Secular Culture*; Kevles, *The Physicists*, 41–44,
53–54; Lowen, »Zur Verflechtung von Politik und Universitäten«; Gilman, *Mandarins of
the Future*.
24 Memo Stewart, 12 April 1954, RFA, RG 3.1, Series 910, b. 9, f. 78.
25 Das gilt selbst dann, wenn man unter »Amerikanisierung« einen komplexen, wechselseitig angelegten, auch von lokalen Eigenheiten dynamisierten Prozess betrachtet; vgl.
Rausch, »Wie europäisch ist die kulturelle Amerikanisierung?«. In den strategischen Konzeptionen war Raum für dezidiert nicht-amerikanische Wege, und umgekehrt lässt sich

Im Kalten Krieg formierte sich ein philanthropisch-politischer Komplex, der in der engen, oft täglichen und über Fragen des Kulturaustauschs weit hinausreichenden Kooperation der beiden Sphären von Politik und Philanthropie rekonstruiert werden kann. Die Stiftungen, namentlich auch die RF, verfolgten das Ziel, die amerikanische Außenpolitik, die Absicherung und den Ausbau der amerikanischen Hegemonie zu unterstützen. Vorstand und »officers« der RF nahmen die Rolle an, »in a time of war« zur intellektuellen Mobilisierung beizutragen, gerade durch die Finanzierung der Area Studies.[26] Doch fand diese Mobilisierungsbereitschaft nicht nur stets da eine Grenze, wo sie wie in der Sowjetologie auf professionelles Eigeninteresse und wissenschaftliche Eigendynamik stieß. Dieselben »officers« erhoben auch prinzipiellen Einspruch, wenn die Linien verwischt wurden: Ein Wissenschaftler konnte Regierungsberater sein, Rollenwechsel waren legitim, aber die Systemdifferenzen mussten grundsätzlich im Sinne des politisch-epistemologischen Objektivitätsideals anerkannt werden. Wissenschaft konnte demnach nicht in Regierungsberatung aufgehen oder getarnte Geheimdienstfunktionen ausfüllen. Die Frage, wo diese Grenze verlief, war freilich umstritten; aber diese Grenze konnte auch von einflussreichen Amtsträgern nicht endlos ausgeweitet werden. Gegen den anfangs der Sache gewogenen Stiftungspräsidenten Chester Barnard konnte zum Beispiel Philip Mosely unter Berufung auf prinzipielle Argumente durchsetzen, dass die Finanzierung eines von George Kennan und dem einstigen OSS-Direktor William Donovan entworfenen quasi-geheimdienstlichen Ostforschungszentrums abgelehnt wurde. Dass es mit Mosely gerade der am besten mit Regierung und Geheimdiensten vernetzte Wissenschaftsmanager und Sowjetologe war, der auf dieser Unterscheidung bestand, lässt die Rollenkonstruktionen deutlich erkennen. Aus dieser Trennung von Funktionen ergaben sich größere Handlungsspielräume für die Wissenschaft, die formal als eigenes System respektiert wurde.[27]

Bei Talcott Parsons, dem Vordenker einer integrativen Sozialwissenschaft und einflussreichsten Soziologen jener Jahre, funktionierten die unter-

argumentieren, dass auch in den ersten Jahren des Kalten Krieges die USA sich von nichtamerikanischen sozialdemokratischen Modellen inspirieren ließen; vgl. etwa Bell, »Social Politics«; Sejersted, *The Age of Social Democracy*, 185–329; grundlegend zur ersten Jahrhunderthälfte Rodgers, *Atlantiküberquerungen.*

26 Minutes Officers' Conference, 18. März 1948, RFA, RG 3.1, Series 900, b. 25, f. 199. Vgl. Müller, *Krieger und Gelehrte*, 251–272.

27 Die Operation firmierte unter dem Namen Eurasia Institute oder Eurasian Research Institute. Siehe etwa Mosely, Memorandum on Eurasian Research Institute, 19. Oktober 1948; Memo Mosely an Willits, 24. November 1948; Memo Willits an Barnard, 16. November 1948, 23. Dezember 1948; Barnard an Donovan, 28. Dezember 1948 RFA, RG 2, Series 200, b. 407, f. 2744; Engerman, *Know Your Enemy*, 40; Cumings, »Boundary Displacement«, 164–165.

schiedlichen sozialen Systeme entsprechend ihrer je eigenen Logik, dennoch bewirkten normative Muster eine soziale Integration.[28] Ähnlich lässt sich die Praxis einer Stiftung wie der RF deuten. Unterschiedlichen Logiken verpflichtete Systeme – Politik, Wissenschaft und die Philanthropie als zwischengelagerte Vermittlungsinstitution – wirkten im Hinblick auf ein strategisches Ziel zusammen, gerade indem sie auf ihrer Eigenständigkeit und ihrem systemischen Eigensinn beharrten. Unabhängigkeit von direkter politischer Einflussnahme war geradezu die Voraussetzung, um politisch langfristig von Nutzen zu sein und das größere strategische Ziel zu verfolgen, die Konsolidierung und Förderung der westlichen, liberalen Moderne – und als deren politische Implikation die globale amerikanische Hegemonie.[29] Im Ringen mit staatssozialistischen Modernisierungsvisionen standen die RF und andere Stiftungen für die offensive Förderung einer sozial-liberal-demokratischen Moderne. Nicht so sehr in der liberalen Vision unterschieden sich die Nachkriegsstrategen von ihren Vorgängen der Zwischenkriegszeit – die sozial-liberale Reformperspektive war im Kalten Krieg in ihrer Reichweite reduziert und sicherheitspolitisch verengt, aber nicht abgeschafft worden. Dass aber diese Moderne nicht von allein wachsen würde, sondern von Staaten und Experten gezielt herbeigeführt und befestigt werden müsse, war eine Vorstellung, die sich erst seit den 1930er Jahren durchgesetzt hatte und nun im Kalten Krieg der Hochmoderne ihren Höhepunkt erlebte.[30]

Und genau dieses Aufeinandertreffen von politischer und wissenschaftlicher Moderne in der Verbreitung liberaler Werte – nach ihrer je eigenen Logik – bezeichnete den Punkt, der mit der eingangs zitierten Formel bestimmt wurde: die Verpflichtung gegenüber den nationalen Interessen der USA wurde als »axiomatisch« anerkannt, sie war unhintergehbare Geschäftsgrundlage der amerikanischen Institution und liberalen Modernisierungsagentur RF. Innerhalb dieses Rahmens, dessen Starrheit oder Flexibilität in der Praxis immer wieder ausgelotet wurde, galt die Verpflichtung der Stiftung ihrer liberalen »reputation for disinterestedness in its international work« und damit der Pflege von wissenschaftlicher Pluralität und Differenz, die am Ende den politischen Interessen des Westens zugutekommen würden.[31] Da ein Grundsatzkonflikt zwischen den beiden Systemen verneint wurde, konnten sie durch eine solche Formel konzeptionell versöhnt wer-

---

28 Zu Parsons und seinem Einfluss vgl. Brick, *Transcending Capitalism*, 121–151; Gilman, *Mandarins of the Future*, 72–112.

29 Der »Westen« wurde als Konstrukt in diesem Sinne im Zuge des Marshallplans geschaffen; vgl. Hitchcock, »The Marshall Plan and the Creation of the West«.

30 Vgl. Heyck, »Die Moderne in der amerikanischen Sozialwissenschaft«; Brick, *Transcending Capitalism*, 145–218.

31 Pro-51: Marshall, Relations of the Foundation with Governmental and Intergovernmental Agencies, 3. November 1950, S. 4, RFA, RG 3.2, Series 900, b. 29, f. 159.

den. Doch Konflikte blieben in der philanthropischen Praxis nicht aus. In den extrem polarisierten McCarthy-Jahren musste die Formel immer wieder neu ihre Tauglichkeit beweisen. Versagte die Idealkonzeption, zeigte sich dann zweierlei: Zwar öffnete sich hiermit ein Einfallstor für politische Instrumentalisierung und geostrategisches Kalkül, doch konnte ebenso die Verteidigung der Forschungsfreiheit im Namen der nationalen Sicherheit legitimiert werden.

4. Politische Praxis im McCarthyismus

Diese Spannung zeigte sich deutlich, als die Organe des McCarthyismus die RF und andere Stiftungen wegen ihrer liberalen Grundorientierung (und nicht zuletzt deren Gegensatz zur rassistischen Politik des amerikanischen Südens) angriffen und zwei aufeinanderfolgende Ausschüsse des Repräsentantenhauses ihnen das Privileg der Steuerbefreiung zu nehmen versuchten.[32] Die Stiftung ließ sich zwar auf Kompromisse mit dem nationalen Sicherheitsrat ein, ging dabei aber nie so weit, wie die extremsten Kongressausschüsse und antikommunistischen Interessengruppen es gefordert hatten. In den frühen 1950er Jahren kam es zu heftigen Diskussion unter den Verantwortlichen in der Stiftung: Die Positionen reichten dabei von einer Sicherheitsfixierung, die nicht allzu weit vom McCarthyismus entfernt war, bis zu einer Ablehnung jeglicher staatlicher Einmischung in die Auswahl von Stipendiaten. Es wurden bei allen Anträgen Sicherheitsüberprüfungen durchgeführt, also ein Abgleich der Namen von Bewerbern mit den wichtigsten offiziellen, von Regierungsbehörden und legislativen Körperschaften (nicht jedoch mit den von privaten Gruppen) herausgegebenen »Listen« vorgenommen, auf denen die angebliche oder tatsächliche, längst vergangene oder noch anhaltende Beteiligung an oder Nähe zu kommunistischen Aktivitäten festgehalten war. Allerdings ließ sich die Stiftung nie zu den Reinigungsritualen drängen, die für den McCarthyismus typisch waren und die vor allem in der Nennung anderer Namen bestanden. Im Gegenteil, wurde ein Name auf den »antisubversiven« Listen gefunden, war damit zwar oft, aber keinesfalls automatisch die Ablehnung eines Antrags besiegelt. Das letzte Wort hatte ein Netzwerk von »close friends« der RF, vertrauenswürdigen und lange bekannten Mitglieder der akademischen und politischen Elite. Dieser liberale, technokratische Elitismus setzte sich durch, je stärker der McCarthyismus sich vom parteipolitischen Establishment, aus dem er hervorgegangen war, löste und als medial aufgeblasenes, eigendynamisch

---

32 Vgl. dazu Schrecker, *Many Are the Crimes*, 407; Müller, *Krieger und Gelehrte*, 293–312.

überdrehtes und angeblich populistisches Phänomen wahrgenommen werden konnte. Ihre liberale politische Epistemologie gab der Stiftung wiederum die Möglichkeit, sich in dieser Situation schließlich auf einen Formelkompromiss zu einigen. Wenn der wissenschaftliche Fortschritt intrinsisch mit der liberalen Moderne verbunden war, gab es auch kein Problem bei der Kandidatenauswahl: »Apart from Communists and Fascists – where the presumption of incapacity for objective scholarly research can be made – RF makes and will make no inquiry into the political, social or religious beliefs of any applicant for Foundation aid. No scholar of repute would accept a Foundation grant if the Foundation attempted to carry on such investigations of applicants' beliefs and values.« Die antikommunistische Linie war offenkundig, doch ebenso waren die Grenzen des Antikommunismus gekennzeichnet. Kommunisten und Faschisten konnten einfach keine guten, förderungswürdigen Wissenschaftler sein; jeder andere aber eben doch.[33]

Die RF machte sich die Begriffe »subversiv« und »unamerikanisch« nicht zu eigen und wies sie schließlich öffentlich zurück. Stiftungspräsident Dean Rusk, der einige Jahre später unter Kennedy und Johnson Außenminister wurde, stützte diese Linie, die sich intern erst hatte durchsetzen müssen. So konnte die Stiftung, als sie sich den Angriffen des Untersuchungsausschusses gegenübersah, ihre Haltung eindeutig erklären: »The chief danger to be avoided is the discouragement by RF of new and adventurous thinking.« Das politische Vokabular des radikalen Antikommunismus wurde nun gegen diesen selbst gewendet: »By preventing adventuring, and insisting on an official line, totalitarian societies shut themselves off from a rich crop of new ideas and one of the basic sources of growth. In combating Communism, it is important that the western world – and the RF as one of its best intellectual symbols – should not encourage the impoverishment of the stream of new ideas.«[34]

---

33 Willits an Barnard, 19. September 1951, RFA, RG 3.1, Series 900, b. 25, f. 199; Kimball an Barnard, 20. August 1951; Fahs, Questions for Discussion with CIB [Chester I. Barnard], 31. August 1951; Barnard an Principal Officers, 12. September 1951; Deane an Willits, 1. Dezember 1952 (Zitat); DeVinney an Willits, Rusk, 20. Januar 1953 (Zitat); Willits an Rusk, 27. January 1953; Rusk an Watson, 1. März 1954; RFA, RG 3.1, Series 900, b. 25, f. 200; Pro-46: Rusk, Notes on Rockefeller Foundation Program, 1. Dezember 1953; RFA, RG 3.2, Series 900, b. 29, f. 158. In Europa führten RF-Mitarbeiter schärfere politische Überprüfungen durch; vgl. Krige, *American Hegemony*, 115–151. Den »best science«-Elitismus betonen Kevles, *The Physicists*; Lowen, »Zur Verflechtung von Politik und Universitäten«.
34 Willits an Rusk, 27. Januar 1953; siehe auch Rusk an Watson, 1. März 1954; Deane an Willits, 1. Dezember 1952; RFA, RG 3.1, Series 900, b. 25, f. 200; Cox Committee: Answers of the Rockefeller Foundation, 31. Oktober 1952, To »Questionnaire Submitted by the Select Committee of the House of Representatives of the Congress of the United States«, S. 52, 55–56, RFA, RG 3.2, Series 900, b. 14, f. 89.

Darin kann man ein geradezu klassisches Statement der liberalen Wissens-machtpolitik sehen, die sich einen politisch motivierten Deutungsspielraum offen ließ, mitunter weitgehende Kompromisse einging und stets nach Mög-lichkeit des Ausgleichs mit den Regierungsinteressen suchte, die aber nicht nur aus normativen Gründen, sondern vor allem aus institutionellem Eigen-interesse letztlich immer wieder zur Bekräftigung der Wissenschaftsfreiheit zurückkehren musste. In der konkreten Auseinandersetzung mit den Unter-suchungsausschüssen lässt sich dieser Kurs ebenfalls erkennen. Fördermaß-nahmen, die hohen wissenschaftlichen Ansprüchen standhielten und die Unterstützung der »close friends« genossen, wurden auch gegen scharfe At-tacken verteidigt, etwa das Cornell Civil Liberties Project, das sich mit der Einschränkung von Bürgerrechten seit dem Ersten Weltkrieg befasste.[35] Das Institute of Pacific Relations hingegen, ein Netzwerk von Asienkennern aus Wissenschaft, Wirtschaft und Politik, hatte nicht nur seine wissenschaftliche Bedeutung an die Area Studies verloren, sondern sich auch politisch angreif-bar gemacht. Das McCarran-Komitee des Senats und die pro-taiwanesische »China Lobby« hatte sich bereits zuvor auf das Institut eingeschossen. Die Stiftung zog sich diskret aus der Förderung zurück, verteidigte Jahre später aber, als das Risiko geringer geworden war, ihr früheres Engagement.[36]

Die Entgegnung der RF auf den Untersuchungsausschuss erfolgte, als sich McCarthy und der von ihm inspirierte radikale Antikommunismus bereits im Niedergang befanden – McCarthy hatte nach seinen Angriffen auf die seit 1953 amtierende republikanische Regierung und schließlich auf die Streit-kräfte die politische Rückendeckung durch seine Partei verloren, auf die er stets angewiesen war. Die Stiftung nutzte den Stimmungswechsel und ver-teidigte ihre Prinzipien mit einer neuen Vehemenz, die offenkundig auch manchen Kompromiss der Jahre zuvor kompensieren sollte. Vorwürfe gegen das RF-Prestigeprojekt Russian Institute wurden unter Berufung auf Präsi-dent Eisenhower zurückgewiesen: »Before the Committee itself condemns foundation support of an institution which is playing such a vital role in our defense against Communism, we respectfully suggest consultation with

35 Willits an Robert M. Hutchins, 16. April 1952; Rusk an Robert Cushman, 18. Juni 1952; Willits an Cushman, 4. März 1953; Willits an Hutchins, 9. März 1954; RFA, RG 1.1, Series 200, b. 327, f. 3903. Zur wissenschaftlichen Relevanz des Cornell-Projekts vgl. die Hinweise bei Schrecker, No Ivory Tower, 343; dies., The Age of McCarthyism, 293–294.

36 Vgl. Schrecker, No Ivory Tower, 161–167, 182, 275–276; dies., Many Are the Crimes, 244–252; Thomas, The Institute of Pacific Relations; Griffith, The Politics of Fear, 115–151; Anderson, Pacific Dreams. Zum Vorgehen der RF siehe Evans an Willits, Fosdick, 2. April 1946, RFA, RG 1.1, Series 200, b. 352, f. 4187; Supplemental Statement of the Rockefeller Foundation Before the Special Committee to Investigate Tax Exempt Foundations, House of Representatives, 83rd Congress, 3. August 1954, Inv-4b, RFA, RG 3.2, Series 900, b. 16, f. 93, S. 10–13.

those who are responsible in executive capacities for the conduct of our foreign affairs and for the defense of the country.«[37] RF-Präsident Rusk sprach davon, dass der Bericht des Untersuchungsausschusses keinen interessiere, weil dieser sich durch sein Vorgehen diskreditiert habe. McCarthys Erzfeind Dean Acheson gratulierte der Stiftung zu ihrem Sieg über »ignorance and know-nothingism«.[38]

5. Strategie und Theorie, politische Philosophie und Marxismusforschung

Die grundsätzlich liberale, aber ambivalente, nicht linear zu erzählende, von Verbindungen und Konflikten zwischen professionellen und politischen, epistemologischen und strategischen Zielen und Praktiken gekennzeichnete Wissens- und Machtpolitik der RF im hochmodernen Kalten Krieg ist nicht nur in diesen politisch sensiblen Zonen zu erkennen. Auch wenn man sich in die einzelnen Projektförderungen hinein begibt, begegnet man variablen Kopplungen. Der Einsatz für die politische Theorie und Ideengeschichte oder für die bereits erwähnte Marxismusforschung sind aussagekräftige Beispiele dafür. In beiden Fällen stößt man auf die konzeptionelle Verknüpfung von wissenschaftlicher Originalität einerseits und Modernisierungspolitik zum Zweck der amerikanischen Hegemoniesicherung andererseits.

Die Initiative zu einer Wiederbelebung der politischen Theorie und Ideengeschichte kam aus der Stiftung. Einige ihrer Mitarbeiter sahen dieses akademische Feld brachliegen, sie erwarteten zugleich aber, mit der Therapie eines intellektuellen Mangels auch einen politischen Defekt zu beheben. In diesem Fall lag die Zuständigkeit bei der sozialwissenschaftlichen Abteilung, die sich bei der Planung und Durchführung des Programms zur »Legal and Political Philosophy« (LAPP) eng mit der geisteswissenschaftlichen Abteilung abstimmte – traditionelle Disziplinschranken spielten keine Rolle, und die angebliche Dominanz der Sozialwissenschaften vertrug sich mit geisteswissenschaftlicher Reflexion. Der Vernachlässigung des politischen Denkens zugunsten behavioralistischer Ansätze sollte entgegengesteuert und das Stiftungskapital vielfältiger investiert werden. Ein Stiftungspapier fasste zusammen: »It was time that approaches other than the quantitative and behavioral be given some encouragement.«[39]

37 Supplemental Statement of the Rockefeller Foundation Before the Special Committee to Investigate Tax Exempt Foundations, House of Representatives, 83rd Congress, 3. August 1954, Inv-4b, RFA, RG 3.2, Series 900, b. 16, f. 93, S. 3–4.
38 Rusk, Statement, 18. Dezember 1954, RFA, RG 3.2, Series 900, b. 14, f. 85; Acheson an Rusk, 14. August 1954, RFA, RG 3.2, Series 900, b. 16, f. 96.
39 Memo Stewart, 12. April 1954, RFA, RG 3.1, Series 910, b. 9, f. 78.

Diese Sicht setzte sich im Ringen mit dezidiert pro-behavioralistischen Stiftungsberatern durch. Sind in der *intellectual history* oft politische Motive hinter wissenschaftlichen oder philosophischen Auseinandersetzungen zu entdecken, so fand hier der agonale Akt auf dem Feld der Wissenschaft statt, mit Schützenhilfe durch politische Argumente, die nur auf den ersten Blick den Ausschlag gaben. Wieder verschränkten sich auf geradezu paradoxe Weise politische und wissenschaftliche Erwägungen: Unter Berufung auf politische Notwendigkeiten wurde ein Programm installiert, das gerade vom (angeblich, aber nicht durchweg) politisch dienstbereiten Behavioralismus wegführen und ein philosophisches Gegengewicht zu den quantitativen Sozialwissenschaften setzen sollte. Auf die behavioralistische Revolution folgte die Gegenrevolution der politischen Theorie – und beide wurden von der RF initiiert, in jedem Fall finanziert und begleitet. Stiftungspräsident Rusk selbst interessierte sich für die Planungen und nahm an der Gründungskonferenz teil. Sein Interesse galt der politischen Selbstreflexion, der theoretisch und historisch fundierten Auseinandersetzung mit den ideenpolitischen Grundlagen des Westens. Intellektuelle Selbstfindung wurde im Zeichen der geistigen Mobilisierung für den Kalten Krieg betrieben. Sie sollte den Westen intellektuell revitalisieren und die Attraktivität des amerikanisch-liberalen Modells in der ganzen Welt unterstreichen. Die geostrategische Dimension dieses Unternehmens bestand darin, Indien oder den Nahen Osten für die »democratic principles« zu gewinnen, deren Rekonstruktion, Deutung und Erneuerung sich die politische Theorie widmete.[40]

Allerdings kann das Programm keineswegs als philosophische Mobilmachung begriffen werden. Es förderte – gemessen an der akademischen Wirkung äußerst erfolgreich – ein breites Spektrum von unterschiedlichsten Denkern und Gelehrten. Politische Revitalisierung konnte offenbar mit scharfer Gesellschaftskritik einhergehen, ein emphatisches Verständnis der Moderne mit der Erkundung ihrer Schattenseiten; in der Tat führte ein wissenschaftlich bewusst offen gehaltenes Profil zu unerwarteten und doch als Zeugnis intellektueller Pluralität erwünschten Ergebnissen. Schon in der Gründungsphase bestimmte, gemeinsam mit amerikanischer Prominenz wie Louis Hartz, Frank Knight und George Sabine, auch ein linker Emigrant wie Franz Neumann den Kurs. Zu den finanzierten Projekten gehörten nicht nur zahlreiche Werke aus dem Kosmos von Leo Strauss, sondern auch Herbert Marcuses *One-Dimensional Man* und andere linksintellektuelle Klassi-

---

40 Proceedings, First Conference on Legal and Political Philosophy, 31. Oktober-2. November 1952, Bd. 1, S. 82–85, RFA, RG 3.1, Series 910, b. 9, f. 81. Siehe auch Rusk's Kommentar, Protokoll, Advisory Committee LAPP, 21. März 1955, RFA, RG 3.1, Series 910, b. 9, f. 78.

ker. Die Kompetenz von Emigranten war gerade auf diesem Gebiet anerkannt und gefragt – die transnationale Koproduktion von Wissen fand hier auf amerikanischem Boden selbst statt.[41]

Der in den späten 1960er Jahren als Kultfigur der Studentenbewegung und der Neuen Linken berühmt gewordene Marcuse war auch an der Ingangsetzung des transatlantischen Marxismus-Leninismus-Projekts beteiligt, vom dem bereits die Rede war. Marcuse hatte die Jahre zuvor als Kommunismusexperte im State Department verbracht. Seine von der Rockefeller Foundation finanzierte Pilotstudie führte zu seinem Buch *Soviet Marxism*, das gleichermaßen eine Intervention im Sinne seiner Auftraggeber in die »Tauwetter«-Debatten um die Entspannungspolitik sowie eine Kritik des sowjetischen Denkens aus der Perspektive des westlichen Marxismus darstellte.[42] Über OSS, State Department und Russian Institute war Marcuse zu diesem Zweck an das Russian Research Center (RRC) der Harvard University gekommen, das in kleinerem Umfang auch Mittel von der RF erhielt, aber in den ersten Jahren hauptsächlich von der Carnegie Corporation und der amerikanischen Luftwaffe – einem Großsponsor gerade behavioralistischer Sozialwissenschaften – finanziert wurde. Das RRC verdient einen Seitenblick, weil es die Machtpolitik der Wissenschaftsproduktion der 1940er und 1950er Jahre besonders deutlich hervortreten lässt. Anders als das Russian Institute legte das 1948 gegründete RRC den Schwerpunkt auf die Forschung. Dort zeigte sich die wissenschaftliche Offenheit, der auch militärische Auftragsforschung folgen konnte (aber nicht musste) und die sich nicht nur in der Rekrutierung zahlreicher Sozialwissenschaftler mit linker Vergangenheit widerspiegelte. Talcott Parsons' strukturfunktionalistische Theorie der Moderne lieferte den Orientierungsrahmen, Parsons selbst war mit dem Center verbunden. Soziologen wie Barrington Moore zeigten auf der Grundlage des für Air Force-Projekte bearbeiteten Materials, dass die Sowjetunion eine moderne, industrialisierte, funktional differenzierte, von politischen Spannungen durchzogene und zugleich stabile Gesellschaft war, deren ökonomische und gesellschaftliche Strukturen eine bürokratisch durchgeführte Reformpolitik erwarten ließen. Der Osten war dem liberal-technokratisch gesteuerten Westen dieser Lesart zufolge, die später in ihren unterschiedlichen Variationen als Konvergenztheorie bezeichnet wurde, gar

41 Zur Gründung von LAPP siehe Proceedings, First Conference on Legal and Political Philosophy, 31. Oktober-2. November 1952, 2 Bde., RFA, RG 3.1, Series 910, b. 9, f. 81–82; eine Liste der geförderten Projekte bis 1962 findet sich in The Rockefeller Foundation: Program in Legal and Political Philosophy 1953–1958 [1962], RFA, RG 3.1, Series 910, b. 9, f. 80.

42 Vgl. zu diesem Forschungsverbund und zu Marcuses Rolle darin Müller, *Krieger und Gelehrte*, 405–538; zu Marcuse und der amerikanischen Linken Wheatland, *The Frankfurt School in Exile*, 311–334.

nicht so unähnlich. Marcuses Buch war kein Fremdkörper in diesen Strukturen, sondern ein Produkt dieses Diskurses.[43]

Diese soziologische Deutung der Sowjetunion als moderne Gesellschaft veränderte auch die Diskussion darüber, ob es sich bei der Sowjetunion um ein (als monolithisch definiertes) totalitäres System handelte – was von den meisten Fachleuten, anders als von Intellektuellen in der öffentlichen Debatte, bereits in den Anfangsjahren des Kalten Krieges bezweifelt oder nur mit erheblichen Einschränkungen und Spezifizierungen vertreten wurde. Das gesellschaftstheoretische Instrumentarium der Soziologie Parsons' und die militärisch-politische Aufgabenstellung führten in einer heuristisch produktiven Kopplung zu einem Innovationsschub, der so in anderen Teildisziplinen der Sowjetologie nicht immer gegeben war. Gerade Moore, Inspiration für spätere Kritiker einer linearen Modernisierungstheorie, an deren Endpunkt die amerikanische Gesellschaft stand, postulierte dabei niemals eine Interdependenz von Industrialisierung und Demokratisierung.[44] In der sowjetologischen Totalitarismusdiskussion ging es darum eher um die Frage, ob modernen Industriegesellschaften generell totalitäre Potenziale inhärent seien, und kaum darum, ob die Sowjetunion nach Stalin noch ein totalitäres Regime wie der Nationalsozialismus sei – diese Frage wurde weitgehend verneint, auch wenn in der Öffentlichkeit die Positionen der Totalitarismustheoretiker Carl Joachim Friedrich und Zbigniew Brzezinski lauter nachhallten. Anhänger der Totalitarismusthese wie der prominente Harvard-Politikwissenschaftler Merle Fainsod, der mit *How Russia is Ruled* ein für lange Zeit verbindliches »textbook« verfasst hatte, differenzierten ihre Ansichten, sobald sie empirisches Material aus sowjetischen Archiven auswerten konnten. Auch hier machte sich die epistemische Eigendynamik der Disziplinen bemerkbar: Die disziplinäre Ausdifferenzierung und Professionalisierung hatte zur Folge, dass eher Fragestellungen verfolgt wurden, die die Sowjetunion in einen größeren, vergleichenden Zusammenhang stellten. Wenn sich dabei politischer Einfluss auswirkte, dann kaum die Linie der antikommunistischen Hardliner. Insoweit die Sowjetforschung politische Implikationen hatte, zeigten diese viel öfter in Richtung Koexistenz und Entspannung. Zugleich darf man die wissenschaftliche Qualität dieser Werke nicht unterschätzen. Sie gingen in ihrer politischen Funktion nicht auf, sie waren nicht von den Intentionen ihrer Geldgeber determiniert und sie konnten zur Dekonstruktion von Feindbildern und zur reformorientierten Kritik der westlichen Gesellschaften beitragen.[45]

---

43 Vgl. Engerman, *Know Your Enemy*, 43–70; zur Luftwaffe als Wissenschaftssponsor Robin, *The Making of the Cold War Enemy*.

44 Zu den soziologischen Debatten vgl. Engerman, *Know Your Enemy*, 180–205.

45 Zur Totalitarismusdiskussion in den »Soviet Studies« vgl. ebd., 206–232.

6. Konvergenz von Macht und Wissenschaft:
Modernisierungstheorien und Modernisierungsagenturen

Die politischen und institutionellen Ambivalenzen hatten eine Entsprechung in der Theorie. Die Modernisierungstheorie (in ihren vielen Schattierungen) war die Meistererzählung der Epoche und die Konvergenztheorie bildete den »historiological kernel of modernization theory«.[46] Doch Modernisierungs- und Konvergenztheorien können nicht allein als auf politische Anwendung zielende Modernisierungsideologien erfasst werden.[47] Von Anfang an operierten mit Moore oder Marcuse innerhalb des modernisierungstheoretischen Diskurses auch scharfsinnige Kritiker von linearen, selbstgewissen, allzu optimistischen und Gewalt einkalkulierenden Modernisierungskonzepten. Als intellektuelle Grundlage für den Vietnamkrieg und andere Interventionen in der Dritten Welt in Verruf geraten, hatten Modernisierungstheorien trotz ihrer diskursiven Gemeinsamkeiten viele Gesichter.[48] Wenn es heißt: »in convergence, there was truth«, so sind damit trotz analytischer Übereinstimmung sehr unterschiedliche politische Wahrheiten gemeint.[49] Im Hinblick auf den Ost-West-Konflikt wohnten Modernisierungstheorien entspannungspolitische Implikationen inne, denn der theoretische Kern aller Entspannungsprognosen war eine modernisierungstheoretische Erwartung. Die prognostizierte Annäherung von Osten und Westen beruhte auf einem den politischen Systemen übergeordneten Strukturwandel, der alle gesellschaftlichen und wirtschaftlichen Bereiche umfasste. Die Verknüpfung von Liberalisierung im westlichen Sinne und industriellem Wandel machte dabei deutlich, dass in diesem Bild von Konvergenz der Westen als Vorbild diente. Modernisierungskonzeptionen integrierten strategische Visionen und hochmoderne Wissenschaftsauffassungen. Die Konvergenz von guter Wissenschaft und westlichen liberalen Werten und die Konvergenz aller modernen Gesellschaften entsprechend westlicher politischer Modelle waren beide Teil einer diskursiven Formation. Die amerikanische globale Hegemonie entsprang beiden Konvergenzkonzepten als indirekte, gewissermaßen natürliche Konsequenz – Hegemonie durch auf Vorbildfunktion gegründete Machtpolitik und durch die Aneignung, Wei-

---

46 Vgl. ders., »The Romance of Economic Development«; Gilman, *Mandarins of the Future*, besonders 1–23, 57, 74–76, 100–103, 190–202, 221–222, 234–235 (Zitat); Metzler, *Konzeptionen politischen Handelns*, 225–231.

47 Vgl. so etwa zur Diskussion in der US-Regierung Latham, *Modernization as Ideology*.

48 Vgl. vor allem Gilman, *Mandarins of the Future*; zur soziologischen Theoriebildung (unter Vernachlässigung der außenpolitischen Bedeutung) Knöbl, *Spielräume der Modernisierung*; zur außenpolitischen Anwendung Simpson, *Economists with Guns*.

49 Gilman, *Mandarins of the Future*, 74.

terentwicklung und Verbreitung von Wissen. Der natürlichen Hegemoniesicherung wurde jedoch gezielt nachgeholfen: In beiden Sphären lag die Steuerung in den Händen sachkundiger Manager und Experten; die hochmodernen Entwicklungs- und Wissenschaftsbegriffe waren zutiefst elitär, womit allerdings noch kein Urteil über ihren Erfolg gesprochen ist.[50]

Für die RF als Modernisierungs- und damit indirekt Hegemoniesicherungsagentur ergaben sich aus diesem ambivalenten diskursiven und institutionellen Gefüge ebenso ambivalente philanthropische Praktiken, die vorangehend nur skizziert werden konnten. Ambivalenz heißt eben nicht, dass machtpolitische Erwägungen immer die Wissenschaftsstrategie dominierten. Intellektuelle Interessen, ja simple Neugier konnte über alle geostrategischen Motive triumphieren. Ein Verständnis der philanthropischen Konzeptionen und Praktiken muss der Eigengesetzlichkeit und Eigendynamik der Systeme Rechnung tragen, wenn auch die Differenzen vermittelt und die Grenzen durchlässig waren. Auf dem Gebiet der Sozialwissenschaften, deren globale Durchsetzung und Ausbreitung selbst ein wichtiges Element in Modernisierungserzählungen war, kommen Verschränkungen und Wechselwirkungen ebenso deutlich zum Vorschein wie Distinktion und Eigensinn – und ebenso wie Konvergenzen von materiellen Interessen.[51]

Es ist gerade die Pluralität der Modernekonzeptionen, die diesen ideenpolitischen Komplex historisch fest im Kalten Krieg verankert. Wenn, um Arne Westad noch einmal aufzugreifen, der Kalte Krieg mehr als alles andere ein »conflict between the two versions of Western modernity that socialism and liberal capitalism seemed to offer« war, beide durch »rule by experts« gekennzeichnet, dann war Modernisierung immer auch – funktional – eine Intervention auf einem strategischen Feld, selbst wenn es sich um unpolitische Fragen handelte. Der Kalte Krieg kann in diesem Sinne als eine Phase globaler, durch den politischen Systemantagonismus dynamisierter Transformationen von wirtschaftlichen und gesellschaftlichen Strukturen betrachtet werden. Die zwei konkurrierenden Modernisierungsmodelle zielten zuerst auf Europa, dann auf die umworbene und umkämpfte Dritte Welt und erstreckten sich auf Bildung, Technologie, Industrialisierung und die gesellschaftliche Ordnung: Liberale Modernisierung durch einen staatlich regulierten Markt – die zeitgenössische Kombination von gezügeltem Kapitalismus, liberaler Demokratie, Wohlfahrts- und Sozialstaat – stand gegen staatssozialistische Modernisierung durch zentrale Planung. Die globale At-

---

50 Zum im Vergleich zur Zwischenkriegszeit inklusiven und gesellschaftsaktivistischeren Elitismus der amerikanischen Natur- und Sozialwissenschaften im frühen Kalten Krieg vgl. Heyck, »Die Moderne in der amerikanischen Sozialwissenschaft«; Lowen, »Zur Verflechtung von Politik und Universitäten«.

51 Vgl. Lowen, »Zur Verflechtung von Politik und Universitäten«.

traktivität der beiden konkurrierenden Systeme hing von ihrem Erfolg bei
der wirtschaftlichen Stabilisierung und der Verbesserung der Lebensbedin-
gungen ab.[52] Der wissenschaftliche Fortschritt und die kulturelle Vielfalt waren untrennbar Teil dieser Vorstellungen von gesellschaftlichen Transformationen. Die technokratische »Verwissenschaftlichung des Sozialen« war ein
Grundzug der Epoche. Die Erfassung des Sozialen und Politischen durch die
Wissenschaft, die politische und gesellschaftliche Nachfrage nach Wissen,
die Ausbreitung von Expertentum, Forschungsuniversitäten und Beratungs-
wesen sowie das zunehmende wissenschaftliche Legitimationsbedürfnis des
öffentlichen Diskurses waren zudem durch eine ideenpolitische Klammer
verbunden, auf die eingangs hingewiesen wurde – die Perspektive einer sozial-liberalen Reformpolitik, die nach dem Zweiten Weltkrieg bis zu den
1970er Jahren vorherrschte. Reformorientierte Sozialisten, Christdemokra-
ten und Liberal-Konservative konnten sich darauf, bei vielen Unterschieden
im Detail, im Grundsatz einigen.[53] Damit war die Position des Westens im
frühen Kalten Krieg bestimmt.

Der Schatten des Kalten Krieges lag also immer auf der Wissensmacht-
politik der RF in den Sozialwissenschaften, doch das macht die geförderten
Sozialwissenschaften – außer in einem zeitlichen Sinne – noch nicht zu »Cold
War social sciences«. Diese Differenzierungsleistung muss jede Wissenschaftsgeschichte des Kalten Krieges erbringen. Komplexität zu reduzieren,
führt hier nicht zu neuen Einsichten. Die Konvergenz von amerikanischer
Macht und moderner Wissenschaft begann in den späten 1960er Jahren zu
zerbröckeln. Auch in dieser Hinsicht ist es sinnvoll, von einem hochmodernen Kalten Krieg zu sprechen. Die Konstellation der 1940er bis 1960er Jahre,
die Versöhnung der Systeme Wissenschaft und Politik durch Scharniere wie
die RF bei gleichzeitiger Aufrechterhaltung der Systemgrenzen, brach zusammen. Dass wir es seit den 1970er Jahren mit einer neuen historischen
Grundkonstellation zu tun haben, stößt mittlerweile auf breiten Konsens.[54]
Auf der Ebene der ökonomischen und gesellschaftlichen Strukturen trat
ebenso ein regional zeitversetzter fundamentaler Wandel ein wie im ideenpolitischen Haushalt des Westens: Dieser Wandel setzte ein mit dem Zusam-

52 Westad, »The Cold War and the international history of the twentieth century«, 10,
16–17.
53 Vgl. Maier, *Recasting Bourgeois Europe*; Brick, *Transcending Capitalism*; Doering-
Manteuffel/Raphael, *Nach dem Boom*; Raphael, »Die Verwissenschaftlichung des Sozialen«.
54 Zusammenfassend etwa Doering-Manteuffel/Raphael, *Nach dem Boom*; Andreas
Wirsching u.a., »Forum: The 1970s and 1980s as a Turning Point in European History?«;
für die intellektuelle Entwicklung in den USA maßgeblich: Rodgers, *Age of Fracture*; zwei
aktuelle Fallstudien zur amerikanischen Sozial- und Wirtschaftsgeschichte: Cowie, *Stayin'
Alive*; Stein, *Pivotal Decade*.

menbruch der sozialreformerischen »Great Society«, dem Vietnamkrieg, dem wachsenden Legitimitätsverlust des Sozial-Liberalismus und dem von der neulinken und »gegenkulturellen« Kritik an der Reformgesellschaft noch verstärkten Aufstieg eines marktradikalen Konservatismus zum dominanten ideenpolitischen Modell. Er resultierte aus den Wirtschaftskrisen und vor allem einer von den liberalen Reformern und Modernisierern selbst beschleunigten Globalisierung, die dem Kapitalismus neue Wege eröffnete, jenseits des nationalstaatlichen Rahmens, auf den gesellschaftliche Reformen noch immer angewiesen waren.[55]

Auf der ideengeschichtlichen Ebene zeigten sich diese Umbrüche im Zerfall der Modernisierungserzählungen. Das hatte direkte Konsequenzen für die Praxis der RF. Auch theoretisch, auf der Grundlage von Modernisierungskonzeptionen und hochmodernen politischen Epistemologien, ließen sich die Missionen der Philanthropie und der Außenpolitik nun nicht mehr problemlos miteinander versöhnen. Die gemeinsamen Grundlagen zerbrachen. Die RF und andere Stiftungen mussten sich neu orientieren und ihre Aktivitäten entpolitisieren. Bestimmten die problem- und anwendungsorientierten, integrierten, interdisziplinären Sozialwissenschaften die von hochmodernem Selbstvertrauen geprägte Förderpolitik des ersten »patronage system« im Kalten Krieg, das für jedes Problem die Lösung finden zu können glaubte, so setzte sich seit den 1970er Jahren ein Fördersystem durch, das an Grundlagenforschung und der Schärfung disziplinärer Profile interessiert war und keine besonderen methodischen oder theoretischen Ansätze bevorzugte.[56]

Ob damit die wissenschaftliche und intellektuelle Vielfalt gewachsen ist, steht auf einem anderen Blatt. Jedenfalls gibt es unter den Kritikern der Modernisierungstheorie, die zugleich ihre besten Kenner sind, auch Tendenzen, das pluralistisch-liberale Wissenssystem der Hochmoderne und geläuterte Modernisierungskonzeptionen historisch zu rehabilitieren, und zwar mit einem vorrangig ideenpolitischen Argument. Was demnach von den intellektuellen Formationen bleibt, die in der hochmodernen Phase des Kalten Krieges ihren größten Einfluss ausübten – das ist der Gedanke an eine globale Reformpolitik, die das ökonomische Diktat des Kapitalismus überwindet. »Some vision of a global welfare state remains the best defense of the Enlightenment as a global ideal«, erklärt Nils Gilman am Ende einer Studie, die minutiös die intellektuelle Arroganz und das politische Scheitern von Modernisierungstheoretikern wie Walt Rostow herausarbeitet: »The aim must

---

55 Diese hier extrem verkürzte Skizze folgt Brick, *Transcending Capitalism*, 219–246, 255–256; Bernstein, *A Perilous Progress*, 148–156; Doering-Manteuffel/Raphael, *Nach dem Boom*; Gilman, *Mandarins of the Future*, 203–240; Rodgers, *Age of Fracture*.
56 Vgl. Heyck, »Patrons of the Revolution«, bes. 433–434.

be to actualize the best parts of 1950s modernization theory«. Und auch Howard Brick schließt mit der von sozial-liberalen Denkern im Kalten Krieg entlehnten Forderung, die konzeptionelle Spannung von reformistischer und revolutionärer Gesellschaftsveränderung ein für alle Mal aufzulösen. »The task remains of shaping a viable successor to the midcentury postcapitalist vision«, betont Brick darum, »one that takes seriously ›transitional‹ strategies for charting a path beyond capitalism, that is, one that recognizes the potential for socializing change in the present without falling back on undue confidence in the given trends of development«.[57] Die Konvergenz von Macht und Wissen, von Wissenschaft und Außenpolitik im frühen Kalten Krieg könnte den Blick dafür trüben, dass wir es im Fall der RF selbst im Kalten Krieg noch mit einer Agentur sozial-liberaler Modernisierung zu tun haben. Liberale Stiftungen wie die RF können zwar auch, aber nicht allein und nicht einmal vorrangig, als Institutionen des Kalten Krieges verstanden werden, so sehr sie immer auch geopolitische Ziele verfolgten und so wichtig sie für die amerikanische Strategie im Kalten Krieg waren.

---

57 Vgl. Brick, *Transcending Capitalism*, 270, 272; Gilman, *Mandarins of the Future*, 276.

Kiran Klaus Patel

Kommentar – Rockefeller Foundation, Kalter Krieg und Amerikanisierung

Am 23. Mai 1949 legte Chester I. Barnard der Öffentlichkeit seinen ersten Jahresbericht als Präsident der Rockefeller Foundation vor. Die Aufgabe, die Entwicklungen des Jahres 1948 zusammenzufassen, war keineswegs einfach: Immerhin befand sich die Welt am Anfang eines neuen globalen Konfliktes, für den man mit dem Ausdruck »Kalter Krieg« bereits einen Begriff gefunden hatte, bevor man sich aller Implikationen und Konsequenzen für die Welt oder auch nur für die Arbeit einer Stiftung wie der Rockefeller Foundation hätte bewusst sein können. Aber es gab noch einen zweiten Grund, der Barnards Aufgabe erschwerte: Der Ökonom, der Harvard ohne Abschluss verlassen hatte, trat nun das Erbe Raymond B. Fosdicks an, der das Präsidentenamt der RF für beinahe eine Dekade innegehabt und die Stiftung vom New Deal durch den Krieg in die Truman-Ära geführt hatte. Es war Fosdick gewesen, der als Teil des Jahresberichts der Stiftung die »President's Review« eingeführt hatte – eine persönliche Stellungnahme des Stiftungspräsidenten zu den Geschehnissen des zurückliegenden Jahres, die zugleich auch selbstständig in mehreren Sprachen veröffentlicht wurde und als ein Aushängeschild der Stiftung diente. Was für die Geschicke der Welt belanglos blieb, musste den Stiftungspräsidenten durchaus umtreiben: die Frage nämlich, wie er sich im neuen Amt öffentlich präsentieren sollte.

Was also tun? Barnard entschied sich dafür, am Format des »President's Review« festzuhalten. Als Einstieg in seinen Jungferntext wählte er 1949 das Naheliegende: eine Reflexion über diese Textform selbst. Die Review stelle ein »personal judgement« dar, zugleich reflektiere sie die »position of official responsibility«. Diese sei bei der RF »unique, because the Foundation represents no private or political interest, and is concerned with the entire range of philanthropic effort throughout the world«. Einerseits, so Barnard, verfügten die Mitarbeiter der Stiftung über eine »detached objectivity«, andererseits sei es unvermeidbar, dass ihre Sichtweise beeinflusst sei »by the biases and preconceptions of their training, and collectively by Judaeo-Christian traditions of long standing, as well as a solid background of American democracy«. Gleichwohl diene die Stiftung dem »welfare of mankind« und sei weder »religiously oriented nor nationalistic in the narrow sense«.[1]

Offensichtlich strebte die Stiftung nach unparteiischer Objektivität, war sich aber zugleich einer besonderen kulturellen Prägung bewusst. Neutralität und Universalismus gingen einher mit einer amerikanisch-westlich fundierten Agenda inklusive entsprechender politischer Wertvorstellungen. Barnard konnte diese Dimensionen beschreiben und miteinander zu vereinbaren versuchen, ohne jedoch das grundsätzliche Spannungsverhältnis zwischen ihnen auszuräumen.

Teil dieses Kräftefelds, in dem sich die Rockefeller Foundation bewegte, war die Förderung der Sozialwissenschaften sowie das Werk der International Health Division (IHD), denen sich Paul Weindling und Tim B. Müller in ihren Beiträgen widmen. Nicht nur, weil es jeweils um die Rockefeller Foundation und den frühen Kalten Krieg geht, sondern auch aufgrund des besonderen Augenmerks auf den wissenschaftlichen Aktivitäten der Stiftung leuchtet die Entscheidung der Herausgeber ein, die beiden Beiträge zu einer Einheit zusammen zu fassen. Denn zu dem Doppelbrennpunkt von übergreifend-philanthropischen Zielen einerseits und politischen Orientierungen andererseits gesellt sich sowohl bei Weindling als auch bei Müller die Frage nach den Eigenlogiken und -dynamiken des Wissenschaftssystems im Zeitalter des Kalten Krieges.

Das Genre des verschriftlichten Kommentars ist eher ungewöhnlich und die folgenden Überlegungen möchten mehr leisten, als die beiden Beiträge zu bewerten, denn sonst bliebe der Erkenntnisgewinn relativ gering. Ich nehme die Texte von Weindling und Müller vielmehr in erster Linie zum Anlass, weiterführende Fragen zu stellen, und ich verstehe es als Kompliment für einen Text, wenn er solche aufwirft. Konkret geht es im Folgenden erstens darum, was man in den Kapiteln Neues über den Kalten Krieg lernen kann. Zweitens sollen die Texte in den Zusammenhang der Debatte über die »Amerikanisierung« und die Rolle der USA in der Welt gestellt werden. Ein knapper dritter Teil wird die Befunde bündeln und zur Gesamtagenda des Bandes in Beziehung setzen.

---

1 Rockefeller Foundation, *Annual Report 1948*, 6; zur Vorstellung des Berichts vgl. z. B. »Rockefeller Fund Report Stresses Importance of Language to Peace«, in: *New York Times*, 24. Mai 1949.

Vielfalt und Einheit im Kalten Krieg

Während der Kalte Krieg in beiden Beiträgen eine zentrale Rolle spielt, liegt ein wesentlicher Wert der Texte darin, jeweils die Rolle der RF im Ost-West-Konflikt differenziert darzustellen und der vor allem in der älteren Literatur vertretenen These einer einfachen Indienstnahme der Stiftung zugunsten der amerikanischen Außenpolitik nuancierte Alternativen entgegenzustellen.

Sehr deutlich wendet sich Müller gegen dichotome Deutungsmuster und die Vorstellung einer direkten Nutzung und Verengung wissenschaftlicher Forschung angesichts des Kalten Krieges. Überzeugend präpariert er vielmehr die relativen Freiräume im Wissenschaftsbereich heraus. Trotz McCarthyismus blieb die sozialwissenschaftliche Forschung in den USA erstaunlich pluralistisch. Stiftungen wie die RF halfen, Spielräume zu eröffnen und gegen politischen Druck zu verteidigen – wie Müllers Beitrag etwa anhand des Cornell Civil Liberties Project skizziert. Überzeugend und plastisch veranschaulicht er, dass Barnards Nachfolger als Stiftungspräsident, der spätere US-Außenminister Dean Rusk, einer monodimensionalen Auseinandersetzung mit dem Kommunismus eine Absage erteilte. Die Stiftung vertrat vielmehr einen Kurs, der die Fähigkeit zur Selbstkritik sowie die Ideale von Meinungspluralität und Diskursivität hochhielt. Der Eintritt in diesen Salon der Gelehrsamkeit sollte Kommunisten und Faschisten grundsätzlich verwehrt bleiben – insofern waren die Freiräume durchaus begrenzt. Dessen ungeachtet kondensierte sich gerade in dieser kontrollierten Mehrstimmigkeit, wie Müller luzide herausarbeitet, die Vorstellung von der Überlegenheit des Westens. Rusk und andere Vertreter der Stiftung meinten, dass allein ein solcher Ansatz es erlaube, den Kommunismus auf dessen ureigenem Terrain zu schlagen. Daraus erklärt sich etwa die Förderung einer westlichen Marxismusforschung, die den Ostblock durch eine Re-Lektüre seiner Säulenheiligen der ideologischen Grundlagen zu berauben suchte. Luhmannianisch angehaucht, fasst Müller das so zusammen: Kritische Sozialwissenschaften galten als Ausweis der westlichen Moderne und dienten ihrer »Selbstreflexion, Selbstkritik, Selbstkorrektur und damit Selbsterhaltung«. Und wenngleich sich die Wissenschaft im Dienste der US-Außenpolitik befand, wurde sie doch nie ganz von ihr determiniert.

Weindlings Beitrag weist zumindest in Teilen in eine ähnliche Richtung. Er sucht darin nach den Gründen, warum die Stiftung 1951 relativ abrupt ihre IHD schloss. Einerseits räumt er dem aufkommenden Kalten Krieg einen zentralen Stellenwert ein, um Veränderungen in der Arbeit der RF zu erklären. Öffentliche Vorwürfe, in der Vergangenheit kommunistische Wissenschaftler gefördert zu haben, die Angst, dass die Stiftung selbst infiltriert werden könnte, sowie die Furcht, den Status der Steuerbefreiung zu verlie-

ren, sind nur einige der Faktoren, die fortan den Kurs prägten. So suchte die
Stiftung nunmehr einen engeren Schulterschluss mit dem US-Außenminis-
terium und setzte besonders auf John Foster Dulles, der bei Barnards Antritt
1948 als möglicher Nachfolger an der Stiftungsspitze im Gespräch war. Aber
wenngleich Weindling der neuen weltpolitischen Lage hohes Gewicht bei-
misst, zeigt der Beitrag auch, dass die institutionelle Dynamik innerhalb der
RF für das Schicksal der IHD eine wichtige Rolle spielte. Die organisatorische Anomalie in der Stiftungsarchitektur, welche die IHD darstellte, das
schmalere Budget der RF angesichts des fallenden Dollars, oder etwa der Ge-
nerationswechsel in den Führungsetagen der Stiftung werden hier in Anschlag gebracht. Sicherlich hätte man versuchen können, den Einfluss dieser
Faktoren noch stärker zu gewichten. Fest steht aber auch so, dass eine mul-
tidimensionale Analyse notwendig ist, um die Geschichte der IHD zu verstehen.

Müllers und Weindlings generelle Stoßrichtung in Hinblick auf ein diffe-
renzierteres Verständnis des Ost-West-Konfliktes bestätigt und nuanciert so
die Tendenz der neueren Forschung zur westlichen Wissenschaft und zu
trans- und internationalen Organisationen im Kalten Krieg.[2] Denn insgesamt hat man sich von der älteren Vorstellung verabschiedet, laut der die Arbeit der US-Stiftungen oder der Wissenschaft direkt mit den Zielen der amerikanischen (Außen-)Politik übereinstimmte und sich im Wesentlichen aus
diesen erklärt. Ein solcher Befund ließe sich für die beiden Texte zugleich in
dreierlei Hinsicht weiter spezifizieren. Erstens bleibt die Position derjenigen
Wissenschafterinnen und Wissenschaftler relativ blass, die sich unter diesen
Rahmenbedingungen zur Mitarbeit an von der RF (ko-)finanzierten Projekten entschlossen. Bei Weindling liegt dies daran, dass ihn vor allem organi-
sationshistorische Veränderungen interessieren. Hauptsächlich geht es ihm
um Einsichten »into Foundation structures and the policy-making process«.
So erscheint die RF hier zwar als durchaus komplexer Koloss mit der IHD als
Subsystem mit phasenweise ziemlich großer Autonomie. Die Spielräume
von Wissenschaftlern und Praktikern an der Basis werden jedoch nicht aus-
geleuchtet. Bedenkt man, dass die IHD »vacillated between laboratory-based
research […] and sanitary measures on the global peripheries«, zwischen
»clinical research, best practice in the organisation of health care, and virology«, dann legt dies nahe, dass diese Spielräume keineswegs klein waren.
Gab es dennoch keine Rückwirkung zwischen den Dynamiken an der Basis
und denen auf der Entscheidungsebene? Und das, obwohl die RF an ihrem
»staff of field officers« vor allem schätzte, dass diese »knew the local public
health circumstances, health problems and governmental agencies of each

---

2 Vgl. dazu z. B. Kott, »Par-delà la guerre froide«; Chou, »Cultural Education«; Tournès, »Introduction«, v. a. 10–11; Manela, »A Pox on Your Narrative«.

geographical theatre of application – such as in the Far East, Brazil, and India«? Angesichts der Entscheidungsstrukturen in der RF könnte das der Fall sein. Aber selbst wenn man lediglich »Foundation structures and the policy process« verstehen möchte, wäre es sinnvoll, diesen Faktor zu diskutieren.

Müller geht demgegenüber weiter und steckt zumindest die Bandbreite möglicher Positionen ab. Er befindet, dass manchmal selbst staatliche Auftragsforschung bemerkenswerte Freiräume für Innovation induzieren konnte, während unabhängige Universitätsgelehrte sich immer wieder selbst mobilisierten und für eine billige Legitimationswissenschaft hergaben. Etwas tiefere empirische Einblicke wären hier interessant gewesen. Zugegeben, kein Buchkapitel kann alle möglichen Forschungsansätze gleichermaßen verfolgen und an anderer Stelle hat sich Müller ausführlich zu dieser Frage geäußert, vor allem in Bezug auf Herbert Marcuse.[3] Im vorliegenden Text gibt es jedoch die Tendenz, die intellektuellen Freiräume primär aus institutionellen Entwicklungen an der Schnittstelle zwischen Staat, Stiftungen und Forschungsstellen zu erklären. Inwieweit individuelle Forscher oder Forschungsgruppen dazu beitrugen, solche Spielräume zu bewahren oder neu zu erstreiten, wird dagegen weniger sichtbar. Das Wechselspiel zwischen Forschung und Lehre bleibt zudem ganz ausgeblendet, wiewohl die Interaktion zwischen Gelehrten und Studierenden gerade im Falle Marcuses interessant ist. Und die Eigenlogik wissenschaftlichen Arbeitens, aber auch die wechselseitige Indienstnahme von Politik und Wissenschaft als Ressourcen füreinander wird hier lediglich angedeutet, nicht aber ausbuchstabiert.[4]

Zweitens laden die Beiträge dazu ein, Grundprobleme wissenschaftlichen Arbeitens zu durchdenken. Um dies zu verdeutlichen, soll zunächst Müllers Kapitel herangezogen werden. Er betont ausdrücklich, dass Exzellenz ein Kernkriterium für die RF bei der Forschungsförderung bildete. Er lässt es dabei bewenden und natürlich kann kein einzelner Beitrag alles leisten. Aus wissenschaftshistorischer und -theoretischer Sicht bleiben so jedoch spannende Fragen außerhalb des Analysehorizonts. Denn die einschlägige Forschung hat längst gezeigt, dass Begriffe wie Innovation oder Exzellenz sozial ausverhandelt sind und sich keineswegs objektiv feststellen lassen – wiewohl es zum Tornistergepäck der meisten Wissenschaftler gehört, die Sonderstellung wissenschaftlich generierten Wissens gegenüber anderen Wissensformen zu postulieren und von klaren Bemessungsmaßstäben in Qualitätsfragen auszugehen.[5] Müller erwähnt, dass Vorstellungen von Qualität und

3 Vgl. Müller, *Krieger und Gelehrte*.
4 Zur wechselseitigen Indienstnahme vgl. Ash, »Wissenschaft und Politik«.
5 Vgl. als Einstiege in die Debatte z.B. Weingart, *Wissenschaftssoziologie*; Vogel, »Von der Wissenschafts- zur Wissensgeschichte«; Lipphardt/Patel, »Neuverzauberung im Gestus der Wissenschaftlichkeit«.

Evidenz gegen Anwürfe von außen in Wissensnetzwerken von »close friends« der RF diskutiert und im Erfolgsfall stabilisiert wurden. Diese Prozesse wären meines Erachtens ein spannendes Feld für Tiefenbohrungen. Sie könnten dabei helfen, den euphemistisch gefärbten Selbstbeschreibungen der Akteure auf die Schliche zu kommen. Dieses Problem erscheint angesichts der auch heute noch oft ungebrochenen Sprache der Hochmoderne in Bezug auf Charakter und Spezifik der Wissenschaft umso dringlicher.

Wenn Müller etwa die »wissenschaftliche Bedeutung« des von der RF geförderten Cornell Civil Liberties Projects mit einer Rezension von James R. Killian zu belegen versucht, dann sollte man Folgendes wissen: Im Jahr vor dieser wohlwollenden Besprechung hatte das Massachusetts Institute of Technology, dem Killian damals vorstand, RF-Chef Barnard als Hauptredner bei der Graduiertenfeier eingeladen.[6] Mehr noch: Genau in dieser Zeit wurde das MIT zu einem der zentralen akademischen Stützpunkte dessen, was in der Literatur teilweise der militärisch-industriell-akademische Komplex der USA genannt wird und wofür der Anthropologe Hugh Gusterson den Begriff »securityscape« geprägt hat.[7] Zugleich konnte das MIT damals auf eine langjährige Zusammenarbeit mit dem RF zurückblicken, die sich genau in den frühen 1950er Jahren noch einmal deutlich intensivierte.[8]

Es geht hier nicht um wissenschaftliche Unredlichkeit seitens der untersuchten Akteure, sondern lediglich darum zu zeigen, dass jene, die über die Qualität anderer befinden, selbst Teil des wissenschaftlichen Feldes sind.[9] Ihre Maßstäbe zur Beurteilung akademischer Texte und Projekte können von einer Vielzahl von Faktoren beeinflusst sein. Die Zuschreibung von Qualität, die Vergabe kulturellen Kapitals und von Prestige fußt nie auf gänzlich objektiven Kriterien – einfach, weil es solche nicht geben kann. Mit Ludwik Fleck könnte man von der Herausbildung von jeweils kulturell gebundenen Denkstilen sprechen, die so tief dringen, dass sie sogar eigene Vorstellungen davon hervorbringen, wie wissenschaftliche Tatsachen aussehen. Der hier beschriebene Denkstil bedient sich demnach der Sprache von Innovation und Exzellenz, ohne diese Kriterien jenseits der Grenzen des zugehörigen Denkstils erzeugen zu können.[10]

Dieser Denkstil ist, wie bereits angedeutet, dem heutigen eng verwandt. Insofern mag es schwerfallen, ihm mit Distanz zu begegnen. Wie uns

---

6 Vgl. zur 84. Commencement Ceremony des MIT: »Barnard and Compton will be Speakers at Commencement«, in: *The Tech*, 12. März 1950, 1.

7 Gusterson, *People of the Bomb*.

8 Vgl. Rockefeller Foundation, *Annual Report 1952*, z.B. 117, 129, 155, 206.

9 Zum Begriff des wissenschaftlichen Feldes vgl. Bourdieu, *Vom Gebrauch der Wissenschaft*.

10 Fleck, *Entstehung und Entwicklung*.

Weindling jedoch erinnert, umfasste in den 1930er Jahren die RF-Definition von Spitzenforschung noch eugenische und rassenbiologische Projekte. Fördermittel flossen bis kurz vor Kriegsbeginn ins »Dritte Reich« und lange Zeit profitierte etwa das von Otmar von Verschuer geleitete Kaiser Wilhelm Institut für Anthropologie, menschliche Erblehre und Eugenik in Berlin von RF-Geldern.[11] Die US-Stiftungen gehörten somit zu einem wissenschaftlichen Feld, das seine Maßstäbe immer wieder neu austarierte. Manchmal unterstützten sie bahnbrechende Projekte, die wir heute als Errungenschaften preisen. Aber manchmal förderten sie Projekte, die zeitgenössisch als ebenso innovativ wahrgenommen wurden und in die Schattenseiten und Abgründe einer wissenschaftsfixierten Hochmoderne führen. Ob die RF dazu gelernt hatte oder ob es nur unfreiwillig komisch war, wenn sie in den 1950er Jahren »Communists and Fascists« per definitionem von ihrer Förderung ausschloss – das sei einmal dahingestellt.

Eine derartige, durch die interdisziplinäre Wissensforschung inspirierte Agenda könnte auch ausgehend von Weindlings Text zu spannenden Fragen führen. Das gilt umso mehr, da er relativ viel über die Zwischenkriegszeit schreibt – ohne dass dies seine These wesentlich prägen würde. Zugleich geht es ihm nicht nur um die Schließung einer Institution, sondern auch um eine intellektuelle und forschungspraktische Neuorientierung der Stiftungsarbeit im Gesundheitswesen. So ließen sich die Gründe, warum es zu einer Reorientierung weg von »Disease Prevention« und hin zu »Population Control« kam, weiter ausleuchten, über die Präferenzen konkreter Akteure wie John D. Rockefeller III oder der Weltgesundheitsorganisation als Alternative hinaus. Eine ausführlichere Analyse wissenschaftlicher Moden, von Wahrheitsvorstellungen und Denkstilen böte sich dann an.

Drittens schließlich könnte man weiter hinterfragen, was sich hinter der Formel »Kalter Krieg« genau verbirgt. Nach wie vor sind in diesem Zusammenhang zentrale Fragen strittig – nicht zuletzt die nach dem Stellenwert der Systemkonfrontation für die Geschichte der zweiten Hälfte des 20. Jahrhunderts. In Bezug auf die beiden hier vorliegenden Texte interessiert besonders das Problem der Prägekraft des Ost-West-Gegensatzes.

Was ist damit gemeint? Manche, wie Bernd Stöver, sehen im Kalten Krieg einen »global und tendenziell total geführten« Konflikt, der alle Lebensbereiche durchdrang und somit *den* Schlüssel zum Verständnis jener Jahrzehnte darstellt.[12] Auf der anderen Seite stehen jene, die im Kalten Krieg lediglich eine Dimension eines deutlich facettenreicheren Bildes der Nach-

---

11 Vgl. Schmuhl, *Grenzüberschreitungen*; ferner problematisch, aber mit interessanten Quellen: Black, *War against the Weak*.

12 Vgl. Stöver, *Der Kalte Krieg*, 19; vgl. z.B. auch Gaddis, *The Cold War*; Westad, »The Cold War and the International History of the Twentieth Century«.

kriegsjahrzehnte sehen. Tony Judts Darstellung der Zeit seit 1945 bildet dafür ein Exempel.[13] Noch weiter geht etwa Matthew Connelly, der bereits vor gut zehn Jahren forderte, man solle die »Cold War lens« ablegen.[14]

Wo nun stehen die beiden hier diskutierten Texte in dieser Debatte? Weindlings Text liefert dafür einige Antworten; zugleich bleiben Fragen offen. Er mustert organisatorische Prozesse innerhalb der RF durch und befragt deren Gewicht im Vergleich zur Prägekraft des Kalten Krieges. Jenes Moment des Selbsterhalts und der institutionellen Eigenlogik, das Müller in seinem Text als Argument in Anschlag bringt, setzt so auch dem Gang der Darstellung bei Weindling seinen Stempel auf. Letztlich hält er die Wirkung des Kalten Krieges allerdings für größer, was er unter anderem mit Zitaten von Barnard belegt. Zu wenig wird jedoch diskutiert, ob solche Argumente nur als Entlastungsstrategie dienten, um stiftungsinterne Gründe zu externalisieren und unangenehme Entscheidungen akzeptabler zu machen. Eine genauere und multidimensionalere Quellenanalyse wäre spannend gewesen. Festzuhalten bleibt zugleich, dass für Weindling der Kalte Krieg somit eine immense Wirkungskraft entfaltete.

Auch Müller versteht den Kalten Krieg nicht allein als Epochenbezeichnung, sondern als verbindlichen Deutungsrahmen für das Aktionsfeld für die von ihm untersuchten Personen und Institutionen. Auf Räume jenseits dieser – gleichwohl pluralistisch gedehnten – Kampfzone scheint sich das Interesse der RF nicht erstreckt zu haben. Wissenschaftsarbeit blieb vielmehr im Wesentlichen auf das Ziel ausgerichtet, in der Auseinandersetzung der Systeme und Ideologien die besseren Argumente zu haben, ohne dass dies – wie oben bereits vermerkt – auf eine Deckungsgleichheit mit der offiziellen Politik der USA hinauslaufen musste. Noch einfacher gesagt, kann man den beiden Texten somit entnehmen: Sozialwissenschaften, die nicht Amerikas Überlegenheit im Ost-West-Konflikt verdeutlichen sollten, spielten keine große Rolle. Interessant wäre die Frage, ob sich dieser Befund so halten und für die gesamte Arbeit der RF und der US-Stiftungen generalisieren ließe. Erst dann könnte man übrigens auch das Problem von Neuausrichtung oder Kontinuität im Vergleich zur Zwischenkriegszeit wirklich beantworten. Auf dieser Ebene betont Müller die Kontinuitäten – was mich überzeugt, aber tendenziell seiner Aussage zum Stellenwert des Kalten Krieges widerspricht. Weindling macht dagegen einen Bruch aus, benutzt zur Charakterisierung der amerikanischen Außenpolitik der Zwischenkriegszeit jedoch wiederholt den Begriff Isolationismus, der bereits seit Längerem überholt ist. Offensichtlich verdient die Frage weitere Aufmerksamkeit, zumal Teile der jüngsten Forschung in eine andere Richtung weisen. Grace Ai-Ling Chou hat etwa

13 Vgl. Judt, *Postwar*.
14 Connelly, »Taking Off the Cold War Lens«.

jüngst die These vertreten, dass Nichtregierungsorganisationen inklusive
der Ford Foundation in jener Zeit in Hongkong keineswegs nur die Logik
des Kalten Krieges bedienten, sondern auch Ziele vertraten, »that were prior
or separate from Cold War concerns«.[15] Auch für andere Themenfelder hat
die Forschung jüngst herausgearbeitet, wie sehr sich Prozesse temporär von
der Dynamik des Kalten Krieges abkoppelten.[16] Und selbst wenn es phasenweise Konvergenz gab, ließe sich weiter nach dem Zeitpunkt fragen, ab dem
das symbiotische Verhältnis von amerikanischer Macht und moderner Wissenschaft zu zerbröckeln begann.

Amerikanisierung: Polyfonie und Appropriation

Schon seit geraumer Zeit hat sich die Forschung von der Vorstellung verabschiedet, dass der interkulturelle Austausch von Wissen oder von sozialen
Praktiken als Diffusion zu verstehen sei. Statt von unveränderten Kopien des
Originals an anderen Orten – oder aber von Missverständnissen und Fehl-
interpretationen – geht man stattdessen von jeweils spezifischen Appropria-
tionen aus, die ihrerseits auf den Ausgangsort zurückstrahlen können. Zudem finden Machtasymmetrien, die konkreten Kanäle der Mittlung sowie
insbesondere die lokalen Konstellationen und Bedürfnisse besondere Beach-
tung. Im Forschungsfeld, das sich mit der Rolle der USA in der Welt befasst,
versinnbildlichen dies die Gänsefüßchen, die »Amerikanisierung« häufig
bekommen hat.[17] So gewendet findet sich der Begriff etwa bei Müller, während andere gleich ganz auf ihn verzichten – was vielleicht erklärt, warum er
bei Weindling gar nicht auftaucht.

Auf programmatischer Ebene dürfte dieser Ansatz mittlerweile weitgehend konsensfähig sein. Entsprechend vermerken Helke Rausch und John
Krige in ihrer Einleitung, wie wichtig für sie die »encounters and negotiations between philanthropists and their potential and actual counterparts,
particularly in Europe« seien. Gleichzeitig zeichnet sich die Historiografie
insgesamt durch eine sichtbare Lücke zwischen zahlreichen überzeugenden
programmatischen Aussagen einerseits und einer deutlich schmaleren Zahl
von empirischen Umsetzungen aus. Vor diesem Hintergrund ist es bedauer-
lich, aber auch nicht besonders überraschend, dass die Beiträge von Weindling und Müller solche Fragen kaum berühren. Beide Texte konzentrieren

15 Chou, »Cultural Education«, 24.
16 Dies trifft etwa für die Forschung zum europäischen Einigungsprozess als einem
anderen Kapitel der Internationalen Geschichte seit 1945 zu; vgl. dazu Ludlow, *European
Integration*.
17 Vgl. z.B. Berghahn, »The Debate on ›Americanization‹«; pars pro toto für die weitere Debatte: Iriye/Saunier, *The Palgrave Dictionary*.

sich vielmehr auf jene komplexen inneramerikanischen Konstellationen, in denen die RF in den 1950er Jahren operierte.

Für die Zwischenkriegszeit entwickelt Weindling zwar einige Überlegungen zum europäischen Engagement der RF und den daraus resultierenden Interaktionen mit Europa, bindet diese jedoch nicht an seine auf die Nachkriegszeit zentrierte These an. Zugleich wagt sich auch Müllers konzeptioneller und empirischer Zuschnitt nicht über festen amerikanischen Boden hinaus. Dabei wäre es bei seinem Thema äußerst ertragreich zu fragen, wie das in den USA an der Schnittstelle zwischen Machtpolitik und Wissenschaft generierte Wissen in der weiteren Welt wahrgenommen und ausverhandelt wurde. Ließen sich – um nur ein Beispiel zu geben – mit einer unorthodoxen Marxismusforschung tatsächlich die »hearts and minds« der Menschen in den beiden Berlins, den beiden Koreas und den vielen (potenziellen) Vietnams gewinnen, um eine Formulierung Che Guevaras aufzugreifen? Hätte man die Frage 1975 gestellt, hätten viele wahrscheinlich mit »Nein« geantwortet, 1990 dagegen mit »Ja«. So schwer es also ist, definitive Antworten zu geben, so spannend erscheint es, diesen Problemen nachzugehen. Cum grano salis gilt dies auch für Weindlings Beitrag, bedenkt man etwa das in den letzten Jahren neu erwachte Interesse an krankheitsspezifischen Ansätzen im Kontext der Gesundheitspolitik. Solche galten, wie Weindling zeigt, Ende der 1940er Jahre als altmodisch. In veränderter Form stellen sie heute dagegen wieder ein wesentliches Standbein philanthropischer Arbeit dar, wie sich etwa an den Schwerpunkten der Gates Foundation als der heute mit Abstand größten Privatstiftung der Welt zeigen ließe.

Zugleich vermerkt Müller en passant, dass in den strategischen Konzeptionen der USA jener Zeit dezidiert Raum für nicht-amerikanische Ansätze gewesen sei – was soweit ging, dass gemäßigt linke Ideen aus Großbritannien, Schweden, Neuseeland oder Australien zu Inspirationsquellen wurden. Das mag für europäische Ohren wenig aufregend klingen, ist im Licht der amerikanischen Debatte aber durchaus bemerkenswert. Denn dort werden solche Austausch- und Appropriationsprozesse, die auf die Vereinigten Staaten im 20. Jahrhundert eingewirkt haben, erst seit Kürzerem in größerem Umfang erforscht; zugleich gilt gerade die Nachkriegszeit als ein Höhepunkt der aufnahmeresistenten Selbstfixiertheit.[18]

Vielleicht noch wichtiger ist etwas Anderes, das sich aus Müllers Beitrag herauslesen lässt. Denn jener Ansatz, der eine kontrollierte Vielfalt von Ansätzen förderte, erstreckte sich nicht nur auf die Rockefeller Foundation und ähnliche Stiftungen. Wie Müller zu Recht vermerkt, wurde das Russian Research Center (RRC), an dem Marcuse und andere Sozialwissenschaftler linker Couleur wirkten, nur in geringem Umfang von der RF finanziert,

18 Vgl. dazu jüngst Bell, »Social Politics«.

während neben der Carnegie Corporation die U.S. Air Force der Haupt-geldgeber war. Zwei Jahre vor Gründung des RRC an der Harvard Universi-tät im Jahre 1948 hatte die Luftwaffe übrigens bei Montgomery in Alabama ihre eigene Universität, die Air University, eröffnet – und war erst ein weite-res Jahr zuvor selbst als eigenständige Teilstreitkraft aufgestellt worden. Ei-nerseits handelte es sich bei der Air Force somit um einen neuen Spieler an der Schnittstelle zwischen Machtpolitik und Wissensproduktion; anderer-seits verfügte die amerikanische Luftwaffe natürlich auch über eine lange Vorgeschichte und hätte mit der Air University eine hausinterne Alterna-tive zu Harvard gehabt.[19] Dennoch entschied man sich für einen Zuschnitt, der vom Renommee der Spitzenuniversität in Cambridge, MA lebte, die besten Köpfe anzog und ihnen zugleich faszinierende Freiräume eröffnete – nicht nur im Sinne einer wenig praxisorientierten Grundlagenforschung, sondern auch im Sinne eines erstaunlich unorthodoxen Forschungspro-gramms.

Müllers knappe Bemerkung zum RRC verweist so auf einen wichtigen Kontext. Staatlichkeit unterschied sich in den USA der frühen Nachkriegs-zeit in zweierlei Hinsicht von früheren Phasen: zum einen aufgrund des im-mensen Kompetenz- und Machtzuwachses auf innen- wie außenpolitischer Ebene, zum anderen aber auch aufgrund der auffallenden Vielfalt der damit verbundenen, gleichzeitig verfolgten Positionen und Ansätze. Vor dem New Deal hatte die Bundesadministration über wenige staatliche Ressourcen ver-fügt. Erst die Roosevelt-Ära hatte die Zahl, die Kompetenzfelder und die Ausstattung staatlicher Behörden dramatisch ansteigen lassen. Infolge der administrativen Kultur der USA wie auch des Führungsstils von Roosevelt glich die Bundesadministration fortan eher einem buntscheckigen Gebilde von untereinander rivalisierenden Behörden und Einrichtungen als einem klar geordneten Gebäude mit funktionaler Aufgabentrennung.[20] Insofern ist es tendenziell irreführend, für die USA der 1950er Jahre von »dem Staat« als monolithischem Akteur mit einer in sich schlüssigen Position zu sprechen. Selbst und gerade in der Zeit des McCarthyismus stießen nicht-staatliche Akteure auf eine beispiellos breite, finanziell gut ausgestattete Landschaft staatlicher Einrichtungen, mit denen sie in- und außerhalb der USA Koope-rationen eingehen konnten. Freilich zielten die meisten dieser Institutionen darauf, Amerikas Rolle in der Welt zu festigen und für ihre Version des ame-rikanischen Traums zu werben. Insofern sollte man nicht von völliger Kako-fonie ausgehen. Dennoch ist die Vielfalt, nicht zuletzt im Lichte einer älteren Literatur, durchaus bemerkenswert.

19 Shaw/Warnock, *The Cold War and Beyond*.
20 Vgl. z.B. Dickinson, *Bitter Harvest*; klassisch ferner Finegold/Skocpol, *State and Party*.

Was hat all dies mit »Amerikanisierung« zu tun? Es verdeutlicht, dass sich die Menge und die Heterogenität der Ansätze und Kanäle, mit denen die USA mit der weiteren Welt interagierten, in der Nachkriegszeit markant vergrößerten. Was nun war Amerika? Das von McCarthy? Oder eben jenes von Dean Acheson oder von George C. Marshall und des nach ihm benannten Plans? Sicher, wer als Spion verfolgt wurde oder in nordkoreanischer Uniform den 38. Breitengrad nach Süden zu überqueren suchte, der bekam ein sehr eindeutiges Amerika zu spüren. Zugleich führen transnationale Kontakte und Transfers immer zu selektiven Rezeptionen und Anverwandlungen. Im Fall der amerikanischen Wissens- und Machtpolitik prägten nicht nur Pluralismus, sondern auch Polyphonie und Polysemie besonders viele Fragen und Bereiche. Sie machten es schwer, »Amerika« als ein politisches oder ideologisches Projekt oder Produkt scharf zu stellen. Dieses Charakteristikum fand sich auch bereits in früheren Phasen amerikanischer Geschichte – nun jedoch spielten die USA global eine deutlich wichtigere Rolle. Zugleich lud dieser Ansatz zu hybrider Appropriation in viel höherem Maße ein, als dies bei anderen Gesellschaften der Fall war, die verbindlicher um eine Position herum formiert waren. Müller hat recht, wenn er in einer Fußnote darauf verweist, dass im nationalsozialistischen Deutschland die Forschung bei aller Pluralität konsequent auf soziale Exklusion und ein rassistisches Zentrum ausgerichtet wurde und dies wesentlich auf das politische System zurückzuführen war. Er verweist so auf einen fundamentalen Unterschied zwischen dem NS-Regime und den USA. »Amerikanisierung« lebte, wie man daraus folgern könnte, von vielerlei, aber nicht zuletzt davon, dass die Vielfalt der Optionen und der Appropriationsmöglichkeiten besonders hoch war – einerseits, weil die USA solche produktiven Anverwandlungen in besonderem Maße zuließen, andererseits aber auch, weil es so viele unterschiedliche »Amerikas« gab, die man als Referenzpunkte wählen konnte.

Um von dieser Überlegung abschließend zu den Ausführungen über den Kalten Krieg zurückzukehren: Wiewohl dessen Prägekraft für die in beiden Beiträgen hauptsächlich untersuchten amerikanischen Akteure zentral gewesen sein mag, würde sich diese Frage neu stellen, blickte man weiter über den amerikanischen Tellerrand hinaus.

Warum ist heute nicht schon morgen?

Das Gros der Forschung zu philanthropischen Organisationen zeichnet sich bislang durch das aus, was ich eine »intrinsische« Analyse nennen möchte: In der Regel wählt man eine Stiftung oder, noch naheliegender, ein Programm oder Institut einer Stiftung oder ein Land, ackert beeindruckend viele Meter des dazu überlieferten Materials durch und schreibt dann über

»Die Rockefeller Stiftung und X«, oder »Die Ford Foundation und Y«. Gelegentlich trifft man sich auf Konferenzen und legt dann die einzelnen Bausteine nebeneinander.

Schöpft man das Potenzial des Themenfelds damit ganz aus? Etwa um den Stellenwert der Stiftungen für Amerikas Rolle in der Welt oder gar das Wechselspiel zwischen lokalen und globalen Dynamiken zu verstehen? Wohl kaum. Dafür wären, wie auch in der Einleitung dieses Bandes angemahnt (oder, genauer gesagt: angekündigt, aber nicht eingelöst), mehr Vergleiche notwendig. Noch wichtiger wären meines Erachtens »extrinsische« Analysen, die globale Verschiebungen und Vernetzungen als Ausgangspunkt nähmen und von dort aus nach der Rolle der Stiftungen fragten.[21] Um nur ein Beispiel zu geben: So gilt es zu bedenken, dass sich das transnationale Engagement philanthropischer Organisationen in einer Welt des Internationalismus vollzog, die sich nach 1945 wesentlich dichter bevölkert zeigte, als dies vor dem Zweiten Weltkrieg der Fall gewesen war. Zum Beispiel gab es 1951 rund ein Drittel mehr international aktive Nichtregierungsorganisationen als vor dem Krieg, und die Gesamtzahl der NGOs stieg zwischen 1951 und 1960 um weitere 50 Prozent, während sich die Zahl der Internationalen Organisationen in jener Dekade um ein Viertel erhöhte.[22] Was hieß dies für den Gestaltungsspielraum der Stiftungen, für ihre Interaktionen mit anderen Akteuren und für eventuelle Effekte? Und welchen Spielraum eröffnete es nichtamerikanischen Eliten, um ihre internen und internationalen Präferenzen zu verfolgen? Solche Fragen betreffen Spielräume gegenüber staatlichen Politiken, wissenschaftliche Innovationsfähigkeit und transnationale Vernetzungen gleichermaßen – um lediglich drei Beispiele für übergreifende Untersuchungshorizonte zu geben. Nur eine Analyse, die nicht stiftungs- und institutionszentriert ist, wird solche wertvollen Erkenntnisse generieren können.

Auf dem Weg zu einer solchen »extrinsischen« Analyse gehen die beiden hier diskutierten Texte erste Schritte. Die Einleitung des Bandes weist explizit in der Sektion »What's next« in eine ähnliche Richtung. Als jemand, der nicht Teil dieses Forschungsfeldes ist, mag man sich jedoch fragen: warum eigentlich länger warten? Was hindert uns daran, solche Fragen jetzt bereits auf die Agenda zu setzen? Würde die Erforschung der amerikanischen philanthropischen Stiftungen in der Welt nicht erst dadurch für Historikerinnen und Historiker mit anderer Spezialisierung spannend? Schade, dass wir nicht heute schon die Fragen von morgen an gestern und vorgestern stellen.

---

21 Vgl. zu dieser Frage z. B. auch die Anregungen bei Tournès, »Introduction«.
22 Vgl. Union of International Association, *Yearbook of International Organization 1986/87*, v. a. Table 2; ferner Iriye, *Global Community*, 43.

The Coproduction of Knowledge

John Krige

The Ford Foundation, Physics and the National Security State

A Study in the Transnational Circulation of Knowledge

In 1956 the trustees of the Ford Foundation made two related grants for the natural sciences under the auspices of the international programme. One was to the Institute for Theoretical Physics in Copenhagen, renamed the Niels Bohr Institute in 1965 (for the sake of convenience NBI hereafter). The other was to CERN, the European Organisation for Nuclear Research, in Geneva. On the face of it these were not the kind of activities the trustees would usually support. The Institute in Copenhagen was already well-established – in fact the NBI had blossomed already in the inter-war years and was regarded as the Mecca of all physicists in the field of nuclear structure. CERN, on the other hand, was a laboratory in embryo with a burgeoning budget provided by twelve European governments that had been persuaded to finance the giant "atom-smashers" needed to close the gap between the Old Continent and the United States in what we now call particle physics.

This was an unusual initiative, then. No case could be made for launching a new and exciting, but otherwise neglected, domain of intellectual endeavour. Other sources of funding were not lacking. On the contrary, nuclear physics in all its varieties was the darling of governments aspiring to global influence and national prestige in the early Cold War, and it was frankly awash with money. Europe was in any case not a priority: the foundation was increasingly concerned about the situation in the "underdeveloped" countries and was determined to intervene substantially in this region of the globe. Notwithstanding these somewhat inauspicious circumstances, Shepard Stone, who had just been made head of the International Affairs Division, managed to get $400,000 for CERN and $200,000 for the NBI approved in April 1956. What is more, these grants were renewed not just once but twice – in 1959 for both organisations and again in 1963 for CERN and in 1966 for the NBI.[1] In sum, in the following decade or so these two estab-

---

1 The amounts were, respectively, $500,000 and $250,000 for CERN and $300,000 and $150,000 for the NBI. The CERN total was thus $1,150,000 and the NBI total was $650,000.

lished organisations in Western Europe dedicated to basic research in theoretical and experimental physics received $1.8 million from the Ford Foundation.

The catalyst for these awards was an exchange between Bohr and Stone soon after the immensely successful international conference on the peaceful uses of atomic energy, which was held at the United Nations in Geneva for two weeks in August 1955, beginning on the tenth anniversary of the bombing of Nagasaki. Stone had received a very positive report on the conference and on CERN from a consultant who had attended the meeting. He was warming to the idea that the foundation should promote what Bohr called "peaceful co-operation in atomic developments". Bohr went on to suggest that his institute and CERN were just what Stone was looking for, "providing stimulus and facilities for international co-operation in atomic science".[2] Thus when Ford Foundation President Rowan Gaither, perhaps surprised at the turn of events, asked Stone to clarify the rationale for the grants, Stone assured him that advancing the frontiers of physics was not the primary purpose;[3] the awards "were specifically for the expansion of international activities and not for the support of science as such". More precisely, the purpose "was to make it possible for Indian and other non-European scientists to receive advanced training both in Copenhagen and in Geneva".[4] The dockets prepared for the meeting of the Board of Trustees in December 1955 made much the same point, though with less emphasis on India and the Third World. The Danish Government and Danish foundations had enabled the NBI to enlarge its facilities. The Ford Foundation grant would pay for non-Danish physicists to spend extended periods of time there. CERN's financial priority was to its European member states; the grant to Geneva was predominantly for fellows from America and other non-CERN countries. Renewals reiterated the point: the money was to support international scientific collaboration by providing fellowships for researchers from non-host countries.

1. Rebuilding European Physics, Exporting American Values

Data on the international traffic facilitated by these awards reveals that American researchers were preponderant among the visitors, with thirty-three of the total fifty-six Ford Fellows supported by the first grant to CERN

2 Letter Bohr to Stone, dated 16 September 1955, Ford Foundation Archives, New York, NY. Unless otherwise specified, all documents cited below are in these archives and associated with Grant 56–154, to the Institute of Theoretical Physics, or with Grant 56–241, to CERN.
  3 Schmidt is wrong to claim otherwise in "Small Atlantic World", 122.
  4 Memo Stone to Gaither, 2 July 1956.

coming from the United States. In 1967 Niels Bohr's son Aage – an outstanding physicist in his own right – reported that 83 of the 222 scholars who had resided in Copenhagen for more than three months with support from the Ford Foundation and other sources had come from America. The Ford Foundation fellows at CERN included Nobel Prize winners for physics like Murray Gellman (who got the prize in 1969), Don Glaser (1960), Leon Lederman (1988), Ben Mottelson (1975), Jack Steinberger (1988), Chen Ning Yang (1957) and Abdus Salam (1979, from Pakistan). Victor Weisskopf from MIT spent time at CERN in the late 1950s as a Ford Foundation fellow and came back in 1961 to serve as the laboratory's Director General.

The intellectual impact of this influx from across the Atlantic was considerable. CERN's Scientific Policy Committee estimated that two-thirds of the money made available by the Ford Foundation in 1961 and 1962 was spent on hosting American scientists in Geneva, and noted that about forty per cent of them had made an "essential contribution" to the laboratory (the remaining sixty per cent made a "useful but less essential contribution").[5] An internal Ford Foundation memo in 1963 claimed that the grants had helped CERN become "one of the most exciting centres for nuclear research in the world", adding that "the leadership and advanced thinking of the American scientists have served to create a stimulating atmosphere and a vigorous intellectual exchange".[6] The paper prepared for the trustees to plead for a third grant to CERN noted that, while "the drive and competence" of the Europeans engaged in developing the laboratory had been of the utmost importance, "a vital element has been the small stream of scientists who have come primarily from America" and who had "transformed CERN into a world meeting place for the best scientists".[7] Aage Bohr agreed: Writing in 1965 and again in 1967, he remarked that "the visitors from the USA, who have included many outstanding senior physicists on sabbatical leave as well as brilliant young scientists, have provided great stimulation to the research atmosphere at the Institute and have contributed very actively to the efforts to promote co-operation".[8] There is no doubt then that the American fellows supported by the Ford Foundation through both CERN and the NBI made a real difference to the intellectual life at these institutions in the late 1950s and early 1960s.

There was more to it than that, though. In my earlier study of these grants I suggested that, by supporting CERN and the NBI, Stone had "joined the

5 CERN/SPC/168, 2 April 1963 (CERN Archives, Geneva).

6 Memo Matthew Cullen to Moselle Kimber, "Request for One Page Memo on Accomplishments of CERN", 19 April 1963.

7 Memo Hill to Heald, Grant Request – International Affairs, 17 January 1963.

8 In his Report of Activities Sponsored by the Grant, attached to letter Bohr to McDaniel, 14 July 1967. See also Bohr's report to Stone, 19 February 1965.

battle to strengthen democratic values in the Free World wherever they were threatened by the Communist menace; to build a positive image of the United States as open, innovative, and giving full scope to individual expression; and to strengthen the Atlantic alliance".[9] I also situated the initiative in the context of a broader American agenda to strengthen Western science in the first two decades of the Cold War. The Ford Foundation's support for physics at CERN and the NBI was part and parcel of a more general effort to raise the level of European science and engineering, for instance, through support for Churchill College, Oxford, and the NATO Science Committee, and to couple it more closely with the military-industrial complex, for example, by underwriting a proposal to develop a "European MIT".

Volker Berghahn, in his study of the intellectual Cold War in Europe, enlarged the scope of the argument beyond the Atlantic community. He emphasised the use of these grants to bring scientists from communist countries to Copenhagen and to Geneva. As he pointed out, the grants were partly inspired by the hope that a dialogue between physicists from opposing political camps "would contribute to easing tensions and building confidence between the two superpowers at a time when the nuclear arms race was gathering speed and Cold War tensions were rising. [...] As long as the creators of the nuclear bomb kept talking in East and West, missiles would not be fired."[10] This argument was widespread among the scientific elite at the time; Bohr too used it in his famous letter to the United Nations in June 1950, where he insisted that full mutual openness of atomic research could avert a nuclear conflagration and foster understanding and co-operation between nations. He was convinced, he told Stone in 1958, that "open exchange among the scientists of the world" was "the best security and best opportunity for the free world".[11] Eisenhower's science adviser, George Kistiakowsky, writing in 1960, claimed that science was "one of the few common languages of mankind", able to "provide a basis for understanding and communication of ideas between people that is independent of political boundaries and of ideologies". As such it could "contribute in a major way to the reduction of tensions between nations".[12] Weisskopf told Stone in 1966 that the NBI deserved further support because it was one of the "tenuous bridges between West and East which will be so essential in the future to preserve some unity among nations". Such bridges, he wrote, had "probably prevented the outbreak of a major war".[13]

9 Krige, *American Hegemony*, 187–8.
10 Berghahn, *Intellectual Cold Wars*, 203, 204; idem, "Philanthropy and Diplomacy", 413.
11 Ibid., 413.
12 Kistiakowsky, "Science and Foreign Affairs", 115.
13 Letter Weisskopf to Stone, 4 November 1966.

Both of these studies situated the grants to CERN and the NBI in the framework of Shepard Stone's cultural agenda in Europe, relating them to his concern to further the cause of peace by constructing an American-led Atlantic community and by maintaining a dialogue with the intellectual elite in the communist bloc. Others saw them differently, however. Stone, taking his cue from Bohr, explicitly invoked the nuclear when justifying his grants to CERN and the NBI: They were for "supporting the development of the peaceful uses of nuclear energy through increasing cooperation among American and European nuclear scientists".[14] This aim inevitably intersected with the foreign policy concerns of some arms of the administration in Washington, most obviously the AEC (Atomic Energy Commission), but also the State Department and even the CIA (Central Intelligence Agency). They were less interested in CERN and the NBI as platforms for cultural diplomacy than as nodes in an international network of knowledge flows in nuclear matters; they were less concerned about the transmission of values than about the protection of national security; they were more interested in maintaining world peace through strengthening America's competitive scientific and technological advantage than through dispelling misunderstandings through dialogue. They did not see American Ford Foundation fellows who went to CERN and the NBI as members of an international scientific community dedicated to the disinterested pursuit of truth, but rather as patriotic citizens embedded in a national research agenda. And they had the power to leave an indelible mark on the scope of the awards that were made.

This article shifts the analysis of the grants provided by the Ford Foundation to CERN and the NBI away from a focus *on culture and on the transmission of values* to one that portrays *the production and circulation of knowledge*. This is tantamount to shifting our gaze away from Stone and the foundation trustees toward their associates in the AEC, the State Department and the CIA, who worked closely with them in defining the physiognomy of the awards. The grants to the NBI and CERN bundled together the interests of different social actors in New York and in Washington, actors who were united in their enthusiasm for international collaboration, but who saw it as serving American cold-war interests in different ways. This convergence was facilitated thanks to the nature of the receiving institutions: Both were international centres that encouraged free-wheeling encounters between researchers in a key cold-war science. They could serve as sites to display the openness of the Western democracies as well as to probe into the closed world of communist regimes. They combined the intangible benefits of cultural exchange with the hope of improved insight into the state of physics behind the

14 Draft docket statement, International Affairs: Atomic Development, CERN and Bohr Institute, undated but around December 1955.

iron and bamboo curtains. The awards made by the Ford Foundation not only helped strengthen Western science and served as an instrument of cultural diplomacy; the face-to-face encounters they financed also facilitated transnational knowledge flows to the advantage of the national security state. In the domain of all things nuclear, the cultural struggle for hearts and minds was distinct from the rivalry for competitive scientific and technological advantage. The former was situated at the level of display and persuasion, the latter at the level of knowledge and power. It is this second aspect of the grants that I want to explore here, taking us backstage behind the performance of the awards to reveal the range of American interests that were embedded in the Ford Foundation's support for CERN and the NBI.

2. "International" Collaboration and National Security

The officers of the foundations always claimed that they had acted independently of the federal Government. Time and again Stone pointed out that the Ford Foundation could do things that were politically delicate and thus unlikely to be authorised by Congress. At the same time, it is abundantly clear that Stone and the Ford Foundation acted in concert with the demands of the national security state.[15] They did not take directives from the agencies of the federal Government. However, they most emphatically ensured that their initiatives were in line with Government policy, and they were willing to accept the boundary conditions that national security imposed on their programmatic actions if and when that was appropriate. Indeed Stone remarked in an interview in 1972 that he went to Washington three or four times a year, and that many people from the nation's capital also visited the foundation's headquarters in New York. As he put it, "I made a point during all of those years of talking, whenever we were developing ideas of programs, with some of the best minds I knew in the Federal governments or in governments overseas."[16] The federal Government did not tell the foundations what to do, though its agencies certainly did suggest desirable areas for intervention. Relevant Government departments were also consulted before ideas were turned into action. In the case studied here Stone assured senior foundation administrator Don Price that "for obvious reasons we would keep in touch with responsible people in the State Department, the AEC and other agencies as we worked out details".[17] The nuclear sciences necessarily engaged sensitive issues of foreign policy and national security. Stone did

15 Berghahn, "Philanthropy and Diplomacy"; Schmidt, "Small Atlantic World", 120.
16 Interview with Stone, 23–4.
17 Memo Stone to Price, 8 December 1955.

not put his proposal for an award to CERN and the NBI on Rowan Gaither's desk until he had been given the green light by Robert Bowie, an Assistant Secretary of State in the State Department, and by William Clarke, the European Regional Director of the US Information Agency, to name two examples.[18] It is on this slim basis that the foundation officers constructed their narrative of freedom of action.

By choosing to embed the grants to CERN and the NBI in the context of atomic energy, Stone had no option but to yield to the foreign policy logic that was inscribed in the promotion of the peaceful atom. Atoms for Peace was a major policy initiative embarked on by the Eisenhower administration beginning with his major speech to the United Nations in December 1953. It was intended to combat a Soviet-inspired image of the United States as a war-mongering nation, and it evolved into "quite possibly the largest single propaganda campaign ever conducted by the American government".[19] A travelling exhibition suggesting that the United States was busy converting all its atoms for war into atoms for peace attracted record crowds in Bonn, Belgrade and Buenos Aires. This internationalisation of nuclear power was given a huge boost at the conference in Geneva, where distinguished scientists and government officials from all over the world were enchanted by an American "swimming-pool" type research reactor that had been flown in from Oak Ridge, and that was regularly brought up to power in a Swiss chalet situated in the gardens of the UN close to the centre of the city. In his opening address, the president of the conference, Homi Bhabha, Secretary of the Indian Department of Atomic Energy, made a spirited affirmation of the importance of nuclear power to the future development of his country.[20] The United States Atomic Energy Commission began to declassify thousands of technical reports and to sign bilateral agreements for research and power reactors beginning with Turkey in June 1955; by 1961 more than forty such arrangements had been signed. This was the context in which Stone mentioned that scientists from Asia and underdeveloped areas – and, more specifically, from India – would be given Ford Foundation fellowships to CERN and the NBI. It was also the context in which he was obliged to restrict the international scope of the grants.

Late in March 1956 Stone informed Bohr that the foundation was planning to support activities "which would increase international exchange at the Institute for Theoretical Physics in Copenhagen". The official letter from the Secretary of the foundation on 14 May 1956 stipulated that the grant was to be used for "young and senior physicists from outside Denmark". Two

18 Memo Stone to the File, 8 December 1955.
19 Osgood, *Total Cold War*, 156.
20 Krige, "Techno-utopian Dreams"; idem, "Atoms for Peace".

weeks earlier Stone had personally explained to Bohr that there were even tighter restrictions than that. As he put it, "It would be very helpful to us if Ford Foundation funds were not used to support persons from Soviet Russia, Communist China and the so-called satellite countries."[21] Stone also saw CERN Director General Bakker personally in April 1956 and came to a "gentleman's agreement" with him that he "would not use Foundation grant funds to finance visits by scientists from the Communist countries".[22] Both Bohr and Bakker agreed to these terms. They were willing to accept foundation money for "international" scientific exchange on terms that respected the geo-political divisions that characterised the Cold-War struggle for nuclear leadership in the mid-1950s.[23] Bohr was sufficiently well known, it seems, for Stone to trust him not to object to a violation of the very principles of "full mutual openness" that the Danish physicist held sacred. Bakker was less prominent, and the foundation asked Lewis Strauss, the Chairman of the AEC, to do a background check on him. He was cleared as being "a staunch friend of the United States and of democratic principles generally".[24]

It was the fear that sensitive nuclear knowledge would leak to the Soviet bloc or to Communist China in the free-wheeling exchanges in Copenhagen and Geneva that delimited the scope of international exchange in the first grants made to the NBI and to CERN. In 1954 Eisenhower's Assistant Secretary of Defence for Atomic Energy Matters wrote that "We are engaged in a life and death struggle against the communist movement in which our principal hope lies in the early exploitation of peacetime [nuclear] power."[25] That same year the Soviets had pumped electricity into the grid from a nuclear power plant for the first time. Nothing was to be done that might enhance their lead.

As the situation in the Soviet bloc changed, so did the political reach of the grants. Khrushchev's speech in February 1956 decrying the crimes of the Stalin era triggered hopes for reform in the satellite states. Resentment burst to the surface first in Warsaw and then in Budapest where hundreds died in standoffs between protesters and Soviet forces. Although it was American policy to try to drive a wedge between Moscow and the states on the periphery of the Soviet empire, little was done by the Eisenhower administration to come to the defence of the beleaguered protesters. Stone and Price took the initiative and managed to persuade the somewhat reluctant trustees to make major grants to assist refugees from Poland and Hungary in De-

21 Letter Stone to Bohr, 30 April 1956.
22 Memo Stone to the File, 9 April 1956.
23 The nationalities of people who received Ford Foundation support through CERN between 1 September 1956 and 31 August 1957 conformed to Stone's wishes.
24 Letter Lewis Strauss to Don Price, 5 December 1955.
25 Abraham, *Indian Atomic Bomb*, 86.

cember 1956. This was soon followed by messages to Bohr and Bakker telling them that the restriction on supporting physicists from these countries was being lifted. By September 1957 even more walls had come down: Don Price told Ford Foundation President Henry Heald that "State Department officials and Allen Dulles, head of CIA, are urging the Foundation to continue to expand the program in Poland, and also in Yugoslavia, Czechoslovakia, Romania, and possibly the Soviet Union".[26] By 1958 relationships with the Soviet Union were also routinised, and Bohr and Bakker were told that Ford Foundation money could be used to support researchers from there as well.

The next step was to relax the constraint on using Ford Foundation money for grants to physicists from Communist China. This happened in 1958: Two Chinese physicists working in America, Tsung-Dao Lee and Chen Ning Yang, were awarded the Nobel Prize for physics in 1957. Levering their prestige, they suggested that Bohr invite a few outstanding physicists from the Chinese mainland to Copenhagen, where they would go to meet them. The State Department was not consulted at once for fear that it might object, but both Robert Amory, the CIA's Chief of Intelligence, and its Director Allen Dulles "strongly favoured such an action". Stone and Price cleared the change of policy with Heald. Bohr was told about it in April 1958, with Stone adding "that we leave all decision as to whom to invite to Copenhagen up to him".[27]

The Ford Foundation used its financial resources to support Bohr's and Bakker's wish to enhance their centres as sites for international scientific exchange – and to restrict the countries that could be counted as members of said "international" research community to conform to the needs of American national security. The boundaries of this community shifted markedly between 1956 and 1958 along with changes in Washington's policies towards the communist bloc. As first one barrier, then another, then another came down, Stone and the foundation moved to build educational and cultural links with scholars in Eastern Europe, and authorised Bohr and Bakker to support scientists from the satellite states as well as the USSR and China. This action forged bonds of solidarity that enhanced the credibility of the West and further undermined the increasingly tenuous grip of the regime in Moscow over its "subjects". Following this line of thought, we can rightly take the redefinition of the scope of the grants to CERN and the NBI – in consultation with the apparatus of the national security state – as indicative of how the Ford Foundation fought the intellectual and cultural Cold War.[28] But as I

---

26 Berghahn, *Intellectual Cold Wars*, 190.

27 Memo from Stone to Price and Heald, Elimination of Restrictions on Grant to Bohr's Institute at Copenhagen, 3 March 1958.

28 Berghahn, *Intellectual Cold Wars*, Ch. 7, 178–213; Krige, *American Hegemony*, Ch. 6, 153–190.

have suggested, there was more to it than that: Foundation money was not used to bring Chinese physicists to Copenhagen solely in order to win hearts and minds. Stone explained: "Yang and Lee had come to Bohr and said it was essential to find out what was happening in physics in Communist China." In turn, Robert Amory "said that Allen Dulles and he strongly favoured such action because the USA needs such information".[29] Later that year Dulles confirmed that "there had been improvement in the information recently about scientific and educational developments in Russia but that we were lagging in respect of Communist China".[30]

The USA needs such information. For Stone and for the senior officials in the Ford Foundation to whom he addressed this explanation, nothing more needed to be said. They apparently understood at once that Copenhagen and Geneva were not simply sites in which the free world's cultural values were on display. What Dulles and Amory valued was the possibility for face-to-face encounters between American nuclear scientists and their colleagues behind the iron curtain and in Communist China. They perceived these laboratories as temporary meeting places for an elite whose members had different national allegiances and were engaged in different national research agendas. Amory and Dulles did not agree to having Ford Foundation money spent on scientists from the Soviet Union or China because they hoped thereby to dissolve misunderstandings in the name of world peace; rather, they wanted American researchers to establish what nuclear scientists were doing in these closed societies that were posing a threat to American security. For the CIA, CERN and the NBI were nodes in an international network of informal intelligence gathering.

3. Lifting the Curtain of Secrecy: Informal Intelligence Gathering

When I attended international scientific conferences in which Soviet, Eastern bloc, or Chinese scientists might be expected to participate, I was invariably contacted by agents of the FBI, CIA, or NSA [National Security Agency] before and after the meetings.

(US physicist Chih-Kung Jen)[31]

The CIA took an interest in the activities of the Ford Foundation as soon as it had decided to expand its activities from the domestic to the international sphere in 1952. The agency was particularly keen to have a list of foundation

29 Stone to Price and Heald, 3 March 1958.
30 Berghahn, "Philanthropy and Diplomacy", 413.
31 Jen, *Recollections*, 221. Jen was a senior physicist at the Applied Physics Laboratory at Johns Hopkins University from 1950 to 1977.

officers and fellows who were working abroad, in order to ask them to "engage in a little free-lance intelligence gathering" in the name of national security.[32] This approach was resisted in-house on the grounds that it would impugn the foundation's reputation. According to Kai Bird, Don Price struck a compromise deal with Allen Dulles and Richard Bissell, who had been a consultant to the foundation in 1952 and who joined the CIA in 1954. The CIA was not to "meddle" with anyone while they were being supported by the Ford Foundation, "but they would be free to recruit them later on". From then on, Bird tells us, "only the names of Ford Foundation fellows whose grants had already expired were regularly forwarded to the CIA".[33]

We know that this was just one dimension of a sustained effort by the CIA and the State Department to enrol intellectual leaders, and scientists in particular, in intelligence gathering. In 1950, a famous report to the State Department written by Lloyd Berkner, entitled "Science and Foreign Relations" included a classified appendix "detailing the value of employing civilian and diplomatic channels to obtain scientific intelligence intended to aid in national security planning".[34] American scientists were instrumental in getting the State Department to establish scientific attaché positions in foreign embassies for intelligence purposes. "To a degree long concealed from colleagues and poorly documented in traditional archival materials," Ronald E. Doel and Allan A. Needell tell us, scientists aided CIA officials in "collecting, gathering and interpreting knowledge about foreign scientific advances."[35] This was achieved in part by "mandatory debriefings of scientists returning from overseas conferences".[36] The approaches made to the Ford Foundation by Dulles and Bissell were therefore in no way unusual: They were typical of the mobilisation of cold-war American scientists as intelligence gatherers, particularly after contact with their colleagues in the Soviet bloc was re-established following Stalin's death in 1953.

Most American scientists apparently did not object to serving as informal intelligence gatherers for their government, especially after the Korean War had broken out. They saw the Soviet Union as a genuine threat to American security and recognised that it was extremely difficult to get reliable information about the state of Soviet science and technology in a closed society. Indeed, they could easily justify their engagement as informal intelligence agents on the grounds that it might make for a realistic, rather than phantasmagoric, defence posture at home. In any event, it is striking how

---

32 Bird, *McCloy*, 426.
33 Ibid., 429.
34 Doel, "Scientists as Policymakers", 219.
35 Doel/Needell, "Science", 67; Doel, "Does Scientific Intelligence Gathering Matter?"
36 Doel, "Scientists as Policymakers", 230.

freely scientists still speak about the approaches made to them by the American intelligence apparatus after they had travelled abroad. Twice they volunteered this information spontaneously when I talked to them about the Ford Foundation's links with the CIA.[37]

It is more than a little ironic, then, to realise that international laboratories that prized openness and mutual understanding were conceived in Washington as prime sites for informal intelligence gathering during the Cold War. And that directors like Bohr and Bakker apparently went along with this without undue difficulty. Indeed, Stone had no compunction about apprising Bohr of the interest that the CIA had in international scientific exchange. In February 1958, around the time that Ford-funded invitations to Chinese physicists were being considered, Stone took Bohr with him to Washington where they "had some fine talks with Allen Dulles and his boys, Senator Clinton Anderson [chairman of the Congressional Joint Committee on Atomic Energy], Senator Flanders [a strong opponent of McCarthy] and other dignitaries".[38]

The timing of the CIA's agreement to let Bohr use Ford Foundation money to support physicists from the People's Republic of China (PRC) was not fortuitous. In 1955 the party leadership in the PRC decided to invest heavily in physics. A nuclear weapons project was launched, and the country joined the consortium of socialist countries that was engaged in the particle physics facility at Dubna in the Soviet Union. The military programme was accelerated after the successful launch of Sputnik in October 1957, when a Sino-Soviet Accord on New Technologies in Defence was signed in Moscow. Thus, when Lee and Yang approached Bohr early in 1958, a number of major programmatic and institutional changes were under way in China. Training and research in physics were being strengthened, the path towards the bomb had been taken, and Soviet assistance had been promised. This was the situation that interested the CIA. The international, free-wheeling and open spirit at the European centres would facilitate exchanges of information that could throw light on the state of physics in China and provide Washington with the kind of data it needed to assess the country's weapons potential.

Over the next few years quite a few Chinese physicists visited the NBI and CERN, some of them on Ford Foundation grants. This was a tumultuous time for the Chinese bomb project. In June 1959, Moscow withdrew support from the Chinese effort, on the grounds that such assistance was incompatible with its support for the test ban treaty that it was negotiating with Wash-

---

37 De Greiff, "Supporting Theoretical Physics", 40, tells us that the International Centre for Theoretical Physics in Trieste was similarly being exploited by all the Western powers, including the British.

38 Berghahn, "Philanthropy and Diplomacy", 413.

ington and London. A year later all Soviet scientific and technical advisers were withdrawn from China. This only renewed the PRC's determination to get a weapon. The party authorised a concentrated indigenous programme, and in October 1964 China successfully tested its first atomic bomb. It was precisely in this time window, from 1961 to 1967, that the Copenhagen institute was host to seven Chinese physicists (from Beijing, Shanghai, Canton and Jilin), for stays of one or two years.[39]

What kind of information could have been acquired from these men through informal intelligence gathering? It is difficult to say. Zuoyue Wang, who has been immensely helpful in characterising this cohort of physicists for me, noticed that many of them did not spend much time in China in the early 1960s, but rather combined a sojourn at the NBI with an extended stay in the Soviet Union.[40] This was the case, for example, with Hsien Ting-chan (Xian Dingchan in Pinyin), who spent a year in Copenhagen in 1962 sandwiched between three years of research at Dubna. It seems unlikely that he was recruited for bomb work. Apparently the Chinese authorities allowed people who were not central to their weapons programmes to go abroad for extended training and research. This is not to say that bomb physicists were never allowed out of the country; on the contrary, a number of them who were deeply engaged in weapons development were regular visitors at CERN in the 1970s.[41]

Much has been made of late of the CIA's clandestine support for the Congress for Cultural Freedom that Stone held so dear.[42] Frances Stonor Saunders, one of the most trenchant critics of this collusion between the Ford Foundation and the CIA, objected strongly to the unwitting enrolment of intellectuals who wrote for leading literary magazines – like the British *Encounter* – in a political agenda that they may not have agreed with. As she put it in an interview with Scott Lucas, "People who were supplying these fantastic articles – you know, no one can argue with the sort of calibre and memorable contributions on the cultural front – were there to supply a kind

---

39 My thanks to Finn Aaserud, the Director of the Niels Bohr Archive, who got the names of these seven for me: Chang, Chun-hsiang (9.65–9.67), Chang, K.-y. (65?, 66?), Chang, Lee (63–64), Cho, Yi-chung (11.64–12.65), Hsien, Ting-chang (1.62–10.62), Liu, Yun-tso (6.65–9.67), and Yang, Fu-chia (64–65), in File 1980-Box10, 65 Samerbejde DK/Kina, NBI Archives, Copenhagen Denmark.

40 Zuoyue Wang (private communication), May 2011; Wang, "Physics in China".

41 Lock mentions some of them in *Origins and Evolution*. These include Tsien San-tsiang (Qian Sanquiang in Pinyin) and Wang Cheng-shu. Qian Sanquiang was one of a handful of key officials who oversaw scientific research on the bomb project, and Wang Cheng-shu was one of the specialists sent to the Gobi desert in the early 1960s to immerse herself fully in bomb work: Wilson/Xue, *China Builds the Bomb*, 249, 46.

42 Stonor Saunders, *Who Paid the Piper?*; Lucas, "Beyond Freedom"; idem, "Revealing the Parameters"; Scott-Smith, *The Politics of Apolitical Culture*.

of veneer, a cultural window dressing. [...] What they didn't realise, and this is what the great deception was, was that the context within which those articles were placed firmly established them as political even if they were written with a disengaged cultural view. So the engagement of people who didn't necessarily want to be engaged in that struggle or on that agenda, that was the problem."[43]

The same "problem" did not arise with the scientific community. Stone was frank with Bohr and Bakker about the interest that the State Department and the CIA had in the awards to their laboratories. They seem to have felt that the constraints on the "international" reach of the grants were acceptable when weighed against the benefits to be obtained by an important influx of foreign, and above all American, researchers. American scientists seem to have had few qualms about serving as informal intelligence gatherers for various branches of their government. Stone and the CIA had no interest in covertly "manipulating" them. Rather, they overtly relied on their sense of patriotic duty and their anxieties regarding national security to get a glimpse of the state of science and technology behind the iron and bamboo curtains.

4. From the Closed World to the Clandestine Programme

The Ford Foundation grants to CERN and the NBI not only facilitated efforts to get indirect information on the state of classified nuclear research in communist societies, they could also be used to gain access to – and to provide a cover for – clandestine weapons programmes in friendly nations. Israel is a case in point. Hard and fast evidence is difficult to come by, of course, but the trajectory of one young Ford fellow, Amos de Shalit, is instructive in this respect.

Amos de Shalit was a brilliant Israeli physicist, one of the first Ford Foundation fellows, who went to CERN from October 1957 to October 1958. Soon thereafter he was nominated to become Head of the Department of Nuclear Physics at Hebrew University in Jerusalem, moving on in 1963 to a succession of top positions in the Weizmann Institute of Science in Rehovoth. He died in 1969 when only 43 years old.[44]

De Shalit was a specialist in the use of particle beams to study nuclear structure, a line of research he actively promoted at CERN's synchrocyclotron accelerator. He and Weisskopf initiated a series of international confer-

43 In Scott-Smith and Krabbendam, *Cultural Cold War*, 19.
44 "Professor de Shalit", http://library.web.cern.ch/library/Archives/biographies/Shalit_A-196910.pdf, accessed 20 April 2010.

ences on high-energy physics and nuclear structure at CERN, the first of which was held in 1963. It was this kind of collaboration that gave CERN an international stamp and that the Ford Foundation grant was intended to foster: a brilliant physicist from a non-member state of the laboratory (Israel) playing an active role in developing a better understanding of the properties of the nucleus using CERN's smaller machine.

That granted, the public persona of de Shalit at CERN left much unsaid, and necessarily so: Back home, Amos de Shalit was actively engaged in the 1960s in Israel's highly secret project to develop a nuclear weapon. There is no need to delve too deeply here into what Avner Cohen, an authority on the history of the Israeli project, has described as the "worst-kept secret". Suffice it to say that already in the early 1950s Israel's first Prime Minister David Ben Gurion actively pursued the nuclear option. De Shalit was initially opposed to the scheme, partly on the grounds that a small country like Israel simply did not have the resources to develop a weapon successfully on its own. This opposition eventually excluded him from the core group that continued to build the installations necessary to produce plutonium at the Dimona complex in the Negev. But in July 1961 de Shalit changed his mind. He was on sabbatical leave in the United States when Israel tested its first indigenously built rocket, Shavit 2, which was a crucial step towards a home-grown strategic missile that could deliver a nuclear warhead to neighbouring countries. De Shalit could not contain his excitement, complimented all those who had been involved in the venture and added, "I am happy to admit, without reservations, that a large proportion of my objections and complaints have been shattered by this achievement."[45] In other words, while de Shalit was actively engaged at CERN doing research and planning his international series of conferences with Weisskopf, he was also involved at home in his country's weapons programme.

The research that de Shalit did at CERN in the early 1960s did not simply express his fascination with nuclear structure. Rather, the public persona that was constructed there was actively used as a decoy to deflect American attention away from what was happening at Dimona. In 1963 President Kennedy stepped up pressure on Israel to allow American inspectors into the Israeli nuclear complex to ensure that it was dedicated entirely to peaceful uses. The Israeli authorities stalled. They would not allow "inspections" – after all they had nothing to hide, they said – but they would permit visits for "scientific purposes". De Shalit hosted some of these visits that occurred roughly annually between 1964 and 1967. Using a variety of subterfuges he ensured that the preparations for the nuclear option, notably the underground plutonium production plant, were not revealed to the American

45 Karpin, *The Bomb in the Basement*, 199

authorities. He also exploited his status as a physicist engaged in fundamental research. In fact, Cohen suggests that de Shalit was apparently chosen to be the guide so as "to highlight the Israeli portrayal of those visits as scientific exchange, and, second, to add credibility to the explanation that Dimona's purpose was for training and scientific research".[46]

In 1962 Weisskopf told a journalist that CERN was "a symbol of what science really means: man's exploration of nature for the sake of pure knowledge". Indeed, the CERN Director General went on, because of its truly international character, because it was "open to all, it might be said to be the only really scientific laboratory of them all".[47] It was an image that could be exploited by the Israeli authorities. De Shalit's engagement at CERN did not simply express his love of basic science and his active participation in an international community of researchers. It also projected an identity that could be mobilised to deflect attention away from the nuclear weapons activities in which he was engaged at home. The Dimona that spoke to visitors – or inspectors – through de Shalit was a research facility like many others of its kind in the world – not a plant producing plutonium for a nuclear weapon driven by a national political agenda.

The capacity of CERN to depoliticise, demilitarise and denationalise scientific interactions was useful to de Shalit and his authorities in another way: It provided a "neutral" venue in which to discuss progress at Dimona with someone like Francis Perrin, the High Commissioner of the French Commissariat à l'Energie Atomique (CEA). Perrin, in his capacity as a professor at the College de France, served on CERN's Scientific Policy Committee (SPC) for the synchrocyclotron from 1960 to 1974. As such he was one of those who evaluated de Shalit's experimental proposals. It was also Perrin, the French authorities and firms like Saint Gobin, that had actively collaborated with Israel in the late 1950s to build the plutonium enrichment plant at Dimona after the American administration refused to do so. Perrin could not make an official visit to the Negev. For one thing de Gaulle had put a stop to the collaboration in 1960 immediately after France successfully tested its own first A-bomb (although he allowed the private contractors to complete the job they had started). But the head of the CEA and eminent member of the SPC could sit and have a coffee with ex-Ford fellow de Shalit at CERN to discuss physics – and to share notes about plutonium production for the French and the Israeli bomb programmes (which used the same technology). The international, scientific agenda embodied in CERN which so attracted the Ford Foundation did not suspend national military ambitions and promote world peace; on the contrary, it created a demilitarised space in

46 Cohen, *The Worst-Kept Secret*, 189; Cohen, *Israel and the Bomb*.
47 Rigby, "Europe Unites", 28.

which sensitive knowledge about bomb programmes could be exchanged under the cover of doing basic science. It was not only the US national security apparatus that benefitted from this; it was also that of Israel and presumably that of all the weapons states whose scientists used CERN.

5. Concluding Remarks

It is possible and plausible to situate the Ford Foundation grants to CERN and the NBI in the context of cultural exchanges and the intellectual Cold War. Physicists insisted that – through dialogue and conversation, to be contrasted with the sabre-rattling and confrontation of the superpowers – they could foster mutual understanding and world peace. This ideal dovetailed with the Ford Foundation's ambitions as enshrined in its founding mission to promote peace and democracy. The support for fellowships to two major European research centres was to improve international understanding, not to advance the research as such.

What needs to be stressed, though, is that international encounters at CERN and the NBI in fact helped to secure a variety of national interests that had nothing whatsoever to do with cultural understanding. The pursuit of national agendas was not transcended in Geneva and Copenhagen; it was intrinsic to them. International collaboration was one of a repertoire of instruments to advance national concerns. For the Ford Foundation, the support for nuclear science was aligned with the foreign policy agenda of the Eisenhower administration, and consciously so: "obviously", as Stone put it, nothing was done without first clearing it with the Atomic Energy Commission, the State Department and, when pertinent, the CIA. The "neutral" space of CERN and the NBI also served as a site for learning more about the covert research activities of rivals, or even as a cover to distract attention away from clandestine bomb-related projects at home. In short, international collaboration provided an opportunity to know and understand others better, and to collectively push back the frontiers of knowledge – all the while advancing national strength, enhancing competition and amplifying rivalry and division rather than overcoming it.

It is difficult to draw a distinction between civilian and military research in the domain of nuclear science. For the purposes of this article we can align the divide with that between what is published in the open literature and what remains classified. The international versus national character of CERN and the NBI mapped onto this cut: They were transparent glasshouses, as the Swiss authorities liked to say, not opaque weapons laboratories.[48] Every

---

48 Strasser, "Coproduction".

physicist and every science administrator in the Cold War learned how to manage this compartmentalisation of practice. The boundary between what was "international", and so public and unclassified, and what was strictly "national", and so kept under wraps if necessary, was constantly put in place and policed.

Visitors to CERN and the NBI came to the international research centres as the nationals of a particular country. It was not simply that the grants made by the Ford Foundation were specifically ear-marked for certain nationalities and not for others – and justified by the laboratory directors and the foundation officers on those grounds, as we have seen. More fundamentally, the researchers from abroad who passed through the portals of the buildings in Copenhagen and Geneva – and who benefited from the resources they had to offer – were usually patriotic citizens engaged in research that often touched on matters of national security. Stone even made a point of mentioning that Lee and Yang had already applied for US citizenship when he suggested that they should go to Copenhagen to meet colleagues from mainland China. Researchers were temporarily released from their national programmes precisely so as to enhance and strengthen them on their return. Ford Foundation fellows who went to the NBI and CERN – be they from the United States, the Soviet Union, China or Israel – did so as members of a national research system with its domestic agendas that often blurred the distinctions in the field of the nuclear that the host institutions did so much to construct and to maintain. They managed two, even multiple, personae; they lived simultaneously in several worlds, worlds that were anchored in their competence as scientists, but that diverged as they mobilised that competence in diverse contexts for different audiences. Their success depended on their capacity to undertake the ongoing boundary work that hid the nationally specific from the internationally universal.[49]

Stone was attracted to these grants by the promise that international scientific exchange could promote mutual understanding and the reduction of global tensions. This was the ideal espoused by Bohr in 1950 and reiterated time and again by the elite of American science. At the same time, as we have seen, Bohr accepted the restrictions on international exchange imposed by the logic of the cold war. In so doing he implicitly recognised that the "republic of letters" had been restructured by the new pact between science and the state after the Second World War. Kistiakowsky's and Weisskopf's appeal to science "as a binding force between men" (see above) was for the most part meaningless, a rhetorical move that obfuscated the science-driven rivalry for national advantage. The Director General's self-indulgent paean to CERN in 1962 as "a symbol of what science really means: man's exploration

49 Forman, "Behind Quantum Electronics", 228.

of nature for the sake of pure knowledge" cast a veil over the use of the "glasshouse" for quite different purposes – and perhaps deliberately so. In the 1960s Weisskopf reportedly met with Ben-Gurion and the leaders of Israel's weapons programme even as he and de Shalit were planning their international conferences at the laboratory in Geneva.[50]

At the most obvious level, this article emphasises that different parts of the American administration shaped, and hoped to benefit from, the award of the grants to CERN and the NBI. This diversity of engagement is a consequence of the nature of the awards themselves, awards that promoted international exchange in a field that impinged directly on the needs of the national security state. This is why the State Department and the CIA had such an important role to play in the grant-giving process. Correlatively, we might expect their role to be diminished the further we move towards knowledge that does not concern them as intimately as did nuclear science in the Cold War. Ford Foundation grants surely did not always engage these arms of the administration so intimately as they did here. But they undoubtedly respected the diverse interests of various branches of the Government whenever their content required it. This is obscured by a too-narrow focus on the officers' arguments for the awards, arguments that have to be framed in terms of foundation aims and objectives and that do not represent the supporting rationales provided by other stakeholders in the process.

This article does not simply emphasise the range of foreign policy considerations that animated those who spoke for these grants in New York and Washington; it also dethrones the official reason given by Stone for making the awards, revealing it as just one of many in favour of the ongoing support for the laboratories from the late 1950s to the early 1960s. Indeed, it is clear that Stone took the widespread and publicly available rhetoric of scientific internationalism as the leitmotif in his arguments to the trustees. The foundation grants doubtless fulfilled that lofty ambition in part, but they were also bearers of a multitude of arguably less noble objectives that were facilitated by the depoliticised spaces created in Geneva and in Copenhagen. Stone was not unaware of those objectives; in fact, he was happy to put foundation dollars to work in the immediate interests of the national security state, as represented by men like Allen Dulles in the CIA. He simply wrote those interests out of the formal script that was used to justify the awards to the trustees, to the laboratories themselves and ultimately to the press.

For the grants to serve these purposes, they had to be embedded in institutional structures both at home and abroad that facilitated the kind of international exchange that Stone and his friends in Washington wanted to promote. The different security agencies of the American State had a well-

---

50 Karpin, *The Bomb in the Basement*, 52. Cohen, *The Worst-Kept Secret*, 353.

established mechanism in place for informal intelligence gathering by the time the grants were made. Research in Copenhagen and in Geneva was organised and administered so as to facilitate the most favourable possible scientific intercourse and the ensuing consolidation of bonds of trust and of friendship between physicists from all over the world. The functionality of the grants, their capacity to achieve their objectives, was parasitic on this infrastructure, and exploited it for the many ends described above. An understanding of this infrastructure as well as of the opportunities it provides is an essential supplement to an analysis of the policy documents in the Ford Foundation archives.

This brings me to perhaps my most important point: To see the Ford Foundation's behaviour through the lens of cultural transmission or of hegemonic outreach is to situate oneself in New York and look out over the world. It is to see the foundation as projecting American knowledge, values and ideals abroad along a vector that is anchored in the United States and that arcs out over the globe connecting "centre" to "periphery". This approach has undeniable merit but it also has its limits. The shift in perspective undertaken in this article away from transmission toward circulation – a shift demanded by the role of the State Department and the CIA in promoting these grants – decentres the foundation and puts CERN and the NBI at the forefront of the analysis. When the language of circulation replaces the language of transmission, vectors are replaced by networks, projection outwards from one pole by interconnectivity between multiple poles. International negotiations between foundation programme directors and laboratory director generals take a back seat to transnational flows of scientists who travel to Denmark and to Switzerland as Ford fellows. Knowledge circulates along with its bearers through this network, serving diverse national agendas from stimulating scientific inquiry to informal intelligence gathering, to discrete conversations about the progress of weapons programmes. With so much to learn, no national entity could apparently resist the opportunity provided by the Ford Foundation to send its nuclear physicists abroad to Geneva and to Copenhagen – not Beijing, not Moscow, not Washington.

When the Scientific Policy Committee and the Bohrs thanked Stone for the extended support for CERN and the NBI, they emphasised the contributions that American fellows had made to strengthening European physics through visits to their laboratories. In doing so they highlighted the single most important reason why these grants mattered to them, and indeed to Stone: after all, that was how he had promoted the awards at foundation headquarters from the outset. What they did not, and could not, speak of was the new resources that international collaboration surely released for these visiting scientists (no matter what their country of origin) when they got back home, the new knowledge that they gained, the new contacts they made, the leverage and the prestige some of them acquired when they rejoined their national programmes. Nor did they allude to the information that American physicists (in particular) acquired at the behest of the CIA and the State Department about nuclear activities in closed communist societies, as well as about a clandestine programme in a country like Israel, through informal intelligence gathering. The co-production of knowledge by Ford Foundation fellows with their international partners in Europe, and the insights that they gained into the research agendas of friend and foe alike as they circulated through Geneva and Copenhagen and back home again, did not simply promote a spirit of mutual understanding. It also satisfied the demands of national security state apparatuses to engage with the multi-layered worlds of nuclear research in other countries.

Giles Scott-Smith

Expanding the Diffusion of US Jurisprudence

The Netherlands as a "Beachhead" for
US Foundations in the 1960s

This article assesses the impact of US foundations, in particular the Ford Foundation, on higher education programmes in law in the Netherlands. It examines two specific cases: the establishment of the Leiden–Columbia Summer Programme in American Law in 1963 and the support given to the Hague Academy of International Law following the Second World War. In both cases the Ford Foundation was a leading partner in supporting the extension of two knowledge circuits: a transatlantic circuit (Leiden–Columbia) and a post-imperial global circuit (Hague Academy). Both institutions promoted the diffusion of US legal thinking and practices as well as educational and jurisprudential norms. US foundations made use of The Hague's location in particular as both a centre for trans-European academic exchange and as a metropole for the post-colonial elites of Asia and Africa (similar to what was happening in London and Paris). This article examines how these Dutch institutions were used as platforms or "beachheads" for furthering US philanthropic designs, and how the Dutch themselves saw their role in this process.

These philanthropic initiatives were linked with the overall drive of US public diplomacy as conducted by the State Department and the United States Information Agency (USIA) during the cold war. Seeking to improve opinion abroad towards the United States, non-state actors like the private foundations could provide additional leverage through financial patronage and nurturing intellectual networks, thereby supplementing and extending official initiatives. Considerable attention was thus given to the field of education and to the establishment abroad of US-related research programmes in the humanities and the social sciences.[1] The strategic value thereof has al-

1 See Skard, *American Studies in Europe*. "American Studies" here refers *not* to a separate "area study", but to "the study of the past and present civilization of the United States through specific courses in academic departments (such as literature, history, geography, government, et cetera)", Walter Johnson, *American Studies Abroad. Progress and Difficulties in Selected Countries*, Special Report from the US Advisory Commission on International Educational and Cultural Affairs, July 1963, 6–7, 45–46.

ways been obvious, as J. Manuel Espinosa of the State Department's Bureau of Educational and Cultural Affairs outlined in 1961: "The study of American subjects in the educational systems of other countries strengthens the basis for a better understanding of American life and institutions on the part of those elements of the population that shape public opinion and give direction to national policy – through educators, students, intellectuals, serious writers, and other leadership elements."[2]

How should we interpret this worldview? Recent research on the relationship between US philanthropy and power, particularly John Krige's notion of "consensual hegemony", has moved beyond the critical view of foundations as "gate-keepers of ideas"[3] by highlighting not only the interests of the various stakeholders involved in foundation-backed projects, but also examples of institutional or individual resistance to these plans.[4] The transmission of the initiative, passing through several players with interests of their own, necessarily gets adapted along the way to its realisation.[5] Yet this should not obscure the fact that a hegemonic project is in operation, however incomplete and haphazard it may sometimes appear to be. As John Ikenberry and Charles Kupchan argue, hegemonic power "relies [...] on ideological persuasion and transnational learning through various forms of direct contact with elites in these states, including contact via diplomatic channels, cultural exchanges, and foreign study."[6] US state and non-state actors combined to marginalise potential socio-economic and intellectual alternatives that were less in tune with US interests.

In the case of the Leiden–Columbia programme and the Hague Academy, US foundations deliberately took the lead, supported by the official institutions of US foreign policy. There were distinct advantages to promoting knowledge of American legal practices in a rapidly integrating Western Europe. The convergence of US and European legal thinking would facilitate transatlantic policy cooperation and back up the State Department's support for the evolution of the European Community (EC). Commercially, such a convergence would assist US corporations to operate within the EC Six and encourage further foreign direct investment. This would be instrumental in sidelining more nationalist and protectionist tendencies present in Europe

---

2 American Studies Abroad: The Role of the Educational Exchange Program of the Department of State, 1961, archive of the Bureau of Educational and Cultural Affairs, Group IV Series 7 Box 166 Folder 10, special collections, University of Arkansas.

3 For critical, often Gramscian-based analyses of US foundations see Arnove, *Philanthropy and Cultural Imperialism*, 1–19; Berman, *The Influence of Carnegie, Ford and Rockefeller*, 1–15; Fisher, "Philanthropic Foundations", 206–233.

4 See Krige, *American Hegemony*.

5 See Fisher, "Double Vision", 141–156.

6 Ikenberry/Kupchan, "Socialization and Hegemonic Power", 290.

and, via the academy in The Hague, other parts of the world. By extension this would also contribute towards bolstering US legal norms more widely within international institutions such as the United Nations. Thus, overall, the implied message was that the United States held the required knowledge to assist Europe with its emerging federal framework, and the benevolent patronage of US philanthropy would make this knowledge available.

The insistence that there was a hegemonic relationship between US and European actors in this respect separates the current perspective from recent work on transatlantic policy networks. The latter rejects the assumption of Americanisation and dominant US influence in favour of a more equal interchange where "the very idea of original and target culture becomes blurred."[7] While mediation was involved, it is still true that the US foundations wanted to achieve certain goals – and they could do so most successfully by working *through* existing European institutions. While the United States Information Agency looked to promote the goals of US foreign policy and foster a pro-American body of opinion, foundation activities were grounded in a conviction that American technocratic efficiency and progressive socio-economic modernisation needed to be exported for the general good. The efforts of these different actors coalesced around the belief that the promotion of US subjects in academia abroad was of paramount importance as a means to legitimise US political and cultural leadership.[8] Western Europe, with its special value for US geo-economic and geo-political interests, was a particular target.[9] Both the foundations and the government assumed that generous patronage and the availability of exchange and research opportunities would produce the desired effect. And on the whole they were right: The American view was typically that if a recipient failed to respond in the expected fashion, it was assumed to be a fault of the individual (or of the apparatus that selected that person) and never of the public diplomacy patronage system itself.

1. The Netherlands: Recipient and Partner

How did the Dutch perceive their role in these American philanthropic endeavours? It is important to emphasise that the Netherlands was an ideal setting for such projects. As the United States Embassy's country plan for 1953

7 Leucht, "Transatlantic Policy Networks", 57. See also Kaiser/Leucht/Gehler, *Transnational Networks*.

8 Reasons given for the export of US culture were phrased both defensively (as a response to propaganda attacks) and offensively (as a logical attribute of the country's "world leadership"). See Johnson, *American Studies Abroad*, 1, 5.

9 See Berghahn, *Intellectual Cold Wars*.

noted, "The Dutch, equipped with a strong democratic tradition at least as strong as our own, are perhaps closer ideologically to the United States than any people in Europe."[10] From the late 1940s onwards, the Netherlands regarded the Atlantic Alliance as the strategic bedrock of its foreign policy and supported American leadership as a welcome balance to French and German designs in Europe. With its economic landscape dominated by several influential multinationals such as Shell, Unilever, KLM and Philips, the Dutch were committed to a free-trade policy, and this reliance on foreign raw materials and markets ensured an internationalist outlook. The Netherlands' position as one of the original Six made it a favoured location for US foreign direct investment and corporate headquarters within the European Economic Community.[11]

The Netherlands had already attracted the attention of American philanthropic interests before 1939, such as the Rockefeller Foundation's support for the Nederlands Economisch Instituut. Nazism and the Second World War ensured a gradual shift throughout Dutch universities away from German models, gradually replacing them with American paedagogic and research techniques through the twentieth century. Efforts by US public diplomacy to increase the circulation of scholars across the Atlantic (such as via the Fulbright Program) contributed to this shift.[12] An article in *Physics Today* from 1948 reported the Dutch as being "very internationally-minded" and "eager to play [their] part in the resumption of international cooperation."[13]

Alongside their Atlanticist orientation, the Dutch were firm believers in the role of the United Nations as a source for international law and development assistance. The Hague Conventions of 1899 and 1907 had established the Netherlands at the forefront of efforts to modernise the rules and norms of warfare and conflict resolution, and this was continued via its membership in the League of Nations. During the 1950s and 1960s the demand grew within national politics for an increase in aid to the poorer countries. No longer a major colonial power after the loss of Indonesia in 1949, the Dutch viewed promoting the socio-economic development of the decolonising regions a politically progressive leitmotif of their post-war international identity. With the aim to reduce poverty and improve living standards, the development approach both allowed for a continuing global role for a post-imperial nation and sought to reduce support for communist alternatives in the Third World. Although financial aid from the Dutch was limited during the 1950s, technical

---

10 Country Plan for USIS The Hague, 30 January 1953, 511.56/1–3053, RG 59, National Archives, College Park (hereinafter NA).

11 Wubs, "U.S. Multinationals", 786–787.

12 Rupp, *Van Oude en Nieuwe Universiteiten*; Scott-Smith, "The Ties That Bind".

13 Gorter, "News from Abroad", 9, 35.

assistance was willingly offered via the United Nations and supported by politicians from both the left and the right. The shifting strategy of the Soviet Union towards a greater influence among former colonies only heightened the need for such a policy, leading Dutch economist (and former Rockefeller research grantee) Jan Tinbergen in 1957 to call for a new "internationalist" social democracy focused on dealing with the development question.[14] Development aid increased from 200 million guilders in 1965 to almost two billion guilders ten years later. By 1980 the goal of providing 1.5 per cent of GDP for overseas causes had been achieved, a higher amount than any other country except Norway.[15] This broad pro-development, modernisation outlook was in line with the views of the main US foundations in their grant-giving activities.

An examination of Ford Foundation support for Dutch institutions during the post-Second World War period fits with this scenario. Three principal groups of recipients are evident: institutions involved in policy-making and planning; institutions involved with international development and cultural awareness; and institutions active in international law. The second and third groups are most important here.

Table: Ford Foundation funding of $500,000 or more for Dutch Institutions, 1951–2004[16]

	Total Funding	Period of Funding
Netherlands Organisation for International Development Cooperation	$997,500	1993–2004
University of Amsterdam	$883,479*	1997–2003
Hague Academy of International Law	$729,293	1952–1991
Institute of Social Studies	$682,000	1959–1972
International Association for the Evaluation of Educational Achievement (NL)	$650,000	2004
Royal Tropical Institute	$525,000	2002–2003
Foundation for Inter-Ethnic Relations	$522,500	1994–1998

* $682,700 of this amount was provided in a single grant in 2003 to strengthen medical anthropological research capacity in reproductive health in Indonesia and the Philippines.

Only two institutions in the 1950s and 1960s are included in the top seven grant recipients for the post-Second World War period: the Hague Academy

14 Tinbergen, "De Internationale Taak van de Sociaal-Democratie", 84–89; de Vries, *Complexe Consensus*, 267–268.
15 Kennedy, *Nieuw Babylon*, 73–76.
16 Funding list from the archives of the Ford Foundation, New York (hereinafter FF).

of International Law and the Institute of Social Studies (ISS). It is also interesting to see that, while there was a hiatus in Ford funding during the 1970s
and 1980s when it moved its interests away from Western Europe, the Hague
Academy continued to receive funds over a period of forty years. Both institutions, in providing a kind of post-colonial "intellectual cosmopolis" for
the elites of the newly independent countries of Asia and Africa, fitted per-
fectly with the international profile that the Netherlands sought to establish
for itself after the Second World War. In 1950 the Netherlands Universities
Foundation of International Cooperation (NUFFIC) was founded to support this goal by promoting international educational exchange, and two
years later the Institute of Social Studies opened in The Hague to offer post-
graduate training in public administration, social policy and economic
planning for the emerging leaders of the under-developed world. In terms of
its international orientation, the institute was from the beginning a part of
the Anglo-American network.[17] Having established itself by 1956 as an independent university within the Dutch system, Ford grants were used for
scholarship and training programmes in Asia and Africa. Dutch institutions
like the Institute of Social Studies and the Hague Academy were ideal "third
parties" for US philanthropy in the field of development because there was
little or no discrepancy between the aims of the foundation staff and those of
the Dutch administrators. Lingering resentment over US diplomatic pressure on the Dutch to withdraw from both Indonesia and New Guinea was
outweighed by the possibility of utilising foundation support for new, post-
colonial developmental goals that maintained both the positive image and
the relevance of the Netherlands in global politics.

So was there no resistance at all to these philanthropic interventions? Occasionally it did surface. In 1962, the United States Embassy, looking to promote the inclusion of American paedagogic methods and materials at the
University of Amsterdam, provided a foreign leader grant for the Rector
Magnificus, Professor Jan Kok, to travel to the United States in March–May
1962.[18] Kok had become rector in 1960, and it was under his leadership that
Amsterdam had assumed full status as a national university. His dislike of innovation, however, literally prevented any real results. In a speech in September 1962, opening the new academic year, Kok spoke out against the
introduction of American approaches to higher education in Dutch universities because they "are in such conflict with the centuries-old development

17 On the ISS see Rupp, *Van Oude en Nieuwe Universiteiten*, 267–74. A US embassy report from 1957 states that "Professor Teaf, a 1953 American [Fulbright] grantee, assisted
in its beginnings", American Studies Inventory and Survey, US Embassy The Hague to
Dept. of State, 31 January 1957, 511.563 1955–1959, Box 2/63, RG 59, NA.

18 Request for academic leave, 5 February 1962, Personeelsdossier Professor Dr J. Kok,
central archives, University of Amsterdam.

of university tradition in our land that it would be very difficult for them to
break through, assuming that one wanted them to."[19] Kok's defence of traditional methods fits in with a general trend amongst old-school cultural elites
opposing Americanised modernisation in the post-war years. Similar
negative views were expressed, for instance, in relation to the mechanisation
of library facilities as a form of "progress".[20] Nevertheless, by the early 1960s
the cutting-edge dominance of US social sciences was having an impact on
Dutch universities, and law was no exception. In promoting these fields,
both US foundations and the United States Information Agency delicately
tried to avoid making the Dutch feel inferior in any way. As the United States
Embassy reported in 1960, "The Netherlands is a small country, and somewhat touchy about its smallness; they should have our constant respect and
reassurance."[21]

2. The Leiden–Columbia–Amsterdam Summer Programme in American Law

The Columbia Summer Programme in American Law is the first example
studied here of US foundations teaming up with Dutch institutions to promote American expertise in a key transnational knowledge sector with clear
policy ramifications.[22] The initiative originated with Columbia law professors Hans Smit (of Dutch background) and Walter Gellhorn, who wanted to
secure a European base for a summer school where American law could be
taught by Americans to Europeans. In 1962 Smit approached Leiden and
Amsterdam, both of which responded positively. The two universities represented quite a contrast: Leiden had conducted legal studies since 1575, while
the University of Amsterdam, which was only able to confer degrees from
1877 onwards, had a reputation as a site of innovation. The dean of the law
school in Leiden at the time was a young professor, Robert Feenstra, an expert in the history of law who had never visited the United States and for
whom intellectually the United States hardly featured as a location of interest. But Feenstra, a respected figure in his field, did possess access to a wide
network of scholars across Western Europe on whom he could call to publi-

19 " ... al deze dingen zijn zo in strijd met in de eeuwen gegroeide universitaire trad-
ities in ons land, dat het wel heel moeilijk zou zijn die te doorbreken, aangenomen, dat
men dit zou willen." *Jaarboek der Universiteit van Amsterdam: Studiegids 1961–62*, 6–7.
   20 Scott-Smith, *Networks of Empire*, 218–222.
   21 Recommended Country Program Plan for FY 1962, 23 March 1960, Country Files
1955–1964, Lot File 66D499, Entry 5118, RG 59, Boxes 212–218, NA.
   22 See http://www.columbiasummerprogram.org/home.html, accessed 20 October
2011.

cise the new programme. He also saw the potential: "I had to find a public. It was also, in that period, still unusual to study abroad like that within Europe. … It was unique, there was nothing comparable."[23]

In December 1962, stimulated by his Columbia colleagues, Feenstra duly approached the Ford Foundation for funding. His application directly stressed the increasing interest among European lawyers in American law due to the unique legal implications of the European Economic Community's supranational institutions. There were few opportunities to satisfy this demand in Europe at this time. The Salzburg Seminar, established in 1948, was a possible option, but this was always intended to provide a broad range of courses in American Studies and so could not satisfy a regular demand for American law.[24] Nevertheless, the Salzburg formula of attracting a multinational group of scholars for a short period of intensive study was one that could be repeated. Feenstra therefore proposed bringing sixty graduate students and young professionals per year from around all Europe for a four-week course to be held in Leiden; only a quarter were to come from the Netherlands itself. Around this programme would be built a more sustained cooperation between Leiden and Columbia, including an exchange of faculty and expertise to enrich their respective law schools.[25] The Ford Foundation initially declined the request, preferring to wait and see how the undertaking would develop.

In July 1963, at the end of the successful inaugural programme, Feenstra petitioned the Ford Foundation again for $125,500 over five years. Sixty-four candidates had been selected out of eighty-five applicants from twelve countries across Europe, representing a cross-section of academia, business, government and other professions. Six members of the Columbia law faculty gave lectures on the American legal method, constitutional law and private international law. The American informal style, which contrasted strongly with what law students from traditional European universities were used to, was a big success for creating a common bond of congeniality.[26] Plans were made to expand the arrangement as a Leiden–Amsterdam–Columbia summer programme and to seek students from a wider array of European nations "outside 'Western Europe', somewhat narrowly defined."[27]

23 Professor Robert Feenstra, interview by the author, Leiden, 14 May 2002.

24 On Salzburg see Schmidt, "Small Atlantic World", and Parmar, "Challenging Elite Anti-Americanism".

25 Feenstra to Joseph Slater (International Affairs), 7 December 1962, Grant 64–117, Reel 2819, FF.

26 Professor Robert Feenstra, interview by the author, Leiden, 14 May 2002.

27 Feenstra to Slater, 25 July 1963, Grant 64–117, Reel 2819, FF. The first year included participants from the Netherlands, UK, Sweden, Italy, France, Belgium, Israel, Switzerland, Germany, Austria, South Africa and Taiwan.

This time the foundation reacted positively. The International Affairs division, which had become more interested in funding international law projects, was prepared to pursue proposals that "increased collaboration between international legal experts in the Atlantic area", that "help[ed] strengthen competence in international law in the developing countries" and that "foster[ed] the acceptance of the rule of law generally."[28] A funding tranche subsequently awarded $290,000 to the British Institute of International and Comparative Law, which possessed close relations with newly independent members of the British Commonwealth, and $95,000 over five years to the Leiden–Amsterdam–Columbia programme. The decision fully recognised the functional value of an expanding knowledge of the American federal legal system for an integrating Europe: "American awareness of European legal and social institutions has been growing in recent years. It has not been matched by a corresponding European understanding of American developments. Given the growing interest in federal legal problems in Europe, an understanding of the American legal system and practice can be especially worthwhile. The legal profession provides a significant portion of the political and intellectual leadership of many European countries."[29]

As usual, the Ford Foundation checked out the programme's development by requesting informal reports from visitors. The report from a participant in the 1965 summer programme in Amsterdam gives a clear indication of the standards being set. The "instruction was organized wholly on the American university pattern and was pursued in the form of seminars and discussions (the case method) [...] the intensity of study was considerable" and the professors maintained a high level of supervision throughout the four-week period. Significantly, the programme had now broadened its intake to include participants from Czechoslovakia, Poland, Yugoslavia, Kenya and Nigeria. The participant noted that while it was impossible to become an expert in American law in four weeks, "of great value was the training received in English conversation and English legal terminology."[30]

With the Ford Foundation backing this increasingly successful venture, the United States Embassy stepped in to expand its educational exchange component. In 1965, a foreign leader programme invitation was given to Feenstra to enable him to tour American universities and expand his contacts in the legal field. Feenstra was involved in selecting Dutch law students for Fulbright grants to study in the United States, and his role in the Leiden–Columbia programme brought him increasingly to the Embassy's attention. In his own opinion, his leader grant was "probably due to the involvement of

28 International Legal Activities, 12 December 1963, Grant 64–117, Reel 2819, FF.
29 Ibid.
30 Some Impressions of the 1965 Course, n.d., ibid.

the Columbia university people, especially professor Gellhorn, who wanted to reward me in some way". While this was true, the Embassy hoped the Dutchman would expand exchanges between Dutch and American institutions. The country plan for 1963 also stated the intention to "[d]evelop chairs, lectureships, and courses in American Studies in specific Dutch universities, particularly in the key faculties of Law, Letters, and Economics where most of the future leaders in government, the mass media, and the political parties are trained", indicating the close connections between law and leadership.[31]

Remarkably, this was Feenstra's first trip to the United States, and in April–May 1965 he visited Columbia, Harvard, Princeton, Yale, the University of Virginia, Louisiana State University, North-West University in Chicago, Ann Arbor, Indiana University, Stanford and Berkeley. His itinerary, which was meant to acquaint him with a broader view of American life and not just "pursuing the interests of the Columbia programme", also included a visit to the Boeing factory in Seattle.[32] Feenstra found the trip "inspirational, rejuvenating", with "the feeling that everything is possible", but did not use it to expand Leiden's connections in the United States. The Dutchman's positive views towards the United States were undoubtedly strengthened, but he was simply not enough of an "entrepreneur" to seize the opportunity as his US benefactors had hoped.

In 1967, with the end of the Ford Foundation grant in sight, informal attempts were made to renew it. This time Walter Gellhorn approached the Ford Foundation to sound out a possible fifty–fifty venture together with the Volkswagen Foundation. Gellhorn remarked that the Ford's initial "speculative investment" had "paid off handsomely". The programme participants were exiting with an appreciation for American legal practice, methods and materials, skills that were increasingly useful in professional settings. Adopting the language of US public diplomacy, Gellhorn stressed that a "multiplying trend" was evident in how participants spread their knowledge after the programme. The programme was "geared particularly to the needs of Europeans", with enquiries even coming in from the USSR.[33] Gellhorn also emphasised that "The Netherlands was deemed to be an appropriate centre of the Program because of its long tradition in international education, its continuingly important role in European affairs and world finance, and its central geographical location". From the Netherlands itself Ernst van der Beugel, associated with the Hague Academy of International Law and from 1966 a

---

31 Revised Section V of the Country Plan for the Netherlands, 7 November 1963, Country Files 1955–64, Lot File 66D499, Entry 5118, RG 59, Boxes 212–18, NA.

32 Feenstra, interview by the author, Leiden, 14 May 2002.

33 Gellhorn to Robert Edwards, 10 August 1967, Grant 64–117, Reel 2819, FF.

consultant for the Ford Foundation,[34] approached Joe Slater with a plea for a continuation of Ford Foundation funding. Van der Beugel was at the time European Secretary for the Bilderberg meetings and a firm believer in the need to introduce new generations into established networks of (transatlantic) influence: "It is vital for the relations between the generations of intellectuals which are now growing up in the United States and Europe that they get involved in each other's problems. The Program helps, in its modest way, to prevent the 'drifting apart' and so fosters American–European contacts at relatively low costs."[35]

These approaches had the desired effect, since in March 1968 the Ford Foundation's International Relations section granted $62,500 over five years. But while the summer programme was praised for "filling an active need in Europe" and its "excellent quality", the grant award stated that "the Ford Foundation … should not continue to bear the full cost of a program designed to benefit Europe." European sources were only bearing ten per cent of annual costs. In other words, the sheer fact of spreading the use and understanding of American law amongst a highly educated cross-section of Europeans, which could also benefit the practice of US business in the region, was not enough on its own to justify continuing Ford assistance. The self-evident need for this service meant that Europeans should pay for it themselves and no longer rely on American philanthropic generosity.

Despite further reports emphasising the quality of the summer programme, fundraising did not go well. Arthur Cyr of the Ford Foundation visited the Dutch board in October 1971 to hear that the Volkswagen people had insisted that German law should be added to the programme and German members added to the board, a move that was rejected. Aside from diluting the essential American focus, the Dutch board members felt that "this would be an ideal excuse for Soviet and East European Governments to use to eliminate participation they now enjoy in the Seminar". The programme was hindered in two ways: There was no tradition of non-governmental support for education activities in the Netherlands (or Europe as a whole), and the Dutch Government was unlikely to back a venture if only a quarter of its intake came from the Netherlands. As a result, Walter Gellhorn and Hans Smit made a new effort in early 1973, focussing on joint projects that covered the significance of the European Economic Community for international law. The heavy demands of the Volkswagen Foundation, which actually wanted to move the entire operation to a German location, were emphasised. US philanthropic support for promoting US legal norms in Eu-

34 Van der Beugel to Henry Kissinger, 8 July 1966, File 7: Correspondence 1963–67, archive of Ernst van der Beugel, National Archives, The Hague.
35 Van der Beugel to Slater, 9 November 1967, Grant 64–117, Reel 2819, FF.

rope was essential, as otherwise alternative models – for instance from Germany – would gain ground. The negative response from other European outlets – the Bernard van Leer Foundation (Netherlands), the Giovanni Agnelli Foundation (Italy) and the Calouste Gulbenkian Foundation (England) – also indicated that US philanthropy was required.

There were two bright spots. One concerned the grants from Dutch-based sources (Foundation for European Culture and the Van den Berch van Heemstede Foundation), both of which indicated the helping hand of van der Beugel and his network. The other regarded the approaches to American law firms, which had produced seventeen grants of $1,000 each, a solid sign of "the interest in American lawyers in advancing understanding and strengthening ties among transnational professional colleagues". The Ford Foundation had laid the groundwork, and US corporate interests were now taking up the slack, the commercial benefits for such a venture being evident.[36] The terminal grant was not reactivated,[37] but it did not need to be: Over the next decade American law firms, supported by Dutch corporations, became the principal financiers of the programme.[38] Ford seed money had served its purpose, and there was no need to take it further.

3. The Hague Academy of International Law

The Hague Academy has a longer heritage than the Leiden–Columbia programme.[39] The academy was founded in the wake of the First World War in the Peace Palace in The Hague, a building paid for by Andrew Carnegie. The aim was to promote the standards of international law as the fundamental principles of interaction between states and peoples, thereby opposing the forces of nationalism and acting to establish a firm set of legal norms in the interests of conflict prevention and resolution. Financial support was provided by the Carnegie Endowment for International Peace, combined with local support from Nobel Peace Prize winner Tobias Asser and Dutch pacifist Dr A. E. H. Goedkoop. Already in the academy's first year, 353 students from thirty-one countries attended courses given in French by lecturers representing fifteen different nationalities.[40]

36 Proposal for Continued Support of the Leyden–Amsterdam–Columbia Summer Program in American Law, 26 February 1973, ibid.
37 A memo from Cyr requesting guidance on the proposal was marked with "No! For goodness sake let terminal grants lie" from someone higher up in the Ford hierarchy. Arthur Cyr to Goodwin, Lederer and Silj, 18 April 1973, ibid.
38 Hans Smit, Report of the 1973 Session, 28 September 1973, ibid.
39 For a detailed account see Scott-Smith, "Attempting to Secure an 'Orderly Evolution'".
40 On the academy's history see Skubiszewski, "Contribution", 68–74, 78–79.

On a regional level, similar to the Columbia summer programme, US foundation support for the Hague Academy after the Second World War also aimed to upgrade traditional European higher education practices by introducing American methods. But there was a more important global dimension: to use the academy to make contact with and influence the elites of the newly decolonising Third World. From the mid-1950s until the early 1970s the academy was part of a broad strategy begun by the Eisenhower administration to ensure a smooth transition from a colonial to a post-colonial world order.[41] While the United Nations was seen as the basis for establishing a consensus on the acceptable behaviour of states and a universal code of international law, the obstacle of the Soviet bloc and the increase in the United Nations' membership from fifty-six states in 1953 to ninety-nine by 1961 ultimately undermined hopes that the United States could successfully manage its agenda.[42] Promoting the dissemination of Western legal norms and practices was one way of bringing Third World elites into line, both ideologically and culturally, with their Western counterparts. As Liping Bu outlined, "when the newly independent nations emphasized education in their nation-building, both the United States and the Soviet Union eagerly offered them educational resources and political ideologies."[43] In this scenario, the Hague Academy served as a "beachhead" institution to create a transnational "epistemic community", sharing an understanding of international order based on Western notions of development, democracy and the free market.[44]

Initially, in the late 1940s, it proved difficult for the academy to revive its pre-Second World War funding channels from the United States. The Carnegie Endowment, which had previously provided $40,000 annually, had decided under its new president Alger Hiss to protect its declining capital and shift its focus instead to supporting the study of international law at domestic centres such as Yale, Harvard and Columbia.[45] Carnegie support was duly terminated in 1949. Efforts by prominent Dutch members of the Hague Academy's governing board (the Curatorium), such as former Foreign Minister Eelco van Kleffens, to replace Carnegie with either the Rockefeller or

41 McMahon, "The Challenge of the Third World".

42 Pruden, *Conditional Partners*, 16–31, 173–175, 188, 197.

43 Bu, "Educational Exchange", 407.

44 On the notion of a "beachhead" institution see Gemelli, "Western Alliance". On epistemic communities see Haas, "Epistemic Communities".

45 Hague Academy of International Law [discussion between Hiss and Rockefeller Foundation officers Joseph Willits and Bryce Wood], 15 March 1958, Record Group (hereinafter RG) 1.2, Series 450, Sub-series 5, Box 8, Rockefeller Foundation archive (hereinafter Rockefeller).

Ford Foundation initially failed.[46] The final word on the issue came from John Foster Dulles, consulted as a Rockefeller Trustee. Dulles, then in his phase of disillusionment with the United Nations, replied with disdain: "He then went on to say that the Communists regarded international law as the means by which those in power keep others in subjection. If there came into view a person who could deal with the problem of the whole philosophy of international law profoundly and wisely, he would favour support."[47]

The Ford Foundation provided a minimal grant of only $22,000 for the 1951 academic year, and at this stage none of the three major foundations were convinced of the need to support an international law institute outside of the United States. Yet the global political environment was changing rapidly. Preparations for a major conference of Afro-Asian nations were already in motion in early 1954, and the resulting event in Bandung in April 1955 was a large step towards a post-imperial world order and "a powerful symbol of solidarity among former colonial possessions."[48] Observing these trends, the Rockefeller Foundation decided that it was necessary to engage with the new elites in order to promote US legal norms as a basis for the emerging post-colonial world order. After spending some time in The Hague during the summer of 1954, Rockefeller vice-president Kenneth Thompson reported to his superior, Dean Rusk, that the Hague Academy's "significance is heightened because of the failures of established agencies like the American Society of International Law (ASIL) and the International Law Association to encourage a free and vigorous debate among responsible scholars of notably diverse viewpoints."[49] He did identify certain administrative problems. While the Dutch ran the Administrative Council, the French-controlled Curatorium ran "policy on educational and scientific matters". The dominant personality was the Curatorium's president, 73-year-old Gilbert Gidel, a professor of law from Paris, and his control was not universally appreciated. Language was a problematic issue. Whereas before the Second World War every lecture had been held in French, after 1945 English was accepted, albeit thanks to the resistance of Gidel only in a minority of courses.

46 In 1956 van Kleffens became an honorary member of the American Society for International Law, a significant sign of recognition. Gilbert Gidel (President of the Curatorium) to Chester I. Barnard (President, Rockefeller Foundation), 27 October 1948; Joseph Willits to van Kleffens, 11 May 1949, RG 1.2, Series 650, Sub-series 5, Box 8, Rockefeller; Record of Dealings between the Ford Foundation and the Hague Academy, 14 June 1956, Grant 51–20, Reel 0552, FF.

47 Joseph Willits, memo: The Hague Academy of International Law: John Foster Dulles, Telephone Conversation, 16 October 1951, RG 1.2, Series 650, Sub-series 5, Box 8, Rockefeller.

48 Newsom, *The Imperial Mantle*, 129–130.

49 Kenneth Thompson, Some Impressions of the Hague Academy of International Law, 13 September 1954, Grant 51–20, Reel 0552, FF.

Modernisation, in the form of more democratic American methods, was badly needed.

Thompson then turned to possible reforms. Above all, he recommended a shift in emphasis away from the old-style *ex cathedra* lecture towards a more open US-style seminar system. Significantly, he had heard "that the French, because of their national educational patterns, have long been opposed to the seminar as a means of instruction at the Academy". Nevertheless, "progressive forces" were gathering strength around van Kleffens and others. Percy Corbett, a Princeton scholar visiting The Hague, agreed: "Five hundred or more students are assembled at The Hague every year. They come from all over the world. If this country has any fresh thought to offer on the elements of an international order, and any interest in spreading such thought beyond its own borders, this channel seems to me open for a great deal of development."[50] In November 1955 the Rockefeller Foundation duly authorised a grant of $122,000, beginning in 1957 and to be spread over five years, to facilitate the creation of a Centre d'Étude et de Recherche de Droit International et de Relations Internationales. Intended to stimulate student–faculty research in a looser, more informal framework, the centre was the first step in redefining the academy's approach.[51]

During the summer of 1956 the momentum picked up. With van Kleffens active on the international lecture circuit emphasising the challenges the West would face through decolonisation,[52] Philip Jessup, a visiting professor of international law and diplomacy from Columbia,[53] drafted an assessment report for the Rockefeller, Ford and Carnegie foundations. Informal networking was a vital part of the institution, and this "shows the possible valuable by-products of the Academy. I was told of it by Boutros-Ghali, the able young Egyptian Assistant Professor of International Law at Cairo whom I had seen there and who studied with us at Columbia last year. This was his fourth consecutive year at the Academy. He is a member of a group of 15–20, many of whom also come back year after year, all of whom are teachers of international law of grades less than full professor. They meet regularly while

50 Corbett to Joseph E. Johnson (president, Carnegie Endowment), 7 September 1954, Grant 51–20, Reel 0552, FF.

51 Record of Dealings, 14 June 1956, Grant 51–20, Reel 0552, FF. On the centre see Boutros-Ghali, "Le Centre d'étude", 139–153, 225–227.

52 In 1956 van Kleffens spoke at the 1956 Bilderberg meeting and at the Aspen Institute on this topic. Van Kleffens, Speeches 1956–61, File 38 Archive of E.N. van Kleffens, National Archives, The Hague (hereinafter van Kleffens).

53 Jessup had been a student at the academy in 1923 and lectured there in 1929. The US representative on the UN Security Council in 1948, he served on the academy's Curatorium from 1957 to 1968 and with the International Court of Justice in the Peace Palace from 1961 to 1970.

at The Hague to discuss teaching methods, substantive topics and general academic and other problems."[54]

The entrance of the Rockefeller Foundation triggered a meeting between the big three foundations on 3 October involving Thompson, Donald Price (Ford Foundation vice-president responsible for its European programme), John Gardner (president of the Carnegie Corporation) and John Howard (director of the Ford's International Training Division). Gardner took a hard line, wanting any grant to be conditional on major changes in management and administration, but the others insisted that the typically European structure of the institution should be respected, and "that the European sensitivities are such that no crude bargaining would have any other than an adverse effect." The fact that Philip Jessup was joining the Curatorium was a major additional factor.[55] Satisfied with the potential, the Ford Foundation approved a grant of $80,000 (subsequently raised to $90,000) over four years. Doubts remained over a lack of American input in the management structure, old-fashioned teaching methods and a lack of engagement with current-day international problems. An emphasis was given "to increas[ing], as far as feasible, the participation of students and lecturers from Asia, Africa, North America, and South America."[56]

By the late 1950s any concerns over the lack of modernisation at the Hague Academy were outweighed by its value as a kind of "listening post" on global affairs. In October 1958 the Department of State sent New York lawyer and former CIA deputy director Loftus E. Becker as an advisor to the United States Embassy in The Hague to increase informal contacts between embassy officials and Hague Academy participants.[57] The Soviet Embassy in The Hague had begun to "cultivate" the students from the Third World, generating a US response, and the establishment of cultural relations with the Eastern bloc meant that the academy was now attracting more participants from Eastern Europe.[58] But the Third World was the key. A new funding re-

---

54 Philip C. Jessup, Report on the Hague Academy of International Law, August 1956, Grant 51–20, Reel 0552, FF. Boutros-Ghali became one of the directors of the Centre d'Études in 1963–1964 and later joined the Curatorium. See Bardonnet, "L'Académie de droit international".

55 Howard to Merillat, 4 October 1956; Merillat to Price, 11 November 1956, Grant 57–145, Reel 0552, FF.

56 International Research and Training: The Hague Academy of International Law (draft), 19 December 1956, Grant 57–145, Reel 0552, FF; Meeting of the Executive Committee, 21 March 1957, Grant 51–20, Reel 0552, FF.

57 In 1959 Becker was the European chief for the legal firm Cahill, Gordon, Reindel and Ohl. See Hersh, The Old Boys, 301; Mader, Who's Who, 56.

58 The Hague Academy Bulletin (1995), 55–61; Budget of the Hague Academy of International Law: 1951, and; Jessup, Report on the Hague Academy of International Law, August 1956, Grant 51–20, Reel 0552, FF.

quest in April 1960 emphasised that "One of the serious problems which face governments of these new States is that of finding persons who possess the knowledge of international law and relations, and the training, required to enable them to act as legal advisors, as diplomats and as representatives at international conferences. From a long term point of view the Academy is making an important contribution to the solution of this problem."[59] Recognising that the academy was "peculiarly dependent on operating grants," the Ford Foundation's Executive Committee approved a further grant of $100,000 over four years beginning in 1962.[60]

In the early 1960s the Hague Academy continued to expand its services. A grant from the Dag Hammarskjöld Foundation led to an annual Dag Hammarskjöld research seminar beginning in 1963 "for persons who have entered upon, or are about to begin, careers in government or diplomatic service, or in the teaching of international law in the countries of Africa and Asia which have become independent within the last two decades."[61] In 1965 the Ford Foundation provided a further five-year grant of $295,000 for modernisation of the Hague Academy's infrastructure, including simultaneous interpretation equipment to finally overcome the English–French issue.[62] An amount of $45,000 was designated for a two-year study on the academy's future potential under the chairmanship of Columbia international law professor Wolfgang Friedmann, with Professor Boutros Boutros-Ghali appointed as one of his colleagues.[63] The group stressed further modernisation of the curriculum, extra scholarships annually for doctoral candidates,[64] and the appointment of five scholars in residence each year.[65]

By this stage the academy was able to count on the interest of several philanthropic organisations. In 1964 the Carnegie Endowment revived its support for an annual lecturer position for a ten-year period. The Rockefeller

59 McNair to Henry T. Heald, 26 April 1960, Grant 57–145, Reel 0552, FF.

60 Jessup to Howard, 20 May 1960; Executive Committee meeting, 8 December 1960, Grant 57–145, Reel 0552, FF.

61 See Dupuy, *Jubilee Book 1923–1973*, 228–229.

62 Report on the Method of Spending the Following Grants from the Ford Foundation to the Hague Academy of International Law and the Achievements Arrived At, September–October 1974, Grant 65–158, Reel 3052, FF.

63 On Friedmann's impressive reputation see Weiler/Paulus, "The Structure of Change".

64 Between 1967 and 1974, 48 doctoral scholars completed their studies at the academy, including 6six Egyptians, 4four Nigerians, 4four Romanians and 2two from the Soviet Union. Report on the Method of Spending the Following Grants, Grant 65–158, Reel 3052, FF.

65 Professor F. Castberg and Professor Dr J. E. de Quay to Dr Howard R. Swearer, 27 November 1968; Report on the Method of Spending the Following Grants, Grant 65–158, Reel 3052, FF.

Foundation continued its support for the Centre d'Études with a grant of $150,000 in 1961 and a $210,000 terminal grant to cover 1966 to 1972. Aiming to expand the curriculum further, the Rockefeller Foundation also provided $1,500 a year for "special courses" from 1965 to 1967, whereby "distinguished exponents of Buddhism, Confucianism, Hinduism and Islam discussed the compatibility of the basic principles of international law with these great religious philosophies." The Asia Foundation contributed towards the participation of Asian scholars.[66] While the number of participants from Asia and Africa was rising – 117 in 1968 compared to 72 the year before – Friedmann's study group recommended the formation of an external programme involving the selection and hiring out of an international "itinerant faculty" who would reside in each applicant country for several weeks, providing a local source of expertise on international legal issues and bringing selected young diplomats, professors and civil servants "who are expected to occupy prominent posts later on" up to date on recent developments in international law. This was described as "a specialised kind of technical assistance" that "would greatly enlarge the effectiveness of the Academy." It would also, according to Friedmann, help to counter the fragmenting tendencies in the discipline, which represented "a definite danger that the unity and universality of international law would increasingly give way to several systems of international law divided by regional, political, economic and other factors."[67] Western legal norms were coming under pressure, requiring some extra proselytising. As van Kleffens formulated the question: "Is International Law solely a product of the West?"[68] The Carnegie Endowment duly provided $173,200 to establish the external programme for its first three years. The first session of the programme was held in Rabat in 1969 and others followed in subsequent years in Bogotá, Mexico City, Tehran, Singapore, Buenos Aires, Yaoundé and Bangkok.[69]

But changes soon came. McGeorge Bundy replaced Henry Heald as the Ford Foundation president in 1966. Under Heald the foundation had been spending part of its capital (over 600 million US dollars above net income by 1962), and Bundy needed to enforce a more sober approach.[70] In March 1970 the Ford Foundation's International Affairs Office proposed a terminal grant of $131,697 for the academy, to be spread over three years. The changing geo-

---

66 Castberg and de Quay to Swearer, 27 November 1968, Grant 65–158, Reel 3052, FF; Dupuy, *Jubilee Book 1923–1973*, 233–239.

67 Castberg and de Quay to Swearer, 27 November 1968, Grant 65–158, Reel 3052, FF.

68 Van Kleffens, Hague Academy of International Law, n.d. [1969], File 58 van Kleffens.

69 Herman van Roijen to Bundy, 27 February 1975, Grant 65–158, Reel 3052, FF. On the programme see Dupuy, *Jubilee Book 1923–1973*, 160–173, 230–232.

70 Berghahn, *Intellectual Cold Wars*, 186–187, 241–249.

political context and the declining strategic value of an institute like the Hague Academy for US foreign policy interests lay behind this decision. By the late 1960s the hope for an "orderly evolution" to a post-colonial international system, with the newly independent nations aligned alongside the West, was a distant memory. Third-World nations had created their own international networks: the Non-Aligned Movement (1960), OPEC (1960) and the Group of 77 (1964). The OPEC price hikes in 1973 and the declaration of a New International Economic Order by the Group of 77 confirmed a dramatic shift in North–South relations. Under these circumstances the effort to foster an epistemic community of Third World elites via the "old-world" academy began to appear as a lost cause and no longer worthy of attention.

A planning document from 1970 explains the resulting transformation in Ford Foundation policy. International law was in danger of becoming irrelevant and having no answers when "confronted with the forces of human reproduction, nationalism, ideological conflict, and the revolutions in science and technology." Traditional concepts and methodology were no longer appropriate for dealing with issues relating to multinational corporations or the exploration (and exploitation) of outer and inner space. As a result, "it seems desirable to allocate the limited resources available primarily to those international aspects of law that are addressed to major challenges to the international political process." Attention was now directed towards the American Society for International Law, which "has taken the leadership in seeking to direct the attention of the international law fraternity to such major challenges as the new technology generated by the continuing scientific revolution [...] and the necessity to incorporate the insights of other disciplines in seeking solutions for problems traditionally styled 'legal.'"[71]

Whereas in the 1950s the Hague Academy had been regarded as a more useful conduit than the American Society of International Law for promoting US legal norms, by 1970 the emphasis was on building new knowledge circuits based on looser professional networks rather than the more static, training-related outlook of the academy. The institute in The Hague was also unable to completely shake off the fact that "many new states tend to see international law as a body of principles whose essential effect, if not design, has been to maintain the colonial stigma."[72] In a coordinated action, the major US foundations collectively withdrew their support, and role of the Hague Academy as a European "beachhead" was over (although, as has been shown, the Ford Foundation did provide some limited grants later on).

---

71 David E. Bell (Ford Foundation Vice-President) to McGeorge Bundy, 25 May 1970, Grant 65–158, Reel 3052, FF.

72 Bell to Bundy, 25 May 1970, Grant 65–158, Reel 3052, FF.

4. Conclusion

Both the Leiden–Columbia–Amsterdam summer programme and the Hague Academy fulfilled particular tasks within the worldview of the US foundations. Through the 1960s they both acted as intellectual "beach-heads": On the one hand, this involved using the Netherlands to promote the "Americanisation" of European academia with the introduction of informal seminars and the Harvard Law School case-study instruction method, supplanting the traditional approaches of the French in the process. On a broader scale, however, it involved promoting US legal norms and models to the detriment of potential alternatives less aligned with US interests, be they on a European (German) or a global, post-colonial scale. In both cases the US foundations took the lead, with the United States Information Agency and the State Department acting only in support when required. A hegemonic impulse – the furthering of US world order – was the driving force behind both of these projects, although the particular ways need to be recognised in which the foundations perceived this. Both the summer programme and the academy acted as platforms to attract participants from other regions – Eastern Europe in the summer programme and the Third World with the academy – although the academy was clearly the more important of the two. Walter Gellhorn's hope that the summer programme could contribute "small steps" towards "relaxing 'East–West tensions'" did not bring the desired result of more funding.[73] In the late 1950s Shepard Stone of the Ford's International Affairs Division initiated a series of arrangements to channel selected Polish researchers and students to Western European universities, a process overseen by European proxies receiving Ford Foundation grants (the British Council, the German Academic Exchange Service, the University of Geneva in Switzerland and the National Bureau of French Universities).[74] Yet the summer programme was not deemed to fit this model: The Europeans and the business sector should fund this operation, since they were the ones benefitting the most. Despite the apparent symmetry of supporting both a European-based and a global-based legal network in the same small nation, the interests behind the two were different. The fact that the summer programme switched successfully from philanthropic to (US) commercial support confirmed this view of the foundation executives.

The experience of the Hague Academy provides revealing insights into both the coordination of American philanthropic and foreign policy interests and the altering posture of the United States towards the Third World.

---

73 Gellhorn to Edwards, 10 August 1967, Grant 64–117, Reel 2819, FF.
74 See grant 5800018, Reel 532 (Germany), Grant 5800070, Reel 532 (Geneva), Grant 5700370, Reel 530 (France) and Grant 5700321, Reel 530 (UK), FF.

Prior to the Second World War the Carnegie Endowment had used the academy to promote conflict resolution and world peace in such a way that, as Endowment Trustee James Brown Scott remarked, the institute should be a neutral vessel through which "international law internationalizes itself."[75] The onset of decolonisation caused support to be more instrumentalised. Between 1956 and 1972 the Hague Academy received $652,000 from the Ford Foundation and $482,000 from the Rockefeller Foundation to extend its impact around the globe. Aside from the normative impact, this also compares to similar US public diplomacy ventures in other post-colonial metropoles such as London and Paris. The so-called Third World programmes run by United States Information Agency personnel in these capitals involved efforts to engage with Asian and African students arriving to study and to approach them with the offer of educational exchange (or overseas student leader grants) to visit the United States: a potent "soft power" weapon to cultivate contacts.[76] But emerging socio-political forces across the developing world rejected the Western concept of international order as a continuation of colonial rule by proxy. Without attention to Third World economic and political concerns, the focus on elites alone could not guarantee success. An "orderly evolution" on these grounds was simply too elitist. The foundations continued to regard the Hague Academy (and the summer programme) as worthy ventures in their own right, though they were no longer effective for promoting US legal norms in a changing global political environment that was challenging Western conceptions of order.

The position of the Netherlands is a significant final issue in these case studies. Alongside the mutual interests in international affairs, transatlantic modernisers such as van Kleffens and van der Beugel were crucial for exerting influence where needed. In their eyes the transition from French to American influence was a central part of the Hague Academy's transition to a more meaningful role. Both the summer programme and the academy signified Dutch eagerness to establish a lead over continental rivals by adopting American pedagogical innovations and – in concert with Dutch global business interests – to play a role as a site for international education. These goals outweighed the need for actual Dutch participation in the institutions themselves. In fact, the summer programme restricted Dutch participants to a quarter of the total, and the academy behaved the same way: In 1965 only eight Dutch auditors attended, about the same number as from Pakistan.[77] For the foundations, The Hague was an ideal location due to its reputation as a centre of legal practice and the fact that the Netherlands, as Dutch Ambas-

75 Hague Academy of International Law, n.d., Grant 65–158, Reel 3052, FF.
76 See Scott-Smith, *Networks of Empire*, 349–351, 388–390.
77 Report to the Ford Foundation 1965, 22 October 1965, Grant 57–145, Reel 0552, FF.

sador to the United States Herman van Roijen put it, "under the influence of historical, social, economic and other factors, has, through the years, generally worked for peace and stability in the world."[78] The impact of these institutions was therefore meant to be as much (if not more) *beyond* Dutch shores as within the local educational system. Significantly, the role of the Netherlands as a "beachhead" for US philanthropic capital did not falter once that capital was withdrawn. Both the summer programme and the academy located other financial sources and continue to this day.[79] Foundation seed money succeeded, both sides of the arrangement benefitted, and dependence was ultimately avoided.

---

78 Van Roijen, "Holland and the Hague Academy", 29–30; Gormley, "The Hague Academy of International Law", 513.

79 Now under the leadership of President Boutros Boutros-Ghali and Secretary General Yves Daudet (University of Paris I), the Academy has successfully diversified its funding sources both internationally and with the private sector. It now receives contributions from 37 countries, and the External Programme has been redirected to focus on the nations of Eastern Europe and Central Asia. See http://www.hagueacademy.nl, accessed 2 November 2011).

Nicole Sackley

Foundation in the Field

The Ford Foundation's New Delhi Office
and the Construction of Development Knowledge, 1951–1970

In 1952, the Ford Foundation consolidated its headquarters at 477 Madison Avenue in New York City, positioning itself at the very centre of an emerging international development regime.[1] Within blocks of Ford's offices lay the Rockefeller Foundation's headquarters and the newly completed United Nations Secretariat building. Out of these headquarters poured a range of plans and proposals for how to define and address the problem of "underdevelopment", from Asia to the Middle East. Meanwhile, the traffic between New York, Washington, DC, and US universities grew ever thicker. Leaders of the Ford Foundation and Rockefeller Foundation moved in and out of high-ranking government positions and consulted regularly with US policy-makers and university experts. Foundation officers spoke frankly about the geo-political urgency of development in the Cold-War battle against the Soviet Union, even as they believed simultaneously in the libratory power of philanthropic funding and American knowledge to, in the capacious mission of the Ford Foundation, "advance human welfare".[2]

In recent years, historians have uncovered a good deal about the domestic production and circulation of development knowledge between US philanthropies and US universities. They have begun to trace as well the role of US foundations in the formation of transnational epistemic communities of experts that cohered around, and defined, developments such as population control, food production and economic planning initiatives.[3] The voice of the foundation in these histories nevertheless remains largely that of the foundation presidents and senior officers in New York. This article, however, intends to shift our perspective on the foundations and the construction of

---

1 To accommodate its first President Paul Hoffman (1951–1953), the Ford Foundation made its headquarters near Hoffman's home in Pasadena, California.

2 Berman, *Influence of the Carnegie*.

3 Lowen, *Creating the Cold War University*; Geiger, *Research and Relevant Knowledge*, Ch. 4; Gilman, *Mandarins of the Future*; McCaughey, *International Studies*; Connelly, *Fatal Misconception*; Cullather, *Hungry World*; Frey, "Neo-Malthusianism".

development from the "centre" in New York to the "periphery" by examining the history of the Ford Foundation's New Delhi office and its representative Douglas Ensminger, who directed the office from 1952 to 1970. As such, it provides the first historical examination of a foundation field office and the critical role such offices played in the making of development knowledge, policy and practice during the Cold War.

The Delhi office was the largest of a network of seventeen field offices that the Ford Foundation established around the world by 1968. In capitals from Jakarta to Bogotá, the foundations' offices operated – along with national planning commissions, research laboratories, United Nations regional economic commissions and statistical centres as well as US Peace Corps offices – as part of the constellation of development institutions "on the ground". The major foundations relied upon their field offices for information, diplomacy and the construction of concrete initiatives. The choices of which projects to fund and how to institutionalise and translate broad foundation missions into local idioms and conditions were often made in the field.

Foundation representatives were the eyes and ears of the foundations, relaying back to New York their portraits of political and economic conditions and assessments of potential grant recipients in receiving nations. They also played a critical role in forging political and institutional relationships and selling the foundation's services to national elites. Central state governments represented the most powerful advocates and engines of development during the 1950s and 1960s; without their assent, US foundations could not function abroad.

Even as field offices represented foundations, their particular institutional roles and geographic positions shaped how they imagined the priorities of development. Field representatives shared with foundation leaders the reflexive anti-Communism and faith in science and expertise that was pervasive among US liberals in the mid-twentieth century. Long-term association with a particular foundation encouraged an "organisation man" ethos, in which foundation officers, cycling between New York and field assignments, became inculcated in the practices and terminology of their philanthropy. Yet, individual field officers held their own programmatic visions, and these could and did change over time with experience in the field. Simply put, the view in Delhi and Bogotá often looked different than in New York. The need to maintain political connections and to insulate the foundation's reputation from potentially controversial or ill-conceived projects meant that field representatives were primed to seek accommodation and discourage projects that smacked of US dominance.[4] As such, the field office proved critical in translating the Cold-War projects originating at the centre

---

4 Bell, "Ford Foundation".

and in crafting development praxis to reflect the priorities of *both* post-colonial elites and US and European actors.

Historians seeking to explain how foundations projected an image of autonomy and independence from US Cold-War policy (even as they supported broad US geo-political goals) have cited the foundations' reliance on
a dual rhetoric of liberal humanitarianism and technocratic social engineering. They have also noted the foundations' relative freedom from the domestic political constraints that shaped presidential and congressional
action in such fields as population control and food production.[5] What has
been less well understood is the role of the foundation field office and
nationalist elites in framing US foundations as apolitical. The case of the
Ford Foundation in India illuminates how individual field offices and
national elites collaborated to build up foundations as essential players in
development practice. This involved critical "boundary work" to distinguish
the field office from US state actors and to position its contributions in India
as merely technocratic and financial support of India's development priorities.[6]

In Delhi, Ensminger invoked humanitarian and technocratic rationales
for the Ford Foundation's raison d'être. A sociologist by training, he believed
fervently that the scientific analysis of social problems could lead to better
policy solutions. At the same time, Ensminger was a political operator who
had been schooled in the politics of knowledge in the US Department of Agriculture during the New Deal and the Second World War. His reading of the
political landscape in India suggested to him that the Ford Foundation could
not gain influence in India supporting projects that appeared to Indian elites
as intrusions on Indian politics and sovereignty. Throughout the 1950s and
early 1960s, he screened expert initiatives originating in the United States for
possible dangers they might pose to the Foundation's or to Prime Minister
Jawaharlal Nehru's position in India. In this way, Ensminger set up the Foundation as a devoted ally to India's powerful Prime Minister at a time when
Nehru and US policymakers were clashing repeatedly over India's foreign
policy and socialist economic framework.

Demarcating the Foundation from US policy, Ensminger also assisted
Nehru domestically by having the Ford Foundation take on projects that
Nehru and his advisers deemed too politically sensitive within India. Nehru
recognised that drawing on Ford Foundation funding and experts allowed
him to promote policies among powerful but potentially sceptical consti-
tuencies such as state-level politicians and the Indian civil service without

5 Hess, "Waging the Cold War"; Krige, "Ford Foundation"; Unger, "Toward Global
Equilibrium".
6 On boundary work, see Gieryn, *Cultural Boundaries*.

bringing in foreign governments or seeming to pit one branch of Indian Government against another. Nehru's more radical political opposition, notably the Communist Party of India, never accepted the Ford Foundation's pose of neutrality and pushed accusations of American imperialism from the early 1950s onward. As his opposition sought to puncture the pose of Foundation neutrality, Nehru and his advisers supported the Foundation's agenda in India. Like Nehru's own Planning Commission of technocratic experts, the Ford Foundation's field office fit his desires to remove development planning and choices from the contested ground of electoral and international politics and vest more power in his own leadership.

In the 1950s, this arrangement ran quite smoothly and effectively: Ensminger forged a tight working relationship with Nehru and other top Indian officials, and the New York headquarters generally deferred to Ensminger's recommendations. Opened in 1952, New Delhi was the very first field office of the Ford Foundation. Arriving just as post-war international efforts to develop India were beginning to stir, the Delhi office became critical for setting patterns and priorities not only for international development work in India but also precedents for other Ford Foundation projects around the world. Under Ensminger's direction, the Delhi office helped establish community development, public administration, population control and urban planning as Foundation priorities. The Delhi office set the pattern for the Ford Foundation's support of government-led projects over private initiatives and its preference for circulating development knowledge through Foundation-selected consultants rather than projects directed by US universities.

Ensminger sought the transfer of American and European knowledge about development – but always selectively and in negotiation with Indian elites. In the 1950s and 1960s, the Delhi office often resisted the wholesale replication of US models advocated by the New York headquarters. Because of Ensminger's assiduous bureaucratic skills, the strong development plans of India's leaders and the powerful importance that US policymakers and foundations attached to India's success in development, the Delhi office frequently succeeded in setting the terms of the Ford Foundation's development work in India. Between 1952 and 1970, the New Delhi office administered approximately 102 million dollars in grants to Indian institutions or the Government of India, far exceeding the Ford Foundation's or any other foundation's contributions to another nation's government.[7] Working with the Government of India, the field office honeycombed the subcontinent from the Punjab to Tamil Nadu with training centres, university pro-

---

7 Ford Foundation, *Foundation-Supported Activities in India*; Ford Foundation, *Annual Report 1969*, 59–60; Ford Foundation, *Annual Report 1970*, 59–61.

grammes and government research institutes whose central goals were to produce applied research for the benefit of India's development projects and to train Indians in "modern" scientific and managerial practices.

The special relationship that the Delhi office forged for the Ford Foundation in India, however, began to unravel in the 1960s. The construction of an international network of field offices, built in part on the New Delhi model, required an exponentially larger New York bureaucracy that tended to centralise and systematise Foundation policy at the centre. Ensminger's power in India depended on his ability to deliver funding and projects quickly to the Indian Government. Foundation bureaucratisation slowed and circumscribed that ability. At the same time, New York reigned in the panoply of Foundation projects in India, narrowing development to an intensive campaign to increase food production and decrease India's birthrate. Indian leaders participated willingly, even eagerly, in the drive to raise agricultural output and curb population with Ford-funded US consultants and Indian research institutions. Yet, as the US government followed the Ford and Rockefeller Foundations into the agricultural and population fields, tying US developmental assistance to efforts to bend India to its policy priorities, Foundation projects became ever more closely associated with US imperial control. By the late 1960s, Indian journalists and intellectuals had begun to regularly accuse the Ford Foundation of setting up projects as fronts for CIA activities. They also tied Ford-funded experts and institutions to a growing transnational, Third-World critique of the use of US social scientists abroad. The Foundation's "academic colonialism", Indian critics charged, dictated intellectual priorities and colonised Indian public discourse.

While Ensminger vigorously refuted such allegations, his own political base of support within India had shrunk. The death of Nehru in 1964 and the subsequent shift in power from the Planning Commission, Ensminger's political base in Delhi, to state and Cabinet ministers shut Ensminger and the New Delhi office out of Indian policy-making circles. In 1970, Ensminger retired from the Ford Foundation. Soon after he left India, the New Delhi office underwent a major restructuring, its programme staff reduced from over a hundred to about ten officers. New York cut its budgets substantially, and the new Ford Foundation representative in Delhi reoriented funding away from large grants to the Government of India and toward modest support of non-governmental organisations.[8] Perhaps more than any other Ford programme, the decline of the Delhi office symbolised the collapse of the alliance that US foundations had forged with the elites of developing nations and the pulling back of the major foundations from the development project.

8 Ford Foundation, *The Ford Foundation, 1952–2002*, 11–12; McCarthy, "From Government", 302.

1. The Ford Foundation Enters India

The Ford Foundation's decision to begin development work in India was guided not by its post-war blueprint, the Gaither report released in 1949, but by the priorities of its first President Paul Hoffman and the context of crises over India in 1951. The Gaither report, an elaborate study to determine the Foundation's guiding principles in the wake of its transformation from a regional charity to the largest philanthropy in the world, sketched a largely domestic programme for "our society" and made only passing reference to "under-developed areas". India was never mentioned.[9] Nonetheless, the report's sweeping call to advance world peace and its robust claims for the importance of applied American knowledge appealed to the ambitions and vision of Hoffman, who assumed the Foundation presidency in January 1951. As administrator of the Economic Cooperation Administration from 1948 to 1950, Hoffman had been a champion of the power of expertise and capital to win the fight against Communism. The Economic Cooperation Administration had, in Hoffman's view, failed in China because the United States had come too late to focus on the problem of Chinese rural development. A long-time supporter of "rural reconstruction" work in China, Hoffman was convinced that China had been "lost" at the "village level" and was determined that the United States should not repeat the mistake in India. "What a different story might have been told if this alternative to Communist strategy had been tried a few years earlier," he lamented in *Life* magazine shortly after taking charge of the Ford Foundation.[10] To Hoffman, India was the next critical battleground of the Cold War.

Hoffman was not alone in his assessment. In 1951, an emerging coalition of anti-Communist liberals had begun to view India as possessing simultaneously tremendous problems that threatened US global hegemony and great possibilities to demonstrate the transformative power of US-led development. India lacked capital and faced what US observers saw as dire conditions akin to those that had produced the Chinese revolution: the "staggering, appalling poverty" of "teeming millions" in "700,000 tiny villages" who had "awakened" to the injustice of their destitution.[11] Yet India seemed to be, among the new nations now labelled "under-developed", the one with the greatest potential for economic transformation. Nehru and his top ministers had set up strong political and economic structures, from a national consti-

---

9 Ford Foundation, *Report of the Study*, 26–27.

10 Raucher, *Paul G. Hoffman*, 75; Hoffman, *Peace Can Be Won*, 105–106; Hayford, *To the People*, 204–224; Hoffman, "Most Courageous", 104.

11 Isaacs, *No Peace for Asia*, 106. See also Vogt, *Road to Survival*, 227; Muehl, *Interview with India*.

tution to a central Planning Commission that had put forward a range of soon-to-be-launched projects in agriculture, population control, urban planning and industrial development. "There is great ferment in the country," Supreme Court Justice William O. Douglas reported after travelling around India in 1950. "Every problem is being attacked; new ideas are pouring out."[12] The plans of the "world's largest democracy", moreover, seemed pragmatic and moderate, eschewing land redistribution or collectivisation. US India supporters stressed Nehru's anti-Communism, his faith in science and expertise, the non-revolutionary nature of India's national birth and its rapid ascendance in world affairs as a voice for newly decolonised nations. If India could achieve economic progress with US assistance, they argued, then it would surely blaze a trail for other nations. But if India were to falter – failing to address what Hoffman's Marshall Plan associate Harlan Cleveland in 1950 had termed a "revolution in rising expectations" among peasant peoples around the world – then India and other developing nations would be tempted down Communist paths to economic growth and social welfare.[13]

Despite these stakes and possibilities, the United States seemed to be failing India. Against the massive military build-up of NSC-68 and the Korean War, Truman's "bold new programme" of technical assistance, Point Four, languished, poorly funded and continually attacked by conservatives in the US Congress. Congressional critics of India's policy of non-alignment in the Cold War, moreover, had stalled passage of legislation to ship emergency wheat to India. While the "wheat loan" passed in June, its politicisation drove Indo-American relations to a new low. Publicly and privately, observers like former TVA administrator David Lilienthal wondered, "Are we losing India?"[14] Chester Bowles, Governor of Connecticut and soon-to-be Ambassador to India, warned Hoffman: "India is the key point in the entire East. [...] If we lose India, as we lost China, we shall certainly lose Southeast Asia with the repercussions running all the way through Africa." Bowles challenged the Ford Foundation to "tackl[e] the job".[15] Hoffman had already begun calling on the Indian Ambassador to the United States shortly after joining the Foundation to seek an invitation to Delhi.

The Ford Foundation programme that emerged by the end of 1951 supported US Cold-War aims but also constituted an implicit critique of US

12 Douglas, *Strange Lands*, 301.
13 Cleveland, *Obligations of Power*, 153; Roosevelt, *India*.
14 Lilienthal, "Are We Losing India?"; McMahon, "Food"; Merrill, *Bread and the Ballot*, 47–74.
15 Chester Bowles to Paul G. Hoffman, 14 September 1951; Chester Bowles to Robert Hutchins, 24 February 1951, General Correspondence, 1951, Bowles, Reel 1139, Ford Foundation Archives, New York/NY (hereafter FFA).

progress in South Asia. Hoffman and his senior staff consulted with senior State Department officials such as Dean Acheson and George McGhee. But plans for the nascent programme grew principally out of a collaboration with officials and experts outside the State Department and the White House. Hoffman and his officers turned to a small group of agricultural experts and New Deal-era officials, many of whom had visited India and saw themselves as India champions. They included Douglas; Bowles; former TVA administrator Arthur Morgan; agricultural economist Howard Tolley, who had left the US Department of Agriculture (USDA) to join the United Nations Food and Agriculture Organisation; and Milburn Lincoln Wilson, USDA Director of Extension Work.[16]

The focus on extension work was significant. Although Foundation officers considered a variety of India projects, including intervention in the Kashmir conflict, they soon settled on a programme of "integrated rural development".[17] Hoffman placed Foundation Vice-President Chester Davis, a former official in the USDA in the 1930s, in charge of the India initiative.[18] Advised by Morgan, Tolley and Wilson, Davis and Foundation officer John B. Howard began to see extension as an ideal vehicle for both raising agricultural output and helping to "build up democracy at the village level" through attention to the "medical, social, and cultural aspects of rural village life".[19] The USDA extension method emphasised the demonstration of scientific farming techniques, but the ferment of the rural New Deal had also transformed extension into a broader project of remaking rural communities through applied expertise in civic engagement, home economics and adult education. Morgan had been the visionary behind the TVA model town of Norris, Tennessee.[20] Now Foundation officials imagined bringing American extension techniques to South Asia.

In fact, the knowledge that Ford officials viewed as "American" was not exclusively American at all. The New Deal's rural policies were born of a

16 George McGhee to Paul Hoffman, 9 February 1951, Rowan Gaither Papers, Box 1, Folder 4; New York Office Report, 20 July 1951; Bernard L. Gladieux to Chester C. Davis, 30 July 1951; John B. Howard, Follow-up on trip to India and Pakistan, 24 September 1951, General Correspondence, 1951, India, Reel 1141, FFA.

17 Chester Davis to Arthur E. Morgan, 3 May 1951; Chester C. Davis to Warren R. Austin, 14 May 1951; Program Planning Division Staff Meeting, 15 May 1951, General Correspondence, 1951, India, Reel 1141, FFA; John Howard, Summary Guides for the Use of Ensminger, Moyer, and Howard in India and Pakistan, 22 October 1951, Report 012093, FFA.

18 Robert M. Hutchins to Chester Bowles, 12 March 1951, General Correspondence 1951, Bowles, FFA; John B. Howard, Oral History, 13 February 1973, FFA.

19 John B. Howard, Economic Development Program in India, 25 June 1951, Reel 0910, FFA; Howard, Summary, Report 012093, FFA.

20 Kirkendall, *Social Scientists*; Morgan, *Small Community*.

transnational circulation of ideas and practices about "rural reconstruction" by missionaries, colonial administrators, social reformers and nationalists from Scandinavia to the Caribbean. India had already been a prime site for village experiments in the 1920s and 1930s. Beginning in 1945, a US architect named Albert Mayer had drawn from these inter-war projects when helping the provincial government of Uttar Pradesh to launch a "pilot project" in rural development in its Etawah district. The project hired "village-level workers" (Indian high-school graduates) and trained them in a variety of expert techniques that they would then demonstrate to peasants in an assigned group of district villages. Indian politicians saw the Etawah project as a collaboration with Mayer that drew upon American ideas but remained grounded in Indian conditions and precedents. But Hoffman and other Ford officers who visited India for the first time in August 1951 envisioned it as an American blueprint for rural development which might be replicated throughout India. "We are greatly impressed by the work that is being done at Etawah," Davis told the Planning Commission; Etawah "aims at the crux of India's rural problem by helping the villagers help themselves in overcoming poverty, disease, and illiteracy." Most importantly, in reporting dramatic increases in yields of wheat and potato crops, Etawah seemed to promise that changing peasant practices through the introduction of low-cost techniques such as crop rotation or manure application could raise agricultural production dramatically.[21]

When Nehru met Hoffman and his party in Delhi, the Prime Minister and his senior officials had reason to receive them warmly. First, Hoffman's record of accomplishment with the Marshall Plan had impressed Nehru. Second, in 1951, Nehru and his advisers were in search of international expertise and financial assistance. The network of international development organisations that would soon descend on India had not yet lodged themselves in the field. While the FAO, the World Bank, the World Health Organisation and UNESCO had all sent survey missions to India, the development field was still open, particularly in the area of village-level development. Finally, Nehru shared the Ford Foundation's admiration for the Etawah project and had begun to think about a national programme built in part on its design. Etawah's focus on mobilising peasant labour resonated with Nehru's own enthusiasm for the voluntary labour of agricultural co-operatives; its apparent success in convincing peasants to change their practices appeared to answer the failures of India's current "Grow More Food" strategy to rally village cultivators. Thus, the Ford Foundation and the Planning Commis-

---

21 Chester C. Davis to N. R. Pillai, 4 September 1951, General Correspondence, 1951, India, Reel 1141, FFA; John B. Howard, Summary Report on Visit to Near East, South Asia, and Far East, 1 October 1951, Report 002576, FFA.

sion came together in 1951 around a strategy of village-level "community development" aimed at raising agricultural production and village conditions.[22] The Foundation would supply funding to train Indian village-level workers in a range of scientific and social scientific methods and techniques.

Foundation officials returned to India in November, with a party that now included the Foundation's new field representative Douglas Ensminger. They left with an agreement to open the first Ford Foundation field office in New Delhi and provide 2.9 million dollars to build and staff regional centres that were to train the first 6,000 village-level workers for what would soon become a nationwide "community development" programme. By this time, Bowles had arrived as the new US Ambassador to India and quickly offered an additional 54 million dollars in Point Four funding to bring hundreds of US experts, primarily in the field of agricultural extension, to India. On 5 January 1952, Nehru and Bowles signed the Indo-American Technical Agreement. Three days earlier, Ensminger opened the Foundation's India field office.[23] With Bowles as Ambassador and Horace Holmes, the agricultural expert at Etawah, now the head of the Point Four extension effort, Hoffman and Foundation officials envisioned little separation between the US Embassy's and the Ford Foundation's efforts in India. While cautioning that the Foundation would "at all times make it clear that it is dealing with the Indians directly and not through or as an agent of any other agencies", they nonetheless imagined that "[r]elations between the Foundation and the responsible US Government mission [would] necessarily be intimate". The Foundation's representative was to be, Davis told Holmes, "someone on the job representing us to work with you in India".[24]

2. Boundaries Against Politics

Ensminger arrived in Delhi ready to work closely with both the US Embassy and India's top policymakers. He set up the Foundation's offices in a two-room suite of the Ambassador Hotel, its rooms filled with US extension agents and their families just arriving in Delhi as a result of the new Point Four agreement. Soon he was consulting with Bowles and key Embassy staff, attending policy meetings and even accepting a desk within the Embassy.[25]

22 Howard, Summary, Report 002576, FFA; Nehru, *Selected Works*, Vol. 16, Pt. 1, 54–55.

23 Merrill, *Bread and the Ballot*, 79–84.

24 Howard, Summary, Report 012093, FFA; Chester C. Davis to Horace Holmes, 24 September 1951, General Correspondence, 1951, India, Reel 1141, FFA.

25 Lyon, *Just Half*, 274; Douglas Ensminger, Program Letter No. 4, 23 February 1952, FFA.

At the same time, he had begun to meet with Nehru and members of the Planning Commission. Through detailed, bi-weekly letters Ensminger kept the Ford Foundation headquarters abreast of his activities. These included not only work in India but also in Pakistan, where, in the interest of regional balance, the Foundation had chosen to open its second field office. Ford Foundation officials pronounced themselves deeply pleased with Ensminger's progress. His reports were "clear, comprehensive, and intensely interesting. [...] Each one opens another window onto Southern Asia," Davis gushed. Ensminger, and thus the Foundation, was "much in the centre of things" both in Delhi and Karachi where his "energy" and accomplishment were "impressive".[26] With no prior knowledge of India, Ensminger had quickly cemented a reputation as an authority on South Asia who could advise on both South Asian conditions and the possible application of India's programmes to other nations. Davis reported with some pride that during a return trip to the United States "so many people want[ed] to see [Ensminger] in Washington that he [was] under great pressure".[27]

By the end of 1952, however, Ensminger had begun to realise the politics of trafficking across national and institutional lines. Maintaining the Foundation's Karachi office took away from his work in India; it also led to suspicion about the kind of information he passed back and forth between the two foes. In January 1953, the Foundation installed a different representative in Pakistan. Meanwhile, relationships with the US Embassy, and specifically its technical assistance, Operations Mission (USOM), had grown more fraught.

USOM Delhi, encouraged by the Truman Administration, had sold the Indian community programme to the US public as an exclusively American creation for the defeat of communism. India's politicians and press decried the Cold-War hyperbole and the casting of Indians as subalterns in their own national programme. Chief ministers in the Indian states soon threatened to block the US extension agents and derail the entire endeavour. Only Nehru's intervention kept the programme afloat. The incident left Ensminger wary of too close a public association with US foreign policy.[28]

---

26 Chester C. Davis to Douglas Ensminger, 25 September 1952, FFA; Raymond Moyer to Douglas Ensminger, 28 February 1952, General Correspondence, 1952, India, Reel 1152, FFA.

27 Chester C. Davis to Carl B. Spaeth, 9 June 1952; Carl B. Spaeth to Douglas Ensminger, 12 June 1952, General Correspondence, 1952, India, Reel 1152, FFA.

28 "County Agent"; "Science: Plows and Sacred Cows"; Truman, *Public Papers*, 13; Douglas Ensminger, The Ford Foundation's Nineteen Years of Involvement with India's Community Development Program, 11 July 1972, Box 14, Folder B21, 51–52, 94–96; Ensminger, Relationships with Nehru, 29 November 1971, Box 1, Folder A8, 21, Douglas En-

More substantive conflicts with USOM advisers had also begun to surface. Trained in rural sociology, Ensminger had entered the US civil service in 1939 as a specialist in rural community organisation for the USDA's Extension Service and Bureau of Agricultural Economics. This background led him to see extension as a method with which to inculcate not only scientific agriculture, but a wide range of civic, cultural and educational goals in rural people. It also taught him the vulnerability of both sociological studies and innovative government "think tanks" to entrenched political interests. The Bureau of Agricultural Economics had been attacked and curtailed in the 1940s by conservative Southern US politicians who objected to the questions its social science studies raised about poverty and race in the US South. Marked by this experience, Ensminger encouraged the Government of India to protect the community development programme from institutional and state politics by establishing it as its own agency, separate from the Ministry of Food and Agriculture and answerable only to the Planning Commission. S. K. Dey, the administrator of the Indian community development agency, shared Ensminger's views. They soon became close collaborators, with Ensminger securing Ford grants to train a range of social scientific, social welfare and public health experts for the Government of India programme.[29] By contrast, USOM leaders in Delhi saw extension as a targeted delivery of scientific farming methods that should be directed by India's Ministry of Food and Agriculture in co-operation with proposed Indian agricultural colleges that would replicate the US system of land-grant universities. In a March 1953 report, USOM critiqued the community development programme for failing to focus on food production and advised the Government of India to reallocate funds to expand university-level agricultural research and village-level training in agricultural methods. With Ensminger's counsel, the Government of India rejected USOM's recommendations.[30] Ensminger had begun to realise that his vision of rural development accorded more closely with Dey than with the US Embassy's technical staff.

Ensminger's distance from the US Embassy grew with the departure of Bowles as Ambassador and the "tilt" in US policy under Dwight Eisenhower toward Pakistan. The change in US Administration was mirrored within the Ford Foundation by the abrupt dismissal of Hoffman and Davis and the in-

sminger Papers, Sterling Memorial Library, Yale University, New Haven, Conn. (hereafter DEP).

29 Ensminger, "Diagnosing"; Sanders/Ensminger, *Alabama Rural Communities*; Ensminger, Program Letter No. 4, 23 February 1952, General Correspondence, 1952, India, Reel 1152, FFA.

30 Ensminger, The Ford Foundation's Contribution in the Field of India's Village and Small Industries, 5 November 1971, Box 3, Folder B2, 40–44, 94, DEP.

stallation of Rowan Gaither as Foundation President. Hoffman's public political stances, inconstant leadership, support for controversial domestic projects and focus on South Asian rural development had combined to tax the patience of Henry Ford II and the Ford Foundation's Board of Trustees. While the new Foundation President continued to support the Ford Foundation's India programme, Gaither never championed the "New India" as had Hoffman and Bowles.[31] An "organisation man" who steered the Ford Foundation from domestic political storms, Gaither emphasised American knowledge of the world in Ford Foundation grant-making, ratcheting up Ford Foundation funding for US areas studies programmes and research fellowships in Asia.[32] These US university programmes and overseas fellows presented new problems for Ensminger, as the New York headquarters began to approve projects for India that Ensminger viewed as politically sensitive and thus threatening to the relationships he had begun to build with Nehru's inner circle.

In the spring of 1953, two high-profile grants for political science research on India came up for consideration in New York. The MIT Center for International Studies proposed a group research project to study the relationship between economic development and political stability in India. Political scientists at Columbia and Berkeley envisioned group field studies to examine Soviet techniques of indoctrination and control in India, Indonesia and Iran.[33] The studies reflected an emerging hypothesis among US social scientists that the "transition" from "traditional" to "modern" societies, though critically important, nonetheless opened a dangerous, temporary period of cultural and social dislocation that Communists could exploit.[34] In discussions of the political science projects, the New York senior staff recognised the "delicate nature of [this] research" but concluded that such studies were "greatly needed and should be undertaken". Ford Foundation officer Richard Bissell (who in later years with the CIA would design the failed Bay of Pigs invasion) argued forcefully that the study of economic

31 Bowles, The Crucial Problem of India: A Personal Report, 4 February 1952; Paul G. Hoffman to Chester Bowles, 28 February 1952; Paul G. Hoffman to Chester Bowles, 11 March 1952, General Correspondence, 1952, Reel 1152, FFA; Bowles, "New India"; Sutton, "Ford Foundation", 71–73.

32 McCaughey, International Studies, 153; A Survey of Asian Studies Prepared for the Ford Foundation, 1951, Report 001066, FFA; Ford Foundation, Annual Report 1954; Sutton, "Ford Foundation", 78–79.

33 Proposal for a Research Program in Economic Development and Political Stability, 13 May 1953, Reel 0115, Grant 52–152, Section 1, FFA; Coordinated Country Studies on Soviet Techniques of Indoctrination and Control, 5 May 1953, Project B-226, FFA.

34 Eugene Staley to Members of the Study Group on Political Implications of Economic Development, 9 April 1952, Box 19, John Kenneth Galbraith Papers, John F. Kennedy Library, Boston/Mass.; Staley, Future.

development must "emphasize its relationship to political and social stability or instability".[35]

Gaither, Bissell and other senior officers worried that the Ford Foundation was pouring millions into the development cure – notably the community development programme – without bothering to study the "disease" that made the cure so necessary. Nehru's Congress Party had sailed to victory in India's first general elections, but to those concerned with Soviet incursion there appeared to be ominous signs of rising Communist strength in the Communist Party of India's electoral victories in several states of southern India.[36] CIA and State Department officials urged the Ford Foundation forward. They offered counsel while assuring Ford Director of Research Cleon O. Swayze that they also felt "that care should be taken to avoid any governmental identification with these projects".[37] To Ford Foundation officers in New York, scholarly projects and Foundation funding offered sufficient distance from US foreign policy-making.

From Delhi, Ensminger protested that political science research could politicise the Foundation's work in India and promptly fought back on multiple fronts. First, he successfully lobbied New York for veto power over Ford Foundation overseas fellows whose research projects he deemed too sensitive in India's political climate. Second, he convinced the Planning Commission to establish its own Research Programmes Committee, consisting of leading Indian social scientists who would screen all foreign social science research for the Government of India. Third, he demanded that all US social scientists doing research on Ford Foundation grants in India should partner with scholars at an Indian university.[38] These new requirements altered the goals of the MIT and Berkeley projects. Pressured by Ensminger, the MIT project in India continued, but compared to the interdisciplinary modernisation theories fabricated by scholars in Cambridge, Massachusetts, MIT research on the ground in India over the next decade employed only economists and focused largely on technical studies of indus-

35 Excerpt from Draft Minutes of Meeting of 5 May 1953, Reel 0408, Grant 54–14, Section 1, FFA; Richard Bissell to Milton Katz, 9 May 1952, Reel 0115, Grant 52–152, Section 4, FFA.

36 Carl B. Spaeth to Cleon O. Swayzee, 22 December 1952, Reel 0408, Grant 54–14, Section 4, FFA; Richard L. Park, Contemporary India Project, November 1953, Reel 0404, Grant 54–14, Section 1, FFA; Irving Kristol to Carl Spaeth, c.1953, FFA; Park, "Indian Democracy".

37 Cleon O. Swayzee to John W. Gardner, 15 June 1953, Reel 0408, Grant 54–14, Section 4, FFA; Paul F. Langer to Philip E. Moseley, Carl B. Spaeth, and Cleon O. Swayzee, 17 May 1953, Reel 0408, Grant 54–14, Section 4, FFA; Cleon O. Swayzee to Carl B. Spaeth, 26 May 1953, Reel 0408, Grant 54–14, Section 4, FFA.

38 John B. Howard Oral History, 13 February 1973, FFA.

trial and agricultural capacity.[39] The director of the Berkeley project abandoned field research altogether.[40] Ensminger's counsel from Delhi thus remade two projects that US policymakers and Foundation officials had seen as urgent.

Curtailing US social scientists' investigations of Indian politics, Ensminger pushed instead the study of public administration within India. The choice of public administration over political science as a Foundation priority represented both a recognition by Ensminger of the political tensions over development in India as well as an attempt to serve Nehru and the Planning Commission by helping them to insulate development planning from politics. Nehru hoped to use science and expertise to topple what he saw as two forces of the status quo: powerful economic and political interests, on the one hand, and the entrenched British-trained bureaucracy of the Indian civil service on the other. The Planning Commission's elite group of advisers supported by various sub-committees of topical experts (on industry, population, agriculture, etc.) was the first mechanism by which Nehru imagined post-colonial India's political and economic transformation.[41] Now Nehru wished to reform the Indian Administrative Service, making its procedures more uniform, rational and responsive to the directives of the Planning Commission at the top and the will of the people from below.

At Nehru's request, Ensminger secured the services of Paul H. Appleby, Dean of Syracuse University's Maxwell School of Citizenship and Public Affairs and, like Ensminger, a veteran of the USDA. Beginning in 1952, Appleby made three extended trips to India as a private consultant to the Ford Foundation. He worked from a desk in the Delhi offices of Chintaman D. Deshmukh, Minister of Finance and a key Planning Commission member, and remained during his visits in regular conversation with Deshmukh, Nehru and Ensminger. Appleby also journeyed out from Delhi to the Indian states to interview thousands of administrators and civil servants at various levels of government.[42] His reports, published by the Indian Govern-

39 Douglas Ensminger, Report 37, December 1953, General Correspondence, 1953, India, Reel 1163, FFA; Sackley, "Passage to Modernity", Ch. 4; On controversies over, and subsequent implosion of, the MIT India project in the 1960s, see Engerman, "West Meets East".

40 Douglas Ensminger to John B. Howard, 2 June 1954; Richard L. Park to Cleon O. Swayze, 13 September 1955; Richard L. Park, Modern India Project: Semi-Annual Report, July 1954, Reel 0408, Grant 54–14, Section 3, FFA; Douglas Ensminger to John B. Howard, 17 February 1955, Reel 0116, Grant 54–88, Section 4, FFA.

41 Prakash, Another Reason; Zachariah, Developing India.

42 Appleby's 1954 appointment diary shows frequent meetings with Ensminger and Nehru. 1954 Diary, Paul Henson Appleby Papers, Box 9, Folder 1, Special Collections, Grinnell College Library, Grinnell, Ia.; Chester C. Davis to Carl B. Spaeth, 9 June 1952,

ment, concluded that Indian administrators had too much "consciousness of rank, class, title, and service" and "too little consciousness of membership in the public service". They needed to replace an "academic and intellectual orientation" with rigorous training in both "human-relations" and specific areas of applied expertise. This analysis fit a common American complaint in the 1950s that British rule had left Indians with a lack of appreciation of applied knowledge and the importance of getting one's hands dirty in the field. Yet, Appleby's report also praised India as "AMONG THE DOZEN OR SO MOST ADVANCED GOVERNMENTS OF THE WORLD". He was careful, moreover, to emphasise that Indian government "must be an outgrowth of its own long history and its own rich culture". American ideas might "stimulate" India but "no practice – certainly none of any importance – can ever be directly copied and simply applied to another".[43]

Appleby's visits to India and recommendations to the Indian Government pleased Nehru and the Planning Commission immensely. The immediate fruit of Appleby's recommendations was the creation of an Indian Institute of Public Administration with Nehru as its honorary chairman. A quasi-government institution, the Indian Institute of Public Administration conducted and published social science research on bureaucracy while also training government officers through the case-study method, a technique popular at the Maxwell School and other US graduate programmes of public affairs and management in the 1950s.[44] But, as far as the relationship between the Government of India and the Ford Foundation was concerned, the effects of Appleby's work in India went deeper. Appleby helped cement in Nehru's mind the Ford Foundation as a source of valuable expertise as well as funding.

For Ensminger, Appleby's work crystallised two models for Ford programming in India: a reliance on consultants placed directly in government offices over US university group projects and a preference for funding government "think tanks" to produce development knowledge. In the 1950s, Ensminger cast his net widely for consultants to bring to India: They included not only US university economists, demographers and agricultural specialists but also furniture designers Charles and Ray Eames, a Danish doll maker, and even the Vice-President of Macy's, then the largest department store in the world.[45] Meanwhile, the Indian Institute of Public Administration became a model for other Ford-funded, Indian Government re-

FFA; Ensminger, Program Letter no. 12, 6 September 1952, FFA; Ensminger, Program Letter no. 42, 10 May 1954, FFA.

43 Appleby, *Public Administration*, 11–12, 1.

44 Braibanti, "Reflections", 6–9.

45 Staples, *40 Years*, 51–2; Ensminger, The Ford Foundation's Relations with the Planning Commission, 21 October 1971, Box 1, Folder A3, DEP.

search institutes during the 1950s and 1960s, from the National Institute of Industrial Design to the National Council for Applied Economic Research, the Institute of Applied Manpower and the Indian Law Institute. Each of these institutes approached development as a technical and managerial problem in which experts brought applied knowledge directly to India's top leadership.

3. Setting Priorities in Delhi

By the mid-1950s, Ensminger had secured a central place in the corridors of power in Delhi. Advice on public administration had shown Nehru, Deshmukh and others the value of Ford Foundation consultants. But it was Ensminger's consistent support of the Indian community development programme and his New Deal experience in rural community projects that embedded the Ford Foundation in the Planning Commission. Ensminger attended Planning Commission meetings on community development, commented on draft policy statements and advised Nehru, Dey and Planning Commission members V. T. Krishnamachari and Tarlok Singh on the subject. In 1956 he even took a six-week sabbatical from the Ford Foundation to draft the Government of India's official guide to community development, writing in the voice of an Indian about "our village people" and "our long struggle for independence". Dey revealed Ensminger as the author of the volume, extolling his "significant contributions" to nearly every aspect of the programme.[46] More often, Indian officials preferred Ensminger's discretion and bureaucratic savvy: He never held a press conference taking credit for the programme and always reviewed the New York headquarters' descriptions of Indian grant projects to ensure that they did not depict Indians as dependent upon American knowledge and largesse. Most of all, Ensminger delivered Foundation funding to Delhi, often in a matter of weeks, for new community development programmes.[47] Perhaps nothing better symbolised Ensminger's new closeness to Nehru and the Planning Commission than the relocation of the Ford Foundation's field office out of the Ambassador Hotel on the outskirts of Delhi and into one of the stately Indian Government bungalows designed by Edwin Lutyens for the British Raj at the very centre of the official city.[48]

46 Government of India, *Guide*, iii, 1; Ensminger, Ford Foundation's Nineteen Years, Box 13, Folder B21, 75, DEP.

47 Ensminger, The Foundation's Image in India, Box 1, Folder A40, 10–12; Ensminger, Foundation's Nineteen Years, Box 13, Folder B21, 1–3, DEP.

48 Ensminger, Program Letter no. 29, 2 July 1953, FFA.

The field office's record of supporting the Indian Government came to matter a great deal in 1954, as the US military pact with Pakistan and Nehru's growing interest in Soviet and Chinese development frayed Indo-American relations. The alliance with Pakistan had infuriated Nehru and provoked him to look more critically at the "increasing activities of Americans" in India:

[T]here are the Technical Aid people [...] Fellowship Exchanges, professors, students, missionaries, and the like [...] a widespread network of activity which is either directly or indirectly aimed at doing intelligence or propaganda work. [...] This was bad enough at any time, but in view of the new developments connected with the US military aid to Pakistan, this widespread activity in India is particularly objectionable and, to some extent, dangerous. [...] I think that we should take stock of all this and [...] check these abuses.[49]

Although he never followed through on the directive, Nehru contemplated "a basic change in policy" that would end the "inviting [of] American experts to India, except in very special cases".

Yet even as he sought a curtailment of American involvement, Nehru explicitly exempted the Ford Foundation from the prohibition. The Ford Foundation had "done good work in India" and as such stood "on a separate footing", he informed his advisers. "I see no reason why they should not be encouraged to continue their activities here."[50] Writing in September 1955, between his state visit to Moscow and the upcoming visit of Soviet leaders Nikita Khrushchev and Nikolai Bulganin to India, Nehru reiterated his satisfaction with the work of the Ford Foundation in India. "[W]e welcome the assistance and cooperation of friends," he assured Foundation president Rowan Gaither.[51] Soviet-built steel mills and Chinese agricultural collectives offered possible development models, but so too did the Ford Foundation and its consultants on community development.[52]

Ford Foundation officers in New York also recognised the importance of its India programme, though for very different reasons than Nehru. In a confidential memo of April 1955, Foundation Vice-President Don K. Price concluded that despite "strong disapproval" of the "socialistic tendencies in the Indian government", any curtailment in the Ford Foundation's development projects in India would constitute "a blow to India in her deadly race with Red China for national development". The Ford Foundation's particular programmes in community development, public administration and social science promoted "vital" economic development and political stability. Even more important "to efforts of the [US] Government in maintaining

49 Nehru, *Selected Works*, Vol. 25, 489–90.
50 Ibid., Vol. 25, 493; Ibid., Vol. 26, 513.
51 Ibid., Vol. 30, 461.
52 Frankel, *India's Political Economy*, 139–40; Merrill, *Bread and the Ballot*, 117–119.

good relations with India" was the very presence of its Delhi field office. Indeed by 1954, New York officers had begun to see field representatives as "projects in themselves". They could, "far better than any foreign official representative[,] influence the Government in new directions by disinterested advocacy of democratic politics".[53] In New York's formulation, the field office achieved a kind of transnational alchemy, turning US Cold-War aims into disinterested advocacy.

In fact, the Delhi field office in the 1950s functioned just as often as a conduit through which Indian development priorities and models flowed back to New York – and from there to the proliferating Ford Foundation field offices around the world. The apparent success of Indian community development encouraged Foundation officials to press for the duplication of India's village programme elsewhere in Asia and the Middle East. The "demonstration in India and Indian leadership" could "help [...] advance planning on Burma, Indonesia, and the Near East countries", Foundation officers explained in 1954. The Delhi field office's focus on public administration also helped shape Ford grants for public administration in Burma, Egypt, Iran and Lebanon. After spreading the word about Appleby's work in India, even the "hypersensitive Government of Indonesia" had "expressed their interest in Foundation assistance in the field of governmental administration", Foundation officers marvelled.[54]

Perhaps most striking, and little studied by historians, was the influence of the New Delhi field office on the Ford Foundation's decision to enter the population field. As Nehru issued the world's first national policy to limit population in December 1952, Ensminger peppered New York with letters about Nehru's commitment to population control and what he saw as the necessity of immediate Foundation action on "India's Number One Problem". Unless international organisations helped India in its efforts, the production and social welfare gains achieved by India's five-year plan would be "lost in the endless race to keep up with the population increases", Ensminger warned New York in 1953. At Nehru's urging, Ensminger engineered initial funding for Princeton demographer Frank Notestein and New York public health official Leona Baumgartner to consult with the Government of India.[55] Foundation officers in New York put off further funding for

53 Don Price, Overseas Development Program, Confidential, 4 April 1955, Report 13365, FFA; Program for Asia and the Middle East, 1954, Report 002832, FFA.

54 Program for Asia and the Middle East, 1954, Report 002832, FFA.

55 Ensminger, Program Letter no. 8, 19 April 1952, FFA; Idem, Program Letter no. 21, 11 February 1953; Idem, Program Letter No. 33, 21 September 1953; Idem, Program Letter no. 34, October 1953; Sutton, "Ford Foundation", 85; Connelly, *Fatal Misconception*, 168–9; Frank Notestein and Leona Baumgartner, Suggestions for a Practical Program

the domestically controversial subject. But conditions changed in the early 1960s with the growth of a transnational population network, new US domestic support and a third five-year plan by the Government of India that placed population control "at the very centre of planned development". And Ensminger was waiting in the wings with a set of population prescriptions. Working with the Government of India and three US public health consultants, Ensminger crafted one of the largest grants in Foundation history. It supported the creation of four intensive family planning districts with the "extension" of public health workers into the Indian countryside and two new government institutes – a Central Family Planning Institute and a National Institute of Health Administration and Education to train public health administrators, conduct demographic research and conduct clinical trials of contraceptives.[56] Ford Foundation population work in India was thus built from designs that the Delhi office had already constructed in the fields of community development and public administration. Its programmes were then vaunted by the Foundation as models for population control in other developing nations.

By 1959, Albert Mayer referred to Ensminger, only half in jest, as the "second most powerful man" in India.[57] His influence could be felt not only in the construction of India's population programme but in India's five-year plans, national agricultural strategy and large-scale projects to redevelop the cities of Delhi and Calcutta. Ensminger instructed the Ford field office to support the Planning Commission's priorities and couch grant requests to New York in terms of the goals of India's five-year plans. Indeed, Ensminger often defended India's centralised co-ordination of public and private sectors and "socialistic pattern of society" to the New York headquarters and the Ford Foundation's Board of Trustees.[58]

Yet, in grant-making decisions from economic planning to agricultural reform, Ensminger and his staff also used their influence in Delhi to try to reshape the goals of Indian development. For example, Ensminger promoted an alliance between MIT economists and a series of Indian economic and social science research centres, created or expanded with large Ford Foundation grants in the mid-1950s. A conscious effort to steer Indian

of Family Planning and Child Care, December 1955 Ansley J. Coale Papers, Department of Rare Books and Special Collections, Princeton University Library.

56 Harkavy, *Curbing Population Growth*, 135–7; Government of India, *Third Five Year Plan*, 675.

57 Albert Mayer to Edward G. Echeverria, 5 November 1959, Albert Mayer Papers on India, Box 21, Folder 17, Special Collections Research Center, University of Chicago, Chicago/IL.

58 Ensminger, Program Letter no. 77, 12 June 1956, FFA; Government of India, *New India*.

economic research to serve government planning, the project also sought implicitly to de-centre the influence of Nehru adviser Prasanta Mahalanobis and his Indian Statistical Institute over Indian policymaking. Mahalanobis had pushed the Planning Commission toward an ambitious second plan that emphasised industrialisation. Ensminger had campaigned to save the second plan when capital and agricultural shortages threatened its goals in 1957 and 1958. Nonetheless, he hoped that Ford-funded Indian institutions, consultants and grants for Indians to study economics in the United States would produce empirical economic studies that pointed to the importance of agriculture rather than the broad input–output sector model and large-scale industrialisation strategy favoured by Mahalanobis.[59]

Meanwhile, in agricultural policy, Ensminger drew upon his credentials as an ally of community development to convince Nehru, in the late 1950s, that India needed a new strategy for raising food production. The Government of India had leaned heavily on the village-level workers of its community development programme to produce food by changing the practices of peasant cultivators. They expanded the programme exponentially from covering six per cent of India's villages in 1952 to over half in 1957.[60] This rapid-fire growth strained the programme both administratively and philosophically, and community development failed as a targeted instrument for food production. Agricultural yields dropped sharply in 1957 and forced the Government of India to devote precious capital reserves to grain imports. Ensminger took to the field to assess the situation. In 1957, he spent three months travelling around India and reported back to Nehru that the problem in the community development programme was largely one of improving administration and organisation.[61] This reassured Nehru, who did not wish to abandon an endeavour he viewed as central to meeting India's social welfare goals and binding India's villagers politically and emotionally to the nation.

When India's monsoons failed for the second year in a row in 1958, however, Ensminger returned to Nehru with a proposal that the Ford Foundation assemble a team of agricultural specialists to examine India's food situation. The idea had originated with the US Department of State, which had requested that the Ford Foundation sponsor the mission so as to avoid the ire of powerful US farm lobby groups who did not wish to see the US Government giving advice that might curtail the lucrative selling of agricul-

59 Engerman, "West Meets East"; Rosen, *Western Economists*, 88–118; Sackley, "Passage to Modernity", 242–254.

60 Nehru, Letters, Vol. 4, 479, 492; Frankel, *India's Political Economy*, 142–144; Pande, *Village Community Projects*, 173.

61 Frankel, *India's Political Economy*; Ensminger, Relationships with Nehru, Box 1, Folder A8; Nehru, *Selected Works*, Vol. 40, 169–171.

tural surpluses to India. Led by USDA economist Sherman Johnson, the Foundation mission implicitly rejected the broad social welfare goals of community development and its premise that national development should incorporate the whole nation. Its report after three months of investigation, *India's Food Crisis and How to Meet It*, painted a stark picture of a Malthusian race between food and population growth in India and recommended a "package" of intensive applications of extension, chemical fertilisers, hybrid seeds and irrigation in a few districts selected for their promise of agricultural productivity.[62] Nehru initially found the report "exaggerated and unnecessarily pessimistic".[63] But under Ensminger's influence and that of his own Ministry of Food and Agriculture, Nehru eventually came around to implementing its recommendations. With Foundation funding, the Government of India launched a new Intensive Agricultural Districts Programme (IADP) in 7 of India's 320 districts in 1961.[64]

Ensminger never formally repudiated the community development approach. Defending the programme to US Congressman Walter Judd in 1960, he explained that the "first step" of raising "the level of aspirations of the village as a whole [...] through providing schools, roads, some health facilities, and a new outlook" had "opened the village to the knowledge [...] of new methods and ideas". Now that villagers had been "awakened", the Government of India would give "top priority to increased food production" and "responsibility for local development to the people themselves". In Ensminger's fashioning, the shift in strategy represented not a desertion of the social welfare aims of development, but the logical next step of an unfolding modernisation process. What he left out of his explanation was any acknowledgement of the role of the Ford Foundation, and Ensminger in particular, in championing community development as a panacea for Indian poverty. Instead, Ensminger rewrote the script and directed the New York headquarters and Indian and US policymakers to focus on the "revolutionary new program" of the IADP that had "tremendous implications for a fully productive agriculture, and the future of a democratic and progressive India".[65]

62 Government of India, *India's Food Crisis*; Rosen, *Western Economists*, 74–77.
63 Nehru, *Selected Works*, Vol. 40, 256.
64 Brown, *Agricultural Development*, 11–13; Perkins, *Geopolitics*, 179–183.
65 Douglas Ensminger to Walter Judd, 10 March 1960, General Correspondence, 1960, Reel 1386, FFA.

4. Imperial Foundation

The simultaneous expansion of Ford Foundation grant making into public administration, agricultural science, social science research, population control, urban planning as well as legal and managerial education increased the reach of the Ford Foundation within India dramatically. It also spurred a rapid growth in the field office. Given the range of its activities, the Delhi field office remained quite small through its first decade. From fewer than 5 US staff in the late 1950s, by 1966 the Delhi office had swelled to 72 foreign permanent staff members or consultants and 177 Indian administrative, clerical or technical employees. To accommodate this expansion, Ensminger demanded and won funding from New York for the construction of a leafy new Foundation campus in Delhi, including a modern office building, an elaborate guesthouse and a swimming pool surrounded by landscaped lawns and cascading fountains.[66]

In his recollections of his Ford years, Ensminger emphasised the humble nature of the field office and his own dealings in India, pointing out what he perceived as his special rapport with Indian farmers as the son of Missourian tenant farmers. He stressed the demands he made on Foundation staff to visit "village India" and his personal habit of carrying his own bags, making his own bed and contributing "an hour digging a ditch, planting trees, or doing whatever work was in progress" whenever he travelled around to India's community development districts. He imagined himself as understanding "the heart-beat" of India's village people far more than most urban and elite Indians.[67]

Observers of Ensminger and the Delhi office in the late 1960s came away with a very different impression. Along with its palace-like headquarters, the Delhi office kept two jet airplanes on hand to transport Foundation staff to projects throughout India. Ensminger lived on his own grand estate tended to by a phalanx of maids, cooks, gardeners and chauffeurs. Each day he arrived at the field office, according to one Foundation official, in a horse-drawn Victoria carriage from which he dismounted to receive a salute from Indian guards and inspected the premises. A self-confident belief in big projects coupled with an "imperial style" characterised the "Ensminger reign in India".[68]

66 Staples, *40 Years*, 6.

67 Ensminger, Ford Foundation's Nineteen Years, Box 13, Folder B21, 78–79, 153, DEP.

68 Harkavy, *Curbing Population Growth*, 130–131; Ensminger, The "Little People" of India, 6 November 1972, Box 1, Folder A39, DEP.

In fact, Ensminger was never simply an imperialist who overwhelmed Indians with Ford Foundation's resources any more than he was the humble populist of his own imagination. Rather, he and the Ford Foundation field office had operated as collaborators with Indian elites since the early 1950s. Indeed, the elaborate gardens and phalanx of subalterns at the Ford Foundation's campus, although better funded than most Indian Government offices, demonstrated just how integrated he had become into the conventions of caste and class in India. The construction of a new campus expressed the seeming solidity of the relationship between the Foundation and Delhi's principal policymakers. Yet, even as Ensminger built up the size and scope of the Delhi field office, its bases of support in both New York and Delhi were crumbling. Ensminger and the Ford Foundation became "imperialists", as the web of political alliances and shared priorities between Foundation headquarters and field office, field office and Delhi politicians, and the US and Indian governments broke down.

In the early 1960s, Ensminger clashed openly with the Foundation's third President Henry Heald, who had no experience in international affairs and expressed deep suspicions of Nehru, India's non-aligned foreign policy and its centralised planning process. To keep Ford Foundation grants flowing to India, Ensminger relied on the rising geo-political importance of India to US policymakers. He returned periodically to the United States, where he maintained a home outside Washington, DC, to meet with US experts and politicians. He also cultivated the Foundation's Board of Directors and used their influence over the New York headquarters to push his priorities. These efforts worked for a time. For example, Ensminger prevented Heald and his Vice-President for overseas development, Forest "Frosty" Hill, from scuttling the IADP programme. Ensminger favoured an "extension" approach of teaching new technologies to India's farmers; Heald and Hill had begun to orient the foundation toward the international laboratory research of hybrid seeds, which would give rise to the Green Revolution. Ensminger invited the Ford Foundation's Chairman, in India by chance on a tiger-hunt, to tour an IADP district and then threatened to resign if the Foundation did not support the programme. New York acceded to Ensminger's ultimatum and extended the IADP programme for five more years. But as US policymakers and the United Nations backed the laboratory strategy, Ensminger's focus on teaching at the village level lost out.[69]

The very success and proliferation of the Ford Foundation's overseas programmes caused further difficulties for the New Delhi office. While Ford

69 Ensminger, The Interaction between the Ford Foundation's India Field Office and New York Office, 30 June 1972, Box 1, Folder A35, 4–12, DEP; Sutton, "Ford Foundation", 45; Staples, *40 Years*, 19; Cullather, *Hungry World*, 162.

New Delhi had provided a model for other field offices in the early 1950s, decolonisation in Africa and Fidel Castro's victory in Cuba had pushed the Foundation to open a raft of new field offices in Africa and Latin America in the early 1960s. Although the Ford Foundation increased its budgets for overseas projects across the board, new field offices meant competition for attention from New York. Foundation officers preferred seeding new programmes rather than re-investing in established ones which, they believed, should be self-sustaining. To manage a far-flung network of field offices, New York increasingly bureaucratised grant-making, adding new subject desks and organisational procedures. Compared to the early 1950s, when Ensminger could give India's leaders an answer on a grant request within a week or two, now his requests required months of planning and paperwork. Ensminger complained bitterly about New York bureaucracy and in his memoirs even likened himself to a Gandhian resister confronting the British Raj.[70]

To many Indians in the late 1960s, it was Ensminger and the Ford Foundation's Delhi office that had begun to seem more like the occupying imperial power. Cracks in the alliance between the Ford Foundation field office and the Government of India began to form with the death of Nehru in 1964. His towering political presence and the overwhelming dominance of the Congress Party had protected foundation programmes and ensured that they would not face sustained political opposition. Nehru's successor, Lal Bahadur Shastri, however, shifted power from the Planning Commission, Ensminger's base of support in India, to the Cabinet and state chief ministers. As a result, the Ford Foundation in Delhi lost the cover of Nehru's mantle and intimate access to development policymaking. This left New Delhi office vulnerable, as increased involvement of US, European and United Nations aid donors in Indian affairs created the perception in India that an interconnected nexus of foreign advisers deployed expertise and funding assistance to bend India to their will. New crises over food shortages, capital reserves and an increased fixation on population control had brought US, United Nations and World Bank missions to India in 1964 and 1965. Their stern counsel and India's dependence on their financial assistance to meet its development targets led Shastri and his advisers to align India's monetary, agricultural and population policies more closely to international prescriptions. In 1966, the US Government under the Johnson Administration increased the pressure on India by tying much-needed grain exports to demands that India should tow the US line in foreign policy from Pakistan to Vietnam.[71] In this context, the careful boundaries that En-

---

70 Ensminger, Interaction, Box 1, Folder A35, 35, DEP.

71 Ahlberg, *Transplanting*, 106–46; Kirk, *India and the World Bank*, 15–16; Rosen, *Western Economists*, 141–143.

sminger had attempted to erect between the US Government and the Ford Foundation began to crumble.

While Ensminger's influence on India's leadership waned, the number of Foundation consultants stationed inside India's central, state and municipal ministries and offices actually rose. These included several Ford-funded MIT economists working with the Planning Commission, eighteen population advisers in the Central Family Planning Institute and the National Institute of Health Administration and Education, as well as over fifty expatriate experts in the massive Calcutta Metropolitan Planning Organisation, charged with redesigning the city of Calcutta. Indian administrators and experts often resented the consultants' high salaries and the esteem that the heads of agencies paid to the "Ford wallahs". Moreover, by the late 1960s, in fields such as economics, demography and regional planning, India had built up considerable indigenous expertise, leaving many to question the continued need for importing foreign advice.[72] Finally, the sheer number of Ford Foundation consultants present in India made it increasingly difficult for Ensminger and the Delhi office to control them. While Ensminger thought first about the preservation of the Foundation's work in India, consultants had other priorities and goals: In addition to advancing their own academic research (many came to India on sabbaticals from US universities), they often imbibed the institutional perspective of the agencies in which they worked. In 1964, MIT economists became embroiled in a political struggle within India over the size of the fourth five-year plan and the relative weight it accorded to agriculture and industry. MIT's computer modelling of the plan pointed toward policy advice favoured by one group of Indian politicians and by USAID.[73] Ford Foundation population advisers assigned to competing bureaucracies took sides in an Indian debate over the relationship between contraception, public health and population control.[74] Ensminger's persistent efforts to wall off technical experts from politics collapsed in the heightened international and national tensions over developments in the late 1960s.

Resentments toward US foreign policy and the role of US experts in India soon cohered around a particular charge: the Ford Foundation and its vast network of grants were operated as a Trojan horse through which the CIA had infiltrated India. Accusations of CIA involvement in India had risen before; Nehru himself had made them following the US alliance with Pakistan.

---

72 Minkler, "Consultants or Colleagues", 413–4

73 Sukhamoy Chakravarty to Paul Rosenstein-Rodan, 12 September 1964; Louis Lefeber to Max F. Millikan, 18 November 1964; Max F. Millikan to Douglas Ensminger, 4 December 1964, Box 10, Folder 7, MIT Center for International Studies Records, Institute Archives and Special Collections, MIT, Cambridge/MA (hereafter MIT).

74 Harkavy, *Curbing Population Growth*, 142; Connelly, *Fatal Misconception*, 200.

But prior to 1964 they had not been directed at Ford Foundation projects. Indian journalists, politicians and intellectuals developed the accusation in part through greater intellectual interchange with the New Left in the United States. As part of the questioning of US policy in Vietnam, US students and intellectuals began to expose collaborations between US social scientists and the CIA as well as the US Defence Department. Publicity about the MIT Center for International Studies Director's previous ties to the CIA as well as CIA funding for the Centre's Soviet Studies provoked an outcry in India. Although the CIA had never funded MIT's India research, Indian politicians and journalists decried the access of an "extended arm of the CIA" to "highly classified information" in order to "sabotage the country's long-term development programme" and build "Indian planning [...] in the image of their predilections". Ensminger demanded that the project shutter its operations in 1965, so as not to endanger other Ford Foundation projects in India.[75] But the charges kept coming. With revelations of CIA funding of the Asia Foundation and US Defence Department funding of the Berkeley study of the politically sensitive Himalayan region, fresh CIA allegations poured in about the Ford-funded Indian Institute of Technology at Kanpur, the Indian Institute of Management and the Calcutta Metropolitan Planning Organisation.[76]

Less specific, and in many ways more damaging to the Ford Foundation field office than the unproven CIA charges, were the ways in which many Indian intellectuals began to think about the place of India in resistance to the United States and its institutions. Indian academics charged that US universities and US foundations used their great resources and access to Indian policymakers to push US visions of the world onto India. In 1967 twenty-six faculty members at the University of Delhi, a prime beneficiary of Ford Foundation social science research grants, issued a public statement against "US infiltration in our Universities". Discussion continued at the Conference of Indian Sociologists and in a special issue of the mainstream monthly magazine *Seminar* on "academic colonialism" in which Indian social scientists identified a "colonization of [Indian] mind[s]" by foreign experts and agencies. In the future, Indians would have to shed the "colonial mentality" and their reliance on the "patrons or masters" of "dominant nations".[77]

75 Stephen A. Marglin to Max F. Millikan, 23 November 1964; Louis Lefeber to Max F. Millikan, 18 November 1964; Douglas Ensminger to Max F. Millikan, 16 November 1965, Box 10, Folder 7, MIT; "Indian Plan, U.S. Model?", *Now* (24 December 1964), 3–4; Blackmer, *MIT*, 180–192.

76 Warren, "Uproar"; "Office of Asia Foundation"; Berreman, "Not So Innocent Abroad"; Leslie/Kargon, "Exporting MIT", 116; Hill/Haynes/Baumgartel, *Institution Building in India*, 120–127.

77 Saberwal, "Problem", 11, 13; Kumar, "Servitude of the Mind", 21, 24; Kothair, "Tasks Within", 16.

In 1970, Ensminger retired from the Ford Foundation. After he left India, the New Delhi office underwent a major review and restructuring in 1973 that cut its budget and slashed its core programme staff to about a dozen Foundation officers. The new Foundation representative, Harry Wilhelm, in collaboration with New York, reoriented Ford Foundation funding away from large, direct grants to the Government of India and toward smaller grants to an array of non-governmental organisations. The changes reflected, in part, a response to the particular context of worsening Indo-American relations. With the Government of India scrutinising visas for foreign scholars and requesting USAID to close out its university technical assistance programmes, Wilhelm declared that the era of the foreign consultant was over.[78] Yet the changes in the Ford Foundation's programmes in India also reflected broader patterns of US philanthropic support for international development, from disillusionment with statist planning to an overall pessimism about the possibilities of engineering massive social and economic changes through expert knowledge and US capital. As the decade's oil shocks reduced the Foundation's endowment, Ford Foundation President McGeorge Bundy oriented the diminished Foundation's resources toward US domestic grant making. From a high of 122 million dollars in 1966, the international division's budget had fallen to 84 million dollars by 1973.[79]

Shortly after leaving the Ford Foundation, Ensminger dictated his memories of his nineteen years in India. "No one looked at me as a foreigner," he asserted. "I shed my foreign cloak, if I ever wore one." Within the Planning Commission he was seen as "Ensminger" and "only rather secondary as [...] the Ford Foundation representative".[80] These comments appear at once deeply naive and self-serving. Indian officials and experts who dealt with Ensminger always remained cognisant that he represented a powerful and wealthy US philanthropy with strong ties to the US Government. Yet, Ensminger's denial of foreignness does capture something important about the nature of the Delhi field office during its first decade in India: While the politics of the Cold War and its differentials of power shaped the Foundation's actions in India, the exigencies of operating on the ground primed Ensminger to accommodate Indian policymakers' visions of development and to shield the Ford Foundation's programme in India from projects and goals he deemed too controversial. In this way, the Delhi field office oper-

---

78 Drummond, "Ford Foundation"; Drummond, "India Curtails Research".

79 Ford Foundation, *Ford Foundation, 1952–2002*, 2–8; McCarthy, "From Government", 302.

80 Ensminger, Relationships, Box 1, Folder A8, 3; Ensminger, Foundation's Nineteen Years, Box 13, Folder B21, 4; Ensminger, Planning Commission, Box 1, Folder A3, 7, DEP.

ated in the 1950s and early 1960s as a critical institutional circuit for the negotiation of development knowledge between the United States and the Third World.

5. Conclusion

The story of the Ford Foundation's field office in Delhi suggests several ways in which we must revise our understanding of the global dynamics of knowledge circulation in the twentieth century. A neat centre–periphery model cannot account for the multiple sites of decision-making within foundations and other powerful American and international institutions. Through their field offices, the foundations also operated from the periphery – and sometimes clashed with the centre. Field offices adapted foundation priorities to local political, ideological and intellectual contexts. And as such this reminds us that the foundations did not simply impose US ways of knowing onto the world. In India, the production and dissemination of such knowledge constellations as community development, population control and public administration involved an intricate transnational process of knowledge production among American and Indian policymakers, scientists and expert advisers.

Ultimately, the contours of knowledge production were shaped by the priorities and power of US and Indian elites. The Ford Foundation altered its agenda to fit local contexts, but it did so to conform to the goals of Nehru and his government. In the case of India, those who criticised Nehru's vision of development, from US free marketers to India's Communist Party to local people, stood outside the circle of Ford-funded knowledge. Acknowledging this narrowness of vision while simultaneously examining collaborations and contestations between centre and periphery allows us to fully investigate foundation-led knowledge production.

Volker R. Berghahn

Commentary – Turntables or Transatlantic Two-Lane Turnpikes?

It is quite a challenge having to comment on three rich and thoughtful contributions to the final section of this book whose arguments are based on plenty of fresh empirical material. Faced with this challenge, I found it best to start my response with a consideration of Nicole Sackley's article, as it is the only one in this volume to explicitly expand the essentially Eurocentric framework relating to the activities of the big American foundations in the Third World.

Designating, as she does, the 1950s as the beginnings of Ford Foundation activity in the non-European world is no doubt correct with respect to resources first being allocated. But apart from the quantitative aspect of the sums of American money spent, there is also the qualitative one, and in this respect it seems there was an evolution of strategic planning. The main focus of philanthropic activity remained on Western Europe from the inter-war period after 1945 into the 1950s, when Western Europe was seen as the main front of the Cold War. It then shifted to Eastern Europe, especially after 1956. Only in the 1960s and 1970s did Latin America, Africa and Asia move to the centre of attention and resource allocation. Only after considering this later period shall I go back in time to the early post-war years and to the contributions by Giles Scott-Smith and John Krige. A further reason for this procedure is that these latter two authors also raise conceptual issues that are different from those broached in Sackley's article, and that will allow me to end with the larger problems encapsulated in the title of this piece.

The Indian Passage

There are two clusters of questions in Sackley's contribution which are inherent in her line of argument but deserve further elaboration. The first one relates to the fact that the big American foundations developed quite complex organisational structures, and that they were run not only by presidents with their own particular agendas, but also by officers who were vying for limited resources – and who as experts in their fields wanted the largest slices of the pie allocated to "their" programmes. Starting with Paul Hoffman, the Ford Foundation's first President, Sackley highlights his interest in Asia and his consequent intention to direct major resources to that part of the world. It is surely also significant, however, that Hoffman had just returned to California from Europe, where he had been the administrator of the European Recovery Program and had experienced at first hand not only the war-time devastation of Western Europe, but also the Soviet threat to that region, for example, during the blockade of West Berlin in 1948–49. Hoffman was therefore arguably more focused on Europe than the Far East when he arrived back from Paris to take over the Ford Foundation presidency.

It may well be that ultimately he had a global vision of foundation activity and, as Sackley demonstrates, clashed with Henry Ford, who seems to have been more orientated toward the reconstruction and protection of Western Europe, perhaps not the least also because the Ford Motor Company had major investments there. It also seems that Hoffman had higher ambitions; there is some evidence relating to the US presidential election campaign of 1952 that he was hoping to become Dwight D. Eisenhower's Secretary of State, though Eisenhower eventually chose John Foster Dulles over the Ford Foundation President.[1] Moreover, there was Hoffman's reluctance to leave California for New York at a time when it had become clear that this city was not only the financial and commercial centre of the United States but, with the United Nations headquartered there, also the centre of international politics. As the Ford Foundation had developed from a small Detroit-based enterprise to the biggest philanthropic organisation of the world with international ambitions, it felt that it needed to be based in New York.

Finally, there were not just the tensions over strategy at the very top, but with the growth of the organisation increasingly interdepartmental rivalries among officers. There was nothing unusual about this: It was a phenomenon to be found in all large bureaucracies.[2] These tensions were exacerbated by the arrival in New York of Dr Shepard Stone and his mentor John J. McCloy; the latter had been the US High Commissioner for Germany, with Stone as his trusted Public Affairs Officer who had received a doctorate from Berlin University in 1932 and knew Germany and Europe well. McCloy joined the Foundation's Board of Trustees, and both men were determined to strengthen its international activities, by which they meant primarily reaching out to Western Europe. To them this was the most precarious front of the Cold War. It took Stone some time to get a European programme firmly established within the Ford Foundation bureaucracy, but by 1955 he had

1 See Berghahn, *Intellectual Cold Wars*, 148.
2 See, e.g., Mommsen, *Age of Bureaucracy*; Macdonald, *Ford Foundation*.

reached his goal. When, after Nikita Khrushchev's speech before the Twentieth Congress of the Soviet Communist party in February 1956, Poland and Hungary blew up in the autumn of that year, Stone's hand was further strengthened and programming was extended from Western Europe to the regions East of the Iron Curtain.[3]

So, while considerable resources were being spent on non-European programmes, it was only in the 1960s that a major shift in the Cold-War struggle took place towards the Third World and South Asia in particular. This was promoted by the Kennedy and Johnson Administrations, not the least also after McGeorge Bundy moved over from the White House to the presidency of the Ford Foundation in New York.[4] Against the background of this shift, Sackley's article opens an intriguing window to Ford Foundation politics. What she says about the evolution of Douglas Ensminger's position within the organisation and in India opens up many questions, some of which she will no doubt have pursued in her research. It is not difficult to understand why a man who had studied rural sociology and had been working for the USDA Extension Service as well as for the Bureau of Agricultural Economics should emerge as the pointman for the South Asian programme. But what in my view deserves further exploration is not only his close relationship with the Indian Government under Nehru, but also the little colonial-style empire and the life he created for himself in New Delhi. There were a "palace-like head-quarters" in Delhi and "two jet airplanes on hand to transport foundation staff to projects throughout India". Ensminger himself "lived on his own grand estate tended to by a phalanx of maids, cooks, gardeners and chauffeurs". To visualise him arriving each day at his office "in a horse-drawn Victoria carriage from which he dismounted to receive a salute from Indian guards" to inspect "the premises" is really quite amazing and raises two questions.

The first relates to the attitudes and lifestyles of India's political elites and the stratification of South Asian society.[5] Had all this remained so unchanged from the British colonial period that an American such as Ensminger had to socially integrate himself into the upper classes if he wanted to get anywhere politically with his philanthropic programmes, which were, of course, also never quite completely separate from the larger national interests of Washington? As Sackley shows, he had to contend with India's non-alignment politics, which were growing stronger over time. But Ensminger's lifestyle also seems to point to how even an American with his pro-

---

3 See Berghahn, *Intellectual Cold Wars*, 178 ff., 187 ff.

4 Ibid., 239 ff., 251 ff.

5 On post-war Indian society see, e.g., Singer/Cohn, *Structure and Change*; Sahoo, *Class Relation*; Sinha, *Social Change*.

fessional background could develop a superiority complex that was quite typical of Western modernisation theorists. Apparently, he was so convinced of the correctness of the American liberal-capitalist progressive reformism in which the American development paradigm was grounded that he remained unaware of the contradictions between his own life and the realities of daily life in India and the Foundation's objectives. If the poverty relief programmes and the ideas of Lyndon Johnson's "Great Society" of the 1960s have increasingly come under critical scrutiny,[6] it may be time to do the same for the development programmes of the big American foundations and to relate them to the conceptualisations of subaltern studies, the field of research that emerged in the 1970s from a reassessment of British colonial rule and the socio-economic impact it had on the structures of South Asia.[7]

American Teaching Methods in the Netherlands

Like Nicole Sackley, Giles Scott-Smith initially also offers fresh empirical material in support of his examination of the diffusion of American jurisprudence. He looks at legal training in The Netherlands and at how the Ford Foundation used that country as a platform to shape Dutch higher education. He disagrees with John Ikenberry's notion of a one-way influence that came into The Netherlands from across the Atlantic. Rather he adopts John Krige's concept of "consensual hegemony". This concept as well as that of "beachhead" – though used in quotes – raise a number of points that may warrant further consideration. As Giles Scott-Smith shows, the Dutch and their legal professions did have great confidence in their own traditions and practices. This absence of an inferiority complex vis-à-vis the United States resulted in a reluctance to adopt American legal principles hook, line and sinker. Instead there occurred – if I have understood this correctly – a blending of indigenous and imported traditions. This is an outcome that has also been found with respect to other spheres of socio-economic and political life in Western Europe after the Second World War. But is this "consensual hegemony" or simply "hegemony" in the Gramscian sense? After all, hegemony meant for Gramsci the percolation of the superior "soft power" of the bourgeoisie into the working class or, as in this case, into another national society that, willingly and almost unconsciously, integrated this influence

---

6 See, e.g., Gettleman/Mermelstein, *Great Society Reader*; Kaplan/Cuciti, *Great Society and its Legacy*; Jordan/Rostow, *Great Society*.

7 See, e.g., Guha/Spivak, *Selected Subaltern Studies*; Chatterjee, *Nation and its Fragments*; Guha, Dominance Without Hegemony.

into its own system of norms and values.[8] If this is how Dutch–American interaction occurred in the 1950s, "beachhead" may also not be the most fortunate term because of the military, "hard-power" connotations that are commonly attached to it. It seems that neither the Americans nor the Dutch perceived their socio-legal encounter in this way.

Giles Scott-Smith then uses the rise of anti-trust law as taught in the Hague Academy to buttress his particular conceptualisation of the Dutch–American relationship in the 1950s. However, if one reads up on the evolution of European anti-trust law as analysed by European business historians, did the push to adopt it not come both very powerfully and "hegemonicly" precisely from the United States whose economic and political elites after 1945 were absolutely determined to wrench European industry and commerce out of its anti-competitive and protectionist traditions? This was not done by force, but by constant nudging, which at times may have been more insistent, though always "hegemonic". This is how anti-trust was first introduced in West Germany, where the United States had the greatest leverage as an occupying power.[9]

Here is a very telling quote relating to American strategy by no lesser person than Hoffman when he appeared before the sub-committee of the Appropriations Committee in Washington in May 1950: The question of decartelisation, he said, filled him with great hopes "for the re-establishment, via Germany, of competition in Western Europe".[10] The goal was to build up in the Federal Republic "the kind of free competitive economy that we have in the United States". Once this had been achieved, West Germany would develop "a very effective economy", whose influence would radiate beyond its western borders because the adoption of the competitive principle in a country like Germany would also lead to increased competition among its neighbours. The European Coal and Steel Community of 1951 and the Rome Treaty of 1957 institutionalised precisely these principles and moved Western Europe towards an American-style oligopolistic competition. European competition law, however, was never an exact replica of the American legal practice, but again constituted a blending of two traditions. Cartels and syndicates, while banned in principle, could be formed with the permission of the High Authority in Luxembourg or that of the Brussels Commission as a temporary emergency measure to overcome an economic crisis.[11]

8 See, e.g., Joll, *Antonio Gramsci*.
9 Berghahn, *West German Industry*, 71 ff., 155 ff.
10 Quoted in *Industriekurier*, 9 May 1950 (my trans.).
11 See, e.g., Diebold, *Schuman Plan*; Gillingham, *Rebirth of Europe*; Leucht, "Transatlantic Policy Networks"; Berghahn, *West German Industry*, 111 ff.

An additional value of Scott-Smiths's contribution lies in his analysis of the further diffusion of American jurisprudence. The choice of a small country with a strong tradition of international law practice and conceptualisation, at Dutch universities and at The Hague, may initially have guided the Ford Foundation to fund the academy there as part of its overall West European funding strategy. But just as Sackley, this author, too, deals with the shift towards the Third World in the 1960s. The reorientation of the Hague Academy towards training jurists from the non-European world fits well into this picture, just as the Foundation saw an advantage in selecting another small country, Denmark, and particularly Nils Bohr's Institute in Copenhagen, to promote exchange programmes in the natural sciences – the theme of Krige's article to be examined in a moment. Nonetheless, in the Dutch case it seems significant that the training of jurists from the Third World took place first in the Netherlands. Bundy as the new President decided in 1966 that an academy in Europe was no longer the right location to influence – in hegemonic fashion – the elites of Latin America, Africa and Asia; this now had to be done by creating centres of legal training in India and elsewhere.

In the end I cannot but agree with Scott-Smith's conclusions. His article is indeed about "American teaching methods" in the Netherlands. The Europeans did make their own contributions to the changes that their law-schools and universities as well as their societies more generally underwent after 1945. Both sides benefitted from the investments, and even though the funding came from the United States, the adage that who pays the piper will hear the preferred tune is too one-sided.[12] So what are the most plausible concepts when we look at American foundations and the "Coproduction of World Order in the Twentieth Century"? These are the problems raised by Krige's article as well, to which we now turn.

The Critique of Political Science

John Krige's contribution builds on research published in his book and several articles in recent years, but it also expands his work conceptually. He has been a pioneer in developing the history of the relations between the big American foundations and the sciences.

To my mind, the most fascinating part of his article is the section on the Israeli physicists who participated in Ford-funded exchange programmes. Not having had access to all relevant archives, Krige is understandably cautious and resists the temptation of relating Israeli nuclear scientists, and

---

12 Stonor Saunders, *Who Paid the Piper?*

Amos de Shalit in particular, to the construction of an atomic arsenal that Israel, notwithstanding persistent denials by its government, is now assumed to possess. At the same time, this particular section, focused primarily on the 1960s, must be seen against the background of Krige's analysis of the complex relationships that evolved between the Ford Foundation, Nils Bohr and European physicists, and the Washington intelligence community. The author is critical of earlier work, which he feels revolved too much around the cultural and intellectual aspects of the Cold War and the involvement of the big American foundations in Europe.

However, the research on foundation activities that he criticises has never denied that powerful interests in Washington played a major role in the complex networks of American Cold-War politics. The role of the CIA in this picture has been covered to the extent that this was possible without access to its archives. Next to Allen Dulles's organisation, the State Department and Pentagon obviously also had a vital interest in science and social science contacts, even across the Iron Curtain with Soviet and East European scientists.[13] This was especially true after 1956, when it became clear that pursuing a hard-line confrontation with the East had become very dangerous after both sides possessed both tactical nuclear devices and the hydrogen bomb, together with the bombers and missiles necessary to deliver their devastatingly destructive power.

The value of this article lies in the fact that it fills gaps and complements received historical knowledge. But it also gives rise to the question of whether the line between "culture" and the "transmission of values" on the one hand, and the "protection of national security" on the other, is really as sharply drawn as Krige would assert. After all, it should not be forgotten that the Cold War was seen by all contemporaries as a comprehensive struggle against Soviet Communism as a political, military, economic, cultural, scientific and intellectual system.

The problem was that, with the development of ever more destructive weapons and the capacity to deliver them to the opponent's population centres, causing millions of deaths, it became increasingly clear that the Western talk about rolling back Communism and liberating Eastern Europe from Soviet rule as well as the idea of reunifying Germany within its 1937 borders (i.e., by revising Poland's borders) were totally unrealistic. They were hot-air propaganda that merely augmented the enormous dangers inherent in the East–West confrontation. This is why, as early as 1952, there emerged an alternative argument to rollback that was best articulated in a memo that Richard Bissell, once on Hoffman's staff and later at the CIA,

---

13 Ibid., *passim*.

wrote for his former boss Hoffman in 1952.[14] While Dulles talked about massive retaliation and mutually assured destruction, this is also the time when other people, like Bissell, began to discuss ways of entering into a dialogue with the Soviets. The aim was to de-escalate the nuclear arms race and the threat of war.

After this and exceptions such as Edward Teller always granted, physicists on both sides of the Atlantic came to favour forays that were later consolidated at top governmental level and called détente. But scientists were not the only advocates. There were also sociologists who, especially after the death of Stalin and Khrushchev's 1956 critique of Stalinism, began to travel, on Ford Foundation money, to Eastern Europe and the Soviet Union. What they brought back was news of a growing intellectual ferment fostered by the exchange programmes that the foundation also began to initiate. Among the travellers were also economists, some of whom even began to discuss the question of whether Western Keynesian welfare policies and East European anti-Stalinist reformism with its search for a democratic socialism "with a human face" were in fact converging. These developments were not "cultural" in the traditional understanding of the European bourgeoisie of "high culture", that is, defined by the arts and elitist *Bildung*. Rather, they were "cultural" in an expanded American sense, where the term included the educational system, the daily practices of civil society and scientific research. The older European definition of culture had never seen the sciences as part of the "high cultural" realm.

To gain an understanding of the shifts that took place under the hegemonic impact of the United States in the 1950s, one merely has to study the agendas and speeches at a number of major conferences held in Berlin, Hamburg and Milan.[15] The Hamburg Congress was specifically devoted to facilitating a dialogue between the natural and the social sciences, with Michael Polanyi as one of its prominent organisers and embodiment of the bridge-building that took place to integrate all academic endeavours under the same umbrella. It is no accident that these big conferences were organised by the Congress for Cultural Freedom. As a number of studies have shown, they were funded by the big American foundations and – no surprise – by the CIA. With Stone negotiating with the Congress for Cultural Freedom for support of the Milan conference devoted to the arts and humanities, there would seem to be plenty of evidence that the new 1950s definition of "cultural" was holistic and shaped by American ideas of what constituted it. They were also attempts to undermine the "hard" military-scientific dynamics of the East–West nuclear confrontation. Indeed, just like

14 For details see Berghahn, *West German Industry*, 145 ff.
15 See, e.g., Coleman, Liberal Conspiracy; Grémion, *Intelligence de l'anticommunisme*.

"culture", the "protection of national interest" also came to have a broader meaning.

To be sure, many of the scientific secrets relating to nuclear power and missile development had to be kept under wraps. But the contemporary notion of national security that became more widely accepted did not end there. It was concerned with the stabilisation as well as constant reformist evolution of Western political systems, and with the gathering of information about the stability and dynamics of the political systems in the East. It is therefore not surprising that the CIA was involved in the Congress for Cultural Freedom, its conferences and its journals, none of which were purely "cultural" in a traditional bourgeois-European sense. The Congress for Cultural Freedom and the foundations also played a key role in the gathering of information on all aspects of life on the other side of the Iron Curtain. For several years after Stalin's death, when restrictions were relaxed, the Soviet Bloc was at the centre of these covert activities. When American or Western European social scientists travelled to Eastern Europe to give lectures or to discuss setting up exchange programmes with their universities, they also reported their observations to Washington, sometimes getting into trouble when the Soviet authorities suspected them of spying.[16]

The Soviet launch of the Sputnik inevitably gave a big boost to the West's quest to learn more about Soviet science and technology, but also about the political system and the economy that had made this feat possible. When Mao triggered the Cultural Revolution in China, the CIA found that it knew very little about that part of the world. No doubt Allen Dulles stepped up the information gathering by the American security apparatus at this time. But, significantly enough, he also nudged Stone at the Ford Foundation to fund the establishment of a Far Eastern research centre at St Antony's College in Oxford under Geoffrey Hudson.

Flow of Knowledge

All these tit-bits are meant to indicate that the value of Krige's article lies in its providing very important and detailed information on what was going on at Nils Bohr's institute in Copenhagen, at CERN and elsewhere in the way of closer contacts between scientists in East and West during the initial years of détente. He conceptualises all these exchanges under the rubric of knowledge circulation. But – and this is my final point – there appears to be a tension in his line of argument here. On the one hand, he speaks of American hegemony that – as I have also mentioned in my comments on Sackley's

16 Berghahn, *West German Industry*, 187 ff.

piece – involves an asymmetric soft-power relationship. The flow of knowledge in this period was primarily from the United States to Europe. And of course the flow of money was also from West to East, from the big foundations to European institutions and organisations.

At the same time it seems that, by introducing the notion of circulation, Krige has bought into the theory, advanced more recently by French scholars, that the Atlantic was in effect a turntable upon which ideas and researchers were constantly being circulated.[17] But this metaphor of circulation does not answer the question of where this process in fact started. This is why it seems to me that it is preferable to see the Atlantic as a two-lane waterway along which the East–West exchange took place over many decades. To stay within the timeframe of this volume as a whole, there clearly was an increased exchange during the inter-war period in which the American foundations played their first major role. However, in terms of the "cultural" ideas (in the broad sense) that moved across the Atlantic, the flow was more from East to West, especially in the 1930s, when European refugees from fascism imported many new perspectives on science and society into the United States.[18]

After 1945, this flow shifted more strongly from West to East, unleashing by the late 1950s a circulation of knowledge that has continued to this day. And yet, this process time and again received a fresh impetus by technological and scientific inventions and innovations that began in North America, as one would expect if one accepts that all these exchanges occurred in the era of an irrefutable American hegemony. This is the era when the United States tried to realise – and comprehensively so – a post-Second World War economic *Pax Americana* in Europe and the rest of the world. This order is now coming to an end due to the "imperial overstretch" (Paul Kennedy) from which the United States is now suffering and also due to the rise of new powers in a world that has again become more multi-polar.

17 See in particular Ludovic Tournès, *Sciences de l'homme et politique*, Paris 2011.
18 See Berghahn, "American Social Scientists".

Thanks

This book is based on a selection of peer reviewed papers given during the Conference *US-Foundations and the Power Politics of Knowledge Circulation in the Global Arena* held at FRIAS in July 2010. The editors warmly thank all participants for their willingness to embark on this common project, including Anne-Emanuelle Birn, Marc Frey, Matthias Middell, Hannes Siegrist, Daniel Spreich and Paul B. Trescott whose voices are unfortunately absent in this volume. We are much obliged to the anonymous reviewers for their thorough and inspiring comments on earlier drafts of the papers. We are also indebted to Agnes Fellner and Jörg Später for their painstaking copyediting of all manuscripts. As with the summer conference, this book profits from the gracious support given by the FRIAS School of History and its directors Ulrich Herbert and Jörn Leonhard whom we thank for including this volume in the FRIAS Weiße Reihe.

Bibliography

"A County Agent Comes to India", *Life,* 31 December 1951, 52–55.

"A Five-Year Plan of Research", *Africa* 5 (1932) 1, 1–13.

"Annual Report. The Work of the Institute in 1935", *Africa* 9 (1936) 1, 100–108.

"Colonial Office Minutes, 3. 1. 1931", cit. in: Lackner, Helen: "Social Anthropology and Indirect Rule. The Colonial Administration and Anthropology in Eastern Nigeria, 1920–1940", in: Asad, Talal (ed.): *Anthropology and the Colonial Encounter* (Ithaca, 1973).

"Notes and News", *Africa* 13 (1940) 1, 68–76.

"Office of Asia Foundation in India to Close", *Los Angeles Times*, 18 May 1968, B5.

"Report of Meeting", *Africa* 9 (1936) 4, 536–543.

"Report of the Commission on the Responsibility of the Authors of the War and on Enforcement of Penalties, with Memorandum of Reservations", *American Journal of International Law* 14 (1920) 1, 95–154.

"Report of the Council for the Year 1928", *Journal of the Royal Anthropological Institute of Great Britain and Ireland [JRAI]* 59 (1929), 3–9.

"Report of the Council for the Year 1930", *JRAI* 60 (1930), 3–8.

"Report of the Council for the Year 1931", *JRAI* 61 (1931), iii–x.

"Report on Progress of Work During the Period 1926–October 1929", *Africa* 3 (1930) 1, 90–102.

"Science: Plows and Sacred Cows", *Time*, 22 January 1951.

"Summary of Proceedings of the Ninth Meeting of the Executive Council", *Africa* 4 (1931) 4, 483–491.

"The Hilton-Young and Wilson Reports on East Africa", *Bulletin of International News* 6 (1929) 1, 3–13.

"The London School of Economics 1895–1945", *Economica* 13 (1946), 1–31.

Abir-Am, Pnina Geraldine: "The Rockefeller Foundation and the Rise of Molecular Biology", *Nature Reviews–Molecular Cell Biology* 3 (2001), 65–70.

Abraham, Itty: *The Making of the Indian Atomic Bomb. Science, Secrecy and the Postcolonial State* (London, 1998).

Ahlberg, Kristin L.: *Transplanting the Great Society. Lyndon Johnson and Food for Peace* (Columbia, 2008).

Akami, Tomoko: *Internationalizing the Pacific. The United States, Japan and the Institute of Pacific Relations in War and Peace, 1919–1945* (London, 2002).

Amrith, Sunil: *Decolonizing International Health. India and Southeast Asia, 1930–65* (New York-Basingstoke, 2006).

Amrith, Sunil/Sluga, Glenda: "New Histories of the United Nations", *Journal of World History* 19 (2008) 3, 251–274.

Anderson, Michael R.: *Pacific Dreams. The Institute of Pacific Relations and the Struggle for the Mind of Asia* (Austin, 2009).

Anderson, Perry: *Considerations on Western Marxism* (London, 1976).

Anderson, Warwick: *Colonial Pathologies. American Tropical Medicine, Race, and Hygiene in the Philippines* (Durham/NC, 2006).

Appleby, Paul H.: *Public Administration in India. Report of a Survey* (New Delhi, 1953).

Arnove, Robert (ed.): *Philanthropy and Cultural Imperialism. The Foundations at Home and Abroad* (Bloomington, 1982).

Ash, Mitchell: "Wissenschaft und Politik als Ressourcen für einander", in: vom Bruch, Rüdiger/Kaderas, Brigitte (Hg.): *Wissenschaften und Wissenschaftspolitik. Bestandsaufnahmen zu Formationen, Brüchen und Kontinuitäten im Deutschland des 20. Jahrhunderts* (Stuttgart, 2002), 32–51.

Baker, G.: "An Experiment in Applied Anthropology", *Africa* 8 (1935) 3, 304–314.

Balibar, Etienne: *Politics and the other Scene* (London, 2002).

Bardonnet, Daniel: "L'Académie de Droit International de la Haye et M. Boutros Boutros-Ghali", in: Boutros-Ghali, Boutros (ed.): *Amicorum Discipulorumque Liber,* Vol. 1 (Brussels, 1998).

Barjot, Dominique/Reveillard, Christophe (eds.): *L'américanisation de l'Europe occidentale au XXe siècle. Mythes et réalités* (Paris, 2002).

Barnard, Chester: *The Functions of the Executive* (Cambridge, 1938).

Barrès, Maurice: *Pour la haute intelligence française* (Paris, 1925).

Bell, Jonathan: "Social Politics in a Transoceanic World in the Early Cold War Years", *Historical Journal* 53 (2010) 2, 401–421.

Bell, Morag: "American Philanthropy, the Carnegie Corporation and Poverty in South Africa", *Journal of Southern African Studies* 26 (2000) 3, 481–504.

Bell, Peter D.: "The Ford Foundation as a Transnational Actor", *International Organization* 25 (1971) 3, 465–478.

Bell, Philip/Bell, Roger: *Americanization and Australia* (Sidney, 1998).

Benessaieh, Afef: "Multiculturalism, Interculturality, Transculturality", in: Idem (ed.): *Amériques transculturelles – Transcultural Americas* (Ottawa, 2010), 11–38.

Berghahn, Volker: "The Debate on 'Americanization' Among Economic and Cultural Historians", *Cold War History* 10 (2010) 1, 107–130.

Berghahn, Volker: "American Social Scientists and the European-American Dialogue on Social Rights, 1930–1970", in: Kessler-Harris, Alice/Vaudagna, Maurizio (eds.): *Democracy and Social Rights in the "Two Wests"* (Torino, 2009), 67–89.

Berghahn, Volker: "1956. The Ford Foundation and America's Cultural Cold War in Eastern Europe", in: Fink, Carole/Hadler, Frank/Schramm, Tomasz (eds.): *1956. European and Global Perspectives* (Leipzig, 2006), 59–76.

Berghahn, Volker: *Transatlantische Kulturkriege. Shepard Stone, die Ford-Stiftung und der europäische Antiamerikanismus* (Stuttgart, 2004).

Berghahn, Volker: *America and the Intellectual Cold Wars in Europe. Shepard Stone Between Philanthropy, Academy, and Diplomacy* (Princeton-Oxford, 2001).

Berghahn, Volker: "Philanthropy and Diplomacy in the 'American Century'", *Diplomatic History* 23 (1999) 1, 393–419.

Berghahn, Volker: *The Americanization of West German Industry, 1945–1973* (New York, 1986).

Berman, Edward H.: *The Influence of the Carnegie, Ford, and Rockefeller Foundations on American Foreign Policy. The Ideology of Philanthropy* (Albany, 1983).

Berman, Edward H.: "Educational Colonialism in Africa. The Role of American Foundations, 1910–1945", in: Arnove, Robert F. (ed.): *Philanthropy and Cultural Imperialism. The Foundations at Home and Abroad* (Boston, 1980), 179–201.

Bernstein, Michael: *A Perilous Progress. Economists and Public Purpose in Twentieth-Century America* (Princeton, 2001).

Berreman, Gerald D.: "Not So Innocent Abroad", *The Nation* 209 (1969) 16, 505–508.

Bertrams, Kenneth: "Le Fonds National de la recherche scientifique en Belgique", *Revue pour l'histoire du CNRS* 16 (2007), 36–39.

Bertrand, Ivan/Delay, Jean/Guillain, Jacqueline: *L'électro-encéphalogramme normal et pathologique* (Paris, 1939).

Bieder, Robert E.: "Marketing the American Indian in Europe. Context, Commodification, and Reception", in: Bosscher, Doeko F.J./Kroes, Rob/Rydell, Robert W. (eds.): *Cultural Transmissions and Receptions. American Mass Culture in Europe* (Amsterdam, 1993), 15–23.

Bird, Kai: *The Chairman. John J. McCloy. The Making of the American Establishment* (New York, 1992).

Birn, Anne-Emmanuelle: *Marriage of Convenience. Rockefeller International Health and Revolutionary Mexico* (Rochester, 2006).

Bischof, Günter/Pelinka, Anton: *The Americanization/Westernization of Austria* (New Brunswick, 2004).

Black, Edwin: *War against the Weak. Eugenics and America's Campaign to Create the Master Race* (New York, 2003).

Blackmer, Donald L.M.: *The MIT Center for International Studies. The Founding Years, 1951–1969* (Cambridge/MA, 2002).

Boas, Franz: "The Aims of Anthropological Research (1932)", in: Idem, *Race, Language and Culture* (New York, 1940), 243–259.

Bonn, Moritz Julius: *So macht man Geschichte. Bilanz eines Lebens* (München, 1953).

Borowy, Iris: *Coming to Terms with World Health. The League of Nations Health Organisation 1921–1946* (Frankfurt a.M., 2009).

Bosscher, Doeko F.J./Kroes, Rob/Rydell, Robert W. (eds.): *Cultural Transmissions and Receptions. American Mass Culture in Europe* (Amsterdam, 1993).

Bourdieu, Pierre: *Vom Gebrauch der Wissenschaft. Für eine klinische Soziologie des wissenschaftlichen Feldes* (Konstanz, 1998).

Boutros-Ghali, Boutros: "Le Centre d'étude et de recherche de droit international et de relations internationales de l'Académie de droit international de La Haye", in: Dupuy, R.J. (ed.): *The Hague Academy of International Law. Jubilee Book 1923–1973* (Leiden, 1973).

Bowles, Chester: "New India", *Foreign Affairs* 31 (1952) 1, 79–94.

Brahm, Felix: *Wissenschaft und Dekolonisation. Paradigmenwechsel und institutioneller Wandel in der akademischen Beschäftigung mit Afrika in Deutschland und Frankreich, 1930–1970* (Stuttgart, 2010).

Braibanti, Ralph: "Reflections on Bureaucratic Reform in India", in: Idem/Spengler, Joseph (eds.): *Administration and Economic Development in India* (Durham, 1963), 6–9.

Bresnan, John: *At Home Abroad. A Memoir of the Ford Foundation in Indonesia, 1953–1973* (Jakarta, 2006).

Brick, Howard: *Transcending Capitalism. Visions of a New Society in Modern American Thought* (Ithaca, 2006).

Brier, Jennifer: "AIDS, Reproductive Rights, and Economic Empowerment: The Ford Foundation's Response to AIDS in the Global South, 1987–1995", in: Idem, *Infectious Ideas. U.S. Political Responses to the AIDS Crisis* (Chapel Hill, 2009), 122–155.

Bright, Charles/Geyer, Michael: "Globalgeschichte und die Einheit der Welt im 20. Jahrhundert", in: Conrad, Sebastian/Eckert, Andreas/Freitag, Ulrike (Hg.): *Globalgeschichte. Theorien, Ansätze, Themen* (Frankfurt am Main, 2007), 53–80.

Brinkley, Alan: "The Concept of an American Century", in: Moore, R. Laurence/Vaudagna, Maurizio (eds.): *The American Century in Europe* (Ithaca, 2003), 7–21.

Brown, Dorris D.: *Agricultural Development in India's Districts* (Cambridge/MA, 1971).

Bu, Liping: "Educational Exchange and Cultural Diplomacy in the Cold War", *Journal of American Studies* 33 (1999) 3, 393–415.

Büschel, Hubertus/Speich, Daniel (Hg.): *Entwicklungswelten. Globalgeschichte der Entwicklungszusammenarbeit* (Frankfurt a.M., 2009).

Butler, Nicholas Murray: "Les attaques contre le libéralisme", *L'Esprit international*, no. 32 (1934), 491–508.

Butler, Nicholas Murray: "National Boundaries as Factors in Trade and Commerce", *Foreign Trade* 1 (1926) 1, 16–17.

Butler, Nicholas Murray: *A World in Ferment. Interpretations of the War for a New World* (New York, 1918).

Butler, Nicholas Murray: *The International Mind. An Argument for the Judicial Settlement of International Disputes* (New York, 1913).

Buxton, William J. (ed.): *Patronizing the Public. American Philanthropy's Transformation of Culture, Communication, and the Humanities* (Lanham et al., 2009).

Bynum, Caroline Waker: "Perspectives, Connections and Objects. What's Happening in History Now?", *Daedalus* 138 (2009) 1, 71–86.

Cahiers pour l'histoire du CNRS (Paris 1988–1991), 10 vols.

Castells, Manuel/Cardoso, Gustavo (eds.): *The Network Society. From Knowledge to Policy* (Washington, 2006).

Ceadel, Martin: *Semi-detached Idealists. The British Peace Movement and International Relations, 1854–1945* (Oxford, 2000).

Cell, J.W.: "Lord Hailey and the Making of the African Survey", *African Affairs* 88 (1989) 353, 481–505.

Chafer, Tony: *The End of Empire in French West Africa. France's Successful Decolonization?* (Oxford, 2002).

Chamak, Brigitte: "Un scientifique pendant l'Occupation. Le cas d'Antoine Lacassagne", *Revue d'histoire des sciences* 57 (2004) 1, 101–133.

Charle, Christophe: *La République des universitaires, 1870–1940* (Paris, 1994).

Chatriot, Alain/Duclert, Vincent: *Le gouvernement de la recherche. Histoire d'un engagement politique, de Pierre Mendès France à Charles de Gaulle (1953–1969)* (Paris, 2006).

Chatterjee, Partha: *The Nation and its Fragments. Colonial and Postcolonial Histories* (Princeton, 1993).

Chomsky, Noam et al.: *The Cold War and the University. Toward an Intellectual History of the Postwar Years* (New York, 1997).

Chou, Grace Ai-Ling: "Cultural Education as Containment of Communism. The Ambivalent Position of American NGOs in Hong Kong in the 1950s", *Journal of Cold War Studies* 12 (2010) 1, 3–28.

Clarke, Sabine: "A Technocratic Imperial State? The Colonial Office and Scientific Research, 1940–1960", *Twentieth Century British History* 18 (2007) 4, 453–480.

Clavin, Patricia: *Bread and Butter Internationalism. The League of Nations and Economic Cooperation, 1919–1946* (Oxford, forthcoming).

Clavin, Patricia: "A 'Wandering Scholar' in Britain and the USA, 1933–45. The Life and Work of Moritz Bonn", *The Yearbook of the Research Centre for German and Austrian Exile Studies* 4 (2002) 1, 27–42.

Cleveland, Harlan: *The Obligations of Power. American Diplomacy in the Search for Peace* (New York, 1966).

Cohen, Andrew B.: *British Policy in Changing Africa* (London, 1959).

Cohen, Avner: *The Worst-Kept Secret. Israel's Bargain with the Bomb* (New York, 2010).

Cohen, Avner: *Israel and the Bomb* (New York, 1998).

Coleman, Peter: *The Liberal Conspiracy. The Congress for Cultural Freedom and the Struggle for the Mind of Postwar Europe* (New York, 1989).

Conklin, Alice L.: "The new 'ethnology' and 'la situation coloniale' in interwar France", *French Politics, Culture and Society* 20 (2002) 2, 29–48.

Connelly, Matthew: *Fatal Misconception. The Struggle to Control World Population* (Cambridge/MA, 2008 & 2010).

Connelly, Matthew: "Taking Off the Cold War Lens. Visions of North-South Conflict during the Algerian War for Independence", *American Historical Review* 105 (2000) 3, 739–769.

Conrad, Sebastian/Sachsenmaier, Dominic (eds.): *Competing Visions of World Order. Global Moments and Movements, 1880s–1930s* (New York-Basingstoke, 2007).

Cooper, Frederick: "Writing the History of Development", *Journal of Modern European History* 8 (2010) 1, 5–23.

Cooper, Frederick: "Development, Modernization, and the Social Sciences in the Era of Decolonization: The Examples of British and French Africa", *Revue d'histoire des sciences humaines* 10 (2004), 9–38.

Cooper, Frederick/Stoler, Ann Laura (eds.): *Tensions of Empire. Colonial Cultures in a Bourgeois World* (Berkeley, 2009).

Cooper, Sandi: *Patriotic Pacifism. Waging War on War in Europe 1815–1914* (New York, 1991).

Copans, Jean: "Œuvre secrète ou œuvre publique. Les écrits politiques de Marcel Mauss", *L'Homme* 39 (1999) 150, 217–220.

Coquery-Vidrovitch, Catherine: "The Popular Front and the Colonial Question. French West Africa: An Example of Reformist Colonialism", in: Chafer, Tony/Sackur, Amanda (eds.): *The French Colonial Empire and the Popular Front. Hope and Disillusion* (Basingstoke, 1999), 155–169.

Cowie, Jefferson: *Stayin' Alive. The 1970s and the Last Days of the Working Class* (New York, 2011).

Cueto, Marcos (ed.): *Missionaries of Science. The Rockefeller Foundation and Latin America* (Bloomington, 1994).

Cullather, Nick: *The Hungry World. America's Cold War Battle Against Poverty in Asia* (Cambridge/MA, 2010).

Cumings, Bruce: "Boundary Displacement. Area Studies and International Studies During and After the Cold War", in: Simpson, Christopher (ed.): *Universities and Empire. Money and Politics in the Social Sciences During the Cold War* (New York, 1998), 159–188.

Curti, Merle: *American Philanthropy Abroad. A History* (New Brunswick/NJ, 1963).

Därmann, Iris/Mahlke, Kristin (Hg.): *Marcel Mauss. Handbuch der Ethnographie* (München, 2011).

Davis, Jackson: "The Christian Mission in Africa. International Conference held at Le Zonte, Belgium, September 14–20, 1926", *Social Forces* 5 (1927) 3, 483–487.

De Grazia, Victoria: *Irresistible Empire. America's Advance Through Twentieth-Century Europe* (Cambridge, 2005).

De Greiff, Alexis: "Supporting Theoretical Physics for the Third World Development. The Ford Foundation and the International Centre for Theoretical Physics in Trieste (1966–1973)", in: Gemelli, Giuliana (ed.): *American Foundations and Large-Scale Research. Construction and Transfer of Knowledge* (Bologna, 2001), 25–50.

de Vries, Tity: *Complexe Consensus. Amerikaanse en Nederlandse Intellectuelen in Debat over Politiek en Cultuur 1945–1960* (Hilversum, 1996).

Delafosse, Maurice: "Sur l'orientation nouvelle de la politique indigène dans l'Afrique noire", *Renseignements coloniaux et documents publiés par le Comité de l'Afrique française* 6 (1921), 145–152.

Devine, Edward T.: "International Implications of Social Work", *Advocate of Peace through Justice* 90 (1928) 8, 499–512.

Diamond, Sigmund: *Compromised Campus. The Collaboration of Universities with the Intelligence Community, 1945–1955* (New York, 1992).

Dickinson, Matthew J.: *Bitter Harvest. FDR, Presidential Power and the Growth of the Presidential Branch* (Cambridge, 1997).

Diebold, William: *The Schuman Plan. A Study in Economic Cooperation, 1950–1959* (New York, 1959).

Dimier, Véronique: "Politique indigène en France et Grande-Bretagne dans les années 1930. À l'origine de l'idéologie développementaliste", *Politique et Société* 24 (2005) 1, 73–99.

Dimier, Véronique: "Le Commandant de Cercle. Un 'expert' en administration coloniale, un spécialiste de l'indigène?", *Revue d'Histoire des Sciences Humaines* 6 (2004) 1, 39–57.

Doel, Ronald: "Does Scientific Intelligence Matter?", *Centaurus* 52 (2010) 4, 165–184.

Doel, Ronald: "Scientists as Policymakers, Advisors and Intelligence Agents. Linking Contemporary Diplomatic History with the History of Science", in: Söderqvist, Thomas (ed.): *The Historiography of Contemporary Science and Technology* (Amsterdam, 1997), 215–244.

Doel, Ronald/Needell, Allan: "Science, Scientists and the CIA. Balancing International Ideals, National Needs, and Professional Opportunities", *Intelligence and National Security* 12 (1997) 1, 59–81.

Doering-Manteuffel, Anselm/Raphael, Lutz: *Nach dem Boom. Perspektiven auf die Zeitgeschichte seit 1970* (Göttingen, 2008 & 2010).

Donati, Pierpaolono: *Relational Sociology. A New Paradigm for the Social Sciences* (London, 2011).

Douglas, William O.: *Strange Lands and Friendly People* (New York, 1951).

Drummond, William J.: "Ford Foundation Tries to Change with the Times in India", *Los Angeles Times*, 3 July 1974, B1.

Drummond, William J.: "India Curtails Research by U.S. Scholars", *Los Angeles Times*, 27 August 1972, 11.

Dubin, Martin: "Elihu Root and the Advocacy of a League of Nations, 1914–1917", *Western Political Quarterly* 19 (1966) 3, 439–455.

Dupuy, R.J. (ed.): *The Hague Academy of International Law. Jubilee Book 1923–1973* (Leiden, 1973).

Eckert, Andreas: "Afrikanische Intellektuelle und Aktivisten in Europa und die Dekolonisation Afrikas", *Geschichte und Gesellschaft* 37 (2011) 2, 244–274.

Ekbladh, David: *The Great American Mission. Modernization and the Construction of an American World Order* (Princeton, 2010).

Engerman, David C.: "Social Science in the Cold War", *Isis* 101 (2010) S1, 393–400.

Engerman, David C.: *Know Your Enemy. The Rise and Fall of America's Soviet Experts* (Oxford-New York, 2009).

Engerman, David C.: "Bernath Lecture: American Knowledge and Global Power", *Diplomatic History* 31 (2007) 4, 599–622.

Engerman, David C.: "The Romance of Economic Development and New Histories of the Cold War", *Diplomatic History* 28 (2004) 1, 23–54.

Engerman, David C.: "West meets East. The Center for International Studies and Indian Economic Development", in: Idem et al. (eds.): *Staging Growth. Modernization, Development, and the Global Cold War* (Amherst, 2003), 199–223.

Engerman, David C./Unger, Corinna R.: "Introduction. Towards a Global History of Modernization", *Diplomatic History* 33 (2009) 3, 375–385.

Engerman, David C. et al. (eds.): *Staging Growth. Modernization, Development, and the Global Cold War* (Amherst, 2003).

Ensminger, J. Douglas: *Diagnosing Rural Community Organization* (Ph.D. Thesis, Cornell University, 1939).

Escobar, Arturo: "Worlds and Knowledges Otherwise", *Cultural Studies* 21 (2007) 2–3, 179–210.

Escobar, Arturo: *Encountering Development. The Making and Unmaking of the Third World* (Princeton, 1950).

Etzemüller, Thomas: *Ein ewigwährender Untergang. Der apokalyptische Bevölkerungsdiskurs im 20. Jahrhundert* (Bielefeld, 2007).

Fangerau, Heiner: "Private Wissenschaft und staatliches Interesse? Forschung am Rockefeller Institute for Medical Research zwischen 1901 und 1925", in: Hüntelmann, Axel C./Scheider, Michael C. (Hg.): *Jenseits von Humboldt. Wissenschaft im Staat 1850–1990* (Frankfurt a.M., 2010), 217–231.

Farley, John: *To Cast Out Disease. A History of the International Health Division of the Rockefeller Foundation 1913–1951* (Oxford, 2004).

Febvre, Lucien: "Quelques aspects d'une ethnographie en plein travail", *Annales d'histoire économique et sociale* 10 (1938) 5, 248–255.

Fee, Elizabeth: *Disease and Discovery. A History of the Johns Hopkins School of Hygiene and Public Health 1916–1939* (Baltimore, 1987).

Ferguson, James: "Anthropology and Its Evil Twin: 'Development' and the Constitution of a Discipline", in: Edelman, Marc/Haugerud, Angelique (eds.): *The Anthropology of Development and Globalization. From Classical Political Economy to Contemporary Neoliberalism* (Oxford, 2005), 140–53.

Ferguson, James: *The Anti-Politics Machine. "Development", Depoliticization, and Bureaucratic Power in Lesotho* (Minneapolis, 1994).

Ferguson, Niall et al. (eds.): *The Shock of the Global. The 1970s in Perspective* (Cambridge/MA, 2010).

Finegold, Kenneth/Skocpol, Theda: *State and Party in America's New Deal* (Madison, 1995).

Fisher, Ali: "Double Vision, Double Analysis. The role of interpretation, negotiation and compromise in the state-private network and British-American Studies", in: Laville, Helen/Wilford, Hugh (eds.): *The US Government, Citizen Groups and the Cold War* (London, 2006).

Fisher, Donald: *Fundamental Development of the Social Sciences. Rockefeller Philanthropy and the United States Social Science Research Council* (Ann Arbor, 1993).

Fisher, Donald: "Rockefeller Philanthropy and the Rise of Social Anthropology", *Anthropology Today* 2 (1986) 1, 5–8.

Fisher, Donald: "The Role of Philanthropic Foundations in the Reproduction and Production of Hegemony: Rockefeller Foundations and the Social Sciences", *Sociology* 17 (1983) 2, 207–232.

Fisher, H.H.: *The Famine in Soviet Russia, 1919–1923. The Operations of the American Relief Administration* (New York, 1927).

Fleck, Christian: *Transatlantische Bereicherungen. Zur Erfindung der empirischen Sozialforschung* (Frankfurt a.M., 2007).

Fleck, Ludwik: *Entstehung und Entwicklung einer wissenschaftlichen Tatsache. Einführung in die Lehre vom Denkstil und Denkkollektiv* (Frankfurt a.M., 1980 [1935]); Reprinted in: Idem: *Denkstile und Tatsachen. Gesammelte Schriften und Zeugnisse* (Frankfurt a.M., 2011), 260–309.

Flint, John E.: "Frederick Lugard. The Making of an Autocrat (1858–1943)", in: Gann, Lewis/Duignan, Peter (eds.): *African Proconsuls. European Governors in Africa* (New York, 1978), 290–312.

Ford Foundation: *Annual Reports* (New York, 1952–1970).

Ford Foundation, Office of the Representative in India: *The Ford Foundation and Ford Supported Activities in India* (New Delhi, 1955).

Ford Foundation: *Report of the Study of the Ford Foundation on Policy and Program* (New York, 1949).

Ford Foundation: *The Ford Foundation and Foundation-Supported Activities in India, Summary of Grants from 1951 to January 1 1968* (New Delhi, 1968).

Ford Foundation: *The Ford Foundation, 1952–2002. Celebrating 50 Years of Partnership* (New Delhi, 2002).

Forman, Paul: "Behind Quantum Electronics. National Security as Basis for Physical Research in the United States, 1940–1960", *Historical Studies in the Physical and Biological Sciences* 18 (1987) 1, 149–229.

Forster, Peter: *The Esperanto Movement* (The Hague, 1982).

Fournier, Marcel: "Marcel Mauss, l'ethnologie et la politique: le don", *Anthropologie et sociétés* 19 (1995) 1–2, 57–69.

Fournier, Marcel: *Marcel Mauss* (Paris, 1994).

Frankel, Francine R: *India's Political Economy, 1947–1977. The Gradual Revolution* (Princeton, 1978).

Frey, Marc: "Experten, Stiftungen und Politik: Zur Genese des globalen Diskurses über Bevölkerung seit 1945", in: *Zeithistorische Forschungen/Studies in Contemporary History*, Online-Ausgabe 4 (2007) 1+2, URL: http://www.zeithistorische-forschungen.de/ 16126041-Frey-2-2007 [20. 12. 2011].

Frey, Marc: "Neo-Malthusianism and Development. Shifting Interpretations of a Contested Paradigm", *Journal of Global History* 6 (2011) 1, 75–97.

Frey, Marc (ed.): *Asian Experiences of Development in the 20th Century. Comparativ. Zeitschrift für Globalgeschichte und Vergleichende Gesellschaftsforschung* 4 (2009).

Friedman, Lawrence J./McGarvie, Mark D. (eds.): *Charity, Philanthropy, and Civility in American History* (Cambridge, 2002).

Fuchs, Eckhardt: "Wissenschaftsinternationalismus in Kriegs- und Krisenzeiten. Zur Rolle der USA bei der Reorganisation der internationalen scientific community 1914–1925", in: Jessen, Ralph/Vogel, Jakob (Hg.): *Wissenschaft und Nation in der europäischen Geschichte* (Frankfurt a.M., 2002), 263–284.

Gaddis, John Lewis: *The Cold War. A New History* (New York, 2006).

Gaillard, Gérald: *Cadres institutionnels et activités de l'éthnologie française entre 1950 et 1970* (Lille, 2003).

Gayon, Jean: "Génétique de la pigmentation de l'œil de la drosophile. la contribution spécifique de Boris Ephrussi", in: Debru, Claude/Gayon, Jean/Picard, Jean-François (eds.): *Les sciences biologiques et médicales en France 1920–1950* (Paris, 1994).

Geiger, Roger L.: *To Advance Knowledge. The Growth of American Research Universities, 1900–1940* (New Brunswick/London, 2004).

Geiger, Roger L.: *Research and Relevant Knowledge. American Research Universities since World War II* (New York, 1993).

Geithner, Peter F.: "The Ford Foundation in Southeast Asia. Continuity and Change", in: Murphy, Ann Marie/Welsh, Bridget (eds.): *Legacy of Engagement in Southeast Asia* (Singapore, 2008), 181–94.

Gemelli, Guiliana: "Western Alliance and Scientific Diplomacy in the Early 1960s. The Rise and Failure of the Project to Create a European M.I.T.", in: Moore, R. Laurence/Vaudagna, Maurizio (eds.): *The American Century in Europe* (Ithaca, 2003).

Gemelli, Giuliana: "Permanent Connections. Paul Lazarsfeld, American Foundations and Europe, 1930s–1960s", in: Idem (ed.): *The "Unacceptables". American Foundations and Refugee Scholars Between the Two Wars and After* (Brussels, 2000), 241–271.

Gemelli, Giuliana (ed.): *The "Unacceptables". American Foundations and Refugee Scholars Between the Two Wars and After* (Brussels, 2000).

Gemelli, Giuliana (ed.): *The Ford Foundation and Europe (1950s–1970s). Cross-fertilization of Learning in Social Science and Management* (Brussels, 1998).

Gemelli, Giuliana/MacLeod, Roy (eds.): *American Foundations in Europe. Grant-Giving Policies, Cultural Diplomacy, and Trans-Atlantic Relations, 1920–1980* (Brussels, 2003).

Gettleman, Marvin E./Mermelstein, David (eds.): *The Great Society Reader. The Failure of American Liberalism* (New York, 1967).

Giannuli, Dimitra: "'Repeated Disappointment'. The Rockefeller Foundation and the Reform of the Greek Public Health System, 1929–1940", *Bulletin of the History of Medicine* 72 (1998) 1, 47–72.

Gieryn, Thomas: *Cultural Boundaries of Science. Credibility on the Line* (Chicago, 1999).

Gilboa, Eytan: "Searching for a Theory of Public Diplomacy", *The Annals of the American Academy of Political and Social Science* 616 (2008) 1, 55–77.

Gillingham, John: *Coal, Steel, and the Rebirth of Europe, 1945–1955* (Cambridge, 1991).

Gilman, Nils: *Mandarins of the Future. Modernization Theory in Cold War America* (Baltimore, 2003).

Ginio, Ruth: *French Colonialism Unmasked. The Vichy Years in French West Africa* (Lincoln, 2006).

Gordon, Leonard A.: "Wealth Equals Wisdom? The Rockefeller and Ford Foundations in India", *Annals of the American Academy of Political and Social Science* 554 (1997), 104–16.

Gormley, W. Paul: "The Hague Academy of International Law. A Study in Intercultural Education and Communication", *Journal of Legal Education* 13 (1961) 4, 512–516.

Gorter, C.J.: "News from Abroad", *Physics Today* 1 (1948) 1, 9.

Government of India, Ministry of Community Development: *A Guide to Community Development* (New Delhi, 1957).

Government of India, Ministry of Food and Agriculture: *Report on India's Food Crisis and Steps to Meet it* (New Delhi, 1959).

Government of India, Planning Commission: *The New India. Progress through Democracy* (New York, 1958).

Government of India, Planning Commission: *The Third Five Year Plan* (New Delhi, 1961).

Greiner, Bernd et al. (Hg.): *Studien zum Kalten Krieg*, 5 Bde.: *Heiße Kriege im Kalten Krieg, Krisen im Kalten Krieg, Angst im Kalten Krieg, Ökonomie im Kalten Krieg, Macht und Geist im Kalten Krieg* (Hamburg, 2006–2011).

Grémion, Pierre: *Intelligence de l'anticommunisme. Le Congrès pour la liberté de la culture à Paris 1950–1975* (Paris, 1995).

Griffith, Robert: *The Politics of Fear. Joseph R. McCarthy and the Senate* (Amherst, 1987).

Guha, Ranajit: *Dominance without Hegemony. History and Power in Colonial India* (Cambridge/MA, 1997).

Guha, Ranajit/Spivak, Gayatri Chakravorty (eds.): *Selected Subaltern Studies* (New York-Oxford, 1988).

Guilhot, Nicolas (ed.): *The Invention of International Relations Theory. Realism, the Rockefeller Foundation, and the 1954 Conference on Theory* (New York, 2011).

Gupta, Akhil: *Postcolonial Developments. Agriculture in the Making of Modern India* (Durham/NC, 1998).

Gusterson, Hugh: *People of the Bomb. Portraits of America's Nuclear Complex* (Minneapolis, 2004).

Haas, Peter: "Epistemic Communities and International Policy Coordination", *International Organization* 46 (1992) 1, 1–35.

Hacke, Jens: "Moritz Julius Bonn – ein vergessener Verteidiger der Vernunft. Zum Liberalismus in der Krise der Zwischenkriegszeit", *Mittelweg 36* 19 (2010) 6, 26–59.

Hailey, Malcolm: "The Role of Anthropology in Colonial Development", *Man* 44 (1944) 5, 10–15.

Hammack, David C./Heydemann, Steven (eds.): *Globalization, Philanthropy, and Civil Society. Projecting Institutional Logics Abroad* (Bloomington/IN, 2009).

Harkavy, Oscar: *Curbing Population Growth. An Insider's Perspective on the Population Movement* (New York, 1995).

Hayford, Charles W.: *To the People. James Yen and Village China* (New York, 1990).

Herbert, Ulrich: "Europe in High Modernity. Reflections on a Theory of the 20th Century", *Journal of Modern European History* 5 (2007) 3, 5–20.

Herman, Ellen: "The Career of Cold War Psychology", *Radical History Review* no. 63 (1995), 52–85.

Herman, Ellen: *The Romance of American Psychology. Political Culture in the Age of Experts* (Berkeley, 1995).

Herren, Madeleine: *Internationale Organisationen seit 1865. Eine Globalgeschichte der internationalen Ordnung* (Darmstadt, 2009).

Herren, Madeleine: *Hintertüren zur Macht. Internationalismus und modernisierungsorientierte Außenpolitik in Belgien, der Schweiz und den USA, 1865–1914* (München, 2000).

Herren, Madeleine (ed.): *Networks in Times of Transition. Toward a Transcultural History of International Organisations* (forthcoming).

Hersh, Burton: *The Old Boys. The American Elite and the Origins of the CIA* (New York 1992).

Hess, Gary R: "Waging the Cold War in the Third World. The Foundations and the Challenges of Development", in: Friedman, Lawrence J./McGarvie, Mark D. (eds.): *Charity, Philanthropy, and Civility in American History* (New York, 2003), 319–340.

Hewa, Soma/Stapleton, Darwin H. (eds.): *Globalization, Philanthropy and Civil Society. Toward a New Political Culture in the Twenty-First Century* (New York, 2005; new ed. 2010).

Heyck, Hunter: "Die Moderne in der amerikanischen Sozialwissenschaft", in: Greiner, Bernd/Müller, Tim B./Weber, Claudia (Hg.): *Macht und Geist im Kalten Krieg* (Hamburg, 2011), 159–179.

Heyck, Hunter: "Patrons of the Revolution. Ideals and Institutions in Postwar Behavioral Science", *Isis* 97 (2006) 3, 420–446.

Heyck, Hunter/Kaiser, David (eds.): "New Perspectives on Science in the Cold War", *Isis* 101 (2010) S1, 362–411.

Hitchcock, William I.: "The Marshall Plan and the Creation of the West", in: Leffler, Melvyn P./Westad, Odd Arne (eds.): *The Cambridge History of the Cold War*, Vol. 1: *Origins* (New York, 2010), 154–174.

Hochgeschwender, Michael: "*The Noblest Philosophy and Its Most Efficient Use*. Zur Geschichte des *social engineering* in den USA, 1910–1965", in: Etzemüller, Thomas (Hg.): *Die Ordnung der Moderne. Social Engineering im 20. Jahrhundert* (Bielefeld, 2009), 171–98.

Hodge, Joseph M.: "British Colonial Expertise, Postcolonial Careering and the Early History of International Development", *Journal of Modern European History* 8 (2010) 1, 24–46.

Hoffman, Paul: "Most Courageous Comeback in History", *Life*, 5 February 1951, 98–114.

Hoffman, Paul: *Peace Can Be Won* (Garden City, 1951).

Hogan, Michael J.: *A Cross of Iron. Harry S. Truman and the Origins of the National Security State, 1945–1954* (New York, 1998).

Holl, Thomas M/Haynes, W. Warren/Baumgartel, Howard: *Institution Building in India. A Study of International Collaboration in Management Education* (Boston, 1973).

Hollinger, David A.: *Science, Jews, and Secular Culture. Studies in Mid-Twentieth-Century American Intellectual History* (Princeton, 1996).

Hull, Terence H.: "Conflict and Collaboration in Public Health. The Rockefeller Foundation and the Dutch Colonial Government in Indonesia", in: Lewis, Milton J./MacPherson, Kerrie L. (eds.): *Public Health in Asia and the Pacific. Historical and Comparative Perspectives* (Abingdon/Oxon-New York, 2008), 139–152.

Hyam, Ronald: *Britain's Declining Empire. The Road to Decolonisation, 1918–1968* (Cambridge, 2006).

Hyam, Ronald: "Bureaucracy and 'Trusteeship' in Colonial Empire", in: Brown, Judith M./ Louis, Roger W. (eds.): *The Oxford History of the British Empire* (Oxford, 1999), 255–279.

Ikenberry, G. John/Kupchan, Charles: "Socialization and Hegemonic Power", *International Organization* 44 (1990) 3, 283–315.

Iriye, Akira: "The Role of International Organisations" & "Internationalism", in: Mazlish, Bruce/Iriye, Akira (eds.): *The Global History Reader* (New York-Abingdon/Oxon, 2005), 182–90 & 202–8.

Iriye, Akira: "Internationalizing International History", in: Bender, Thomas (ed.): *Rethinking American History in a Global Age* (Berkeley-Los Angeles, 2002), 47–62.

Iriye, Akira: *Global Community. The Role of International Organizations in the Making of the Contemporary World* (Berkeley, 2002).

Iriye, Akira/Saunier, Pierre-Yves (eds.): *The Palgrave Dictionary of Transnational History. From the mid-19th Century to the Present Day* (New York, 2009).

Isaac, Joel: "The Human Sciences in Cold War America", *Historical Journal* 50 (2007) 3, 725–746.

Isaacs, Harold: *No Peace for Asia* (New York, 1947).

Jacoby, Russell: *Dialectics of Defeat. Contours of Western Marxism* (Cambridge, 1981).

Jay, Martin: *Marxism and Totality. The Adventures of a Concept from Lukács to Habermas* (Berkeley, 1984).

Jeffries, Charles (ed.): *A Review of Colonial Research, 1940–1960* (London, 1964).

Jen, C.K.: *Recollections of a Chinese Physicist* (Los Alamos, 1991).

Joll, James: *Antonio Gramsci* (New York, 1977).

Jordan, Barbara C./Rostow, Elspeth D. (eds.): *The Great Society. A Twenty Year Critique* (Austin, 1986).

Jordan, John M.: *Machine-Age Ideology. Social Engineering and American Liberalism, 1911–1939* (Chapel Hill, 1994).

Judt, Tony: *Postwar. A History of Europe since 1945* (New York, 2005).

Jureit, Ulrike: "Wissenschaft und Politik. Der lange Weg zu einer Wissenschaftsgeschichte der 'Ostforschung'", *Neue Politische Literatur* 55 (2010) 1, 71–88.

Kaiser, Wolfram/Leucht, Brigitte/Gehler, Michael (eds.): *Transnational Networks and Regional Integration. Governing Europe 1945–83* (Basingstoke, 2010).

Kaplan, Marshall/Cuciti, Peggy L. (eds.): *The Great Society and its Legacy. Twenty Years of U.S. Social Policy* (Durham, 1986).

Karpin, Michael: *The Bomb in the Basement. How Israel Went Nuclear and What that Means for the World* (New York, 2006).

Kay, Lily: *The Molecular Vision of Life. Caltech, the Rockefeller Foundation and the Rise of Molecular Biology* (Oxford, 1993).

Keith, Arthur: "Presidential Address. How Can the Institute Best Serve the Needs of Anthropology?", *Journal of the Royal Anthropological Institute of Great Britain and Ireland* 47 (1917), 12–30.

Kennedy, James C.: *Nieuw Babylon in Aanbouw. Nederland in de Jaren Zestig* (Amsterdam, 1995).

Kevles, Daniel J.: *The Physicists. The History of a Scientific Community in Modern America* (Cambridge, 1995).

Khurana, Rakesh/Kimura, Kenneth/Fourcade, Marion: "How Foundations Think. The Ford Foundation as a Dominating Institution in the Field of American Business", *Harvard Business School Working Paper* (Boston, 2011).

Kirk, Jason A: *India and the World Bank. The Politics of Aid and Influence* (London, 2010).

Kirkendall, Richard Stewart: *Social Scientists and Farm Politics* (Columbia, 1966).

Kistiakowsky, George: "Science and Foreign Affairs", *Bulletin of the Atomic Scientists* 16 (1960) 4, 115–117.

Knöbl, Wolfgang: *Spielräume der Modernisierung. Das Ende der Eindeutigkeit* (Weilerswist, 2001).

Kohler, Robert: "A policy for the Advancement of Science. The Rockefeller Foundation, 1924–1929", *Minerva* 16 (1978) 4, 480–515.

Korey, William: *Taking on the World's Repressive Regimes. The Ford Foundation's International Human Rights Policies and Practices* (New York, 2007).

Kothair, Rajni: "The Tasks Within", *Seminar*, no. 112 (1968), 14–19.

Kott, Sandrine: "Par-delà la guerre froide. Les organisations internationales et les circulations Est-Ouest (1947–1973)", *Vingtième Siècle* 109 (2011) 1, 143–154.

Kott, Sandrine: "Une 'communauté épistémique' du social? Experts de l'OIT et internationalisation des politiques sociales dans l'entre-deux-guerres", *Genèses* 71 (2008) 1, 26–46.

Krige, John: "Die Führungsrolle der USA und die transnationale Koproduktion von Wissen", in: Greiner, Bernd/Müller, Tim B./Weber, Claudia (Hg.): *Macht und Geist im Kalten Krieg* (Hamburg, 2011), 68–86.

Krige, John: "Building the Arsenal of Knowledge", *Centaurus* 52 (2010), 280–96.

Krige, John: "Techno-Utopian Dreams, Techno-Political Realities", in: Gordin, Michael/Tilley, Helen/Prakash, Gyan (eds.): *Utopia/Dystopia. Conditions of Historical Possibility* (Princeton, 2010), 151–175.

Krige, John: *American Hegemony and the Postwar Reconstruction of Science in Europe* (Cambridge/MA-London, 2006).

Krige, John: "Atoms for Peace, Scientific Intelligence and Scientific Internationalism", in: Idem/Barth, Kai-Henrik (eds.): *Global Power Knowledge. Science, Technology and International Affairs* (Chicago, 2006), 161–181.

Krige, John: "The Ford Foundation, European Physics, and the Cold War", *Historical Studies in the Physical and Biological Sciences* 29 (1999) 2, 333–361.

Krohn, Claus-Dieter/Schildt, Axel (Hg.): *Zwischen den Stühlen? Remigranten und Remigration in der deutschen Medienöffentlichkeit der Nachkriegszeit* (Göttingen, 2002).

Kuisel, Richard: *Seducing the French. The dilemma of Americanization* (Berkeley, 1993).

Kuklick, Henrika: "Personal Equations: Reflections on the History of Fieldwork, with Special Reference to Sociocultural Anthropology", *Isis* 102 (2011) 1, 1–33.

Kuklick, Henrika: *The Savage within. The Social History of British Anthropology, 1885–1945* (Cambridge, 1992).

Kumar, Girja: "Servitude of the Mind", *Seminar* no. 112 (1968), 20–24.

Kuper, Adam: "Alternative histories of British social anthropology", *Social Anthropology* 13 (2005) 1, 47–64.

L'Algérie en 1928. Discours prononcés par M. Pierre Bordes, Gouverneur Général de l'Algérie aux Délégations Financières Algériennes, Janvier-Mai 1928 (Algier, 1928).

L'Estoile, Benoît de: "Internationalization and 'scientific nationalism'. The International Institute of African Languages and Cultures between the wars", in: Tilley, Hellen/ Gordon, Robert J. (eds.): *Ordering Africa. Anthropology, European Imperialism and the Politics of Knowledge* (Manchester, 2007), 95–116.

L'Estoile, Benoît de: "'Africanisme' & 'Africansim'. Esquisse d'une comparaison franco-britannique", in: Piriou, Anne/Sibeud, Emmanuelle (eds.): *L'Africanisme en questions* (Paris, 1997), 19–42.

L'Estoile, Benoît de: "The 'natural preserve of anthropologists'. Social Anthropology, Scientific planning and Development", *Social Science Information* 36 (1997) 2, 343–376.

L'Estoile, Benoît de/Neiburg, Federico/Siagaud, Lygia: "Savoirs Anthropologiques, Administration des Populations et Construction de l'État", *Revue de Synthèse*, no. 3–4 (2000), 233–263.

Labouret, Henri: "Ethnologie coloniale. Un programme de recherches", *Outre-Mer* 4 (1932) 48–89.

Lagemann, Ellen Condliffe: *The Politics of Knowledge. The Carnegie Corporation, Philanthropy, and Public Policy* (Chicago, 1992).

Laqua, Daniel: "Transnational Intellectual Cooperation, the League of Nations, and the Problem of Order", *Journal of Global History* 6 (2011) 2, 223–47.

Latham, Michael E.: *The Right Kind of Revolution. Modernization, Development, and U.S. Foreign Policy From the Cold War to the Present* (Ithaca, 2011).

Latham, Michael E.: *Modernization as Ideology. American Social Science and "Nation Building" in the Kennedy Era* (Chapel Hill, 2000).

Lawrence, Christopher: *Rockefeller Money, the Laboratory and Medicine in Edinburgh, 1919–1930. New Science in an Old Country* (Rochester, 2005).

Lawrence, Jon: "The transformation of British Public Politics after the First World War", *Past and Present* 190 (2006) 1, 185–216.

League of Nations (ed.): *Handbook of International Organisations* (Geneva, 1938).

Leffler, Melvyn P./Westad, Odd Arne (eds.): *The Cambridge History of the Cold War* (Cambridge, 2010).

Leffler, Melvyn P./Westad, Odd Arne (eds.): *The Cambridge History of the Cold War, Vol. 1: Origins* (Cambridge, 2010).

Leslie, Stuart W./Kargon Robert: "Exporting MIT: Science, Technology, and Nation-Building in India and Iran", *Osiris* 21 (2006) 1, 110–130.

Leucht, Brigitte: "Transatlantic Policy Networks in the Creation of the first European Anti-Trust Law", in: Kaiser, Wolfram/Leucht, Brigitte/Rasmussen, Morten (eds.): *The History of the European Union. Origins of a Trans- and Supranational Polity 1950–72* (London, 2009).

Lévy-Bruhl, Lucien: "Institut d'Ethnologie", *Annales de l'Université de Paris* 1931, 346–351.

Lévy-Bruhl, Lucien: "Rapport d'activité de l'Institut d'éthnologie pour 1929", *Annales de l'université de Paris* 1929, 417–422.

Lévy-Bruhl, Lucien: "L'Institut d'éthnologie pendant l'année scolaire 1928–29", *Annales de l'Université de Paris* 1929, 417–422.

Lévy-Bruhl, Lucien: "L'Institut d'éthnologie pendant l'année scolaire 1925–26", *Annales de l'Université de Paris* 1927, 90–94.

Lévy-Bruhl, Lucien: "L'Institut d'ethnologie de l'université de Paris", *Revue d'ethnographie et de traditions populaires*, no. 23–24 (1925), 233–236.

Levy, Roger: "Indo-China in 1931–1932", *Pacific Affairs* 5 (1932) 3, 205–217.

Lewis, John Wilson/Xue, Litai: *China Builds the Bomb* (Stanford, 1988).

Lilienthal, David: "Are we losing India?", *Colliers*, 23 June 1951.

Lipphardt, Veronika/Patel, Kiran Klaus: "Neuverzauberung im Gestus der Wissenschaftlichkeit. Wissenspraktiken im 20. Jahrhundert am Beispiel menschlicher Diversität", *Geschichte und Gesellschaft* 34 (2008) 4, 425–454.

Litsios, Socrates: "Malaria Control, the Cold War and the Postwar Reorganization of International Assistance", *Medical Anthropology* 17 (1997) 3, 255–78.

Lock, William: *Origins and Evolution of the Collaboration Between CERN and the People's Republic of China, 1971–1980* (Geneva, 1981).

Louis, William R.: "American Anti-Colonialism, Suez, and the Special Relationship", in: Idem, *Ends of British Imperialism. The Scramble for Empire, Suez and Decolonization* (London-New York, 2006), 589–608.

Louis, William R./Robinson, Ronald: "The Imperialism of Decolonization [1994]", in: Louis, William R.: *Ends of British Imperialism. The Scramble for Empire Suez and Decolonization, Collected Essays* (London, 2006), 451–502.

Lowen, Rebecca S.: "Zur Verflechtung von Politik und Universitäten in Amerika", in: Greiner, Bernd/Müller, Tim B./Weber, Claudia (Hg.): *Macht und Geist im Kalten Krieg* (Hamburg, 2011), 31–49.

Lowen, Rebecca S.: *Creating the Cold War University. The Transformation of Stanford* (Berkeley, 1997).

Lucas, Scott: "Beyond Freedom, Beyond Control. Approaches to Culture and the State-Private Network in the Cold War", in: Scott-Smith, Giles/Krabbendam, Hans (eds.): *The Cultural Cold War in Western Europe, 1945–1960* (London, 2003), 53–72.

Lucas, Scott: "Revealing the Parameters of Opinion: An Interview with Frances Stonor Saunders", in: Scott-Smith, Giles/Krabbendam, Hans (eds.): *The Cultural Cold War in Western Europe, 1945–1960* (London, 2003), 15–40.

Ludlow, N. Piers (ed.): *European Integration and the Cold War. Ostpolitik – Westpolitik, 1965–1973* (London, 2007).

Lugard, Frederik D.: "The International Institute of African Languages and Cultures", *Africa* 1 (1928) 1, 1–12.

Lugard, Frederik D.: *The Dual Mandate in Tropical Africa* (London, 1922).

Lunden, Rolf/Asard, Erik: *Networks of Americanization. Aspect of the American Influence in Sweden* (Stockholm, 1992).

Lyon, Jean: *Just Half a World Away. My Search for the New India* (New York, 1954).

MacCurdy, George G.: "Extent of Instruction in Anthropology in Europe and the United States", *Science* 10 (1899), 910–917.

Macdonald, Dwight: *The Ford Foundation. The Man and the Millions* (New York, 1956).

Mader, Julius: *Who's Who in CIA* (Berlin, 1968).

Maier, Charles S.: *Among Empires. American Ascendancy and its Predecessors* (Cambridge/MA, 2006).

Maier, Charles S.: "Consigning the Twentieth Century to History. Alternative Narratives for the Modern Era", *American Historical Review* 105 (2000) 3, 807–31.

Maier, Charles S.: *Recasting Bourgeois Europe. Stabilization in France, Germany, and Italy in the Decade after World War I* (Princeton, 1988).

Maigron, Gilles: "Résistance et collaboration dans l'université de Paris sous l'occupation", in: Gueslin, André (ed.): *Les Facs sous Vichy* (Clermont-Ferrand, 1994), 133–142.

Mair, Lucy S.: "Applied Anthropology and Development Policies", *British Journal of Sociology* 7 (1956) 2, 120–133.

Mair, Lucy S.: "Review", *Man* 37 (1937), 196.

Mair, Lucy S.: "Chieftainship in Modern Africa", *Africa* 6 (1936) 3, 305–316.

Mair, Lucy S.: "Colonial Administration as a Science", *Journal of the Royal African Society* 32 (1933) 1, 366–371.

Malinowski, Bronislaw: "The Pan-African Problem of Culture Contact", *American Journal of Sociology* 48 (1943) 6, 650.

Malinowski, Bronislaw: "The Present State of Studies in Culture Contact: Some Comments on an American Approach", *Africa* 12 (1939) 1, 27–48.

Malinowski, Bronislaw: *Methods of Study of Culture Contact in Africa* (Oxford, 1938).

Malinowski, Bronislaw: "The Rationalization of Anthropology and Administration", *Africa* 3 (1930) 4, 405–430.

Malinowski, Bronislaw: "Ethnologie Pratique. Résumé de son Article: Practical Anthropology", *Africa* 2 (1929) 2, 186–190.

Malinowski, Bronislaw: "Practical Anthropology", *Africa* 2 (1929) 1, 22–38.

Malinowski, Bronislaw: "Ethnology and the Study of Society", *Economica* 6 (1922), 208–219.

Malinowski, Bronislaw: "The Primitive Economics of the Trobriand Islanders", *The Economic Journal* 31 (1921) 1, 1–16.

Manela, Erez: "A Pox on Your Narrative. Writing Disease Control into Cold War History", *Diplomatic History* 34 (2010) 2, 299–323.

Margairaz, Michel: *Le Front populaire* (Paris, 2009).

Marks, Shula: "Doctors and the State. George Gale, Social Medicine and the State in South Africa", in: Dubow, Saul (ed.): *Science and Society in South Africa* (Manchester, 2000), 188–211.

Marrin, Albert: *Nicholas Murray Butler. An Intellectual Portrait* (Boston, 1976).

Masseys-Bertonèche, Carole: *Philanthropie et grandes universités privées américaines. Pouvoir et réseaux d'influences* (Bordeaux, 2006).

Mauss, Marcel: "L'ethnographie en France et à l'étranger", *Revue de Paris* 20 (1913), 537–560 & 815–837.

Mazower, Mark: *No Enchanted Palace. The End of Empire and the Ideological Origins of the United Nations* (Princeton-Oxford, 2009).

McCarthy, Kathleen D.: "From Government to Grass-Roots Reform: The Ford Foundation's Population Programmes in South Asia, 1959–1981", *Voluntas* 6 (1995) 3, 292–316.

McCaughey, Robert A.: *International Studies and Academic Enterprise. A Chapter in the Enclosure of American Learning* (New York, 1984).

McMahon, Robert J.: "The Challenge of the Third World", in: Hahn, Peter L./Heiss, Mary A. (eds.): *Empire and Revolution. The United States and the Third World since 1945* (Columbus, 2001).

McMahon, Robert J.: "Food as a Diplomatic Weapon. The Indian Wheat Loan of 1951", *Pacific Historical Review* 56 (1987) 3, 349–377.

Melland, F. H./Lugard, Frederik D./Harlech, Lord et al.: "Lord Hailey's African Survey", *Journal of the Royal African Society* 38 (1939) 1, 1–70.

Merrill, Dennis: *Bread and the Ballot. The United States and India's Economic Development, 1947–1963* (Chapel Hill/NC, 1990).

Metzler, Gabriele: *Konzeptionen politischen Handelns von Adenauer bis Brandt. Politische Planung in der pluralistischen Gesellschaft* (Paderborn, 2005).

Michelet, Charles: "L'empire français et la constitution impériale", *Outre-Mer* 4 (1932) 1, 30–48.

Mills, David: "Professionalizing or Popularizing Anthropology? A Brief History of Anthropology's Scholarly Associations in the UK", *Anthropology Today* 19 (2003) 1, 8–13.

Mills, David: "British Anthropology at the End of Empire. The Rise and Fall of the Social Science Research Council, 1944–1962", *Revue d'histoire des sciences humaines* 6 (2002) 1, 161–88.

Minkler, Meredith: "Consultants or Colleagues. The Role of US Population Advisors in India", *Population and Development Review* 3 (1977) 4, 403–419.

Missiroli, Antonio: *Die Deutsche Hochschule für Politik* (Sankt Augustin, 1988).

Mitchell, P.E.: "The Anthropologist and the Practical Man", *Africa* 3 (1930) 2, 217–223.

Moebius, Stephan: "Intellektuelle Kritik und Soziologie. Die politischen Schriften und Aktivitäten von Marcel Mauss", in: Moebius, Stephan/Schäfer, Gerhard (Hg.): *Soziologie als Gesellschaftskritik. Festschrift für Lothar Peter* (Hamburg, 2006), 142–160.

Moffett, Samuel E.: *The Americanization of Canada* (Toronto, 1972).

Mommsen, Wolfgang J.: *The Age of Bureaucracy. Perspectives on the Political Sociology of Max Weber* (Oxford, 1974).

Morgan, Arthur E.: *The Small Community, Foundation of Democratic Life* (New York, 1942).

Muehl, John Frederick: *Interview with India* (New York, 1950).

Müller, Tim B.: "Reform und Rationalität. Der Erwartungshorizont der Moderne und die Verwissenschaftlichung des Politischen im Kalten Krieg. Neuere Beiträge zur Ideen- und Wissenschaftsgeschichte", *Mittelweg 36* 20 (2011) 3, 65–80.

Müller, Tim B.: *Krieger und Gelehrte. Herbert Marcuse und die Denksysteme im Kalten Krieg* (Hamburg, 2010).

Nehru, Jawaharlal: *Selected Works of Jawaharlal Nehru, second series*, vol. 40 (New Delhi, 2009).

Nehru, Jawaharlal: *Selected Works of Jawaharlal Nehru, second series*, vol. 30 (New Delhi, 2002).

Nehru, Jawaharlal: *Selected Works of Jawaharlal Nehru, second series*, vol. 26 (New Delhi, 2000).

Nehru, Jawaharlal: *Selected Works of Jawaharlal Nehru, second series*, vol. 25 (New Delhi, 1999).

Nehru, Jawaharlal: *Selected Works of Jawaharlal Nehru, second series*, vol. 16, pt 1 (New Delhi, 1994).

Nehru, Jawaharlal: *Letters to Chief Ministers, 1947–1964, vol. 4* (New Delhi, 1988).

Nemchenok, Victor V.: "'That So Fair a Thing Should Be So Frail'. The Ford Foundation and the Failure of Rural Development in Iran, 1953–1964", *Middle East Journal* 63 (2009) 2, 261–84.

Newsom, David: *The Imperial Mantle. The United States, Decolonization, and the Third World* (Bloomington, 2001).

Ninkovich, Frank: *The Diplomacy of Ideas. U.S. Foreign Policy and Cultural Relations, 1938–1950* (Cambridge, 1981).

Ory, Pascal: *La belle illusion. Culture et politique sous le signe du Front Populaire* (Paris, 1994).

Ory, Pascal: "L'américanisation, modernisme et culture de masse", in: Compagnon, Antoine/Seebacher, Jacques (eds.): *L'esprit de l'Europe*, tome 3 (Paris, 1993), 252–261.

Osgood, Kenneth: *Total Cold War. Eisenhower's Secret Propaganda Battle at Home and Abroad* (Lawrence, 2006).

Page, Benjamin B./Valone, David A. (eds.): *Philanthropic Foundations and the Globalization of Scientific Medicine and Public Health* (Lanham, 2007).

Paligot, Carole R.: "L'émergence de l'antisemitisme scientifique chez les anthropologues français", *Archives Juives* 43 (2010) 1, 66–76.

Palmer, Steven: *Launching Global Health. The Caribbean Odyssey of the Rockefeller Foundation* (Ann Arbor, 2010).

Pande, V.P.: *Village Community Projects in India* (New York, 1967).

Park, Richard Leonard: "Indian Democracy and the General Election", *Pacific Affairs* 25 (1952) 2, 130–139.

Parmar, Inderjeet: "Challenging elite anti-Americanism in the Cold War. American foundations, Kissinger's Harvard Seminar and the Salzburg Seminar in American studies", in: Parmar, Inderjeet/Cox, Michael (eds.): *Soft Power and US Foreign Policy. Theoretical, Historical and Contemporary Perspectives* (London, 2010).

Parmar, Inderjeet: "Engineering Consent. The Carnegie Endowment for International Peace and the Mobilization of American Public Opinion, 1939–1945", *Review of International Studies* 26 (2000) 1, 35–48.

Parmar, Inderjeet/Cox, Michael (eds.): *Soft Power and US Foreign Policy. Theoretical, Historical, and Contemporary Perspectives* (Abingdon, 2010).

Pells, Richard: *Not Like US. How Europeans Have Loved, Hated and Transformed American Culture since World War II* (New York, 1997).

Perham, Margery: *Native Administration in Nigeria* (Oxford, 1937).

Perkins, John H.: *Geopolitics and the Green Revolution. Wheat, Genes, and the Cold War* (New York, 1997).

Pestre, Dominique: "Le nouvel univers des sciences et des techniques. Une proposition générale", in: Idem/Dahan, Amy (eds.): *Les sciences pour la guerre, 1940–1960* (Paris, 2004), 11–47.

Pestre, Dominique: "Science, Political Power and the State", in: Idem/Krige, John (eds.): *Science in the Twentieth Century* (Amsterdam, 1997), 61–76.

Pestre, Dominique: *Physique et physiciens en France, 1918–1940* (Paris, 1984).

Picard, Jean-François: *La fondation Rockefeller et la recherche médicale* (Paris, 1999).

Picard, Jean-Francois: *La République des savants. La recherche francaise et le CNRS* (Paris, 1990).

Picard, Jean-François/Pradoura, Elisabeth: "La longue marche vers le CNRS (1901–1945)", in: *Cahiers pour l'histoire du CNRS*, Vol. 1. (Paris, 1988).

Pinault, Michel: *La science au Parlement. Les débuts d'une politique des recherches scientifiques en France* (Paris, 2006).

Plant, Arnold: "An African Survey", *Economica* 6 (1939), 205–212.

Plé, Bernhard: "Lucien Lévy-Bruhl", in: *Biographisch-Bibliographisches Kirchenlexikon*, Bd. 4 (Herzberg, 1992), Sp. 1580–1589.

Plé, Bernhard: *Wissenschaft und säkulare Mission. "Amerikanische Sozialwissenschaft" im politischen Sendungsbewußtsein der USA und im geistigen Aufbau der Bundesrepublik Deutschland* (Stuttgart, 1990).

Porter, Theodore M./Ross, Dorothy (eds.): *The Modern Social Sciences* (New York, 2003).

Prakash, Gyan: *Another Reason. Science and the Imagination of Modern India* (Princeton, 1999).

Pruden, Caroline: *Conditional Partners. Eisenhower, the United Nations, and the Search for a Permanent Peace* (Baton Rouge, 1998).

Prudhommeaux, Jules Jean (ed.): *Enquête sur les livres scolaires d'après guerre* (Paris, 1924).

Prudhommeaux, Jules Jean: *Le Centre Européen de la Dotation Carnegie pour la Paix Internationale 1911–1921* (Paris, 1921).

Raphael, Lutz: "Ordnungsmuster der 'Hochmoderne'? Die Theorie der Moderne und die Geschichte der europäischen Gesellschaften im 20. Jahrhundert", in: Schneider, Ute/Raphael, Lutz (Hg.): *Dimensionen der Moderne* (Frankfurt a.M., 2008), 73–92.

Raphael, Lutz: "Die Verwissenschaftlichung des Sozialen als methodische und konzeptionelle Herausforderung für eine Sozialgeschichte des 20. Jahrhunderts", *Geschichte und Gesellschaft* 22 (1996) 2, 165–193.

Raucher, Alan R.: *Paul G. Hoffman. Architect of Foreign Aid* (Lexington, 1985).

Rausch, Helke: "Verordnetes Wissen? Amerikanische Forschungsförderung in Deutschland und Frankreich nach 1945 als Moment einer transatlantisch vergleichenden Wissen(schaft)sgeschichte", *Archiv für Sozialgeschichte* 49 (2009), 185–214.

Rausch, Helke: "Wie europäisch ist die kulturelle Amerikanisierung?", *Aus Politik und Zeitgeschichte*, no. 5–6 (2008), 27–32.

Rausch, Helke: "US-amerikanische 'Scientific Philanthropy' in Frankreich, Deutschland und Großbritannien zwischen den Weltkriegen", *Geschichte und Gesellschaft* 33 (2007) 1, 73–98.

Regal, Brian: *Henry Fairfield Osborn. Race and the Search for the Origins of Man* (Aldershot, 2002).

Rettig, Tobias: "French Military Policies in the Aftermath of the Yên Bay Mutiny, 1930. Old Security Dilemmas Return to the Surface", *South East Asia Research* 10 (2002) 3, 309–331.

Richardson, Malcolm: *Weimars transatlantischer Mäzen. Die Lincoln-Stiftung 1927 bis 1934. Ein Versuch demokratischer Elitenförderung in der Weimarer Republik* (Essen, 2008).

Rietzler, Katharina: "Before the Cultural Cold Wars. American Philanthropy and Cultural Diplomacy in the Interwar Years", *Historical Research* 84 (2011) 223, 148–164.

Rietzler, Katharina: "Philanthropy, Peace Research, and Revisionist Politics. Rockefeller and Carnegie Support for the Study of International Relations in Weimar Germany", *GHI Bulletin* Supplement 5 (2008), 61–79.

Rigby, Robert: "Europe Unites to Explore the Atom", *The Rotarian* 101 (1962) 5, 26–29.

Robin, Ron: *The Making of the Cold War Enemy. Culture and Politics in the Military-Intellectual Complex* (Princeton, 2001).

Rodgers, Daniel T.: *Age of Fracture* (Cambridge, 2011).

Rodgers, Daniel T.: *Atlantiküberquerungen. Die Politik der Sozialreform, 1870–1945* (Stuttgart, 2010).

Rodgers, Daniel T.: *Atlantic Crossings. Social Politics in a Progressive Age* (Cambridge, 1998).

Rojas, Fabio: "The Ford Foundation's Mission in Black Studies", in: Idem: *From Black Power to Black Studies. How a Radical Social Movement Became an Academic Discipline* (Baltimore, 2007), 130–66.

Roosevelt, Eleanor: *India and the Awakening East* (New York, 1953).

Rosanvallon, Pierre: *Demokratische Legitimität. Unparteilichkeit – Reflexivität – Nähe* (Hamburg, 2010).

Rosen, George: *Western Economists and Eastern Societies. Agents of Change in South Asia, 1960–1970* (Baltimore, 1986).

Rosenthal, Michael: *Nicholas Miraculous. The Amazing Career of the Redoubtable Dr. Nicholas Murray Butler* (New York, 2006).

Ross, Dorothy: *The Origins of American Social Science* (Cambridge, 1991).

Rupp, Jan: *Van Oude en Nieuwe Universiteiten. De Verdringing van Duitse door Amerikaanse Invloeden op de Wetenschapsbeoefening en het Hoger Onderwijs in Nederland, 1945–1995* (The Hague, 1997).

Rydell, Robert/Kroes, Rob: *Buffalo Bill in Bologna. The Americanization of the World 1869–1922* (Chicago, 2005).

Saberwal, Satish: "The Problem", *Seminar,* no. 112 (1968), 11–13.

Sachse, Carola: "Gereinigte Wissenschaft. Die Rockefeller Foundation und die Max-Planck-Gesellschaft im Kalten Krieg", in: Hofmann, Birgit et al. (Hg.): *Diktaturüberwindung in Europa. Neue nationale und transnationale Perspektiven* (Heidelberg, 2010), 36–52.

Sackley, Nicole: *Passage to Modernity. American Social Scientists, India, and the pursuit of development, 1945–1961* (Ph.D. Thesis, Princeton University, 2004).

Sahoo, Basudeb (ed.): *Class Relation in Indian Society* (Bhubaneswar, 1980).

Sanders, Irwin T./Ensminger, Douglas: *Alabama Rural Communities. A Study of Chilton County* (Montevallo, 1940).

Sarraut, Albert: *La mise en valeur des colonies françaises* (Paris, 1923).

Sasse, Dirk: *Franzosen, Briten und Deutsche im Rifkrieg 1921–1926. Spekulanten und Sympathisanten, Deserteure und Hasardeure im Dienste Abdelkrim* (München, 2006).

Saunier, Pierre-Yves/Tournès, Ludovic: "Philanthropies croisées. A joint venture in Public Health at Lyon (1918–1940)", *French History* 23 (2009) 2, 216–240.

Schlesinger, Arthur M., Jr.: *A Thousand Days. John F. Kennedy in the White House* (Boston, 1965).

Schmidt, Oliver: "Small Atlantic World. US Philanthropy and the Expanding International Exchange of Scholars after 1945", in: Gienow-Hecht, Jessica/Schumacher, Frank (eds.): *Culture and International History* (New York, 2003), 115–134.

Schmuhl, Hans-Walter: *Grenzüberschreitungen. Das Kaiser-Wilhelm-Institut für Anthropologie, menschliche Erblehre und Eugenik 1927–1945* (Göttingen, 2005).

Schneider, William H.: "War, Philanthropy, and the National Institute of Hygiene in France", *Minerva* 41 (2003) 1, 1–23.

Schrecker, Ellen: *The Age of McCarthyism. A Brief History with Documents* (Boston, 2002).

Schrecker, Ellen: *Many Are the Crimes. McCarthyism in America* (Princeton, 1998).

Schrecker, Ellen: *No Ivory Tower. McCarthyism and the Universities* (New York, 1986).

Scott-Smith, Giles: *Networks of Empire. The US State Department's Foreign Leader Program in the Netherlands, France and Britain 1950–1970* (Brussels, 2008).

Scott-Smith, Giles: "Attempting to Secure an 'Orderly Evolution'. American Foundations, the Hague Academy of International Law, and the Third World", *Journal of American Studies* 41 (2007) 3, 509–532.

Scott-Smith, Giles: "The Ties That Bind. Dutch-American Relations, US Public Diplomacy, and the Promotion of American Studies since WW II", *Hague Journal of Diplomacy*, 2 (2007) 3, 283–305.

Scott-Smith, Giles: *The Politics of Apolitical Culture. The Congress for Cultural Freedom, the CIA and Postwar American Hegemony* (London, 2002).

Scott, James C.: *Seeing Like a State. How Certain Schemes to Improve the Human Condition Have Failed* (New Haven, 1998).

Sealander, Judith: *Private Wealth and Public Life. Foundation Philanthropy and the Reshaping of American Social Policy from the Progressive Era to the New Deal* (Baltimore, 1997).

Sears, John F.: "Bierstadt, Buffalo Bill, and the Wild West in Europe", in: Bosscher, Doeko F.J./Kroes, Rob/Rydell, Robert W. (eds.): *Cultural Transmissions and Receptions. American Mass Culture in Europe* (Amsterdam, 1993), 3–14.

Sejersted, Francis: *The Age of Social Democracy. Norway and Sweden in the Twentieth Century* (Princeton, 2011).

Seybold, Peter J.: "The Ford Foundation and the Triumph of Behavioralism in American Political Science", in: Arnove, Robert F. (ed.): *Philanthropy and Cultural Imperialism. The Foundations at Home and Abroad* (Bloomington, 1980), 269–303.

Shaw, Frederick J./Warnock, Timothy: *The Cold War and Beyond. Chronology of the United States Air Force, 1947–1997* (Washington, 1997).

Shepherd, Chris J.: "Imperial Science. The Rockefeller Foundation and Agricultural Science in Peru, 1940–1960", *Science as Culture* 14 (2005) 2, 113–37.

Sibeud, Emmanuelle: "The Elusive Bureau of Colonial Ethnography in France, 1907–1925", in: Tilley, Helen/Gordon, Robert J. (eds.): *Ordering Africa. Anthropology, European Imperialism, and the Politics of Knowledge* (Manchester, 2007), 49–66.

Sibeud, Emmanuelle: "Marcel Mauss. Projet de présentation d'un bureau d'ethnologie (1913)", *Revue d'histoire des sciences humaines* 10 (2004), 105–115.

Sibeud, Emmanuelle: *Une science impériale pour l'Afrique? La construction des savoirs africanistes en France 1878–1930* (Paris, 2002).

Simpson, Bradley R.: *Economists with Guns. Authoritarian Development and U.S.-Indonesian Relations, 1960–1968* (Stanford, 2008).

Simpson, Christopher (ed.): *Universities and Empire. Money and Politics in the Social Sciences During the Cold War* (New York, 1998).

Sinclair, Upton: *The Goose Step. A Study of American Education* (Pasadena, 1922).

Singer, Milton/Cohn, Bernard S. (eds.): *Structure and Change in Indian Society* (Chicago, 1968).

Sinha, Raghuvir: *Social Change in Indian Society* (Bhopal, 1975).

Skard, Sigmund: *American Studies in Europe. Their History and Present Organization, Vols. I & II* (Philadelphia, 1958).

Skubiszewski, K.: "The Contribution of the Academy to the Development of the Science and Practice of Public Law", *Recueil des Cours* 271 (1998) 1, 57–100.

Smith, Edwin W.: "The Story of the Institute. A Survey of Seven Years", *Africa* 7 (1934) 1, 1–27.

Solomon, Susan Gross: "Through a Glass Darkly. The Rockefeller Foundation's International Health Board and Soviet Public Health", *Studies in the History and Philosophy of the Biomedical Sciences* 31 (2000) 3, 409–418.

Solomon, Susan Gross/Krementsov, Nikolai: "Giving and Taking across Borders. The Rockefeller Foundation in Russia, 1921–1928", *Minerva* 39 (2001) 3, 265–298.

Solomon, Susan Gross/Murard, Lion/Zylberman, Patrick (eds.): *Shifting Boundaries of Public Health. Europe in the Twentieth Century* (Rochester-Woodbridge/Suffolk, 2008).

Sparrow, James T.: *Warfare State. World War II Americans and the Age of Big Government* (Oxford, 2011).

Speich, Daniel/Nützenadel, Alexander (eds.): *Global Inequality and Development after 1945. Journal of Global History, Special Issue* 6 (2011).

Staley, Eugene: *The Future of Underdeveloped Countries. Political Implications of Economic Development* (New York, 1954).

Staples, Eugene S.: *Forty Years. A Learning Curve* (New Delhi, 1992).

Stein, Eric Andrew: *Vital Times. Power, Public Health, and Memory in Rural Java* (Ph.D. thesis, University of Michigan, 2005).

Stein, Judith: *Pivotal Decade. How the United States Traded Factories for Finance in the Seventies* (New Haven, 2010).

Stephan, Alexander: *Americanization and Anti-Americanism. The German Encounter with American Culture after 1945* (New York, 2005).

Stocking, George W. Jr.: *Malinowski. Rivers, Benedict and Others* (Madison, 1986).

Stockwell, Sarah (ed.): *The British Empire. Themes and Perspectives* (Oxford, 2008).

Stoecker, Holger: *Afrikawissenschaften in Berlin von 1919 bis 1945. Zur Geschichte und Topographie eines wissenschaftlichen Netzwerkes* (Stuttgart, 2008).

Stonor Saunders, Frances: *Who Paid the Piper? The CIA and the Cultural Cold War* (London, 1999).

Stouman, K./Falk, I.S.: "Health Indices. A Study of Objective Indices of Health in Relation to Environment and Sanitation", *Quarterly Bulletin of the Health Organisation* 5 (1936), 901–996.

Stöver, Bernd: *Der Kalte Krieg, 1947–1991. Geschichte eines radikalen Zeitalters* (München, 2007).

Strasser, Bruno: "Coproduction of Neutral Science and the Neutral State in Cold War Europe. Switzerland and International Scientific Cooperation 1951–69", *Osiris* 24 (2009) 1, 165–184.

Stuchtey, Benedikt (ed.): *Science Across the European Empires, 1800–1950* (Oxford, 2005).

Suri, Jeremi: *Henry Kissinger and the American Century* (Cambridge, 2007).

Sutton, Francis X.: "Nation-Building in the Heyday of the Classic Development Ideology: Ford Foundation Experience in the 1950s and 1960s", in: Fukuyama, Francis (ed.): *Nation-Building. Beyond Afghanistan and Iraq* (Baltimore, 2006), 42–63.

Sutton, Francis X.: "The Ford Foundation. The Early Years", *Daedalus* 116 (1987) 1, 41–91.

Sweetser, Artur: "The Non-Political Achievements of the League", *Foreign Affairs* 19 (1940) 1, 179–192.

Temple, Richard C.: "'Tout Savoir, Tout Pardoner.' An Appeal for an Imperial School of Applied Anthropology", in: *Man* 21 (1921), 150–155.

Temple, Richard C.: *Anthropology as a Practical Science. Address delivered at Meetings of the British Association at Birmingham, the Antiquarian Society of Cambridge, and the Anthropological Society of Oxford* (London, 1914), 26–32.

Thomas, John N.: *The Institute of Pacific Relations. Asian Scholars and American Politics* (Seattle, 1974).

Thomas, Martin: "French Empire Elites and the Politics of Economic Obligation in the Interwar Years", *The Historical Journal* 52 (2009) 4, 989–1016.

Thomas, Martin: *The French Empire between the Wars. Imperialism, Politics and Society* (Manchester, 2005).

Tilley, Helen: *Africa as a Living Laboratory. Empire, Development, and the Problem of Scientific Knowledge, 1870–1950* (Chicago, 2011).

Tinbergen, Jan: "De Internationale Taak van de Sociaal-Democratie", *Socialisme en Democratie* 14 (1957), 84–89.

Tournès, Ludovic: "Comment devenir une superpuissance intellectuelle? La fondation Rockefeller et la documentation scientifique", in: Hauser, Claude/Loué, Thomas/Mollier, Jean-Yves/Vallotton, François (eds.): *La diplomatie par le livre. Réseaux et circulation internationale de l'imprimé de 1880 à nos jours* (Paris, 2011), 165–180.

Tournès, Ludovic: *Sciences de l'homme et politique. Les fondations philanthropiques américaines en France au Xxe siècle* (Paris, 2011).

Tournès, Ludovic: "Introduction. Carnegie, Rockefeller, Ford, Soros. Généalogie de la toile philanthropique", in: Idem (ed.): *L'argent de l'influence. Les foundations américaines et leurs réseaux européens* (Paris, 2010).

Tournès, Ludovic: "La Dotation Carnegie Pour La Paix Internationale et l'invention de la diplomatie philanthropique", in: Idem (ed.): *L'argent de l'influence. Les fondations américaines et leurs réseaux européens* (Paris, 2010), 24–44.

Tournès, Ludovic: "La fondation Rockefeller et la construction d'une politique des sciences sociales en France (1918–1940)", *Annales. Histoire, sciences sociales* 63 (2008) 6, 1371–1402.

Tournès, Ludovic: "Le réseau des boursiers Rockefeller et la recomposition des savoirs bio-médicaux en France (1920–1970)", *French Historical Studies* 29 (2006) 1, 77–107.

Tournès, Ludovic (ed.): *L'Argent de l'influence. Les Fondations américaines et leurs réseaux européens* (Paris, 2010).

Truman, Harry S.: *Public Papers of the Presidents of the United States, January 1 1952 to January 20 1953* (Washington/DC, 1966),

Tyrrell, Ian R.: *Reforming the World. The Creation of America's Moral Empire* (Princeton, 2010).

Tyrrell, Ian R.: *Transnational Nation. United States History in a Global Perspective since 1789* (Basingstoke, 2007).

Uma, Warren: "Uproar over CIA imperils Fund's Work in India", *Washington Post*, 3 March 1967, A3.

Unger, Corinna R: "Toward Global Equilibrium. American Foundations and Indian Modernization, 1950s to 1970s", *Journal of Global History* 6 (2011) 1, 121–142.

Unger, Corinna R.: *Ostforschung in Westdeutschland. Die Erforschung des europäischen Ostens und die Deutsche Forschungsgemeinschaft* (Stuttgart, 2007).

Unger, Corinna R.: "Cold War Science. Wissenschaft, Politik und Ideologie im Kalten Krieg", *Neue Politische Literatur* 51 (2006) 1, 49–68.

Union of International Association (ed.): *Yearbook of International Organization 1986/87, Vol. 2.* (München, 1986).

van Roijen, J.H.: "Holland and the Hague Academy of International Law", *Recueil des Cours*, 138 (1973) 1, 29–30.

Vogel, Jakob: "Von der Wissenschafts- zur Wissensgeschichte. Für eine Historisierung der 'Wissensgesellschaft'", *Geschichte und Gesellschaft* 30 (2004) 4, 639–660.

Vogt, William: *Road to Survival* (New York, 1948).

Wagner, Peter: *Sozialwissenschaften und Staat. Frankreich, Deutschland und Italien 1870–1980* (Frankfurt a.M., 1990).

Wagnleitner, Reinhold: *Coca-Colonization and the Cold War. The Cultural Mission of the United States in Austria After the Second World War* (Chapel Hill-London, 1994).

Wang, Jessica: *American Science in an Age of Anxiety. Scientists, Anticommunism, and the Cold War* (Chapel Hill, 1999).

Wang, Zuoyue: "Physics in China in the Context of the Cold War, 1949–1976", in: Trischler, Helmuth/ Walker, Mark (eds.): *Physics and Politics. Research and Research Support in Twentieth Century Germany in International Perspective* (Stuttgart, 2010), 251–276.

Wartelle, Jean-Claude: "La Société d'anthropologie de Paris de 1859 à 1920", *Revue d'histoire des sciences humaines* 10 (2004), 125–171.

Weiler, J.H.H./Paulus, Andreas: "The Structure of Change in International Law", *European Journal of International Law* 8 (1997) 4, 545–565.

Weindling, Paul: *John Thompson, Psychiatrist in the Shadow of the Holocaust* (Rochester, 2010).

Weindling, Paul: "The Extraordinary Career of the Virologist Eugen Haagen", in: Hulverscheidt, Marion/Laukotter, Anja (Hg.): *Infektion und Institution. Zur Wissenschaftsgeschichte des Robert Koch-Instituts im Nationalsozialismus* (Göttingen, 2009), 232–249.

Weindling, Paul: "American Foundations and Internationalizing of Public Health", in: Murard/Solomon/Zylberman (eds.): *Shifting Boundaries of Public Heath. Europe in the Twentieth Century* (Rochester, 2008), 63–86.

Weindling, Paul: "'Out of the Ghetto'. The Rockefeller Foundation Confronts German Medical Sciences after the Second World War", in: Schneider, William H. (ed.): *The Rockefeller Foundation and Biomedicine: International Achievements and Frustrations from World War I to the Cold War* (Indiana, 2002), 208–222.

Weindling, Paul: "From Moral Exhortation to Socialised Primary Care. The New Public Health and the Healthy Life, 1918–45", in: Rodríguez-Ocaña, E. (ed.): *The Politics of the Healthy Life. An International Perspective* (Sheffield, 2002), 113–130.

Weindling, Paul: "Modernising Eugenics. The Role of Foundations in International Population Studies", *Minerva* (2002), 167–179.

Weindling, Paul: "An Overloaded Ark? The Rockefeller Foundation and Refugee Medical Scientists, 1933–1945", *Studies in the History and Philosophy of Biology and Biomedical Science* 31 (2000) 3, 477–489.

Weindling, Paul: *Epidemics and Genocide in Eastern Europe* (Oxford, 2000).

Weindling, Paul: "The Rockefeller Foundation and German Biomedical Science, 1920–40. From Educational Philanthropy to International Science Policy", in: Rupke, Nicolaas (ed.): *Science, Politics and the Public Good. Essays in Honour of Margaret Gowing* (Basingstoke, 1988), 119–140. (Reprinted in: Gemelli, G./Picard, J.F./Schneider W.H. (eds.): *Managing Medical Research in Europe. The Role of the Rockefeller Foundation 1920s–1950s* (Bologna, 1999), 117–136.)

Weindling, Paul: "Philanthropy and World Health. The Rockefeller Foundation and the League of Nations Health Organisation", *Minerva* 35 (1997) 3, 269–81.

Weindling, Paul: "Public Health and Political Stabilisation. Rockefeller Funding in Interwar Central/Eastern Europe", *Minerva* 31 (1993) 3, 253–267.

Weingart, Peter: *Wissenschaftssoziologie* (Bielefeld, 2003).

Werner, A.: "Rezension", *Bulletin of the School of Oriental Studies* 4 (1928), 889–891.

Westad, Odd Arne: "The Cold War and the international history of the twentieth century", in: Leffler, Melvyn P./Westad, Odd Arne (eds.): *The Cambridge History of the Cold War*, Vol. 1: *Origins* (New York, 2010), 1–19.

Westad, Odd Arne: *The Global Cold War. Third World Interventions and the Making of our Times* (Cambridge, 2005).

Westermann, Dietrich: "Das Internationale Institut für Afrikanische Sprachen und Kulturen", in: Brauer, Ludolph/Mendelssohn-Bartholdy, Albrecht (Hg.): *Forschungsinstitute. Ihre Geschichte, Organisation und Ziele*, Vol. 2 (Hamburg, 1930), 413–417.

Wheatland, Thomas: *The Frankfurt School in Exile* (Minneapolis-London, 2009).

Wilder, Gary: "Framing Greater France between the Wars", *Journal of Historical Sociology* 14 (2001) 2, 198–225.

Wilder, Gary: *The French Imperial Nation-State. Negritude and Colonial Humanism between the Two World Wars* (Chicago, 2005).

Wilson, Godfrey: "Anthropology as a Public Service", *Africa* 13 (1940) 1, 43–61.

Winn, Joseph: "Nicholas Murray Butler, the Carnegie Endowment for International Peace, and the Search for Reconciliation in Europe, 1919–1933", *Peace & Change* 31 (2006) 4, 555–584.

Wirsching, Andreas et al.: "Forum: The 1970s and 1980s as a Turning Point in European History?", *Journal of Modern European History* 9 (2011) 1, 7–26.

Wubs, Ben: "U.S. Multinationals in the Netherlands. The Cases of IBM, Dow Chemical, and Sara Lee", in: Krabbendam, Hans/van Minnen, Cornelis/Scott-Smith, Giles (eds.): *Four Centuries of Dutch-American Relations* (Amsterdam, 2009).

Zachariah, Benjamin: *Developing India. An Intellectual and Social History, c. 1930–50* (New Delhi, 2005).

Zunz, Olivier: *Philanthropy in America. A History* (Princeton-Oxford, 2011).

List of Authors

Volker R. Berghahn is Seth Low Professor of History at Columbia University, NY

John Krige is Kranzberg Professor in the School of History, Technology and Society at the Georgia Institute of Technology, Atlanta, GA

Madeleine Herren is Professor of Modern History at Heidelberg University

Tim B. Müller is Postdoctoral Research Fellow at the Hamburg Institute for Social Research

Kiran Klaus Patel is Professor of European and Global History at Maastricht University

Helke Rausch is Senior Lecturer at the Institute of History at Freiburg University and a former Junior Research Fellow of FRIAS

Nicole Sackley is Assistant Professor of History and American Studies at the University of Richmond, VA

Giles Scott-Smith holds the Ernst van der Beugel Chair in the Diplomatic History of Atlantic Cooperation at Leiden University

Ludovic Tournès is Professeur des universités for the History of International Relations at the Université Paris Ouest-Nanterre La Défense

Jens Michael Wegener is PhD Research Fellow at the European University Institute, Florence

Paul Weindling is Wellcome Trust Research Professor in the History of Medecine at Oxford Brookes University

Schriftenreihe der FRIAS School of History

V&R

Band 3: Marie-Janine Calic /
Dietmar Neutatz (Hg.)

The Crisis of Socialist Modernity

The Soviet Union and Yugoslavia in the 1970s

2011. 231 Seiten, gebunden
ISBN 978-3-525-31042-7

Die westliche Industriemoderne stieß in
den 1970er Jahren an ihre Grenzen. Ein
ausgeprägtes allgemeines Krisenbewusst-
sein war die Folge. Wie aber stellte sich
die Lage in den sozialistischen Staaten
dar? Trifft die Charakterisierung dieses
Jahrzehnts als Epoche des Übergangs
auch auf die Gegenentwürfe zur kapi-
talistischen Moderne zu? Die Beiträge
gehen dieser Frage anhand von Politik,
Wirtschaft, Gesellschaft und Kultur der
beiden Vielvölkerstaaten Jugoslawien
und Sowjetunion nach und zeigen, dass
sich beide in einer verborgenen Krise
befanden.

Band 2: Jörn Leonhard /
Christian Wieland (Hg.)

What Makes the Nobility Noble?

Comparative Perspectives from the Sixteenth to
the Twentieth Century

2011 396 Seiten, mit 22 Abb., gebunden
ISBN 978-3-525-31041-0

Die Geschichte des Adels in Europa ist
häufig »zweigeteilt« betrachtet worden: Für die Frühe Neuzeit spricht man
meist von »Herrschaft«, für das 19.
und 20. Jahrhundert vom »Kampf ums
Obenbleiben«. Die Beiträge dieses Bands

überschreiten bewusst die Grenze zwischen Vormoderne und Moderne. Aus der
Perspektive des Adels heraus stellen sie die
Frage nach Kontinuitäten und Brüchen
der Neueren Geschichte auf neue Weise.
Anhand der Kategorien Recht, Politik und
Ästhetik werden wesentliche Handlungs-
felder und Modi der adligen Selbstdarstellung und Selbstbehauptung analysiert.

Band 1: Ulrike von Hirschhausen /
Jörn Leonhard (Hg.)

Comparing Empires

Encounters and Transfers in the Long Nineteenth
Century

2. Auflage 2012. 556 Seiten, mit 19 Abb.,
gebunden
ISBN 978-3-525-31040-3

Europas Großreiche waren geprägt von
ethnischer Differenz und räumlicher Vielfalt. Gerade der Umgang mit Pluralität, die
lange als Ursache für Scheitern und Zerfall galt, interessiert heute als typisches
Signum Europas. Die Beiträge dieses
Bandes vergleichen systematisch vier
europäische Empires im 19. und frühen
20. Jahrhundert – das Britische Empire,
die Habsburgermonarchie, Russland und
das Osmanische Reich – und erklären, was
die Beziehungen zwischen Zentrum und
Peripherie sowie zwischen Herrschern und
Beherrschten so spannungsreich und viel-
fältig machte.

Weitere Bände sind in Vorbereitung

Vandenhoeck & Ruprecht

Band 1: Jörn Leonhard /
Ulrike von Hirschhausen

Empires und Nationalstaaten

im 19. Jahrhundert

2. Auflage 2010. 128 Seiten mit 4 Abb.,
kartoniert
ISBN 978-3-525-32300-7

Noch immer dominiert der Nationalstaat
unser historisches Bewusstsein. Die Großreiche Europas waren dagegen bereits
in den Augen der Zeitgenossen anachro-
nistische Gebilde. Aber Empires prägten
die Geschichte Europas weit länger und
stärker als die historisch relativ späte Erfindung des Nationalstaats.

Ulrike v. Hirschhausen und Jörn Leonhard zeigen, wie die Habsburgermonarchie, das Zarenreich, das Osmanische
Reich und das Britische Empire im 19.
Jahrhundert auf die Vielfalt ihrer Herr-
schaftsstrukturen und Ethnien reagierten
und sich so zugleich mit dem Modell des
Nationalstaates auseinandersetzten.

Band 2: Gerd Koenen

Was war der Kommunismus?

2010. 143 Seiten, kartoniert
ISBN 978-3-525-32301-4

Gerd Koenen untersucht eines der inte-
ressantesten Kapitel des 20. Jahrhunderts: Die Dynamik und den raschen Zerfall der kommunistischen Bewegungen
und Staatsgründungen.

»Gerd Koenen hat ein selten dichtes,
gedankenreiches und pointiert geschrie-
benes Buch vorgelegt.« *Rolf Hosfeld,
Deutschlandradio Kultur*

»Kenntnisreich, tiefgründig, einsichtig
legt er Eigenarten und Entwicklung des
Kommunismus zwischen seinem Kern-
reich, der UdSSR, und China, Südame-
rika, Europa dar.« *Immo Sennewald, blog.
literaturwelt.de*

»... kompetent und prägnant ...«
Erhard Eppler, Süddeutsche Zeitung

Vandenhoeck & Ruprecht